PEARL BUCK

A Woman in Conflict

TO

GRACE SYDENSTRICKER YAUKEY

In Admiration & Gratitude

CONTENTS

ACKNOWLEDGMENTS

I am deeply indebted to the following for their generous support, help and invaluable reminiscences and information: Dawn Akins; John Anderson; Roger Baldwin; Erik Barnouw; Lillieth Bates; Dr. James Bear; Margaret Bear; Marcella Berger; Judge and Mrs. Edward Biester; George Breen; Jackie Breen; Clifford Buck; Lomay Buck; Paul Buck; Lois Burpee; George Carabeau; John Mack Carter; Professor G. A. Cavasco; Chen Chi; Josephine Churchill; Alexander Clark; Malvine Cole; Natalie Walsh Coltman; Zerrita Colvin; Marc Connelly; Dr. Roberta Cornelius; Nan Craddock; Helen Daniels; Judge Howard Douglas; Lietta Dwork; Eva Eshleman; Dr. Isadore Falk; Dorothy Farrell; James Farrell; Phyllis Fenner; Mary Ferguson; Margaret Fischer; Harriet Fitzgerald; Florence Galla; Annie Kate Gilbert; Fay Glover; Mary Graves; Elizabeth Haines; Dorothy Hammerstein; William Hammerstein; Harry Hansen; Robert Hill; Hope Hollingshead; Alta Hoylman; Professor Chih Tsing Hsia; Dorothy Hughes; David C. Hyer; Alexander Itkis; Julia Jeffrey; Emily Johnson; Dorothy Jones; Nannine Joseph; Jeanette Kamins; Emi Kamiya; Dean and Ray Kelsey; Mary Kennedy; Dr. Ellen Finley Kiser; Joan Kracke; Dr. and Mrs. Ardron Lewis; Freeman Lewis; Naome Lewis; Andrea Lloyd; Isabel Lundberg; Aline MacMahon; Florence McNeil; Gertrude Macy; Alice Mathias; Aldo Merusi; Martha Moore; Priscilla Morse; Kathryn Nash; Dorothy Olding; Ruth Osborn; Robert Parsons; Patricia Powell; David Quintner; Bertha Reisner; Charles Robbins; Paul Roebling; Sara Rowe; Sheila Sadowski; Miki Sawada; Grace Shannon; Carol Johnstone Sharp; Dr. and Mrs. Henry Shissler; Ruth Sills; Cornelia Otis Skinner; Joan Skirtland; Grace Smith; William Arthur Smith; Helen Foster Snow; Shepperd Strudwick; Margot Studer; Dr. Katherine Sturgis; Jean Swain; Charles Sydenstricker; Henriette Walsh Teush; James C. Thomson, Jr.; Nan Thornton; Frances Tompkins; Isabel Tozzer; Lester

Trauch; Alan Tucker; Cynthia Vartan; Nancy Waller; Janice Walsh; Richard J. Walsh, Jr.; Greg Walter; Dr. William Westcott; Emma Edmunds White; Mollie Winfree; Lillian Wolfson; J. Sellman Woollen; Grace Sydenstricker Yaukey; Viola Yoder; Lucille Zinn.

Special thanks go to Dr. Richard Hocking for permission to print the letters of his father, Professor William Ernest Hocking.

Also, thanks to the Trustees of the Pearl S. Buck Family Trust for permission to quote from Pearl Buck's personal letters.

PROLOGUE

Nanking, China, March 24, 1927

In the brick house on Big Horse Road the Thomson family huddled on the second floor out of range of the guns. The gate in their wall had been demolished, and shouts and laughter accompanied the smashing of their front door. A horde of ragged Hunanese soldiers barged up the stairs demanding "Money—watches—rings," as their leader shouted to the crowd of beggars and vagrants who followed: "Take what you want. It's all ours now."

Eyeing the white family who stood helplessly before him, he ordered: "Money. Rings." The elderly woman quickly hid her left hand behind her back, but the movement caught the leader's eye. Grabbing her hand he attempted to pull off the wedding ring but the enlarged knuckle prevented it. As he pulled out his knife, her daughter screamed to her son, "No! No! Johnny, get that file in your carpentry set." The soft gold in the ring soon gave way.

Another soldier grabbed the spectacles from the eight-year-old daughter. Her mother protested:"But you're already wearing a pair." The Chinese soldier grinned as he placed the child's pair on his nose atop the others.

Farther down Big Horse Road the house of Dr. Hutchison went up in flames as looters darted in and out with pieces of furniture. The soldiers had also gone in search of money here, but Dr. Hutchison had left by the back door to hide in the coal bin under a scattering of coal.

Across the road the wife of a university professor was preparing to bathe her baby in their second-floor bathroom. Hearing shouts in the street she looked out and saw a soldier struggling with the vice president of the university over something he held in his hand. Seconds later there was a shot and Dr. Williams fell, his forehead torn away.

Farther along Big Horse Road the Lossing Buck family gathered at its accustomed place for breakfast, protected from outside disturbances by the high garden wall. During the spring the city's whole white population had lived in safety under an international treaty, more or less independent of the martial clashes of two Chinese armies battling for supremacy.

For several days, however, the two armies had been converging on Nanking. Chiang Kai-shek's Nationalist army, with its infiltration of Communists, was moving up from the South to meet the helter-skelter troops of the local warlord coming down from the North. Judging by past experience, Nanking's citizens anticipated minor clashes within the city walls, possibly even a siege, certainly disorder and lawlessness, but eventual victory for the Nationalists. Serious fighting had begun three days before with a dull boom of cannon and the crackle of guns outside the wall, and rumor had it that the Nationalists were advancing. As usual when the city became a battleground, the Buck household took in Chinese friends seeking asylum, since the international treaty extended its protection to the friends of whites, and the night before they had poured in bringing their own food. A dull roar emanated from the nether regions of the house, and Pearl Buck had commented to her sister Grace that the cellar was so full of refugees she could almost feel the floor heaving.

Grace and Jesse Yaukey and their son, David, had slept peacefully, as had Pearl and her two children, while Lossing Buck patrolled the road. But on this morning Pearl had started up, wakened not by noise but by dead silence—no boom of cannon outside, no rumbling within the house. The refugees, she discovered, had left in a body, and as she sat down to breakfast she wondered if peace had come or if there was another less assuring reason for the silence.

Their breakfast began as usual with cereal, eggs, toast, coffee and tinned milk. The big hall stove gave off a cozy warmth, and Pearl had just settled her children at the table while the amah placed their food before them. Lossing Buck, weary from his late night patrol, sat down, remarking, "I think I heard some shooting outside." As Pearl poured his coffee, the front door suddenly banged open, and the tailor who lived nearby rushed in screaming, "Get out quickly! They're shooting white people. They just shot Dr. Williams. Hide! Quick, hide!"

The Nanking Incident, which was to become the turning point in so many lives, both white and Chinese, had begun on March 24, 1927.

No one had believed it could happen. The treaty of 1900 under the terms of which Europeans and Americans, chiefly missionaries and traders, were guaranteed safety, even for their Chinese friends and associates, plus immunity from Chinese laws, became, overnight, null and void, as the brooding hatred for the white intruders erupted.

Indecision paralyzed the Buck household. Where could they go? Who were their friends now? But here the bread that they had cast upon the waters returned to them. The Buck family, as missionaries, teaching these people to love, trying to abide by the Christian doctrine they preached, received an outpouring of devotion from their Chinese servants and friends.

Pearl's and Grace's elderly father, Absalom Sydenstricker, had just left for his office, and the houseboy ran to fetch him back. Lossing Buck rushed upstairs for a precious manuscript that always lay beside his bed. Pearl and Grace, their first thoughts for the children, frantically grabbed up caps and coats. As possible hiding places were suggested and rejected, a back gate in the garden wall opened and an unkempt woman, hair straggling, stumbled on badly bound feet into the house.

"Wise Mother," she gasped to Pearl, "come with me. No one will look for you in my shabby hut." Certainly the cluster of tiny houses outside the wall would seem unlikely places in which to find foreign devils. Across the fields the Bucks and the Yaukeys raced, to be greeted lovingly by the local Chinese.

The room they entered was scarcely big enough for a bed of woven string, a chair, a table, a stool and a pot. There was one small window high under the thatched roof accessible only to the tallest, and in this semidarkness the five adults and three children stood together panting. "You will be safe here," Mrs. Lu told them. "My friends will see to it if the soldiers come. And if your children cry, I will slap my own son till he cries, too, so no one will know the difference."

Left alone, the five adults tried to comprehend all that had happened. Tall Absalom Sydenstricker, the missionary with forty-seven years of preaching and teaching experience, looked out through the hole under the roof. "They are burning the Theological Seminary," he reported sadly. "Why would they want to burn the place where God's word comes from?" No one responded; there was nothing to say. The hatred suddenly erupting around them was alien and terrifying.

Mrs. Lu slipped through the door with a pot of tea and food for the children. Grateful but concerned, Pearl begged her not to endanger herself, but she replied, "Should I not help you, Wise Mother, who twice saved the life of my son?"

The uproar seemed closer now. The group could hear the front of their house being battered and shouts of glee as looters raced through the rooms. Everything they owned was being ravaged, their past swept away.

In the face of such peril each person responded in his own way. Seventy-five-year-old Absalom Sydenstricker, serenely sure of the mercy of God and the goodness of the Chinese people, waited quietly for whatever lay in store. The two young husbands pondered the future in dismay. Grace Yaukey, twenty-seven years old and perilously near childbirth, drew her small son close and prayed. Pearl Buck held young Janice on her lap while seven-year-old Carol, normally so boisterous, leaned against her mother, mute and still. In grateful wonder at this silence Pearl looked down into her daughter's vacant eyes. Was it a guardian angel, a felicitous prayer, that kept this helpless creature from betraying them? She had given up praying years before, but perhaps there were still prayers that were granted.

Pearl realized how close they were to death. If Carol cried out in English as a soldier passed, they could all be killed. What if they were indeed discovered? Dr. Williams's death could have set off a wave of murders. Her skin prickled at the thought of a coolie remembering an insult by an arrogant white. And what if only the grownups were murdered? What would become of the children?

Chilled by such horrendous thoughts, Pearl put her mouth close to her sister's ear. Grace turned to listen. "If they come to kill us . . . make sure the children go first." Grace met her eyes steadily and nodded.

Hour after hour they huddled together in the cramped hut. Waiting in silence for something to happen, Pearl's mind raced through a jumble of emotions. Memories of her past washed over her in waves of pain and self-condemnation for her meager accomplishments. At thirty-five what had she to show? A few trivial stories sold, an empty marriage endured, a decade of service to an ill mother and a stubborn father—and worst of all, the anguish of a handicapped child.

At that moment, in that place, her burden of despair became intolerable and her spirit suddenly rebelled. In a kind of fury Pearl Buck swore that if she were, by the grace of God, to live through this day, she would make a new life for herself. Long afterwards, she would dismiss the years before this day as "having spent part of my life in jail . . . in a queer submerged sort of state."

1

Not every child has a nurse with feet measuring only three inches long who hatches baby chicks in her undergarments; nor does every child participate in the overthrow of an empire. Pearl Comfort Sydenstricker had all this and much more. Though born in West Virginia on June 26, 1892, during her missionary parents' home leave, she grew up in China, the only white child in their city, speaking Chinese before English and considering herself to be Chinese. The house in which the Sydenstrickers lived was rented to a white couple because Chinese tenants were annoyed by its resident ghost, a woman murdered not long before by her husband, which the whites, strangely, seemed to ignore.

At this time the missionary couple had lived in China for ten years. Absalom Sydenstricker, tall and homely, an intellectual, had been stricken early by the missionary fever of the 1880s and had married young Caroline Stulting not because she was attractive but because a missionary had to have a wife willing to travel. Carie in turn seems to have married him on the rebound from a handsome rogue who drank. Love had never entered their bargain.

It was typical of Absalom, an abstracted saver of souls, that in preparing for their journey to China, he had absent-mindedly bought a single railroad ticket. Also typically, Carie good-naturedly overlooked this symbolic foretaste of the future and gallantly went on to make a life and seven babies for God and His zealous servant.

Pearl Comfort was the sixth of seven children (three had died), named for her pink and white glow of health. A sturdy child, lively and precocious even at four, she drove her mother frantic with questions.

"Not another Why for fifteen minutes," Carie would snap, and Pearl, drawing up her small rocking chair before the clock, would sit mute, watching, and on the tick of fifteen would ask her next question.

There was much to investigate. "Mother," Pearl asked one day, "what makes the red marks on Father's forehead at breakfast?"

"Your father prays for an hour every morning," Carie explained. "Those red marks are where he leans his head on his hands." Pearl, deeply impressed, looked for similar marks on her mother's forehead. "Why don't you pray too?"

With a touch of spirit Carie answered, "If I did who would get your breakfast and clean the house? The Lord will just have to understand that I have to condense my prayers."

The mismatched couple, in their twenties, had braved a nine-thousand-mile journey to a land of which they knew little—only that men wore pigtails and ate birds' nests and women bound their feet and walked on the stumps. The only important fact known was that these ignorant millions lacked the benefits of Christianity—their souls doomed to eternal hell-fire unless others more fortunate could save them.

Still relatively unknown were fifty centuries of Chinese art and literature and invention, for only a few years earlier had white traders and missionaries finally penetrated the proud privacy of this Middle Kingdom and come back to report their findings.

At first the Sydenstrickers' Gospel message had been met with iron resistance. Under Absalom's ardent eloquence in his newly acquired Chinese, however, resistance gradually softened. In water shops and tea houses, wherever the men gathered to gossip or trade, Absalom explained the goodness of his God and the worthlessness of theirs. Carie, meanwhile, listened with womanly understanding to their wives' tales of hardship, quick to look for ways to help. Distressed Chinese women told her, "I am only a woman ignorant and worthless, yet you listen and try to help me. What you believe I will believe for it must be true to make you so kind."

Thus the missionaries did their jobs, slowly winning converts through an honest love for the people that they had come to save. After initial shock at outlandish Chinese superstitions and brutal practices such as killing girl babies, the Sydenstrickers enjoyed mutual respect and trust, Absalom going so far as to wear Chinese clothes and grow a pigtail to counteract the foreignness of his blue eyes and prominent nose.

Their oldest child, Edgar, had survived the diseases that had killed three other children before Pearl was born, and after their sabbatical year, Clyde was born in the "haunted" T'singkiangpu house.

Carie taught her children at home while Absalom went into the fields on donkeyback armed with Bibles, tracts and a stick to beat off the dogs. Pearl quickly learned to read, almost instinctively, absorbing everything in print that was available. Carie realized, however, that the adolescent Edgar was ready for an American education. After sending him to her brother in Hillsboro, West Virginia, she concentrated on Pearl and young Clyde. But when Pearl was six, death again struck the family, and her brother Clyde was buried behind the locked gates of the Christian cemetery.

By now Pearl was foreshadowing her own future. An avid reader of the *Christian Observer*, a religious paper published in Louisville, Kentucky, which featured a Letters to the Editor column, she wrote on the subject of death. Under the headline, "Our Real Home in Heaven," her letter appeared in the April 5, 1899 issue: "I am a little girl six years old. I live in China. I have a big brother in college who is coming to China to help our father tell the Chinese about Jesus. [A plan that never came to pass.] I have two little brothers in heaven. Maudie went first, then Artie, then Edith, and on the tenth of last month my little brave brother, Clyde, left us to go to our real home in Heaven. Clyde said he was a Christian Soldier and that Heaven was his bestest home. Clyde was four years and we both loved the little letters in the Observer. I wrote this all by myself, and my hand is tired, so goodbye. Pearl."

After the exhilaration of this literary achievement Pearl began writing regularly for the *Shanghai Mercury*, an English language newspaper which offered prizes each month for the best stories and articles by children. Acceptance by the *Mercury* became a source of regular pocket money.

At the age of eight, Pearl Sydenstricker began to step out in the world. Though forbidden to go down the hill to the Chinese homes she was completely comfortable in the neighborhood, unfazed at having her fair hair examined because of its odd color or being asked if her skin was white because she was bathed too often. There, in front of her, was life in the raw, quarrels in a language that made her ears tingle, lepers displaying their rotting flesh for alms, childbirth discussed with clinical precision, and death in the fields. Highly ceremonial funerals were conducted near her home, and she joined the mourners companionably, watching the dead laid to rest under the handsome mounds built over the graves. For babies a shallow grave was dug and the tiny nude body dropped in the ground. Starving wild dogs often found such graves and more than once a tearful Pearl beat them off, then dug the grave deeper to provide a decent burial.

After Clyde died, Pearl's life was lonely. To compensate Wang Amah, Pearl's brown gnome of a nurse, took her to the theater. Since Wang's taste ran to the melodramatic, Pearl spent many hours on a hard bench stiff with excitement. The plays often pitted Chinese heroes of great virtue against villainous white foreign devils. Traditionally, the white villain wore a persimmon-colored wig, and Pearl hissed the foreign devil as heartily as the Chinese audience. Red, Pearl knew, was the wrong color for hair; her own pale shade was bad enough, but obviously there could be no virtue in a persimmon shade.

Wang Amah was indeed Pearl's amah in the actual Chinese meaning—foster mother. It was to her Pearl ran in time of trouble, onto her lap she climbed, for Carie, apparently so benumbed by the lack of warmth in her marriage, never, in Pearl's memory, petted or hugged her children.

Wang Amah also provided entertainment. She told stories of dragons and gods and, even better, of her own youth, when she had been, so she swore, an irresistible beauty. Pearl found it hard to believe of the wrinkled old woman with shoe-blacking on her bald spots and only two teeth that met, but the tale of having been lowered down a dry well to save her from lusting bandits was convincing enough. And her trick of hatching baby chicks by carrying the eggs in her undergarments made her unique among all adults.

Like all girls of proper Chinese parents, Wang had had her feet bound at three. It had proven so painful before numbness set in that her father had made her sleep in the kitchen to muffle the noise of her weeping. But the rewards were sufficient. At fifteen her feet measured only three inches in length, and her parents were able to marry her off profitably.

At Pearl's insistence, she took off her cloth shoes and white socks and unwound the long, white bindings. The four lesser toes and the heel of each foot had been squeezed together under the instep, so that she stumbled along on the big toe and a mass of mangled bones. The flesh was a strange dead color, and Pearl, sickened but satisfied, was relieved when they were re-covered.

By the age of seven, young Pearl had read everything the book shelves provided, Plutarch's *Lives*, Fox's *Book of Martyrs*, the Bible, church history, sermons, Tennyson and Browning. One afternoon, hungrily hunting for new fare, she found on a top shelf a long row of books bound in blue. At random she opened the one titled *Oliver Twist*.

Many years later she wrote, "I have long looked for an opportunity to pay a certain debt. And I know of no better way than to write what Charles Dickens did in China for an American child." She had read all of Dickens and then read them all again. This reading schedule she maintained for ten years and ever after kept a Dickens novel always at hand. "He opened my eyes to people," she observed. "He taught me how to love all sorts, high and low, rich and poor, the old and little children. He taught me to hate hypocrisy and pious mouthing; that beneath gruffness there may be kindness, and that kindness is the sweetest thing in the world. He made Christmas for me a merry, roaring English Christmas full of goodies and plum puddings and merriment and friendly cheer. I went to his parties, for I had no other. Charles Dickens made himself a part of me forever."

Encouraged by Carie to write something every week, Pearl, not surprisingly, decided to be a novelist. However, Carie had hardly intended this, having been brought up to regard Dickens as belonging to the lower order and all novels as frivolous time-wasters.

In this she was abetted by Mr. Kung, the stately Confucian scholar who came six days a week to tutor Pearl. To Mr. Kung, novels were not literature at all. Pearl therefore kept her ambitions to herself. Instead, Mr. Kung instructed her in classic literature and Chinese philosophy, with emphasis, of course, on Confucius.

Confucius's primary principle, "What you do not like to have done to you, do not do to others," paralleled the Golden Rule set forth in Matthew 7:12, and he chose the word *reciprocity* to express the whole. Other ideas, however, were his own. Society, he taught, consisted of five relationships: ruler and subject; husband and wife; father and son; older and younger brother; and friend and friend. Command belonged to one; submission to the other. The health of society rested on this order, and the superior's duty was to maintain it, thus setting an example for the inferior.

Rather than any Christlike figure, the Superior Person was Confucius's ideal, a man of self-discipline and self-control. The pragmatism of Confucianism exactly suited the practical Chinese mind and apparently Pearl's as well, for while at home she was exposed to Presbyterian orthodoxy, she was also absorbing Confucian secularism, and throughout her life the word *superior* served as her highest encomium.

In 1900 Grace, the last of Carie's and Absalom's children, was born, a considerable surprise to the tall stranger who turned up periodically from the field. At Christmas the father would return, though somewhat disapprovingly, for Christmas used up money better spent on chapels and Bibles, and there was also a pagan taint about the festivities. But even he joined in when the mail-order boxes arrived from America. They contained coffee and sugar and small items not found in Chinese shops, such as safety pins and peppermint candy. Aside from the necessities, there was for each person a special article, with a dollar limit, chosen from the catalogue. This Dream Book occupied hours of Pearl's time, Satan leading a small child into covetousness and envy.

Yearly she yearned for the beautiful baby doll with a round, bisque face and chubby hands, dressed in a frilly bonnet and frock. "Life size," the catalogue read, but it cost $3.98, and Pearl dared not ask. For years she prayed for a miracle, and her unfulfilled yearning persisted to such a degree that some of her friends are convinced that this led to her later infatuation with babies—all babies.

It seemed to Pearl that there was always something thwarting her desires. For years it was her father's New Testament. Possessing a scholar's familiarity with the New Testament in the original Greek, Absalom fretted over the only existing Chinese translation. There should be, there must be, a proper Chinese translation, both accurate and unadulterated. For years he worked with an elderly Chinese scholar, and at last the feat was accomplished. But then it had to be printed. Again and again revised editions of the New Testament consumed the odd dollars that might otherwise have gone for a book or a doll. Pearl would ask wistfully, "Mother, when Father is finished with the New Testament, may I buy something I want?" But it was never finished, and for years Pearl bore an irrational ill-will toward the New Testament.

Their father, for years almost the only white man the Sydenstricker children knew, was accepted as the norm. White fathers, it seemed, rarely touched or caressed their children, or even their wives, and often seemed not to know they were there. He cared only for his mission work. And indeed the Chinese people were to Absalom what some men's wives were to them. He had grown to love the souls he had come to save, and given the choice between believing a white man or a Chinese, the latter always won. "I've learned I can trust them more," he said bitterly. It was the same in differences of policy. A humble Chinese pastor, struggling to maintain his meager church on ten dollars a month, might ask the Mission Board for help and be refused. Absalom, however, would dig into his pocket, even though it meant leaner rations at home.

Carie had a hard time making her husband establish a balance between his children and his converts. Instinctively, she knew that some Chinese were "rice Christians," preying on his trust. But an unperturbed Absalom would not listen, turning a deaf ear to anything he did not want to believe.

Pearl's first eight years were relatively free of calamities. Within the house Father remained a distant and shadowy figure, Mother an adored object, alternately gay and incomprehensibly sad, turning aside worried queries with a flippant, "Am I never allowed to be quiet?" Wang Amah, however, was always there, comforting lap accessible, arms ready with a hug, no child's grief or fear too trivial to be smoothed away. Outside the house were other children Pearl's age who accepted her in spite of her strange looks. Playing their favorite game of Empress and Son, the girls took turns being the legendary Empress Tzu Hsi in her Forbidden Palace, while some small boy was pressed into service as the child Emperor. Often accused of having the wrong looks for the part of the Empress, Pearl would shout: "I don't care if I do look different from her; I'm just as Chinese as any of you."

Doubtless during these years many events took place that might have awakened Pearl from her peaceful world—worried conversations between her parents, the curious behavior of neighbors. But for eight years she had picked up no clues. Then one morning her father came home covered with blood after having been called to the bedside of a dying convert. Ruffians had broken into the woman's house, and finding Absalom there, had bound him to a post, forcing him to watch while they tortured her to death. It was the raising of a curtain on a dreadful, unsuspected world.

Pearl now saw many things with new eyes—the slurs cast on her fair hair and white skin, the departure of playmates. She realized that her mother had fewer visitors, and at Sunday service the chapel was almost empty. A worried Pearl questioned her mother, who explained sadly that it was nothing they themselves had done; it was the white race they belonged to that was so despised. Then Absalom defined the hatred.

For the past hundred years or so white men from England and Europe had entered China forcibly, humiliating their people. They had overrun the land with their armies and won treaties granting special privileges and advantageous ports and properties. Up to that time China had lived a life secure from the West in comparative calm under the Manchu T'sing Dynasty.

Heading the dynasty was Tzu Hsi, a woman chosen at seventeen to be one of the Emperor's concubines. Through a combination of beauty, brains and willpower, she had become the Emperor's favorite wife and, after his death, the Dowager Empress, ruling China in the name of their son and heir. When the heir died and she saw her power threatened, she boldly placed her nephew on the throne, thus continuing as regent and supreme ruler.

In the last years of the century, however, the power of the Empress and the T'sing Dynasty visibly declined. As as it fell apart, other powers moved in. Japan invaded Korea, which China had always claimed as her own, while the white men hastened to establish markets for their goods, laying down shipping routes along her coastline and railroads between her cities.

Meanwhile, China attempted to fight off the Japanese invaders, only to be soundly defeated and saddled with an enormous indemnity. In desperation, she applied for loans from Germany, France, Russia and Britain, thus finding herself virtually in hock to the white race. "We are being carved up like a melon," shrilled an outraged Tzu Hsi.

Upon reaching manhood, the young Emperor, Kwang Hsu, acknowledged his country's helplessness before the West's superior technology and, aided by advisors, tried to adapt to the westerners' methods of warfare in order to defeat them on their own terms. Tzu Hsi would countenance no compromise, however. Determined to wipe out western influence with one annihilating blow, she allied herself with a ferocious secret society, the Boxers, who claimed supernatural powers. Turned loose on the foreign devils, a wave of mayhem and murder swept through the white settlements, where hundreds died along with the Chinese who tried to protect them.

During the first half of 1900 the whites of Chinkiang, among them the Sydenstrickers, watched daily as the danger crept closer. At first they had refused to flee to Shanghai where American gunboats waited, but in July the U.S. Consul warned everyone:"Keep packed and ready to leave. When the consulate raises its red flag, go straight to the ship at the dock."

In August Absalom rushed home; the red flag had gone up. While the adults grabbed their belongings, Pearl wandered about the house miserably bidding her books and dolls goodbye. She was being driven from her home for a crime she had not committed and barely understood—the crime of belonging to a race different from those about her. On that day the term "race" took on a new and sinister meaning.

Absalom, having despatched his family to Shanghai, stayed behind, the only white man in the area. His work with the Chinese who remained faithful continued, though now as he passed he was often spat upon or stoned. But this was all part of his mission—after all, he reasoned, Jesus himself had been stoned and spat upon.

In Shanghai, Carie took Pearl and her baby, Grace, to a boarding house near Bubbling Well Road. They went for walks to the Bund to watch United States liners docking, and Carie, in a wave of homesickness, described what the voyagers would find at home—wide meadows and rich fruit orchards, barns for children to play in and trees for them to climb, sweet-smelling clover—beauty everywhere. To Pearl America sounded like Heaven.

They waited out the Boxer Rebellion as the surrounding countryside was ravaged, neighborhoods torched, and hundreds of missionaries killed. Japanese and German officials were also murdered and foreign properties pillaged by the ravening Boxers. The chaos lasted until the combined forces of Britain, Russia, France, Germany, Austria, Italy, the United States and Japan routed the Boxers. By that time the Empress's court had fled six hundred miles inland where she lived out the holocaust.

After surrender came retribution. If the Boxers had been destructive, the conquerors were no less so, looting the Imperial Palace, burning and decimating indiscriminately. When the consortium of nations finally announced the terms of surrender, the Chinese were appalled: civil service appointments suspended wherever foreigners had suffered; no arms sold to China for five years; and a fine of $330 million to be paid over the next thirty-nine years. China was stripped of everything save hatred and despair.

One day, as Carie and Pearl walked down a Shanghai boulevard, their way was blocked by a portly Chinese gentleman in a blue satin robe wearing a long queue. In a childish gesture the eight-year-old Pearl gave the queue's tassel a quick tug. Instantly the Chinese turned and, seeing a white child, gave her a murderous look. Carie, seeing the look, blanched. "Please," she gasped, "she's only a child. She's very naughty, and I'll punish her." She pulled her daughter away, and they hurried down a side street. "Never," she snapped, "never do such a thing again. It might be very dangerous." Pearl never forgot the terror on her mother's face.

After nearly a year, Absalom came for them. Grace stared at the gaunt stranger. Pearl's dutiful prayer, "God, please keep our father from the Boxers," was answered, and Carie, relieved at leaving Shanghai, rejoiced further to hear that her husband planned a long furlough at home.

At the turn of the century, missionaries had no scheduled leaves, so Absalom, weary and somewhat discouraged, was now ready for a rest. For Pearl it would be an exciting adventure. For her mother it would be an exile's return.

2

San Francisco, rising out of the early morning mist, its hills clothed in gleaming white houses climbing tier on tier, presented a thrilling picture. Absalom had allotted a few days to sightseeing, and every moment in this unique city was precious. Pearl, accustomed to kerosene lamps and water delivered in pitchers, stared breathless at streets bright with gaslight, and though she had heard of wealthy Shanghai households with running water, nothing had prepared her for the streams gushing out at a turn of a tap. Nor had she dreamed of cable cars rushing uphill at breakneck speed unassisted by horse or man, or the seven-story towers with cages inside that moved up and down.

Carie, her memory focused on West Virginia farm life, had forgotten to describe other American customs, and Pearl, watching the hoisting of trunks and the making of hotel beds, whispered in awe, "Mother, the coolies here are *white* people!"

After several days of surprises the train brought them to Hillsboro, where further surprises awaited. The tall Edgar preparing for an M.A. at Washington and Lee, in solemn eyeglasses and a stiff collar, was hard to reconcile with the brother she remembered climbing trees. Her grandparents' white house had tall columns, a wide lawn and enormous maple trees in front and, far off, there were the Alleghenies. The surprise here was the spaciousness of everything.

Carie's brother and father, both silver-haired and erect, led the travelers indoors to a parlor with horsehair furniture and Stulting portraits, among them one of great-grandfather Meynheer, who had led a colony of Hollanders to Virginia two hundred years before.

Taking Pearl upstairs Carie showed her the six bedrooms dominated by the large front one where she had been born.

Soon thereafter Pearl met Grace Stulting, the cousin with whom she would play all summer, pick apples and berries and join the grown-ups butter making. The months passed, uneventful and happy until fall, when the family took a house in Lexington so Edgar could enter college and Pearl the third grade.

For Absalom this was a return to days when, too poor to eat in the college mess hall for eleven dollars a month, he had cooked in his room, and graduated magna cum laude. His son Edgar knew the same was expected of him, for Absalom, when shown a report card bearing a 99, would say merely, "A hundred would have been better."

But Edgar did well enough. Pearl, listening to their discussions around the fireplace, would hear her father make a remark in Latin and her brother shoot back an answer in Latin at which they both laughed. Occasionally Carie joined in, and Pearl realized proudly that her family were intellectuals, a cut above the rest. Leaning against Edgar by the fire, holding his hand, she knew not only pride but close personal friendship.

But strain was also present. One night Pearl woke to hear her mother crying. Creeping downstairs, she saw Carie sitting in Edgar's room weeping. Edgar, sprawled across the bed, lay on his stomach, one arm hanging off the bed, his face red. A strong, acrid odor filled the room.

Pearl understood the reasons for her mother's distress only vaguely. But tears she did understand, and she sat on the floor holding Carie's hand against her cheek. Finally they went to bed, and the incident was never mentioned. This encounter with alcohol left Pearl with a certain unease in its presence, and she never lost a sense of powerlessness as, in later years, she often watched it take its toll.

With the scholastic year at an end, it was time for China again, reminding them of the possibility of a return of animosity. But externally, their return was reassuring. The male servants were still polite, and Wang Amah, except for growing even more gnomelike, was the same devoted foster mother.

After a year's absence, Pearl really saw her Chinkiang home for the first time. Built for missionaries, purely practical, it made no claim to beauty: dining room and living room off a central hall, Carie's room with its flowers and white curtains on one side and next door the girls' room with a thin wall between. Her father's room, however, was a place apart—no carpet or flowers or curtains here, only wall bookcases crowding his desk into the middle of the room. The household, accustomed to scholarly visitors arriving to discuss the fine points of Scripture, were relieved to discover the reappearance of these gentlemen upon their return.

Gradually, the missionaries learned that China was changing. In place of anti-white hostility, the Chinese had adopted a creeping servility. Absalom was now flattered and fawned upon, his chapels crowded, his advice sought, and soon his diocese encompassed two hundred churches and schools. It became evident that attendance at the white man's church bestowed priority status, and Absalom exulted in this new acceptance of the Word. Even Pearl met with obsequiousness in the houses she visited. Puzzled, she sought out Teacher Kung.

The Chinese nation, Kung explained, was paralyzed with fear. The whites' revenge for the Boxer Rebellion and their crushing indemnity demands were so exorbitant, so intimidating, that like a beaten dog, China cowered before the master with the whip.

Behind the Chinese submissiveness, he went on, lay more than a normal military defeat. The Boxers believed that the whites possessed a supernatural power superior to their own, and that this Christianity they espoused had been responsible for their defeat. So for a while the Christians' missions and industries enjoyed great prestige, and China could only watch as the foreign devils' power increased.

Seeing China prostrate, Russia began a move into Southern Manchuria. Japan's reaction to the move was a proposal that between them they should divide up coastal China into "spheres of influence." Russia, believing herself militarily superior to Japan, refused to share, and the result was the Russo-Japanese War. To the world's amazement, Russia was defeated, and Japan had suddenly become a world power.

In all the skirmishing, China was virtually ignored except as a battleground. But this had an arresting effect. From the Japanese defeat of Russia the Chinese absorbed the exhilarating knowledge that a yellow race could overwhelm a white race—thus, when Orientals learned Occidental methods they too would be able to win battles.

Pearl, through Teacher Kung, imbibed the lessons of history daily. He spoke in solemn tones: "Little Sister, listen while you can. It will be peaceful here in China for a while. But the storm is rising, and before it breaks, you must go far away. Go to America and stay there lest next time you be killed with all your kind." At these words Pearl put her forehead on the table and wept.

Never again would Pearl feel that China was her home. She was an American, white, a person separate from others, speaking across a gulf. Thus she would often describe herself in later life . . . different . . . alone.

As Pearl approached adolescence, she examined herself in the mirror with mixed feelings. Tall enough and slim enough, she approved of her long braids and fine eyes but deplored the uneven teeth and prominent nose too strong for girlish prettiness. She could boast a vast general knowledge and such feminine graces, forced upon her by Carie, as knitting, sewing, cooking, painting with water-colors, even some facility on an old Mason and Hamlin piano wangled somehow by her mother.

Alone too much, since Grace was seven years her junior, Pearl tended to be morose. And after the death of Teacher Kung, too old for another male tutor, she was sent to a girls' school where she met other American and English expatriates like herself. But with the advent of 1907 everything stopped, for there came that year one of the worst famines in Chinese history.

Absalom spent that winter in the North administering American aid, and as starvation worsened refugees poured south. In Chinkiang Carie dispensed mission funds, moving among sickening sights— husbands and wives fighting over a fishhead, mothers snatching scraps from their babies' hands; rumors ran rife of cannibalism. After a day of horrors she would go home, but having been seen dispensing food, she was followed by crazed people staggering up the hill. In the morning there would be corpses lying outside the gate, their arms outstretched.

Shiploads of aid arrived from America, and Carie was proud to tell of its origin. But sometimes she laughed grimly at the contents— corsets, high-heeled slippers, chiffon ballgowns. There were hundreds of slightly aged cheeses which proved equally useless, for to the Chinese cheese was spoiled milk and therefore inedible. Nevertheless, Carie went to every white home selling this gourmet's delight, ripe cheese, and turned a profit for relief.

The famine lasted through the winter. There could be no Christmas; instead that day was spent cooking huge vats of rice and passing it through the gate. The stresses of the year had left Pearl with a more mature sensitivity. Things she had always known unconsciously became sharply clear. Her mother's references to West Virginia's beauty and cleanliness bespoke her homesickness. And through the bungalow's thin walls had come sounds of an argument, Carie's angry voice high and sharp, Absalom's low and defensive, and, occasionally, the plaintive sound of weeping, which only much later would she understand. In her most personal novel *The Time Is Noon*, Pearl Buck would put those feelings into words: "I thought there would be something more than this."

For the first time she saw her mother's pathetic attire—fresh and dainty and somehow elegant but actually mended and darned. And this while all their extra cash went into her father's hated Testament. Envisioning her mother as something of a martyr, Pearl developed a healthy hatred for her father. In the Confucian culture of respect for parents, however, one made no scenes of rebellion, and Absalom may never have noticed his daughter's feelings.

The barrenness of her parents' marriage was emphasized by the proximity of a marriage rich in love. For years Carie had taken in young missionary couples, and this time it was the Hancocks from Texas. He was lean and sunburned and talked with an intriguing Texas twang; she was slender and wore stunning American clothes. One night after dinner Hancock excused himself to study and his wife rose to follow. "Why don't you stay here?" Pearl begged. "Why do you have to go in there with him?"

The wife replied simply, "Because I love him."

These years were not happy ones for Pearl. Sensitive, emotional, she swung wildly from playing practical jokes to entertaining end-of-the-world forebodings. And there was contention over the question of college. Pearl favored Wellesley, expensive of course, but she would earn money coaching. West Virginia, however, was still in her mother's blood. "Wellesley!" she scoffed. "Why that's a *Northern* college!"

So Pearl abandoned the North. Among Southern colleges, the best seemed to be Randolph-Macon in Lynchburg, Virginia. It had Methodist-Episcopal affiliations—not Presbyterian, of course, but better than nothing. It was inexpensive; and it had a curriculum that made no concession to femininity, stressing a thoroughly masculine list of courses. Clinching the selection was the fact that her brother Edgar would be working on a Lynchburg newspaper.

Absalom's sabbatical, however, was still a year away so until she could travel to Lynchburg with her parents Pearl attended the Jewell School in Shanghai.

At sixteen she was approaching adulthood. The girls in school had introduced her to the pompadour, a hirsute structure padded by a "rat" made of false hair. Carie had maintained her silence when her daughter appeared in one, for she knew this to be a prelude to the subject of new clothes.

Chinese tailors were employed to copy the dresses and coats in American magazines (the *Delineator* was the favorite) and from them she and Pearl chose her wardrobe. But Chinese tailors were no match for American hats. Carie had a box filled with old hats in their attic and now she suggested gaily, "Let's go to Paris and buy you a *chapeau*." The result, after steaming, pressing and trimming, silenced, if not entirely satisfied, Pearl's demands.

The girl who arrived in Shanghai with her parents appeared somewhat taller than her actual five feet five. Her hair, worn in a single braid caught at the nape of the neck, was tied with a wide flat bow. The tailor had outdone himself on her clothes, and Carie presented her at the well-known school with confidence.

The Misses Jewell, Martha and Eugenia, had come from Vermont, their stern Puritan consciences directing them to found a school for missionaries' daughters. Situated in an unfashionable neighborhood, it was nevertheless the repository of all the daughters of whites, including the well-to-do.

Pearl's first impression was of a ground floor heavily barred, dark rooms hung with biblical texts, a fireplace smouldering without a flame. Miss Eugenia was equally dark. Years of dispensing discipline had cured her of any tendency toward cheerfulness, and the atmosphere exuded a disheartening piety reassuring to the most rigid parent.

Two missionaries' daughters were to be Pearl's roommates. Soon after her arrival she remarked recklessly that Christianity and Buddhism had much in common, and perhaps Jesus had taken his golden rule from Confucius. Her heresy was quickly reported to headquarters, and for the good of the school, she was transferred to a single room. A delighted Pearl could now read after lights were officially out.

In her studies she was selective, giving her heart only to English, philosophy and literature. The Friday Literary Club was impressed by the novel she was writing and astounded by her remark that she read

Alice in Wonderland once a year for its deeper insights. By common consent she was allowed to be different from the rest.

Born with a writer's curiosity, she spent time exploring Shanghai, fascinated by its racial make-up: English, French, Russian, German, Indian, Japanese and American. Also comprising part of the mixture were the Chinese of mixed blood, miserable blue-eyed citizens who belonged nowhere. Pearl often visited the foreign park where certain intruders were banned by a sign, NO CHINESE, NO DOGS.

The city's showplace was the Bund, a tree-shaded promenade bordering the Yangtse River, which at this point was over a mile wide. One section, the French Concession, was made up of land taken from the Chinese under an early treaty, now the home of the wealthy of all races. Next to it, in the International Settlement, British industry and banking reigned, while the American Settlement, home of the Jewell School, was considerably less elegant than either.

The Jewell sisters insisted on their charges making a contribution to the common good, not with money but in service, and one of the opportunities presented was at the "Door of Hope." This institution, a rescue home for girls forced into prostitution and slaves owned by tyrannical mistresses, was supported by the municipal authorities. Its mission was to free the slaves and find them regular work, and Pearl was asked to teach them sewing, knitting and embroidery. The girls, sold by their families during times of crisis, were trained as servants in wealthy households. (Many of the prostitutes had been children bought and traded for this purpose.) If the family was kind the slave might be freed at eighteen and given in marriage; if not she might be beaten or raped.

"At the Door of Hope I saw the dreadful fruit of evil . . ." Pearl Buck later wrote. "Many a night I woke . . . to ponder the stories the girls told me . . . I had early to accept the fact that there are . . . men and women incurably and willfully cruel and wicked. But forced to this recognition I retaliated spiritually by making the fierce resolution that wherever I saw evil and cruelty at work I would devote all I had to delivering the victim. This resolution has stayed with me throughout life and provided a conscience for conduct. It has not always been easy to follow."

At the end of that winter Pearl returned home to prepare for college life.

Since Edgar was married and living in Lynchburg, Virginia, it was appropriate that the family reassemble there, and so the house was closed and the long journey begun. Pearl's sister Grace recalled the trip. "It was two weeks, Peking to Moscow. We went up through Mukden and Harbin and then the ten days across Russia, all four in one cabin with Pearl and me in the upper bunks. There wasn't any lavatory and facilities were a hole in the floor at the end of the passage. We took a basin to wash in and canned milk, coffee, peanut butter, jam and so on. When the train stopped along the way we ran out and bought thick black bread and hard-boiled eggs and cheese.

"In Moscow we saw the Kremlin, and we stayed a month in Neufchatel where Pearl was tutored in French to get into a second year class. In Paris we went to museums, but my father was disgusted at the naked statues and wouldn't look."

Pearl's sightseeing in Russia depressed her deeply, the wealthy noblemen and priests contrasting with the filthy peasants. "I felt a fearful premonition of a world to come," she wrote, "the innocent would suffer because of the anger of an outraged people. I remember hoping . . . that when the peoples of Asia rose up against the white men who had ruled them, Americans could be recognized as different."

After France they visited England, which Pearl came to love passionately. But remembering England's legal admonition in the park, NO CHINESE, NO DOGS, she felt that they would be oblivious to any uprising. This uprising, her father predicted, would begin in Russia where people were the most wretched, and then move to all of Asia. There, he decided, it would be against the entire white race because they had been the oppressors.

When Pearl reminded her father of the good works accomplished by America in China, the new hospitals and schools, he shook his head. "We missionaries went to China without invitation and solely from our own sense of duty. The Chinese therefore owe us nothing. We have done the best we could but that was our duty and so they still owe us nothing. And if the United States had taken no concessions, we have kept silence when others did, and we too have profited from the unequal treaties. I don't think we shall escape when the day of reckoning comes."

In September 1910, Pearl spent her first day at college. She and her parents had arrived at the twenty-acre Lynchburg, Virginia, campus via interurban streetcar and, after the formalities of registration, Absalom and Carie kissed their daughter goodbye and returned to Edgar's house in town. A teacher led Pearl through a dark uncarpeted corridor to West Hall and her room. There alone she suddenly realized, for the first time in her life, that she was on her own.

Depression was settling in on her. Dreams of the world's great universities—Heidelberg, Cambridge, Princeton—had prepared her for mellowed stone buildings clothed in ivy, tree-shaded lawns and dedicated students scurrying earnestly from one majestic hall to another. After descending from the streetcar onto a row of stepping-stones embedded in thick red mud, she had picked her way to a cluster of raw brick buildings, graceless and nondescript. The guest hall was drab and uninviting, and though there were fellow students rushing about, their din was, for the most part, high-pitched shrieks of recognition.

Supper was served at six, and Pearl found her way to the dining hall, guided by the distant hum of voices and clattering dishes. Slipping into a chair at the door, she glanced about. Everyone seemed to know everyone else. Only Pearl, concentrating on hiding her misery, seemed like an outsider.

Another girl, small and fair-haired, sat at a nearby table. She, too, looked around inquiringly. "I remember my first day at college," Emma Edmunds recalled. "I'd grown up in this little village, and when I got to college the girls all seemed at home and so sophisticated, and I felt so countrified. Then I saw this one girl and she looked even more countrified than me. Her dress was made of Chinese grass linen and nobody else had anything like that. It had a high neck and long sleeves, and her hair was in a braid turned under at the back. Most of the other girls had those little artificial curls stuck on that everybody was wearing, and big puffs. Pearl looked terribly *different*. I felt sorry for her, somehow, I knew how she felt, and so I dared speak to her. That's how we met." Theirs became a firm friendship that would endure for sixty years.

The Sydenstrickers were to leave America before too long, and Pearl spent her free time at her brother Edgar's house. Though her unusual background had won her immediate attention in the classroom, outside of it the other girls did not drift toward her, and with only Emma as a friend, she felt truly alien. Unbearably lonely, as the weeks passed she concentrated on learning the minutiae of her college.

The Randolph-Macon student body was expected to live "in accord with the principles of honor and of good breeding," and a Student Government Committee was responsible, under the Board, for their conduct. On entering each girl pledged to observe the honor code, which covered everything from off-campus limits to plagiarism and cheating. Living conditions were spartan—two iron cots in each room, two chairs, a bureau and one gas burner. The bathrooms contained three bathtubs for every twenty girls, which had to be reserved in advance. Daily chapel was compulsory, as were Sunday services and vespers. Free time was three to six and ten until lights out. Gym was required and so was the detested gym uniform, ballooning black serge bloomers and black cotton stockings worn with a white middy blouse and black sailor tie.

Social life was confined to the campus, and many girls never left it except at Christmas and Easter, though until Pearl's parents returned to China she was allowed to spend weekends at Edgar's. Girls could invite boys to Sunday night group parties, carefully chaperoned, but dancing and card-playing were forbidden, except for Flinch, a children's card game deemed less harmful than most. And the Victrola played popular as well as sacred music.

Saturday night dates were allowed in the parlor, and the giggling undergraduates were supervised by the Hall monitor. The weekly highlight, however, was the party after Sunday vespers. Everyone dressed in her finest and as entertainment a story was read aloud. "The Casting Away of Mrs. Lecks and Mrs. Aleshine" was the current favorite. On other evenings there was music or elocution performed by the students, and imitations were extremely popular.

The local YWCA was affiliated with a Student Volunteer group and among their activities were meetings aimed toward those students interested in becoming missionaries. Pearl had privately considered the principle of foreign missions, and in her loneliness decided that belonging to a missionary group was better than belonging to nothing at all.

When certain freshmen began sporting mysterious twists of ribbon on their blouses, Pearl learned that they were pledge badges to a sorority. That Emma too had been excluded from pledging provided some consolation, and the two young women felt more than ever like two exiles in a hostile land.

At Christmas Emma went home while Pearl joined her family at Edgar's for what would be their last Christmas together for four years. She dreaded the separation, for her mother was not in good health and Edgar's home life was far from ideal. His wife contributed little to the union and was regarded as inferior to him by her in-laws. Pearl realized that she was witnessing the slow death of a marriage.

After the holidays she discovered that back at college things had also

gone awry. The usually lively Emma seemed uncomfortable and eva-
sive in her presence, and Pearl, sensitive to her moods, waited for an
explanation, which came on the day Emma appeared wearing her Chi
Omega pledge ribbon.

"I hurt Pearl," Emma acknowledged, "never telling her. I had just
thought it was so secret I wasn't supposed to tell anybody. If the
positions had been reversed I know I'd have been hurt."

This was the final blow for Pearl. Aware that four years in America
had to be endured, she faced her situation coolly. Her life somehow
depended on these strange American college girls. Snobbish and brain-
less they might be, but she would have to take life on their terms. She
would adapt herself to their ways, follow them, indeed be like them.
But she would not merely copy them; she would be American like
them, and furthermore become a leader as well.

Her academic courses would present no problem; she would score
well. But outside of class she would study the college leaders, their
clothes and speech, even their points of view, and step by step she
would remake herself in their image.

She had known from the beginning that her clothes were all wrong,
"tacky" and had even attempted some alterations. Now she would
indeed go out and buy a new wardrobe. From the best shop in town.

She would have to earn her spending money. Coaching slow learners
was profitable so coaching lessons began. And she not only acquired
the accepted slang vocabulary but even such fads as sleeping late and
skipping breakfast. "By the end of my freshman year," Pearl boasted
proudly, "I was indistinguishable from any other girl of my age and
class."

Her studies, meanwhile, moved along predictable lines. Latin and
mathematics proved to be her *bêtes noires*, and physics she brushed
off, to her later regret. But her English, psychology and philosophy
teachers seemed hard pressed to keep up with her, one complaining,
"In marking her English papers, I used to run out of synonyms for
excellent."

Her contributions to the college periodicals were also predictable.
"The Valley by the Sea," published in *The Tattler*, was a Chinese story
written in pseudo-poetic style, as was "By the Hand of a Child" in the
Helianthus; but these brought her some attention, and that was a
beginning.

The school year passed, routinely on campus but not off campus, for Edgar's marriage was a shambles, and Pearl visited the couple only for the sake of the children. Even a longed-for vacation at Emma's had to be sacrificed for them and she was happy when college reopened.

This year found her happier and more self-assured. Her wardrobe, though modest, was *right*, and she was an "old girl" now, putting new girls at ease, at last comfortable enough to joke about herself. When another student laughed about losing ten dollars, Pearl admitted: "If anybody in *my* family had lost ten dollars, we'd have gasped and fallen dead."

Still excluded from the inner college circles, she joined other groups. Traditionally every girl was either an Odd or an Even according to her year, and the two waged eternal warfare. There were parades and battles, and an afternoon of horseplay would leave the grounds thick with false hair lost in the fray. "We had loads of fun letting off steam," Emma remembered, "and Pearl was not too dignified. She got kind of involved."

For college girls in 1911 there was no radio or television, no automobiles, no solitary dates, no dancing even with each other. They had to invent their entertainment, and Emma described a party in which her friend Pearl participated to the hilt. "The Odds were planning an Undersea party to dress up like mermaids and drape fishnets around the gym. We Evens decided to break it up. We spent two dollars for a sack of old fish and gave them time to ripen. And that night Pearl dressed up as an old fisherman with a beard and a pack on her back and went to the Odds' party and dropped one of those awful fish in every net."

Pearl now belonged. For the literary societies where she was outstandingly eligible, she presented outstanding papers. And she ended her year a member of the Student Committee and treasurer of her class.

At that year's commencement a senior chose her to be "attending squire" in the graduation ceremony, a special honor. And finally, taking a giant step, she was elected president for the coming year. Few of her later honors gave her the satisfaction of this juvenile triumph.

"The best year of my college life," she called it. Popular now, busy, a power in her tiny world, Pearl was a radiant class president, and more glory was to follow. Am Sam, the most prestigious society on campus, its membership limited to sixteen, decided they had to have her as a member. Pearl sat with the Am Sam leaders in their own house, drank hot chocolate and discussed the crucial issues of Randolph-Macon College. Finally, the prominent sorority, Kappa Delta, broke precedent in pledging her. Their image was one of "cute" girls, not intellectuals, and in choosing her they apparently considered her both.

In the spring she represented the college at the YWCA conference at Bryn Mawr. What to wear was a major problem, but West Hall contributed several dresses, some so new and stylish Pearl had never seen anything like them, and discovered much later that she had worn one of them back to front.

Before she left for the conference, a delegation of Kappa Delta presented Pearl with a long, narrow package. They said they knew that women in China didn't wear corsets, and Pearl didn't have to on campus, but for the national honor of Kappa Delta, would she please wear this corset at Bryn Mawr?

Her letters home resulted in both pride and mystification. *Am Sam, Kappa Delta, rushing, pledging, hazing* were incomprehensible terms to her family, but the overall picture was of a college girl happily involved, and Carie was happy and Grace proud. But to Absalom all the doings his daughter described were costing an enormous amount of money. When she presided at meetings before five hundred girls it was embarrassing, she wrote, to stand up there week after week in the same dress. She had a certain position to maintain; please, could she have a bit more money? This was a new Pearl.

That spring Pearl received sad news; her dear, wrinkled Wang Amah was dead. Pearl wrote, "She left her share in us her white children. Part of her went into us, as mothers are part of their children, so that now and forever her country is like our own." Later she learned that her mother was not well. Pearl had noticed her frail condition before she left Lynchburg and she was worried. Her happy year was taking a downward turn.

Spring elections for the fall's two biggest offices, President of Student Government and President of YWCA, were imminent, and the campus was abuzz with speculation. The delegate to the Bryn Mawr YWCA conference, Pearl knew, usually became president of the Student Committee. When she was asked who she thought would be Student President, she answered simply, "I think I will."

Her candor did not sit well, and resulted in her achieving neither post. A friend observed, "She *was* slated for Student Committee, but she didn't have the political savvy to keep her mouth shut." In time, this would prove to be a lesson well learned.

In their senior year Emma and Pearl had planned to room together but suddenly there was a crisis with Edgar's career. He had been studying economics and a good position demanding considerable travel was offered him in Washington. He turned to his sister. Would Pearl move into his house and look after his children and his wife, Alice, who was afraid to be alone?

This not only meant living with a woman she disliked, but forfeiting editorship of *The Tattler*, a job customarily held by a boarder, plus an hour's streetcar ride each way to the campus. But Sydenstricker blood prevailed, and Pearl did her duty.

Soon afterwards additional sisterly help was required when Edgar, considering divorce, asked Pearl to break the shocking news to their parents. Her beloved brother asked and so she complied. The aftermath was a tear-stained letter from Carie mourning the wrong she had done her son in sending him away so young. Edgar, sensing the depth of her pain, put off his divorce until after his parents' deaths.

For Pearl the year was one strictly of work, coaching and marking freshman psychology papers. Having learned her lesson in diplomacy, she gracefully "accepted" the presidency of the Franklin Literary Society, the Senior Club and the exclusive Modern Literary Club. *The Tattler* published several of her poems and stories. Although the poems still reveal a juvenile fascination with poetic phrases and myths, her fiction was beginning to embrace reality. "The Hour of Worship," written in the archaic style later used in *The Good Earth*, relates the problem of a missionary woman who has lost her faith in religion. Superficially it reflects Pearl's mother's dilemma, for Carie had never attained the unquestioning faith of her husband, suffering, as a result, pangs of guilt. But it also reveals Pearl's growing skepticism of the missionary establishment. This conflict was beginning to give her trouble.

Her writing was moving from myth to experience, and her last two contributions were proof of literary progress. In the year-end competitions for best story and best poem, Pearl Sydenstricker won both prizes.

However, her memories of her collegiate literary successes were painful. Forty-five years later she wrote: "Many honors do not make one better loved.... What astonished and wounded me was that in the congratulations of my fellows I discerned a slight hostility, a hint of complaint that one person had been given the two best prizes.... The same criticism fell upon me when the Nobel Prize for Literature was given me. I felt almost apologetic for having received it."

After commencement exercises everyone but Pearl went home. She had not decided what to do next, but America beckoned. There was more to see than just Bryn Mawr and West Virginia, so when the psychology professor offered her an assistant's post, she settled down to teach.

Meanwhile, distressing news arrived from China. Carie had developed sprue, a painful disease of the red blood corpuscles which offered no long-term hope. A frantic Pearl applied to the Presbyterian Board of Missions for a teaching job in Chinkiang.

In 1914 world events made traveling precarious, and Pearl was asked to postpone her trip. But with further depressing medical reports from China, she insisted on leaving. Emma Edmunds agreed to take over her faculty job, and on a gray November day in 1914 Pearl began the month-long journey home.

On the ship Pearl met a young man with the Standard Oil Company, ten years her senior, whom she referred to as "a part of my education."

"I suppose the first time I was in love was on that ship," she commented briefly. "I didn't want to marry anyone, yet the shipboard experience was good for me. It was the first time I ever kissed a man with all my heart.... Yet I knew perfectly well I did not really care for him. I knew I would be too much for him because he wasn't my equal. I suppose I was in need of some physical expression, but I was very grateful I had not let it go too far. Nevertheless, I was first conscious then of my own looks. He did that for me, he made me value my looks." To her sister Grace she confided that he "almost proposed," and wanted her to go with him to Manila.

By the time she reached Shanghai, however, she had made a decision. Her first priorities would be her mother's health and the education of her teen-age sister.

She was met by Absalom, tall, spare as ever and aged only slightly, and by Grace, no longer a child but still in awe of her sister. On the train to Chinkiang Pearl learned that she had arrived home none too soon.

It also became immediately apparent how much China had changed. The political reforms of the Empress's nephew attempted to satisfy the westernized element among the younger generation of Chinese. Some schools were teaching western ideas and technologies, and American colleges had accepted Chinese students as partial payment of the Boxer Rebellion indemnity. Literature was becoming westernized; military schools were flourishing and the army, hitherto despised, was being upgraded. The judicial system was also in the process of being overhauled (without, however, abolishing extraterritoriality, the treaty granting aliens exemption from local laws). A shift to constitutional government from the Manchu monarchy was being considered and trade with the outside world encouraged.

The Empress's efforts to block reforms had proven futile and when both she and Kwang Hsu died in 1908, the Manchu dynasty appeared doomed.

Three years of chaos and strife followed, out of which emerged China's great leader, Sun Yat-sen. A Christianized doctor turned revolutionary, Sun had spent twenty years working both overseas and in his own country for a republican form of government, and in 1911 his Kuomintang Party fathered the Republic of China. When Pearl returned in 1914 the Kuomintang, "the Nationalists" were firmly ensconced, though the remnants of the Manchu government still resisted change, and as in all contests there were impassioned arguments for both sides. Pearl kept up with the news diligently, but had to concentrate primarily on her mother's baffling disease.

Tropical sprue attacked the mucous membrane of the mouth, throat and intestines, making eating and digestion painful and difficult. A diet of rice, gruel, fresh fruit, soft boiled eggs and liver seemed to help, and Pearl felt hopeful. Meanwhile, she assumed her mother's mission work with the exception of seeking converts, which she found awkward. But, like her mother, she listened eagerly to the trusting Chinese women's confidences, deeming it a priceless experience.

Pearl had obtained a position in the local mission school, and with teaching, nursing and church work, her days were full. She enjoyed teaching, for her students were high school seniors profoundly eager to learn, and while teaching she also discussed ethics, philosophy and government. "They taught me far more than I taught them," she observed later. "It was a wonderful time to live in China. I was young, interested in everything, able to read both Chinese and English, and surrounded by friends far beyond the Christian mission circles. I found myself stirred and stimulated."

The young Chinese intellectuals, western-educated students, were attempting to create a new China, quarreling bitterly over the laws of government. Opposing them were the cruel and selfish warlords still squabbling over their separate empires. Firmly between the two factions stood the zealous Sun Yat-sen fighting for his own ideals. "Sometimes," Pearl wrote, "I felt as I read the papers that I was a juggler trying to keep a dozen balls in the air at once."

During the fall and into the following spring, Carie lay ill and fretful. The same deep love from childhood existed between the two women, but now Carie criticized dresses with low necklines and love songs with suggestive lyrics, and the twenty-two-year-old Pearl resisted the older woman's criticism. Still, mutual affection held them together and Pearl longed only for her mother's recovery.

But there was also a gnawing urge within her to get on with her life. Recalling her impatience she wrote later, "I knew of course that I would be a writer, but I was not ready yet. I still felt empty." No writer, she believed, should attempt a novel before thirty, and then only if he had been hopelessly involved in life. He must live at full tilt and for nothing but the experience itself. Later the experience might transmute itself into literature.

But how, she asked herself, could one live at full tilt in her tight missionary circle? More and more she rebelled at the idea that only one religion had a right to exist. She wrote to Emma, "I have not seen kindness among missionaries, because they are not kind to the people who disagree with them. When I came back from America I was already disagreeing with them."

Before long the need to lead her own life elsewhere drove her to cast about for an escape. A teacher in the distant Yunnan Province needed workers for a challenging cultural experiment, and Pearl volunteered. Unfortunately, the teacher's letter of acceptance fell into Carie's hands. An hysterical Carie cried that she would die if Pearl left, reproaching her daughter for ignoring the Chinese tradition of filial devotion. Pearl reminded her mother that she had left home against her father's wishes, and Carie cried out bitterly, "I know it. I wish I had obeyed him." The abyss this cry disclosed shocked Pearl into silence.

When Carie's condition worsened, she was ordered to the health resort at Kuling. Accepting defeat, Pearl reentered the nursing ward.

Kuling, a mountain retreat far from the sweltering Yangtse Valley, had been established years before by white missionaries. With cool clean air where heat, cholera and malaria were relatively unknown, it was a two-day journey by steamer, a summer residence for women and children and a vacation spot for the men. Absalom had built a small stone cottage there when Pearl was a child, and every summer she had relished running barefoot among the wild flowers and bathing in the icy pool. Its fame as a health resort had attracted whites who considered it their special property, and now, large and cosmopolitan, it had white shops and a tuberculosis sanatorium. On the fringes of town wealthy Chinese had built large stone mansions.

"We must let the Chinese in," Carie had remarked. "I can see that. Perhaps we white people should never have built a separate place for ourselves. . . . Some day the Chinese will take everything back again."

But there were no visible signs of animosity, and that summer was pleasant enough. Grace arrived from her Shanghai school and there were both old and new Kuling acquaintances in residence. When Grace returned to school in the fall, however, Pearl stayed on with her mother, and there she spent what she called "the loneliest winter of my life," with only one couple and one sanatorium patient as companions.

By February her sense of duty had been replaced by desperation. Leaving her mother with the doctor, she walked down the mountain, finally returning to Chinkiang where alone with the self-absorbed Absalom she hoped to make new friends.

Unfortunately, all the young Chinese women were busy with husbands and babies, for their parents had planned their futures early. A Chinese marriage was a family affair, and for stability and happiness a daughter's husband was chosen by birth and breeding to fit into the family circle. What was begun by the parents was expected to result in companionship and love for the children.

Pearl's parents had neglected the matter of marriage, and her friends worried for her. Secretly she worried for herself. Whenever the subject of matrimony had arisen Absalom had favored a Chinese husband, but Carie, stoutly American, wished otherwise, and Pearl, after four years in the States, agreed. Now it was time to look around for herself.

Chinkiang's white male population consisted of two or three men who worked for British concerns and a few who were with the Standard Oil and American Tobacco companies. They too were looking around, and when the handsome American with her magnificent blue

eyes and radiant smile appeared, interest in her ran high. Dates followed: horseback rides, walks, dinners at friends' homes. But one day
an older woman, a missionary, approached Pearl, and Pearl angrily
recorded their conversation:

"You cannot continue in both ways of life," the woman warned her.
"If you go with the business people, you must leave the missionary
circle."

"But I am not a missionary," Pearl had protested. "I'm a teacher."

"You are a teacher in a mission school. And your parents are
missionaries."

"My parents don't mind."

"The rest of us do," the woman snapped. For the sake of her parents,
Pearl gave up the business people.

During this period she had kept up her correspondence with Emma
Edmunds, who had finished out Pearl's term at RMWC and was now
preparing to marry a young missionary and come to China. "I think
there was a missionary doctor whom she had a good many dates with,"
she reported of Pearl. "She sort of intimated she could have married
him. But then another girl came along and he married her. Then there
was somebody else that she was very much interested in but for some
reason she didn't feel she should marry him. I tore up the letter and I
don't remember any more than that."

When school finished, Pearl returned to her mother in Kuling with
the endless days stretching ahead of her like a road across a desert.

3

John Lossing Buck was born on a farm outside Poughkeepsie, New York, in 1890, the eldest of four sons and a descendant of early English, Dutch and French settlers, hard-working, no-nonsense farmers. Except for an annual call on nearby relatives, his father and mother adhered strictly to life on their farm, where they brought up their sons to be honest, reverent and frugal, and to avoid frivolities.

Lossing Buck revealed his drive and self-reliance early, skipping a grade in school and supporting himself through Cornell Agricultural College with a variety of jobs. Concentrating in college on his major, he spent his few leisure hours in the environment he knew best. Because of his interest in foreign missions, he joined a small group that met every Sunday morning in Cornell's religious center, Barnes Hall, under the leadership of John Reisner, a graduate student.

Among the group also studying agriculture was a young Chinese with whom he soon became friends. Hu Shih, although less than impassioned about farming, was given as a class assignment the identification of New York apples and, finding the task monumentally boring, switched to arts and science. In this major he pursued such a spectacularly successful course that, upon returning to China he would in time be responsible for altering the way in which the Chinese language was written, ultimately serving as Ambassador to the United States. Another important contribution was his encouragement of classmate Lossing Buck's interest in China.

After graduation from Cornell in June 1914, Lossing went to work on a reformatory farm teaching young prisoners improved methods of farming. He had accepted the job only in the missionary spirit, but after a year he left the prison farm and applied officially to the Presbyterian Board of Foreign Missions for a post. New York City's Madison Avenue Church currently supported a mission station at Nanhsuchou in China's wheat region, two hundred miles north of Nanking, where American methods were being introduced. An interview with the Church's eminent pastor, Dr. Henry Sloan Coffin, clinched the job.

The project was only two years old. Dr. John Williams, Vice President of Nanking University (later killed in the Nanking Incident), had gone to Cornell looking for a teacher for its College of Agriculture. John Reisner, with an M.A. in agriculture, left for Nanking in October. When Buck applied a few months later, his teaching experience made him a natural choice for the Nanhsuchou experiment.

Bidding his parents and brothers goodbye, he left on October 29, 1915. He wrote his first letter home while crossing the "great American desert": "There are mountains on all sides, plants growing are greasewood bushes (about four or five feet high, many branches and with small brown leaves, certain plants five feet high, mostly three or four feet high). Tumbleweed, a finely branched weed . . . is so-named because it is easily blown about by the wind. . . ." He interrupted his numerous descriptions of mountains and rivers: "Train just stopped. I went out and got a sample of greasewood and tumbleweed. Will send you a sample. You can tell the difference by the greasiness. Grease is to keep water from evaporating from the plant. The other is fuzzy for the same reason. I notice from the color on my fingers that greasewood has other characteristics as well."

Soon after docking at Shanghai in June 1916, the tall, auburn-haired New Yorker found himself struggling with the Chinese tongue eight hours a day in the School of Languages of the University of Nanking. With characteristic detail he sent his mother a description of his "fine room" in Mr. and Mrs. Small's boarding house. "Southwest corner second floor of a new house." After several pages covering the interior and exterior of the house, he described the landscape beyond, the servants' wages, the population of Nanking (350,000) and the region's mean temperature.

Between all-day sessions at the school he explored the city and decided "the great pressing need of China is Christianity and education. I am mighty glad I have come, the field is unlimited." After reporting that he had seen John and Bertha Reisner, been invited to dinner and met some future Nanhsuchou colleagues, he kept his parents abreast of his financial affairs. "It costs me $25 a month for board, heat and light, at the present rate of exchange just half of my salary. I have visions of paying my debts and my life insurance and getting rich all in a hurry!"

In late June he went to Kuling for a two-month vacation, staying with a Mrs. Adams, a motherly Englishwoman. Kuling's social life appeared to be unusually brisk. Its international atmosphere—British, American, Swedish, Norwegian, German, French and Russian—provided gay though decorous activities: picnics, tea parties, walks and bathing. Dinner parties and music provided by local talent enlivened the evenings, and a handsome young bachelor was not likely to be lonely.

After settling in at Mrs. Adams's, Lossing had attended church and surreptitiously looked around. His monthly salary of fifty dollars did not allow for much extravagance, but manfully he put fifty cents in the collection plate. He would have to be very frugal. A white suit ($14) and a pith helmet ($4) being compulsory attire, he would be wise to move cautiously before committing himself to any social engagements.

All this he relayed to his mother along with bulletins about a girl at home named Mildred and a joyous report about meeting Dean Joseph Bailie's daughter, who said her father, the American agriculturist, might come to China the following year. He had also met another Cornellian, Dean Kelsey, and had been invited to dinner, at which time Mrs. Kelsey had mentioned a picnic the following Sunday when "that darling Mrs. Sydenstricker's daughter, Pearl," would probably be present.

On July 26 Lossing wrote his mother: "I have just met a nice missionary's daughter (last Sunday) and managed to find out her age already through mathematics. Have seen her three times this week and have a date for tonight. How's that for a beginning? *Now don't say that I'm going too fast.* You'll hear more later."

Actually Mrs. Buck didn't hear for five weeks. In the meantime gossip had apprised Lossing that Pearl Sydenstricker was taking walks with an unattached missionary named Mr. Gish, though no one knew how serious it was. Lossing wondered. Then one afternoon the colony was shocked by the news that Mr. Gish had drowned in the pool at the foot of the mountain. Lossing had started down to help but half-way there was met by a group of coolies carrying the body back up.

In Lossing's presence Pearl gave no sign of being more than normally upset and he tactfully didn't mention the tragedy. No one would ever know whether Mr. Gish represented more than just another eligible man of the right age and profession. But now Pearl and Lossing Buck spent long walks and tea parties and picnics together. He was also invited to meals at the Sydenstrickers' house in Kuling, which provided Absalom and Carie the opportunity to look him over. Pearl's only contribution to this period's history was the statement that both parents heartily disapproved of him.

Absalom Sydenstricker held all uneducated people in contempt, and the dinner-table conversation revealed that young Mr. Buck had only an agricultural degree, which did not really qualify as an education. Furthermore, teaching farming was not considered to be missionary work. Altogether, in languages, literature, the arts, history and comparative theology, Mr. Buck failed miserably. Carie also compared his limited vista with her daughter's broad scholarship and agreed with her husband. Through their tight-lipped silence there was no mistaking their attitude.

Pearl, however, made her own assessment. Lossing Buck was an American, and unmarried. He was clean and kind and honest. As for herself, she had recently turned twenty-four. And the restrictive perimeters of the missionary circle were choking her.

Lossing's next letter home was from Nanhsuchou. He described his three-room house minutely and then went on: "I left September 2nd. The nicest girl in all Kuling came down on the same boat (which I had arranged beforehand). We had a good time getting better acquainted. Her parents are Virginians, so she is really a Southern girl. She has the most sense of any girl I've seen yet. . . . I said goodbye on the boat but later ran down to see her for a day. Was mighty glad I did; she had some delicious ice cream for dinner. . . . Well, this is enough about girls, you will think I've fallen in love with her which is not the case. She is just one peach of a girl. Speaking of girls, Mildred wrote me a letter which makes me sit up and take notice. . . . I wrote her a letter which told her more or less about some of her failings and shortcomings, and for which she has thanked me several times since."

This letter also mentioned certain bills incurred before leaving home. "As you can see from the dentist bill, I can't send any money home yet for a while. I landed back in Nanhsuchou with just three dollars to my name. I can truthfully say I haven't spent any money unwisely since coming to China. I can also say that if a man is carrying life insurance a missionary's salary (at least a single man's) is not adequate, even without spending anything for books, magazines, side trips for observation, etc. There is a single man in Nanking who did not take a vacation just because his salary did not allow it. The whole thing is this, if the Board wants efficient missionary work done it has got to give a man enough to keep awake to what is going on. I like my job very much but the money question is a serious one. I'll simply have to ask Father to pay my insurance bill again if he will."

Back in Chinkiang, Pearl Sydenstricker returned to her teaching, and very shortly a copious correspondence had sprung up. Lossing considered asking Pearl to visit Nanhsuchou. Before she could come, however, he had received a letter from Mildred which seems to have caused him some confusion about his feelings, for, writing to his mother, he failed to mention Pearl but spoke enthusiastically of Mildred. Indeed his confusion was not confined to a choice of girls but included his future as well. He thanked his mother "for paying that Student Volunteer pledge. . . . Thanks also for seeing about the insurance. I honestly don't know what is going to happen to me financially. It's only the bigness of my job that keeps me here. I am sure it's God's will and I suppose He will find a way of helping me, but if I wasn't already here I would seriously consider dropping mission work until I could get on a sound financial basis."

He was not the only person in a state of indecision. Mildred seemed not to know her own mind; and Pearl was seeing both Lossing and another man. However, as the winter of 1916–1917 wore on Lossing, desperate for solvency, did make up his mind. He may have been influenced by the fact that in the world of foreign missions, when a man married he received a second salary for his wife.

At all events, he invited Pearl to Nanhsuchou for a visit, announcing it to his colleagues in an offhand manner. They, playing along with him, received the news in the same casual spirit.

For Pearl, being looked over must have been an agonizing experience. But by all accounts she played the scene perfectly—easy-going, lively but dignified, charming. Her colleague Marian Gardner remembered her first impression. "Really a very pretty girl, an oval face, slender and wearing her hair done attractively. She had lovely eyes and a lovely smile."

Naturally Pearl was doing her own observing, and Marian provided an immediate relief. A small, perky New Englander, a Phi Beta Kappa from Smith College, she had been sent out to manage a school for girls. With her wit and ready laugh she had become known as the Hot Hearted Little Sister (translated as "energetic and earnest" in Chinese). She was semi-engaged to another missionary she had met at the Language School, but at the moment she was fighting her way through the thickets of the Chinese language and managing to make fun of her struggles.

Also warmly welcoming Pearl were an attractive couple, Dr. Van Wiltsie and his wife Marian, who were striving for some kind of an accommodation between medical practices and Chinese patients.

The Carters, Tom and Dagney, were veterans of a year or more of missionary service, and, as Pearl saw immediately, as promising as potential friends as Marian Gardner.

The Nanhsuchou community was relieved, congeniality in such close quarters being a prize above rubies. Marian recalled: "I fell for her immediately. I knew we would be very good friends, and was glad that Lossing had chosen such a fine and able person." She did, however, have some reservations about Lossing as a husband. "He was a very dear person and a dependable one. But there were areas which I felt he could never penetrate. . . . Agriculture was his whole life."

Lossing also felt some trepidation about Pearl's reactions. After showing off his array of charming people, he took her for a tour of the city. Nanhsuchou, he knew, would prove a dreary contrast to the lush greenery of Chinkiang. Dry and desolate, it boasted no single thing of beauty except its magnificent brick wall encircled by a moat, garnished at the corners with towers and interspersed with gates which were locked at night against bandits. Much later Pearl Buck shared her first impression: "It was a complete change of scene. . . . Outside the walls and beyond the moat the countryside stretched as flat as any desert, earth and houses were all dust color, even the people, for the fine sandy soil was dusted into their hair and skin by the incessant winds." To Pearl, almost obsessively sensitive to visual beauty, this arid land and the stark half-furnished "houses of the whites" compound must have struck something like terror to her heart. Outside their compound there would be no intellectual contacts, no libraries, no bookshops, no treasures either of art or nature. When she finally said goodbye and went home to think, there must have been a number of No's as well as Yes's to weigh in the balance.

One definite plus certainly would be the people she had met. Another was the fact that Nanhsuchou was two hundred miles from Chinkiang, and a third that escaping that world through marriage would be more acceptable to her parents than through a job.

On the other hand, with Pearl's missionary background, marriage would be forever and she a wife in the full meaning of the word—helpmate, lover, mother, homemaker, counselor, hostess, supporter. It also connoted thriftiness, resourcefulness, tolerance and patience, understanding, imagination and wisdom, diversion and inspiration, selflessness and nobility—above all, partnering a husband in every endeavor. Partnership with Lossing Buck would entail joining hands in missionary work, and this, given her disaffection in college, must have caused agonized uncertainty.

By now, however, Pearl had passed several self-tests. She had arrived at Randolph-Macon a stray dog and ended up a Kappa Delta, Am Sam, a leader on campus. It had taken concentration and study, but by careful observation of her models she had made herself into a perfect replica. So now, why not success again, for she had been observing missionaries all her life.

Whatever her reasons, she decided she could make it, and when Lossing proposed, she said yes. Indeed, so complete was her metamorphosis that she applied to the Kiangan Mission Board for membership and assignment to educational and evangelical work in Nanhsuchou.

When she informed her parents, they objected strongly, stressing Lossing's incompatibility with the Sydenstricker style. "You are behaving like Chinese parents," Pearl protested. "You think whomever I marry has to suit the family first."

But Carie reasoned: "We know you better than you imagine. How can you be happy unless you have someone who understands what you are talking about? He never reads and you are never without a book."

"He will read when he has the right atmosphere," Pearl insisted, never admitting until long after that at the moment she said yes a voice in her head had told her emphatically, "This is a mistake. You will be sorry."

Undeterred, she wrote Emma, who had recently announced her own engagement to a young missionary: "I am happier every day. Lossing is all any woman would wish him to be and makes me completely happy. He is *thoroughly good* and so fine and true. I hear such splendid things of your man . . . but he will have to be mighty fine to be good enough for you. To tell the truth, *my* man is the only one good enough for you, but unfortunately I can't very well spare him. Six weeks from tomorrow is the great day."

On May 30, 1917, the wedding, a Presbyterian service, took place with Dean Kelsey as best man and Grace standing beside her sister in the rose arbor of the Sydenstricker house. Pearl's dress was crêpe de chine and chiffon, and somehow she acquired a bride's trousseau. She had asked Grace to buy yards of delicate lace in Shanghai as trim for her lingerie. And though Grace was by now accustomed to Pearl's expanding expectations, she had been a bit shocked at this extravagance.

Marian Gardner represented the Nanhsuchou station, making herself useful by arranging the flower bell in the arbor and holding down the white cloth runway to keep it from blowing away.

The newlyweds took the boat to Kuling for a honeymoon in the Sydenstricker cottage, which her parents had vacated, retaining their private views but bowing to the inevitable.

Pearl soon had her first experience as hostess in her own home at a luncheon the Bucks gave in honor of the distinguished Dean Bailie. Lossing had been promised that if Bailie came to China, he should have some time with him and now, all aquiver, he was entertaining the head of Nanking's College of Agriculture and Forestry in his own home. They were ten at table, with Lossing at the head and his wife at the foot.

This occasion was, so far, the apogee of his career, a fact evident in a letter to his mother a month after the wedding: "I am especially happy just now because Dean Bailie is up here at Kuling. I expect to see quite a bit of him." He went on to describe Bailie's work in detail. And again, a month later, he wrote: "Dr. Bailie gave a talk on his impressions of the rural situation in China. I am enclosing a copy. . . . Pearl took the notes in longhand but got most of it down." Finally, he commented on his marriage. "Pearl and I are looking forward to this year at Nanhsuchou together. I certainly am a much happier man this year than last at this time. The longer we are together the surer we are that we made no mistake."

Marian herself was exceptionally happy these days, for Lloyd

Craighill had come to Kuling and they were to be married the following year. At a bridal shower celebrating their engagement, Pearl read aloud her congratulatory poem:

> "All of us who've been and done it
> Are very glad to hear you've won it—
> A heart, you know.
> For even tho it's "Piscopalian"
> You never can become an alien
> From Nanhsuchou.
>
> Please then accept our hopeful wishes
> For your exchange from Miss to Missis,
> It's lots of fun!
> And so for good advice,
> Just this, love is mighty nice,
> When all is said and done."

Pearl was at her most carefree that summer, off-duty and not yet responsible for setting any examples. "She was bubbling over with humor in those early days," Marian remembered, "seeing funny things everywhere and telling about them with relish. We laughed a great deal."

And when their time in Kuling was over, there came the fun of starting their own household in Nanhsuchou. Instead of Lossing's tiny rooms they were given a small house left by a departed couple. Pearl described it as "a lovely little Chinese house. We had a lawn and a flower garden enclosed in a compound wall. We lived in the shelter of the city wall nearby. There were only four rooms but what pleasure to arrange the furniture, hang the curtains, paint a few pictures for the wall, hang the Chinese scrolls! I was happy and busy."

For her role as wife, she chose her mother as model. She undertook to write to Lossing's family every other week, and in an early letter to her mother-in-law, she wrote: "We haven't any money to speak of but having always had a missionary home, I am used to seeing what one can do with very little expense."

An opportunity soon arrived for her to call upon her wifely resourcefulness. Marian Gardner, who was living with the Bucks, described it to her family. "The Bucks are having their walls tinted and sent to

Shanghai for yellow powder to put in whitewash. When the stuff came it looked like a hot mustard foot bath and we knew it would give us all jaundice. But trust Pearl! 'Bring some red mud!' she commanded. 'Pour water on it. Stir it thoroughly and add to the yellow.' Behold, a beautiful tan! We are quite rapturous."

The total wife also became her husband's partner in his work. Sitting down at Lossing's typewriter for a letter to his mother, she confessed: "I am not very proficient in typewriting but I want to become proficient enough to help Lossing out with some of the many letters he has to write."

As watchdog over the family budget, she cheerfully reassured her mother-in-law on that tricky subject: "It takes very close managing, but I like to make ends meet. We will have enough for a new suit for Lossing this winter, which he needs. And of course good food is a vital necessity for a man's health. Mother, I certainly should appreciate it if you would send me the recipe for the whole wheat bread you used to bake. He enjoyed it so much."

After Lossing developed eye trouble, which interfered with his reading the countless charts and tables of figures associated with his work, Pearl read them aloud to him. And when the sunlight bothered him, she bought cotton cloth and improvised window shades.

She seems to have genuinely enjoyed her wifely duties, for a year after the wedding she wrote to Emma, now Mrs. White: "I was so happy to get your letter and to hear that you are happily married to a good man. After all, it is simply the *only* life for a woman. Of course, one can go on and fill one's life with other things . . . but for fullness of satisfaction with life, there is nothing like marriage and a home. . . . We live in a tiny semi-Chinese house with very few conveniences: out here one's home means so much, especially in such a very isolated place. I owe it to Lossing to make his home cheerful and pleasant and be so myself. He has far too heavy a burden, and a man depends so on his wife for his well-being. I can't help but smile sometimes at these great men we women marry—how like children they are and have to be mothered and coddled and loved—and yet what a tower of strength they are to us in our turn!"

And in a letter to his mother, she wrote: "Lossing has a great future before him here. I try to help him all I can. Mother, he grows better every day. We are happier all the time. He is so good to me in every little way and makes life so happy for me in the little things even, little things that make all the difference."

The trio in the semi-Chinese house seem to have meshed admirably Marian, the Hot Hearted Little Sister, with her language problems found Pearl invaluable in helping her settle differences. "There was a grand fuss yesterday between the Chus and the Wongs. It's a quarrel and it has the added nervous strain for me of being in a foreign tongue. It's wonderful to have Pearl here and her Chinese language and experience. When one of the evangelists came in to tell the fuss she translated. She has a lot of good sense. . . ."

While Marian, small, brisk and spectacled, was called Little Sister, Pearl, taller, more dignified and quite handsome, was addressed as Learned Lady or Wise Mother. As time went on Marian discovered there were a thousand such fine points of etiquette to be learned: In China one did not use a person's real given name, since to speak it was to seize hold of his spirit. Servants might call the mistress Elder Sister; a father addressed his children as Second Son or Third Daughter; a man was My Husband to his wife, and she My Wife or My Son's Mother. Such were the many nuances of speech to be learned by a foreigner to avoid giving offense, and the three different modes of conversation—truth, falsehood and politeness—were included in every teacher's course. Politeness was the formal or Outside mode. To the question, "How is your honorable wife?" a gentleman answered, "My miserable slave does very well." The husband was the Outside person, the wife the Inside person, with no position of her own outside the home. The gentleman derogated his own belongings while exalting the other's. "May I invite you into my wretched hovel?" called for the response, "I shall be honored to enter your magnificent castle."

It was offensive, Marian learned, to touch another person physically under ordinary circumstances. In the crowded living conditions of Chinese life personal identity was difficult to preserve, so that no one, not even street coolies, made any avoidable contact, greeting a friend by bowing instead of shaking hands. Oriental manners at table also differed from the Occidental, with a loud belch serving as a tribute to the quality of the host's dinner.

Marian delighted in learning the racial characteristics and found Pearl's running translation during social crises an insight into personalities and events. "Our houseboy got married the other day," she wrote her family. "He was determined to have a Christian wedding, but the bride was a slave of a wealthy family and we feared she might be too independent for him. Well, our fears were amply justified. A gorgeous red wedding chair stuck at the gate; the bride was asked to get out. She refused, saying firmly that she was not a church member nor had she been baptized, therefore she was not to be married in a church and she would not stir one step. The boy is a good simple sort and she is a very gay bold sort and probably a very bad lot. The boy informed her that they were to have a blessing with their meals whereat she said she would eat no blessed food. He further told her he was going to love her and treat her like a Christian and never beat her. At which she replied that if he did not beat her it was because he was afraid of her. The boy spent the day on his bed in tears and came to Pearl in a lachrymose condition to find out what to do. Pearl wanted to say beat her but restrained herself. Instead she told him to refuse to quarrel but to go on and have grace and let her starve a few meals and she would come round. The next day she refused to attend to some housekeeping detail and so mortified the poor groom he spent the day in bed weeping. Already he looks henpecked."

Pearl had also written her in-laws about the luckless groom and added a sequel: "In disgust the boy bought a second slave in exchange for the first. Well, he has been having a hard time. It seems a friend of the girl, an ex-slave also from the same family and now married, is the person who arranged the wedding, and she didn't get paid as much as she expected, so she has been alienating the young wife's affections and she has left her husband. Being for the first time really free from slavery, she has been having a good time about town and her poor husband is perfectly disgusted."

Pearl's first months were spent chiefly on domestic matters. Later, however, her insatiable curiosity about people asserted itself and she began looking outward. She once wrote: "The Chinese were delightful in my Northern city. Since my little house was so accessible a fairly steady stream of visitors came and went and I was pressed with invitations to birthday feasts and weddings and family affairs. I enjoyed it all and soon was deep in the lives of neighbors, as they were in mine. I played with their babies and talked with young women about their problems with their mothers-in-law and other relatives, and as usual I felt profoundly the currents of human life.

"The longer I lived there, however, the more deeply impressed I was not by the rich folk but by the farmers and their families, who lived in the villages outside the city wall. They were the ones who bore the brunt of life, who were the most real, the closest to the earth, to birth and death, laughter and weeping. To visit the farm families became my search for reality, and among them I found the human being as he most nearly is.

"More than once I almost began to write, but each time I put it off, deciding to wait a little until mind and soul were fully grown."

The novelist Pearl Buck was gradually emerging, storing up ideas, seeking out experiences and adventures. When Lossing planned to check on a mission station sixty miles away, his wife decided to accompany him.

She wrote to Lossing's mother: "We left home early one morning, I in a very uncomfortable Chinese chair and Lossing on his bicycle. The chair (enclosed by curtains) was carried by four coolies, who shook me up and down a great deal, so it was not a pleasure trip. All day we rode through barren flat country, stopping at villages whose people had never seen a white woman and were wildly curious about me. In one place they tried to take the top off the chair to see me better. I got quite nervous, as Lossing had ridden ahead, and there were literally hundreds of people packed against my chair. Fortunately, Lossing returned and we got out without trouble.

"Late that night we came to an inn where they put us in the stable to spend the night, the place reeking of manure. At least we were alone, however, but Lossing had to go back for our luggage and I had a little discomfort as a large crowd gathered and were peering in the windows and tried to burst open the door. When Lossing got back we pinned sheets over the windows and locked the door as tightly as we could. Next day we traveled all day and again created a sensation. But we finally arrived at our destination where the people were very friendly and we got some evangelistic work started."

Occasionally Pearl did not have to seek adventure but found it at home. As no real government existed in China at this time altercations between local warlords often took place in and around the city. "This week" she wrote, "we had a real battle. Once Lossing ran outside and a bullet just missed his head, so after that we all stayed indoors and away from windows. The wounded soldiers began to come in. One poor woman, just a young thing, came with a bad wound in the abdomen, and I went out to help her but she died in just a few minutes. She had been struck by a stray shot. I couldn't forget about it . . . she was dying and begging for help and there was no help to be given."

Pearl became familiar with the bandit-warlords and their battles. "At least once or twice a year bullets would fly over our town. The battle usually ended at sundown, or if a thunderstorm came up they returned to keep their uniforms dry. The city fathers always locked the gates when a battle threatened, and the wounded were brought in through a side gate. Actually they preferred treachery and strategy to open warfare, and sometimes over a dinner table, when the terms of a truce were to be discussed, there was a surprise assassination of the guests and that comfortably ended the problem for the time being." Thus did the dramatic incidents of her life during those years feed the imagination of the author who would later write *Dragon Seed* and *Sons*.

Often she found herself precipitated into a scene that would haunt her for days. "Last Friday night Dr. Wiltsie got a call to see a woman who was dying. He asked me to go with him to give the chloroform. We found her in a miserable hovel, nearly dead from neglect and ill-usage. It was a strange scene . . . the wretched room covered with filth and grime of years, at the door a fire built on the earth floor and the room full of smoke, the woman lying on the bed surrounded by her mother, husband and numerous neighbors, both men and women. Then the American doctor, with his case of instruments, so shining and clean and himself so spotless. Then when the operation began, I crept over the filthy bed to get at the woman's head to give the anaesthetic, and the doctor began.

"It was a very serious business and we expected the woman to die at any minute. They had called in ten Chinese doctors before they called us, and they had each administered all sorts of stuff, and she was in a very bad way. However, she rallied and was better for two or three days. Then as soon as she was conscious she refused to have the foreign doctor and he had to drop the case. Of course she was not cured, but the Chinese have no idea of medical treatment and the time necessary for recuperation, and the last we heard she was worse again and I suppose will die. Well, death is a very common thing here and one must get hardened or life would be unendurable."

She described to the Bucks the tragedy of a young married woman whose mother-in-law's cruelty had driven her to attempt suicide. Pearl was called to the home. "I got there and found the whole yard packed with curious outsiders, and on the walls sat lots of people beating gongs and shouting '*Sha-lai, sha-lai*' which means '*Come back, come back.*' She had hanged herself and they were calling back the soul of the girl which was supposed to have wandered away. I went into the house, a dark hole full of people and foul air, and there was the poor girl propped into a half-sitting posture. To my horror, they had stopped her ears and nose and had gagged her so she could not breathe. I told them that if she were not already dead she should certainly be smothered. I wanted them to let me unwrap the face but they would not. So I had to go away, knowing the girl was being murdered. For it was murder. Even the girl's mother helped. The reason they do that when people hang themselves is that since nearly all breath is out of the body they want to keep in what little is left inside. There is no limit to their ignorance."

For all the gruesomeness, Pearl and Marian still found much to admire and love, and many of the Chinese women became close friends. The Chou family in particular had shown them such generosity that a gracious return of hospitality was indicated. "Last night we gave a real feast," Marian wrote her family. "We invited five of the Chous, married and single, and they are such perfect ladies that even though it was the first time they had had foreign food we knew it would be easy. Pearl had everything just like a nice American dinner and they were so impressed by the cleanliness—a white table all shiny with silver is such an absolutely novel sight. I explained what the butter was, and forewarned them about things as I would have been glad to have someone do for me in the case of sea slugs. They liked the bread and sat holding it in their hands and crumbling it up like little squirrels. Mrs. Jhan, always equal to any occasion, drank down a glass and a half of water in much the same spirit of bravado that I would have shown in tackling champagne. All showed the most marvelous good manners, just very cordial and polite interest. The peppers and salts they examined with great interest. I saw Mrs. Jhan unscrewing one of the tops and peering into its depths, one eye shut to get a better view, and they were so tickled by the bread-and-butter knives. They seemed to like the corn and the cake best of all. I was busily taking notes for future events all evening."

Marian's departure to be married in June 1918 was more of a blow to Pearl than she had foreseen. She missed her as a witty, light-hearted and stimulating companion. The gap was further widened when the Wiltsies returned to America. Most of the time the Carters were the only other whites in the city. However, making the best of what she had, she continued to help her husband in his work, acting as translator when he discussed soil and seed and irrigation matters with Chinese farmers. Thus Pearl was constantly gaining insight into their problems.

As wheat was China's prevailing crop, the kind of seed planted became of vital concern, and Lossing's immediate task was to test over a hundred varieties from all parts of the world. It was finally decided that the seed already in use was still the best for that locality, so the next task was to devise new ways to cultivate it.

At first he tried to teach the farmers what he had learned at Cornell, but it soon became apparent that American agriculture differed greatly from that of China and that an understanding of Chinese farm conditions was crucial. Pearl recalled: "One worrisome evening when there seemed no solution to this problem, I suggested that perhaps the wisest plan would be to discover first the facts about Chinese farming and rural life. No questionnaire had ever been used on the subject and yet the Department of Agriculture was full of students who had come to learn. . . . This . . . moved me to help as much as I could. Chinese students took questionnaires on rural life to Chinese farmers, and when the replies were assembled and organized the findings went into a book on Chinese farm economy. When this book was published by the University of Chicago it so impressed the Institute of Pacific Relations that a more significant study of Chinese rural life was made."

The events of several years were telescoped by Pearl, who may have been taking too much credit for the inception of the monumental survey. Certainly she did help devise the questions and collate the replies and no doubt assisted with the editing. But as Marian Gardner observed later: "After Lossing and she divorced he accomplished so much on his own that I can't help thinking he would have had a distinguished career anyway."

Throughout this period Pearl studiously continued to do her best in her role as helpmate. Schooled from childhood in the *modus operandi* of mission work, she plunged into the role of missionary needing no instruction. She wrote Emma White: "This winter I am going to try to do more mission work than ever before. I get oppressed sometimes with a realization of how much there is to do. I have *sole* charge of teaching the gospel to *all* the women in a population of *two million* people! It is absurd, of course, but it weighs on me terribly at times."

Much of the work consisted simply of visiting the Chinese women, sitting, chatting socially, which was, in reality, a gentle indoctrination.

"She told me once," Marian Gardner recalled, "that she never allowed her calls to be merely social ones. She felt that she had wasted an opportunity if she didn't at least manage to bring in the story of Christ—and I suppose His atonement."

Periodically she was required to write to the wife of Dr. Coffin at New York City's Madison Avenue Church. Her year-end report for 1918 was a full one, describing her daily work. She and a convert, a Chinese woman, would visit nearby villages carrying tracts and pictures to illustrate their talks. As a white woman she invariably caused a sensation with her jutting nose and huge feet, but after a period of general gossip and joking, she and Mrs. Hsu would turn to serious matters. Sometimes they conducted classes on hygiene accompanied by enormous blown-up photographs of houseflies with germs on their feet, causing one Chinese matron to remark that certainly any fly as big as *that* would be frightening! At other times they conducted classes in child care, admonishing gently against abandoning the girl babies. Inevitably, however, they turned to the subject of worship, explaining to the women that they were worshiping the wrong gods. "This catches their attention," Pearl wrote, "and they listen avidly, while we tell them of the One who took their sins upon Himself and atoned for their sins for them." Some women, she discovered, thought they had to atone for their sins by burning incense or becoming vegetarians. Her way, she was convinced, appealed to them. In all of China, she went on in her report, there was so much corruption, so much drunkenness, so much opium addiction that she wondered when China would awaken to its own weakness. The letter ended plaintively, "How can we save China from her own weaknesses? How can we touch her heart to her own dreadful wickedness? These are the thoughts that burn in us by day and night."

This letter, written just before Christmas 1918, does not appear to be the letter of a happy woman. A revulsion at the life around her had already begun appearing in letters home. One was written to Lossing's mother less than a year after their marriage: "In a place like this we have little opportunity for rest and pleasure apart from our work. It is not only the work which is so wearing on one—most of all it is the constant contact with the terrible degradation and wickedness of a heathen people . . . with things which one cannot tell because of their unspeakable horror. . . . I often think the real hardships of missionary life are not the material deprivations or the discouragements of the work. . . . One may have all those anywhere. The greatest hardship is having to deal with and know about all kinds of horrible sin. No one can know what it means until he has lived here where human life is valued as nothing almost and vice of all kinds is unspeakably prevalent. One can realize little of what it must have meant to Christ, who hated sin so much more than any human can, to have to live in a world like this.

Whether Pearl expressed these feelings as harshly to her husband is not known. But it appeared that communication between them was becoming attenuated. By nature Lossing Buck was wholly a compendium of facts and figures while Pearl was the more sensitive, more responsive of the two. One had nothing of the other. Misunderstandings were inevitable, accompanied by boredom and impatience.

The following spring she wrote with even greater intensity: "I have been trying to find out how much infanticide goes on in this city. It is very prevalent over all China. . . . Knowing these people as I do it makes me thoroughly angry to have China considered as even a semi-civilized country. There is entirely too much idealism of China in the United States, and the common idea of her is very far from the sordid truth. She is a country given to the devil."

Actual animosity seems evident in this communique, almost as though she had immersed herself in the thundering wrath of a Jonathan Edwards who had shaken his fist at "sinners in the hands of an angry God." Several of her contemporaries, reading her letters, could not reconcile them with the Pearl they had known, and felt that they reflected not only a deepening disillusionment with her own situation but a psychic shock resulting from the contrast with her former life.

Or, some asked, was it merely frustration, an outraged exasperation at having one's best efforts met by stern resistance?

It became obvious that she was torn between savagely condemning a people and loving them deeply. To Pearl the Chinese peasant woman, exhausted from child-bearing, enslaved by her menfolk, yet patient and humorous, was a creature of gigantic strength and courage.

Singly and in groups these women came to Pearl as they had to her mother, grateful for a receptive ear. Not all of them were poor. One girl, married to the heir to a great fortune, caught Pearl's eye when Pearl dined at her home. Surreptitiously she led her guest to her sumptuous bedroom, locked the door and then asked timidly, "Will you tell me, is it true that your husband speaks to you in the presence of other people?"

"Yes," Pearl answered.

The girl sighed. "I am not allowed to speak to mine except in this room at night." Wistfully she poured out her loneliness. Though deeply in love with her husband she was prohibited verbal contact with him in the public rooms of the house. Her father-in-law had never addressed her, and even the older women of the house were silent in her presence. Only with the servants and slaves was she free to talk. For all these women, whatever their class, Pearl Buck became a bottomless well of compassion.

During the almost three years the Bucks lived in Nanhsuchou they learned a great deal. But that phase was about to end. The mission needed their house to expand the boys' school and they were given a sum of money with which to build a new one. When the house construction was underway, Lossing, who had planned to expand his agricultural work on the basis of his survey, was suddenly informed that the funds from New York were to be cut off and his project canceled.

Then, ironically, this stunning blow turned instead into a timely opportunity. John Reisner, at Nanking University, was introducing a course in Agricultural Economics and invited Lossing to develop a department of field work. Thus his efforts in the barren North were to bring him finally to a rich and fruitful haven.

Before they could leave, however, Pearl found, to her intense joy, that she was pregnant, and Dr. Horton Daniels, a recent addition to the mission station, became her physician. While Lossing began winding up his work, Pearl packed their household goods.

A few months later Dr. Daniels, having decided that Pearl's pregnancy was not progressing altogether satisfactorily, suggested that she go on ahead to Nanking. Since Lossing was not ready to leave, the Reisners invited her to share their large house and she and Bertha Reisner, also pregnant, spent their days making happy plans.

In January Lossing joined Reisner at the university. The Reisners were due to leave for a two-year sabbatical in May and during Dean Reisner's absence Lossing was to double as acting dean and instructor in Agricultural Economics, Farm Management, Rural Sociology and Farm Engineering. Suddenly the Bucks' life was full and vibrant with a joyful future looming ahead.

A day in late December or early January had been designated as the time of their first child's birth, but January came and went without a sign. There were re-evaluations and re-examinations, and on March

20, two months behind schedule, Pearl was confined and Caroline Grace was born, a beautiful, lively baby weighing seven pounds and eight ounces.

Pearl remembered that special moment: "The first time my little girl and I saw each other . . . was a warm mild morning in March. A Chinese friend had brought me a pot of budding plum blossoms the day before, and a spray of them had opened. That was the first thing I saw when I came out of the ether. The next thing was my baby's face. The young Chinese nurse had wrapped her in a pink blanket and she held her up for me to see. Mine was a pretty baby, unusually so. Her features were clear, her eyes even then, it seemed to me, wise and calm. She looked at me and I at her with mutual comprehension and I laughed. I remember I said to the nurse, 'Doesn't she look very wise for her age?' She was less than an hour old.

"'She does indeed,' the nurse declared. 'And she is beautiful, too. There is a special purpose for this child!'

How often have I thought of those words!"

4

Carol Buck, it was generally conceded, put other babies to shame. The Reisner's son John, born a week after Carol, was compared with Pearl's daughter. "Carol was beautiful," Bertha Reisner remembered, "lots of dark hair, pretty and very alert. We put the two babies in an upholstered chair and mine settled down and kind of looked like a potato, and Pearl's was so alert, looking around."

Soon Pearl would be taking up her active life again. She had arranged to teach English literature at the Christian-supported Nanking University and the Chinese-supported National University, where the two salaries would contribute nicely to the household budget. This plan also gave her time to enjoy Carol's first fascinating months. After three weeks in the hospital, however, Pearl was not convalescing normally, and to Dr. Daniels's horror, he discovered a tumor in her uterus which accounted for the confusion regarding her child's birth date. She was ordered to return to the United States and go directly to New York where her in-laws' farm would be handy for her recuperation.

The Pleasant Valley farmhouse was alerted; Mr. and Mrs. Buck would be waiting, and her sister Grace at a small college in Tennessee would come when called, as would her brother Edgar in Washington. The Mission Board in Troy, New York, Lossing Buck's sponsors, had agreed to take care of the medical bills.

At the end of June, Lossing, Pearl and baby Carol arrived at the Buck farm. Mrs. Buck, a sweet, kindly woman, though willing, seemed unable to cope, and Grace, equally inexperienced, had to assume her niece's care.

On July 10, Edgar and Lossing took Pearl to the Presbyterian Hospital in New York. With the removal of her appendix and a benign tumor, there was great rejoicing. But other medical news was heart-wrenching. Pearl, at twenty-eight, was now barren, the dream of many children gone forever, and Carol became doubly precious.

They spent that summer on the farm, with Lossing helping outdoors and Pearl joining in the household chores, and in November Lossing, Pearl and their daughter returned to Nanking.

Pearl put aside her sadness in her devotion to her child. She was worried about recurrent attacks of the baby's eczema, but otherwise all seemed normal. Their large new house with its garden and bamboo grove presented a delightful change from the four-room Nanhsuchou house.

Lossing, back at work as department head, seemed deliriously happy. He wrote his parents proudly that an exhibit his department had sent to the International Silk Exchange in New York had been the only one accepted from China. And Pearl, after settling into the big house, set out to explore the city.

The city's wall, she learned, was its citizens' chief pride, twenty-five miles around and so wide at its top that three vehicles could race abreast. Its situation also was pleasant—hills at the back and water at the front on a site reportedly chosen by an astrologer. But the astrologer had neglected to consider the climate, for the Yangtse Valley, with its steamy rice paddies, was overpoweringly humid. As one ex-resident described it: "You felt as if you had an iron band around your head and it was being screwed tighter every minute. In summer you just couldn't sleep. One family came home one night to find their coolie sleeping on top of the grand piano—the coolest place." The missionary women and their children escaped to Kuling while the men pooled resources with a cook and then went up to Kuling for the last weeks of summer.

The Bucks' street, narrow and cobble-stoned, had an eight-foot compound wall on either side. Each house or cluster of houses had its encircling wall, with a gateman to keep out robbers. Few streets had names, but the Bucks', being near Nanking University, had achieved the status of Big Horse Road. The missionary residences, designed by European architects with no thought to the local terrain, were large, commodious and hideous, great brick squares relieved only by bamboo groves and gardens. On Big Horse Road the Kelseys lived catercornered from the Bucks, the Thomsons next door, Dr. Williams (the vice president of the university) a few doors down and the Reisners opposite. The business district and the diplomatic communities were centered several miles away near the river.

Pearl was grateful, she wrote later, for her beautiful garden. "When I found that my windows opened to Purple Mountain I chose an attic room from which I could look over the compound wall upon the vegetable gardens beyond." But they were not to have their house to themselves. New missionary arrivals had to live somewhere while learning to speak Chinese, and because the Language School was five miles from the university, the permanent residents were required to take in transients. There was always someone billeted with them, for a night or sometimes a year. Servants were needed and the Bucks had a male cook, a housewoman, an amah for Carol, and a gateman-gardener who also delivered messsages since there were no phones. Transportation was by coolie-drawn rickshaw or horse-drawn carriage and one rarely walked. One missionary remarked wryly, "In China we all live like lords and kings on fifty-five dollars a month." Which was the truth since $1300 was the yearly salary for a couple.

Nanking society was a rich mix of missionary, faculty, consulate and Standard Oil personnel. Gatherings were divided sharply into the wets and the dries, with the missionaries teetotalers and the rest according to preference. With servants plentiful, dinner-parties were endemic.

As Pearl's health returned, she plunged into the thick of things, mixing with couples her own age, both Chinese and American. And in her class she found a wide array of types. The Nanking University students had traveled in the West, spoke English and were often wealthy and sophisticated, while those at the National University were nearly all poor, spoke little English, dressed shabbily, ate sparingly and in winter sat in icy classrooms. But these young people were avid for an education and Pearl enjoyed her sessions with them. Many, she learned, lived in towns like Nanhsuchou and were from similar superstitious peasant families. One eminent Chinese Ph.D. had come from a home where there had been only one pair of shoes for the whole family. Desperate for an education, he had walked eight miles to school each day carrying the shoes and, because they were painful to wear, putting them on only when he arrived.

The city of Chinkiang where Pearl's parents lived was two hundred miles away and Pearl divided her time between her baby and her mother, who was by now losing a battle with pernicious anemia. "Come home," Pearl wrote Grace in America, and by the time she arrived there were only a few sad months left of their mother's life.

Carie, striving valiantly to be the old Carie, ordered a bewildered Pearl to get a stick of chewing gum. When her younger daughter walked in, she was lying in her prettiest lavendar gown, white and gaunt, but she cried out, "Well, here you see your old mother, chewing gum. I hear it's the latest thing in America."

Pearl was torn between conflicting loves and needs. Carie, she knew, could not last much longer, and she treasured every moment that remained. But Carol, in Nanking, was being tortured by eczema and needed constant treatment. Weighing obligations, she decided to return to her child and relinquished Carie into Grace's hands. A nurse had been found, a spritely woman with dyed red hair and bad teeth but, mercifully, a glorious sense of humor, who told wild tales of her adventures all over the world. Creating a lively atmosphere in the midst of death, she made the last weeks more bearable for both the dying woman and Grace.

Near the end Pearl hurried back to find Carie lying in bed smiling weakly while Grace and the nurse stumbled through their version of a foxtrot. Her mother had begged to see how it was done. "I wish I had learned to dance," she told them wistfully.

"She did not want to die," Pearl wrote. "That was plain. . . . I could not hide from myself that she was doomed, and I tried to face a world in which I would never see her face again." She slipped away in her sleep on a gray October afternoon while Absalom and his daughters sat waiting. At last the nurse came in and nodded. Absalom and Grace rose but Pearl stood, unable to move. Grace recalled that moment. "She sort of gave me a push and said, 'You go in, I won't go,' and she waited for me outside. Afterwards when we were getting Mother ready for burial, she touched her hand and said, 'It is like marble.' She never cried. . . . She was a very strong person. Enormous control."

Carie was buried in the rain, in the Chinkiang foreign cemetery where her little son lay. So now Grace and Absalom were there for Pearl to care for, and it was hard to know which needed care the most. Grace was twenty-one, sweet, shy, sensitive, always, to her own mind, moving in Pearl's shadow. As there had been a bond between the volatile Carie and the positive, self-confident Pearl, so there was an implied understanding between the intense, inarticulate father and his unassuming younger daughter.

From childhood Grace had been a lonely girl, much too young for Pearl's companionship. At night, on the verge of tears, she would hear her parents' angry voices through the wall. "I used to feel sorry for my father when my mother would fly up at him," she said. "I knew he only meant to do what he thought was right. But he couldn't tell her how he felt. I was the same. I couldn't express myself."

Absalom accepted his wife's death mutely, moving like an automaton, displaying no grief, hardly mentioning her name. The two, father and sister, seemed suspended, waiting for some force to set them in motion again.

Pearl acted typically. Grace would come and live with her, attending the Language School to perfect her Chinese. Absalom also would live with her; but this would take more careful planning. Absalom, even after a slightly disabling stroke, retained his fierce pride and would resist being given orders. Living in China, however, had taught Pearl the art of saving face.

During his ministry years Absalom had usually sided in any dispute with the Chinese against the whites. This had not sat well with some of the younger preachers who worked with him. His stubbornness had nettled them into active opposition, and finally he faced a new rule— retirement for all missionaries at age seventy.

When his Chinese friends heard the news, they protested, but facts and figures were produced proving how casual Absalom's ministrations had been and how misdirected his funds. For the first time his blind confidence wavered and when his resignation was presented to him calling for a general housecleaning, he signed.

All through the winter he remained numb and silent, but Carie had warned her daughter, "Look out for spring. When April comes, he'll get restless and hard to manage." And indeed, in April he mounted his old white horse and started down the road preaching. His churches and schools, however, had been closed, their members scattered. Appalled, he began to suspect he was too old and—unthinkable—unwanted.

Quietly Pearl took over. Her father had once administered a correspondence course at the Nanking Theological Seminary, test papers for preachers in the field. Swallowing her pride, she went before the Mission Board. Would they take Absalom on, turn these courses into a correspondence school with an office and a title and—most vital—

conceal her part in the transaction? (Salary could be ignored, his regular stipend would suffice.)

The Board proved difficult. But Pearl would not give up. Finally, with great solemnity the seminary tendered Absalom an invitation to form a correspondence school for the field. After due consideration, he accepted and Pearl, breathing a sigh of relief, sold the Chinkiang house and moved Grace and Absalom to Nanking. There for the last ten years of his life he went contentedly to his office and ate silently at the table, still nurturing his contempt for his illiterate son-in-law.

Pearl Buck later wrote in *My Several Worlds*: "When I went back to Nanking after my Mother's death I was filled with the need to keep her alive, and so I began to write about her. I thought it was for my own children, that they might have a portrait of her. I did not think of it as a book. I put it in a box and placed it in a closet to wait until they were old enough to read it."

Certain events, however, suggest there was another reason as well— the primitive instinct of the living to propitiate the dead. Pearl had known how Carie had dreaded Pearl's leaving her, yet she had done so, seeking escape first in a job and then in marriage. Loving her mother but still craving her freedom, she no doubt felt remorse. Thus in building a monument to her she went beyond life and lovingly produced a likeness with a bit too much virtue and a shade too few faults . . . certainly adorable; just not perfect. Finishing the portrait of her that winter cleansed and shriven, Pearl put her notes away and went on to other matters.

Pearl's four years of isolation had occurred during a period of profound change in China. For three thousand years the country had refused to change its ways, its language or its concept of itself, and now suddenly such continuity was shattered. Sun Yat-sen had taken over with ideas brought from the West by trade and missionaries and students who had traveled abroad. The earth appeared to quiver under the impact of his thinking: all citizens should have an equal voice; women had rights as well as men; self-questioning could be healthy and change sometimes for the better.

Since 1911 Sun had struggled to promote the concept of democracy but at last had to recognize that it suffered from a lack of strong organization. To compound the difficulty a schism had developed between China's North and South paralleling the earlier one in the

United States, and a civil war was in the offing. The North, home of the tradition-bound aristocracy, functioned under warlord dynasties while the more progressive South supported Sun. Into this divided country Japan thrust itself in 1915, presenting its Twenty-one Demands for territorial concessions which would have rendered China a virtual colony.

While rejecting the demands, China was thrown by Japan's aggression into even worse confusion and Sun, while cherishing his ideal of a reborn China, still lacked the power to make it work. Then in Petrograd, in 1917, the October Revolution exploded and the Communist Party was born. Sun observed and took note.

In war-torn Europe, Britain, France and Italy, hard-pressed by Germany, persuaded China to join them in return for a seat at the up-coming peace talks. China, hoping to regain some of the lands now in Japanese and German hands, acquiesced. However, in what China regarded as an outright betrayal, the Versailles Peace Treaty terms announced on May 4, 1919, ceded Germany's former concessions in Shantung to Japan.

As a result, thousands of students in Peking rioted and thirteen colleges and universities joined in a march on the Palace, setting fire to the house of the Minister of State and giving the Foreign Minister a thrashing. A student strike spreading to other big cities marked the start of a new era, and the May Fourth Movement soon embraced other areas of Chinese life.

Pearl Buck, still isolated in Nanhsuchou, may have seen an occasional newspaper, but she could not have been aware of the secret conclaves taking place in Peking. There Li Ta-chao and Ch'en Tu-hsiu, two admired professors who had learned about the growth of Russia's Communist Party, decided this was the philosophy to save their own country. Proclaiming "What we must prove to the world is not that the old China is not dead but that a new youthful China is in the process of being born," they founded the Society for the Study of Marxism at Peking University. For thousands of eager Chinese youths this program, with its concrete form and plan for action, seemed the answer. By the fall of 1921 there was a fledgling Communist Party in China.

Such was the political situation when Pearl began teaching in Nanking, and great was the division she found among her students. Those from the tradition-bound North rejected Sun's Nationalists while impoverished Chinese university students, thrilled by the May Fourth Movement, rushed to join Sun's revolution.

Still invisible behind the scenes were Russia's maneuverings, but Sun watched with growing interest the Communist Party's growth. On the horizon stood Borodin, the Russian who would turn up as Sun's advisor in the reorganization of his party. Russian money and Russian know-how would pour eastward to build a party along Leninist lines; and a young Chinese general would rise to eminence, Chiang Kai-shek.

Of these changes Pearl Buck has written: "The aspect of the revolution which interested me most was still the literary one." While the country struggled to find a political form for the modern age, a profound change took place in the writing and reading of books. Since the age of Confucius China's aristocracy was based on achievement in scholarship. In the Imperial Examinations the candidates were judged on archery, horsemanship, music, rites and mathematics. Deviation from established form was considered heresy, and the intellectuals who excelled became respected mandarins, China's elite.

While this intellectual elite was barred by tradition from expounding new ideas, they had to confine their activities to learning and perfecting the language of literature and its myriads of words—which in truth, were not words at all but pictures representing objects and ideas.

The Chinese pictogram for *love* was a combination of three pictorial elements: one, a bird in flight suggesting "excited breathing" or "passion," superimposed on the one for "heart" and the third "a man walking with dignity and grace"—all together signifying not only *love* but *envy* and *admiration* as well. The three-hundred-year-old K'ang Hai Dictionary contained 44,000 pictograms from which the scholars labored to bring forth essays, poems, philosophical treatises, all in endless repetition.

At the same time, however, other literature was being written *sub rosa*, novels pertaining to arranged marriages, wars and family intrigue. Being widely read but not yet officially recognized, they thus escaped the critics' barbs while basking in the freedom and prosperity of the disreputable.

These maverick authors wrote simply for the pleasure of writing flouting traditional subjects in favor of lively stories of everyday men and women. *The Red Chamber Dream*, considered one of China's great early novels, frankly commemorates Chinese women, depicting them as admirable and their men as a bad lot. Two other popular novels, *Gold Vase Plum* and *Shui Hu Chuan* were reputed to be written by respected mandarins moonlighting pseudonymously for fun and profit.

Liberation from China's literary "laws" arrived with the abolition of the Imperial Examinations shortly before the 1911 revolution, and in 1915 the first hint of freedom appeared. In the magazine *The Tiger*, the journalist Huang proclaimed, "We must endeavor to bring Chinese thought into direct contact with the contemporary thought of the world . . . the life of the average man. The method seems to consist in using plain and simplified language . . ."

The use of the vernacular became the key to reformation. Respectable writing had been formal for centuries, full of esoteric allusions to other esoteric writings incomprehensible to the uninitiated. This style, the abstruse *Wenli*, served as a wall between the intelligentsia and the uneducated. In contrast, the *paihua* speech of the popular novels was the actual speech of the common man, always readable, often exquisitely beautiful.

Almost immediately another magazine, *New Youth*, published two pieces in the vernacular which caught the eye of a young Chinese, Hu Shih, recently returned from the United States—the same Hu Shih whom Lossing Buck had watched rebel at classifying New York State apples so many years before. Hu Shih proposed a set of eight literary principles beginning with "Avoid the use of classical allusions" and ending with the eminently sensible "What you write should have meaning or substance."

Hu Shih was hailed as the leader of the "Literary Revolution" and soon magazines, newspapers, and poems began appearing in the liberated tongue. By 1919 when the May Fourth Movement took place, the literary revolution was waiting, and the two forces merged like streams joining to form a torrent. Within four years China had accomplished the fastest language reform in history, no doubt because it was so long overdue.

All this was of vital interest to Pearl Buck. Now she dared to acknowledge her passion for the popular novels and discovered her friends equally addicted, many even busy writing themselves. The freedom to express unashamedly one's thoughts and feelings brought enormous release. But in her classes, she noted later, the new freedom had also produced "a mass of experimental material. The young Chinese who called themselves modern cut themselves off too abruptly and superficially from the traditional. They began to write imitatively after the western style. It even became the fashion to ape the western poets. . . . One handsome and rather distinguished and certainly much beloved young poet was proud to be called The Chinese Shelley. He used to sit in my living room and talk by the hour and wave his beautiful hands in exquisite and descriptive gestures, until now when I think of him I see first his hands. . . . He was a Northern Chinese, tall and classically beautiful in looks . . . and his hands were big and perfectly shaped and smooth as a woman's.

"These young writers, in the effort to repudiate all Confucian tradition, became rigorously candid. . . . They began to reveal themselves in the most intimate moods of their minds . . . their feelings and their actions, which shocked their elder relatives. It was almost as though they now felt compelled to tear off their clothes and walk the streets naked."

Writing thus in *My Several Worlds* thirty years after these events, Pearl Buck was critical of the young imitative poets who exposed their passions in the exhilaration of freedom. But this was hardly her attitude toward them at the time.

During these early years Pearl often observed that she felt "like a juggler trying to keep a handful of balls all aloft at once." There was the household of servants and boarders to supervise, her husband to assist, their child to care for and two college courses to teach. Grace and Absalom had been settled for the moment, but as the wife of the acting dean there were increasing demands on her time. She wondered when there would be an interval for her writing.

Another distraction, but a pleasant one, was the arrival in January 1922 of the Locke Whites. They were at the Language School, billeted at a home only a half mile from the Bucks. Years later Emma would write an article in which she recalled their Nanking days.

"We landed in the Nanking station and as we drove over the cobbled street, through the big gate in the city wall past the picturesque Drum Tower, beneath beautiful Purple Mountain that overlooks the ancient city, Pearl explained the Chinese sights and sounds. . . . The atmosphere of peace and charm that she created was a marvel. Her living room was very large, and in it her husband and her father were almost continuously entertaining Chinese guests. Her desk was in the far corner but she wanted a little privacy. Finally she called her faithful Chinese carpenter, showed him the back of her upright piano and asked him to carve dragons on a piece of wood that could be put on this back. The next time I called she had her little den, the piano being the dividing wall. The living room side was a panel of handsome redwood carved with intricate dragons for which she had paid the princely sum of one dollar . . . Never a week passed but there were overnight guests, as well as other people invited for tea, lunch or dinner. Incidentally, hers was the first home in Nanking to use a woman cook rather than a man. So successful was her experiment that she later brought other women into her kitchen and trained several cooks for her friends."

The meticulous training Pearl gave her cook was not a personal idiosyncrasy. Everything eaten in China, even fruits and vegetables, had to be thoroughly cooked before it was safe to eat. A young missionary had contracted amoebic dysentery and suffered with it for fifteen years because her cook, in scalding a banana, had missed a small break in the skin. This toxic result was caused by the use of night soil as fertilizer. Great earthenware jars, called gungs, were set into holes in the ground to collect human and animal wastes, after which water was poured over them and left to stand. The gungs were then set out for the gardeners to use. No fertilizer equaled night soil for richness, but as a former Nanking resident sighed, "When the gardeners went around at eventide watering their plants we thought we would just *die*."

Careful householders like Pearl forbade their gardeners the use of night soil on pain of dismissal and were thus able to serve home-grown lettuce, but so resistant to new ways were most Chinese gardeners that everything was disinfected automatically.

Pearl's graciousness as a hostess was useful to Lossing. Nanking was a junction point for travelers going north or west, and though his term as acting dean ended with the Reisners' return, his department was attracting interest with its research into the improvement of cotton crops and the production of disease-free silkworm eggs. He was eager to be in touch with people visiting the university and to keep up with outside developments. "Pearl helped Lossing not only with ideas and suggestions," Grace recalled. "If he met a man who might help him in some way, she would invite him to dinner."

Fortunately there was one place where Pearl could follow her literary pursuits. Margaret Thomson, wife of a chemist-nutritionist at Nanking University, and her mother, Mrs. McIntosh Seabury Cook, lived next door. Margaret Thomson's daughter, Nancy Waller, recalled their early days: "I think this friendship between Pearl and Mother was an intellectual enjoyment. Mother was older and was considered probably the brightest woman in the crowd. She taught English Literature and History at Ginling Women's College. There were many other bright women in Nanking, graduates of Smith and Bryn Mawr, who taught music or other courses. They had a club to read plays and a woman's club that gave lectures. I remember Mother and Pearl together, two dark-haired, blue-eyed, good-looking women talking together a great deal."

Nancy Waller's brother James Thomson added: "Pearl and my mother being married to rather non-literary, non-articulate scientists, found in each other's company great warmth. Pearl also found in my mother's mother, a very, *very* literary woman of the mid-Victorian era, great company. Pearl would go over and they would recite Browning to each other."

Margaret Thomson presented another picture of her friend. "She was a very *gay* sort of girl. She would talk to people on the street." This comment is matched by another woman's revealing anecdote: "Pearl was very daring. Once while we were walking down the street Pearl pulled out of her pocket a handful of peanuts and offered some to me. I didn't take them, of course."

Daring, indeed, for Chinese women never talked to people or ate peanuts on the street. In fact, proper Chinese women did not even walk on the street. Since missionaries endeavored never to offend their hosts, Pearl Buck was indeed somewhat of a rebel.

One day a year or so after the Bucks had left Nanhsuchou, a bedraggled woman with half-bound feet, wearing baggy trousers and a padded jacket appeared at Pearl's door. "Wise Mother," she asked, "do you remember me?" She reminded Pearl of her kindness to the wife of her gardener in Nanhsuchou. Her husband had run off during a famine, and her five children had died in "the ten-day madness." "And now," Mrs. Lu said, touching her belly, "this is the only one left. I have come to you, Wise Mother, because I have no one else."

Pearl listened appalled, as the woman rushed on. "There is a little house behind your garden. If I could live there till the child is born, I would not trouble you, and afterwards I would find work." Melting, Pearl offered her a better cottage, for the house she referred to was really for chickens. The woman said she knew about birthing and would need no help.

The hut was cleaned and supplied with bed, table, and chair, curtains, and a padlock, food, and a brazier. And—for the event ahead—bandages, scissors and a bottle of iodine.

The baby arrived, a fine boy lovingly named Little Meatball, and Pearl provided clothes and two good luck silver dollars, for which Mrs. Lu expressed such gratitude that Pearl fled in embarrassment. The next day the cook rushed in to report that the baby was dying from iodine burns on his belly. "Wise Mother," Mrs. Lu moaned, "I thought if the medicine was good why not use it all." Offered the help of a foreign doctor, she recoiled in fright but allowed Pearl to take Little Meatball. In a few days Pearl restored him healed to his mother. But next year she had to save Little Meatball again. This time his naked bottom had been burned. "I thought now he is so big," Mrs. Lu moaned, "I need not use the water cloths you gave me. . . . We lay our babies on a bed of sand so when they wet there is no washing. Here there is no sand so I used ashes from the stove." His urine, mixed with ashes, had formed lye. It took two weeks to heal the child, but now Mrs. Lu belonged to Pearl Buck body and soul.

There was, it seemed, something in Pearl that went out to all women, and Bertha Reisner recalled another instance of her instinctive compassion. "Many of the missionary wives formed a club for the wives of farmers at the university's experimental farms. We met once a week and gave them various classes and suggestions. Nanking is very cold in winter and farmers' houses would be unheated and frightfully cold. Everybody just wore very heavy padded clothes, and it was difficult for a woman to take a bath. There were public wash-houses for men but nothing for the women. Pearl invented a cabinet made of bamboo frames, four walls and a roof on a hinge. She bought matting and covered the frame to make a sort of sauna, big enough for a woman to sit inside on a low stool with a tub of hot water in front of her. They'd put the hot water in first to heat the air and then go in. They'd even bathe the babies in there. It could be folded and put away when not in use and it was a very great boon, the women loved it." Years later the best-selling author, Pearl Buck, made a substantial donation to the city to build a bathhouse for women.

In the midst of all these activities her internal voice had kept ordering her to write, but something had always interfered. But with the anguish of her mother's death, a pain sharper than any before, a pen had literally been forced into her hand. "That summer," she wrote, "I remember quite clearly one August afternoon. I said suddenly, 'This very day I am going to write, I am ready at last.' . . . I sat down . . . in my robe of blue Chinese silk . . . and I wrote a little essay and sent it off to *The Atlantic Monthly.* . . . When this was done I enjoyed a delightful exhilaration. I had begun what I always knew I would do when I felt rich enough in human experience. And after the essay was published I had a letter from the *Forum* asking for an article. . . . The year was 1922 and I was thirty years old. It was high time indeed."

Her "In China Too" is a short essay purporting to be written by a middle-aged Chinese woman who, having read in American magazines about divorce, cigarettes, suffragettes, flappers and other phases of American life, compares the two cultures and admits that China is liberalizing too, and that she likes it. There is humor and charm in it which resembles the delicate drawing of a fine miniature.

"Beauty in China" is an ode to the visual beauty of a single poppy in a glass or the sun's rays filtered through a screen onto a Chinese rug. To Pearl Buck visual beauty was food and drink, parts of a necessary diet.

She began to write in earnest. "It was to have been my first big novel," but she told no one about it. "This was not secretiveness, for if there had been anyone I would surely have told. But I had no friends or relatives to whom I could speak about my writing, and it did not occur to me that this was strange or even a deprivation. I was long ago used to living in many mansions."

"Many mansions," revelatory words about her marriage. During the first year she had written Emma that she was very happy, but after a while the word *love* is missing from her letters. (She did, however, write lovingly of Lossing to his mother, but that seems to be for his mother's sake.)

A comment by a friend around 1923 seems significant: "Pearl was terribly fat about this time, like a bag of meal with a string around it. And her hair was always thrown up just anyhow. I had a dress that she liked and she asked me to let her have it copied. I was as thin as a beanpole. . . . We happened to go to the same party . . . in the same dress—she enormously fat and me like a rail. We looked so funny together. We laughed about it a lot."

This is a new Pearl, fat and sloppy, uninterested in her appearance, accepting her ungainliness as a joke. Such indifference suggests despair, and there would be more of that.

Marian Gardner, visiting in 1922, had noticed something disturbing. "Carol's eyes looked queer to me, unfocussed," she wrote her family. "I tried to make friends with her, and she burst into tears. Pearl tried to brush it aside and said, 'Carol is funny that way, she just cries when people speak to her.'" The following year Marian wrote, "Carol is nearly three and is not talking at all. She doesn't act like a sensible human being. It would be too dreadful . . ."

Grace also was disturbed by her niece's inability to walk. "I soon felt something was wrong. Pearl thought her terrible eczema might be contributing to her slowness, her arms and legs tied up because of that terrible scratching."

Pearl finally consulted Dr. Daniels. "But," her friends recalled, "Dr. Daniels was such a gentle person he probably couldn't bear to tell her." Her anxiety growing, Pearl would drop in at the Kelseys to ask casually when Rey's child had started to smile or, drinking tea with Bertha Reisner, draw her out about first steps, first words.

Pearl Buck wrote about that traumatic period in her life. "I think I was the last to perceive that something was wrong. I did not think of such a possibility. Everything had always gone well with me. I was one of the fortunately born. I took good fortune for granted."

Meanwhile, she could control her fears long enough to write a short story for a missionary magazine. She could run her household on excess energy, and she could accept a new missionary in her home. Jesse Yaukey, a bachelor from Pennsylvania attending the Language School, was a warm, intelligent young man who played unselfconsciously with Carol and won a fitful response. His kindness was balm to an open wound; he and Pearl would sit before the big pot-bellied stove and discuss politics and religion while her mind suppressed its hidden terror.

She could even play Cupid in the love affair between Jesse and Grace, and on June 10, 1924, Yaukey and Grace were married. The ceremony was to have been held outdoors, but suddenly the rains came. Ordering the servants to cut tall bamboo stalks, the ever-competent Pearl planted them in pots at the back of the living room and then set up shorter stalks as candle holders in a line behind the minister. So Grace had a pretty wedding after all and the newlyweds sailed up the Yangtse to Yoyong to join Yaukey's new mission station.

In 1924 Pearl tried to face the truth about her daughter. It was becoming harder to blame eczema or her own imagination. When she and Lossing discussed Carol, he had little to contribute. Carol would probably grow out of it, he thought, and he could offer his mother's word that all her children had been slow to develop. Pearl seized on this news eagerly. If the trouble was hereditary it came from his side, not hers, and this was not only comforting but food for resentment. For years she cherished this thought because it was all she had. Neighbors recalled that Lossing was considerate of Carol and there are snapshots of the two at play, but he was inarticulate, unable to offer the solace that Pearl needed.

His preoccupation increased as his work became more engrossing. His survey of farm conditions begun in Nanhsuchou had won favorable comment at the college and since the year 1924 was his sabbatical, he planned to use his data on 17,000 farms for a Master's degree at Cornell. He intended to work in North China first, so that summer the Bucks vacationed on the seacoast near Tsing Tao. Pei Ta Ho was a popular resort with beautiful beaches, Mongolian ponies and cottages facing the sea, and while Lossing came and went on his explorations and the amah stayed with Carol, Pearl rode the hills thinking and praying.

At a lecture on the pre-school child by a visiting American pediatrician, Pearl first learned the signs of normal growth as well as the abnormal and, facing her panic, she asked for a private consultation with the pediatrician and two other doctors. She listed for them her child's healthy habits: Carol could feed and dress herself, except for buttons, look at picture books, listen with rapt attention to music. Under questioning she admitted certain damaging facts she had not recognized as germane: the eczema, the meaningless bursts of laughter, the sudden tears. Their decision was that she should take Carol to America.

Thus began what Pearl Buck referred to as "that long journey which parents of such children know so well . . . seeking over the surface of the whole earth the one who can heal." Stony-faced, heartsick, she returned to Nanking to prepare for the year ahead, going through the motions of finding a housekeeper for Absalom, alerting Grace to possible emergencies, dismissing servants, preparing clothing, closing the house. Her control was almost perfect, and Grace never saw her sister cry.

But Rey Kelsey would never forget a morning when a haggard-faced Pearl stumbled through her front door. Reaching out for Rey, she threw herself into her arms, sobbing uncontrollably, "What am I going to do? Oh, God, *God! What am I going to do?*"

On the surface Lossing and Pearl Buck, returning to Ithaca for a year of study, must have seemed a normal family going through the normal routine of settling down. Lossing taught Sunday School in exchange for use of the Mission parsonage and Pearl, no longer earning salaries at two colleges, economized by doing her own housework. Foreseeing expensive doctors' bills for Carol she signed up for courses toward a Master's degree qualifying her for higher pay later, and between classes she and Lossing took turns caring for Carol.

All seemed moving well and in order. Actually, Pearl told Grace much later, "During those years I felt as if it was all I could do just to *exist*." Driving her brain to perform its assigned tasks, her real mind was absorbed with the grinding problem of Carol, and reaching out for help in every direction, she consulted child psychologists, children's clinics, gland specialists. One doctor suggested that Carol was too much alone and that a sister might stimulate her development. Thankfully she wrote Emma White, "We are going to adopt a little girl," and for months this hope carried her along.

Costs, meanwhile, were eroding Lossing's salary and their savings. New York's winter weather proved too much for Pearl's thin coat and she needed warmer clothes. "So," she wrote, "casting about I thought of a story I had written on the ship coming over. . . . Since it was about a Chinese family whose son brings home an American wife, I sent it to *Asia Magazine*."

The hundred-dollar check from *Asia Magazine* encouraged her, and she attempted a sequel which proved unsuccessful. However, the university offered monetary prizes for essays, $250 being the highest, for "the essay giving evidence of the best research and the most fruitful thought to the field of human progress or the evolution of a civilization during some period in human history or during human history as a whole." Pearl's English professor warned her that the prize was usually won by a graduate student in history, but undaunted Pearl chose as her subject the impact of the West upon Chinese life. A lengthy manuscript, it won the prize, and a gleeful Pearl Buck waved her check in the face of her doubting professor.

This Laura L. Messenger Memorial Prize essay would later serve as the basis for a speech before the American Academy of Political Science in Philadelphia, but the immediate effect of its success was to lift its author's spirits. "I got back my faith in myself," she confided, "which was all but gone in the sorry circumstances of my life."

Although she made few friends in Ithaca, she did make one memorable one. Eleanor Roosevelt came to lecture to the Home Economics Department and Pearl, a member of the reception committee, met her at the railroad station at seven in the morning. Pearl described their meeting. "She came off the train wearing . . . a long ankle-length purple satin dress, a brown tweed coat and men's bright tan oxford shoes and a nondescript hat. She carried a stuffed attache case and got off the train filled with good humor and a disarming kind of shyness. . . . She explained the purple satin dress by saying that she knew she wouldn't have a minute all day to change. . . . She made a good speech to the Home Economics Department and we were given a luncheon, mostly raw cabbage, which they were very proud of because it cost only seven cents a person. Mrs. Roosevelt ate it with great gusto and congratulated the head of the department in her gay, high-pitched voice.

"At the end of a long day she went off, still in her evening clothes. In later years she grew far more graceful. . . . In fact she grew better looking the older she grew. At the time I met her she had difficulty with her prominent teeth. Later a merciful automobile accident broke those teeth and a dentist improved on nature, so that even her teeth looked better."

There were strong parallels between the two women. Both taught themselves how to dress and improve their appearances. Both possessed high-pitched voices, though Pearl's was mellifluent and pleasant while Eleanor Roosevelt's tended to invite parody. Both women had protuberant front teeth. A dentist altered Pearl's while it took an automobile accident to correct Mrs. Roosevelt's.

There also existed a sisterhood in both women's sense of responsibility for those outside their own circle, and inexhaustible vitality.

From time to time Lossing and Pearl visited his parents' Pleasant Valley farm. Mrs. Buck (also named Grace) and Pearl were on affectionate terms, but Pearl could not forget that Lossing had described his mother as "a very quiet, lonely, solitary woman who used to talk to herself." Could that be, Pearl wondered, an explanation for Carol's condition? She asked Lossing's brother, Clifford.

"I'll trace up the family history and see," he promised her, but he failed to uncover a relative any more eccentric than his mother. So the search went on. And then the answer came, as she recorded later.

"The end of the journey for my child and me came one winter's day in Rochester, Minnesota. We had been sent finally to the Mayo Clinic, and day after day we spent in the endless and meticulous detail of complete examination. My confidence had grown as the process went on. Surely so much study, so much knowledge, would tell me the truth and what to do with it. We went into the office of the head of the children's department. . . . He held in his hand the reports sent in from all the departments where my child had been examined, and he made his diagnosis . . . all the physical parts were excellent. My child had been born with a fine body.

"There were other things good too. She had certain remarkable abilities, especially in music. There were signs of an unusual personality struggling against some sort of handicap. But—the mind was severely retarded.

"Any parent who has been through such an hour knows that monstrous ache of the heart which becomes physical and penetrates muscle and bone. 'Is it hopeless?' I asked him.

"Kind man, he could not bear to say that it was. Perhaps he was not really sure. At least he would not say he was sure. 'I think I would not give up trying,' was what he finally said. So again my child and I went out of the doctor's office and walked down the wide empty hall. The day was over and I had to think what to do next.

"Now came the moment for which I shall be grateful as long as I live. I suppose to be told that my child could be well would have meant a gratitude still higher; but that being impossible I have to thank a man who came quietly out of an empty room as I passed. . . . I had seen him in the head doctor's office once or twice. He had, in fact, brought in the sheaf of reports and then had gone away without speaking. . . . He came out almost stealthily and beckoned me to follow him into the empty room. I went in, half bewildered, my child clinging to my hand. He began to speak quickly, in broken English, his voice almost harsh, his eyes sternly upon mine. 'Did he tell you the child might be cured?' he demanded.

" 'He—he didn't say she could not,' I stammered.

" 'Listen to what I tell you,' he commanded. 'I tell you, madame, the child can never be normal. Do not deceive yourself. You will wear out your life and beggar your family unless you give up hope and face the truth. She will never be well—do you hear me? I know. I have seen these children. Americans are all too soft. I am not soft. It is better to be hard, so that you can know what to do. This child will be a burden on you all your life. Get ready to bear that burden. She will never be able to speak properly. She will never be able to walk properly. She can never read or write and she will never be more than four years old. Prepare yourself, madame! Above all, do not let her absorb you. Find a place where she can be happy and leave her there and live your own life. I tell you the truth for your own sake.'

"I can remember these words exactly as he spoke them. I suppose the shock photographed them upon my memory. I remember, too, exactly how he looked, a little man, shorter than I, his face pale, a small clipped black mustache, under which his lips were grim. He looked cruel, but I know he was not. I know now that he suffered while he spoke. He believed in the truth.

"I don't know what I said or even if I said anything. I remember walking down the endless hall again alone with the child. I cannot describe my feelings. Anyone who has been through such moments will know, and those who have not cannot know, whatever words I might use. Perhaps the best way to put it is that I felt as though I were bleeding inwardly and desperately. The child, glad to be free, began capering and dancing, and when she saw my face twisted with weeping she laughed. It was all a long time ago and yet it will never be over as long as I live. That hour is with me still."

She then concentrated on finding a sister for Carol. One or two adoption agencies had already turned them down because they would be taking the child to China. The solution came unexpectedly, through their own church. An individual church often supported a particular mission; Lossing's sponsor was the First Presbyterian Church of Troy, New York, and at Christmas he and Pearl were invited to visit the board. He had been asked to speak on his work in famine control, and had been warmly received.

In this friendly atmosphere the Bucks mentioned their search for a baby and the church's pastor took Pearl to a small, local orphanage where she was led into a large room full of cribs.

She wrote, "I went from crib to crib. At last I came to one where a very small, very pale little girl lay, her eyes closed. She seemed scarcely to breathe. 'How old is she?' I asked. 'Three months,' the director said, 'and she has never gained since birth. She weighs only five pounds. She will not eat.' 'I want her,' I said. He argued against it immediately, why should I take a child doomed to death? But I insisted. I felt a strong instant love for the exquisite dying child. I took her in my arms and carried her away. The very next day she began to eat. In a fortnight she was so different one would not have known her. She was actually plump."

Pearl Buck's account was told to a close friend. She omitted, however, the fact that the child was not only thin but utterly bald, and having lain for weeks on the same side, her face was deformed, an ear stuck forward rather than back against her skull. Bertha Reisner, asked why Pearl chose her, replied, "That was typical of Pearl. She was the kind to take this helpless little thing and feed it and love it and bring it back to life."

Emma White offered the same explanation. "Janice couldn't have been attractive looking, but she was so pitiful that she moved Pearl to take her. And then, to have her turn out so lovely—golden curls and those big brown eyes . . ."

A third person close to Pearl held a different opinion. "She had just had that failure with Carol. . . . I think she had to prove to herself that she could make it. Because nobody in their right mind, after having one badly retarded child, would then take another deformed one. It was a challenge. She had to prove something."

Janice did indeed blossom, and when her new parents took her to the farm she was universally admired.

In June Lossing and Pearl received their degrees, Pearl an M.A. and Lossing an M.S. Pearl's brother, Edgar, joined them for the summer; he and Lossing had discovered many common interests during their 1920 visit and when they returned to China Edgar accompanied them on the four-week trip.

After a year in the United States there were readjustments to be made. A new set of servants had to be found and established in their various ranks, with protocol strictly observed. Each man's duties were precisely defined and any infraction was cause for battle—one man used the dish towels, another laundered them, and woe betide him who overstepped. After a year without servants, Pearl was confronted anew with the time-honored graft known as *squeeze*. As head servant the cook did the marketing, taking for himself a certain percentage of the price. The laundry man's squeeze came in the form of soap or other supplies, the amah's cash or clothing. Even the gateman who simply accepted packages received his squeeze for taking them in.

Soon the household seemed to be running smoothly. Then Mrs. Lu walked in. Little Meatball had died the previous winter. Mrs. Lu had heard that Pearl was back, and now she insisted on working as table boy. In vain Pearl protested, finally bowing before the greater force.

A few months later Mrs. Lu's contours changed drastically; Pearl found it necessary to inquire and tearful Mrs. Lu explained that she had been working in the fields when a soldier passed and, entirely against her will. . . . She seemed to Pearl rather strong to be so defenseless, but Pearl as usual softened and offered the same amenities as before.

A few weeks later, investigating a hue and cry in the servants' quarters, Pearl stepped literally into a pool of blood. Mrs. Lu had aborted herself with a potent Chinese drug, nearly killing herself, but after weeks in a hospital she finally recovered. Her gratitude was overpowering.

Gradually Pearl began to slip into the old grooves—all except one. Worship in Union Church had been to her second nature, and as long as there had been hope for Carol's recovery she had entered to pray. But now she confessed to her husband that there was nothing there to pray to; no one was listening. Whatever faith she had had, she had lost. And she could no longer listen to music. Her piano, once her great joy, now stood closed.

She did what she could for her daughter, developing her capacities, reaching for the mind inside. "The experience taught me patience with dull people," she told her sister. "I came to know that people cannot help being as they are." As the sturdy Carol grew, coping with her irrational behavior presented more of a test. When one day she poured a spoonful of porridge into her mother's typewriter the impulse to react proved almost irresistible. Pearl's consolation was Janice, a quiet, normal toddler with almost fairy-tale beauty, gold ringlets and enormous black eyes.

Absalom, after a brief illness, had given up his correspondence school, but, now recovered, was growing restless again. Pearl found another solution. "Why don't you revise your book of Chinese idioms?" she suggested, and he went happily to work.

Though Pearl had sold a few short articles and stories, she had been working secretly for some time on a novel. Her pride kept her from mentioning it, however, for what one has not attempted one has not failed at. In the meantime, like the other white residents of Nanking, she watched the political situation closely. Since Sun Yat-sen's death in 1925, Chiang Kai-shek had emerged as leader of the party; and now the Kuomintang planned to move against the North's warlords and unify China under one central government.

Nanking, its missionary population included, believed that victory for these revolutionary forces was China's only hope. The warlords would fight for their own territories but such disruptions would be worth it if they brought about democracy.

During the winter of 1926 Chiang faced internal problems as he moved north. Leaning toward the right (he would marry shortly into one of China's wealthiest families) he was already in contention with Moscow's advisors, and their split widened as the armies moved north. Most whites moved out of the battleground areas and waited tensely.

On March 7 Pearl wrote Emma: "We are fast approaching the crisis with thousands of soldiers here. We expect the South any day and only hope we will escape without a siege. Grace and her little family were driven out of their homes and are here with us. She is expecting another baby in May. They have had a pretty hard time, their house has been completely looted."

Lossing kept the Missionary Board in America abreast of events: "For the past eight months we in Nanking have been spectators upon the present revolution, Nanking being one of the places of contention between the North and the South. Northern soldiers have been pouring into Nanking to stem the coming of the Kuomintang (Nationalist) army and it is believed the Southerners will be here within a week. . . . The extent of the looting will depend upon how well the Nationalists can keep order.

"The missionaries in the Hunan area were requested by their consuls to leave. Washington wanted them to leave in case the United States was planning a show of force and they don't want any missionary to be held as a hostage. As a result of this possibility 107 of us Nanking missionaries cabled the State Department supporting negotiating with China and opposing any show of force as dangerous to all interests. We support the Nationalists' principle of China for the Chinese. It is the best for mission work . . ."

The whites, obviously on the Nationalists' side, expected to be regarded as their friends in the coming struggle. Thus the events of March 24, 1927, came as a shock. This fight then was not simply Chinese against Chinese but yellow against white, the Chinese against the foreign devils, and was nurtured by a blazing hatred.

As always, the missionaries, remaining aloof but offering aid, had opened their doors to their Chinese friends and neighbors. The university president had requested the male faculty members to patrol the streets to help keep order. But on that morning, like the shot at Fort Sumter that began the Civil War, the shot that killed university vice president Williams was the beginning of a new phase in Chinese history.

When the Buck's tailor rushed in screaming, "Get out quickly! They're shooting white people.... Hide! Quick, hide!" and throughout that terrifying day when the five adults and three children were hidden by Mrs. Lu, while the Nationalist soldiers looted and burned, the sisters stuck to their grim decision, "If they come to kill us . . . make sure the children go first."

Pearl declared that that day in March turned her life around. "In those hours in that little hut I realized that I had not been living in the world. I had lived in a Chinese community, my house, my garden, my neighbors, the community events. I'm convinced that had it not been for that day I would never have left China because my whole life was there. On that day my cord to China was broken. . . . If I lived . . . it would have to be in the entire world."

During the many hours spent in that hut, Mrs. Lu slipped in and out with food and tea. A university colleague of Lossing stopped by with the news that many Chinese were working to save the whites. A friend brought hot soup and a bedroll for Absalom. There were even moments of comic relief as when devoted Mrs. Lu staggered in carrying a bedspread filled with aluminum pots and pans from America, presumably priceless, and once with a large mirror slung across her back.

Amazingly, during the whole thirteen hours the three children made no sound. "An answer to prayer," someone commented, and Pearl did not deny it.

One of Pearl's private thoughts was of the novel she had finished only the day before. Lying on her desk, the manuscript was now at the mercy of the looters.

By mid-afternoon the silent waiting made the constant sounds of gunfire and the distant crackle of flames almost unbearable. Then suddenly there was the screeching noise of shells. "American gun-boats," one of the men whispered. Indeed the United States consul had managed to reach a destroyer seven miles up the river, and it was laying down a barrage, two parallel lines of shellfire between which the foreigners were to make their escape.

Pearl looked at her watch. Five o'clock. On a grateful impulse she shoved the watch under Mrs. Lu's pillow. Soon it grew dark and there were footsteps outside as Mr. Chou entered accompanied by a National-ist soldier whose presence guaranteed safe conduct. The shelling had produced the desired effect and it was now safe for the whites to gather at the university's Bailie Hall.

As the Bucks walked through the city with their military guard, they saw the destruction—faculty houses burned out to their brick walls, others charred, some simply broken into and unwanted loot discarded. When a hundred whites, ashen and shaking had assembled in the hall it was learned that the treasurer of the Presbyterian Mission had been shot in the hip but that Dr. Williams, killed at the start of the rioting, was the only mortality.

The following morning a number of Chinese tearfully apologized for the troops' unexpected hostility. Their friends had defied the soldiers to bring clothing and toilet articles, money and food, insisting that this explosion of hatred was the work of Communists and that the mis-sionaries must not think that all the good they had done had been forgotten. The affection and sincerity of these Chinese visitors did much to assuage the whites' hurt.

The next afternoon the commander of the warship managed to negotiate their release, and the Chinese Red Cross drove them to the dock among silent, watching Chinese, some friendly, others hostile. Lossing and Pearl, regretting the show of force that had saved their lives, went aboard the ship in some shame. "I was glad not to die," Pearl wrote, "but I wished that I had not needed to justify, against my will, what I knew to be wrong."

Shanghai, filled with refugees from all over the country, was in-sufferably crowded, hotels and rooming houses mercilessly gouging everyone. The Yaukeys, with Grace's confinement imminent, moved on to Kobe in search of an American doctor. Absalom, who disliked Shanghai, decided to visit missionary friends in Korea and set off alone. The Reisners stayed on, but the Thomsons, who had rented a cottage in Japan, suggested that the Bucks go with them to Unzen.

A small hot springs resort near Nagasaki, Unzen had a few shops and a golf course in a pine woods setting. Their bungalow, cool but fragile, was constructed of paper with one large room divided by screens.

Pearl wrote Bertha Reisner, "Unzen is a very diminutive Kuling. We seem to be about the only white people here in a little group of seven bungalows. I keep busy cooking, etc. and trying to make some spring clothes. We left Nanking with just what we had on, like everyone else, and of course have nothing. Lossing keeps regular hours, and we don't speak to him between eight and twelve and one and five. (He did salvage his survey manuscript.)

"I am having to make one of the hardest adjustments I've ever made about China. There is an element of lawlessness in the Chinese I didn't dream of. For centuries they have had no functioning religion, and thus have not had one of the strongest human social controls. They have depended on mere custom and now that is weakened under the impact of the West. I believe the Chinese are *glad* that the foreigners were driven out. While individuals were genuinely ashamed and sorry, others were secretly glad. The returned students are just rotten with pride and envy, determined to be 'equal' without the faintest conception that the only way to be equal is to get a government and *do* something."

Isolated in Unzen the Bucks were unaware of the latest events. While they hid in Mrs. Lu's hut, Chiang Kai-shek, in Shanghai, held negotiations with Chinese and western bankers. Hostile now toward his Russian advisors, he was determined to expel the Communists from China, and within a few days the Nationalist soldiers who had overrun Nanking's foreign population found themselves to be outlaws. Advisor Borodin was expelled and the Russian consul sent home. The crushing of the Communist party and its suspected sympathizers was under way.

The possibility of the Bucks' eventual return to Nanking arose, for Chiang was planning to make that city the national capital. But confusion reigned as the Bucks learned that their house was being used as a barracks for the Southern soldiers. They could only wait out events.

In May Pearl wrote to Emma: "It was a terrible experience. But it seems productive of some good since it awakened the better Chinese to the Red influence in the Nationalist party. We do know that we have loyal and true Chinese friends at the University and want to go back to China, for surely such men and women are worth working with and for. I feel that the experience we have gone through together will bind us, Chinese and foreigners, so closely that no small differences can ever make us doubt each other's loyalty to a great cause. All this makes our personal losses sink into insignificance. I have my bad times of homesickness for all that is gone, but if the Chinese are served my loss is gain somehow."

For two months all was quiet in Unzen. "Then one morning," Pearl wrote, "I heard a loud familiar voice from the back porch." It was Mrs. Lu, the heroine of March 24. "This hearty and indomitable creature had decided that it was her duty to find me because she was sure I needed her. She had gone to Shanghai, had inquired of friends where I was, and then with her own money she had bought a steerage ticket and found her way, not speaking a word of Japanese, to our mountain-top. I have no idea how she accomplished this but when I saw her standing there, her belongings tied up in a flowered kerchief, and her round lively face all smiles, I suddenly knew that I did need her. We fell into each other's arms and within minutes she was managing everything."

The summer passed and gradually Pearl Buck found her creative drive reasserting itself. She began viewing events in terms of stories, reaching out for half-formed ideas and pinning them down for later development. A hurricane that summer became, years later, *The Big Wave*, a book for children. And the Nanking Incident on March 24 inspired a story "The Revolution" whose hero Wang Lung would appear again in a novel titled *The Good Earth*.

5

When the weather in Unzen made the paper house uninhabitable, the Bucks moved on, but not to Nanking, still in the hands of Red soldiers. Funded for the daily essentials by the Mission Board, they could afford a modest rent, and both the Bucks and the Yaukeys chose Shanghai.

A house on Avenue Joffre in the French Concession was surprisingly presentable but too large and expensive for them alone. Pearl mulled over possible housemates, and two old friends, fellow refugees, seemed "the least incompatible."

"Pearl suggested our sharing a house," Sara Burton (not her real name) reported. "She offered us the first floor. The Yaukeys and Mr. Sydenstricker would have the second, and she and Lossing and the kids would take the third. She said, 'Frankly, we'd have liked the house alone but since we can't afford it we decided we could stand you better than anyone else.' It worked out very well. Each couple could have our own guests if we didn't want them together, but very often we did. My husband and I went to the Christian church in the morning, but I don't remember Pearl going much. I think her religious feeling was a pretty shifty thing at this time. She seemed to have lost a good deal of her faith. Pearl had two amahs she was trying to help, one for Carol, and the ubiquitous Mrs. Lu. She used to say there were two kinds of amahs, the bright and sharp and the dumb and reliable. 'Mine are all the latter kind,' she said, but it was well to have someone there at all times with Carol."

Lossing was anxious to return to Nanking to work on his survey which, with Pearl's help, he had been assembling all summer. The Thomsons and the Reisners lived nearby, and the three husbands, defying the anti-white feeling in Nanking, slipped in and out unnoticed to hole up in Professor Thomson's laboratory all winter, working and sleeping under the noses of the Communist-Nationalists.

Theoretically, the three wives ran the Joffre Avenue household, but actually Mrs. Lu reigned supreme over the kitchen and everyone therein. For a time there was a noisy truce. Then from the basement came a loud and angry male voice. When questioned Mrs. Lu confessed that she had a man imprisoned below. After the Bucks had left Nanking Mrs. Lu had fallen in love with a neighbor's table boy, who had promised to marry her, but in all the confusion another woman had carried him off. Yesterday, however, Mrs. Lu had seen the two in the marketplace. Tearing him away from his captor, she had dragged him home and locked him in the cellar.

Pearl mildly suggested that Mrs. Lu's prize might have something to say about all this and demanded to see him. A personable young man appeared who admitted with some pride that both women wanted to marry him. A virgin would have been preferable, but virgins cost money so he was willing to marry Mrs. Lu if she would not lock him up. The marriage was performed and all went well until he brought in the other woman. This Mrs. Lu would not countenance. He argued that many Chinese men had two wives, but she countered by citing Chiang Kai-shek, who before marrying Soong Mai Ling had banished all three of his previous wives. As usual, Mrs. Lu got her way. And later, eager for a family, she triumphed over other difficulties. The aging woman, who had mothered uncounted babies, discovered that her abortion had made her sterile. But ever resourceful, she bought her husband a nice ugly concubine who obligingly produced a fine boy which Mrs. Lu appropriated as her own.

This happy ending occurred after the Bucks' return to Nanking. At the moment Mrs. Lu was preoccupied with running her kitchen. Sara Burton taught in the American school while Grace, with two children and Absalom back from Korea, had her hands full caring for them.

"Grace," Sara Burton recalled, "was a lovely person. Her father was very difficult to live with, so sure he was always right. Pearl snapped at him sometimes, but Grace never."

"I felt very sorry for Pearl altogether. She had a hard time with Carol up there on the third floor. I could see a fine spirit inside her. Of course

I knew her weaknesses but I knew her virtues too and they far out-weighed the faults. For instance, later, when my younger boy had to wear hand-me-down clothing he hated wearing things that didn't fit. Well, she sent him a whole new little suit that fit him exactly, and you should have seen the joy on that child's face. That's the kind of thing she did all the time. I loved her very much."

Living in communal style Mrs. Burton developed intense loyalties. "Pearl should never have married Lossing," she declared. "She had to ask him for every cent. Lewis and I had a joint bank account and one day when Pearl saw me buying a table, she said, 'Can you do that without asking Lewis?' I thought that was terrible for a bright woman like her. He wanted to keep all the money in his account, even though she was earning a salary as a teacher. Someone said it was probably because he was brought up in a poverty-stricken home."

Poverty existed in the Joffre Avenue home as well, with perhaps the greatest pressure on Pearl who carried the extra burden of a helpless child.

Some time earlier she had recognized that the responsibility for Carol was to be hers alone, for Lossing on his limited salary opposed lavish expenditures, and if Carol was to have the kind of care she visualized, she would have to provide it. Alone on the top floor of the house, with a borrowed typewriter, Pearl Buck set to work.

Her writing could only be done at night, for both Carol and Janice required a great deal of attention during the day. Pearl spent hours trying to teach Carol the simple proprieties and regularly took her out for a walk. Sara Burton remembered her returning home one day, her face drawn. "'Sara,' she told me, 'I hope you'll never know what it's like to walk in the park and see people draw aside . . . you can almost hear them whispering, 'There's that woman with that strange child.' It's so awful to be known as the mother of such a child.' Pearl was really remarkable. I don't know how she got any sleep. Carol was always waking at night and asking for water. You could hear her stomping around up there."

Janice also could prove difficult. For lessons in table manners Pearl felt children should eat with the adults. "But Janice disdained food," Sara Burton stated. "Before she was three she had decided not to eat and she just kept her mouth closed. Pearl would say, 'All right, you can have it warmed up at your next meal,' and once she kept her sitting there all day except for going to the bathroom. Pearl was so frustrated

. . . the child needed food, she was very thin, but the doctor said she was medically healthy. Finally Pearl altered her tactics somewhat, but it was years before Janice ate naturally. I guess it was just a battle of wills."

So far Pearl had made a few literary sales—three short pieces to *Asia Magazine*, three to *The Nation*, one each to *The Atlantic Monthly* and *Forum*, and three to missionary magazines. Other manuscripts mailed to New York were rejected, and she agonized over the two months lost in transit. To find a publisher and to make money she must acquire an agent.

In an old English *Writer's Guide* she found the names of two literary agents with offices in New York and timidly she wrote them describing her work. One replied that American readers were not interested in China, but the other's response was more positive, and she sent segments of *A Chinese Woman Speaks* to David Lloyd suggesting that together the two sections might make a novel with the title *Winds of Heaven*.

This period in Pearl Buck's life proved to be the most meaningful professionally, for on the third floor of the Shanghai house she was writing a novel which she thought of as *Wang Lung*. Everyone in the house knew she was busy at something on those nights alone, but politely no one inquired. One spring day Pearl asked Margaret Thomson if she would mind reading a long manuscript and tell her what should be cut.

Two days later Margaret returned it. "I'm absolutely *stunned!*" she had cried. "Overwhelmed! It's marvelous; it's like Dostoyevsky. I sat up all night reading it. . . ."

In the subsequent excitement Sara Burton asked Grace if she had known about this marvelous manuscript. "No," Grace had replied somewhat wistfully. "You don't think she'd tell her little sister about it? She never tells me anything she's doing."

Her response was no exaggeration. The year they lived in the same house Grace, tied to her restless father and two small children, knew nothing of her sister's activities. She remembered Pearl leaving Carol with the amahs. "She was out a great deal, I believe. You see, she was a gifted speaker; she had written some articles and she could speak with wit and color about Chinese people and their literature. Shanghai had a great many foreigners and there was a lively literary set."

Christine Lewis, a high school student in Shanghai, remembered

Pearl Buck's speech in their assembly hall. "We thought it was very interesting that a missionary's wife, somebody pretty heavy and not at all well dressed, would actually be selling stories and articles about the people all around us—ordinary people."

"At this period of my life," Pearl wrote later, "I was keenly aware of the Chinese peasant—his wonderful strength and goodness, his amusing and often alarming shrewdness and wisdom, his direct approach to life." Nothing, she admitted, enraged her like the Communist term for the peasant, "the packhorse of a nation." "To what heights may not these packhorses rise if they are considered human beings instead of beasts of burden!" However, there is no reference to the period ten years earlier when she raged to her mother-in-law about the "terrible degradation and wickedness of a heathen people . . . so stupid and ignorant and superstitious." Pearl Buck had changed a great deal.

Now for the first time she had the opportunity to go anywhere and see anyone she chose. Cosmopolitan Shanghai was not conservative Nanking, a white woman was not considered out of place and it was possible to live one's life fully, if done inconspicuously. On a certain social level the two cities were so westernized that they could bear comparison with America in the Roaring Twenties—its new-found freedom, the kicking over of traces epitomized by Scott and Zelda Fitzgerald. Some of this libertinism had ruffled the surface of old-fashioned Nanking but not its missionary circles. There Pearl had shared the political and cultural upheaval in the classroom, even inviting groups of ardent young students into her living room for discussions. But otherwise she had simply been the wife of a dull statistician, housekeeper for other missionaries, and mother of a handicapped child. In Shanghai she had an opportunity to enjoy more than objective observations.

The romantic news that Pearl had had a lover was known for some time by three of her intimates—Emma through Pearl's letters, Sara Burton because the two women shared a house, and much later a private secretary who was also a close friend. Rumors existed, but no one actually knew the lover's identity until an interview with Sara Burton in 1978.

Hsu Chih-mo, whose name in another dialect was Hsu Tze-mo, was a well-known poet during the twenties and thirties. Born in 1896, he was four years younger than Pearl, rich and socially prominent from a famous banking family. Educated in a westernized school he had been married at twenty in the Chinese tradition and fathered a son. He had left China to study social science in the United States and from there gone to England where at Cambridge University he felt he had found his spiritual home.

In the serene beauty of the English countryside, the poetic and impractical Hsu developed an almost mystical relationship with nature and mankind. Submerging himself in the romantic literature of the English poets, he rebelled against his own mundane marriage, and like Shelley, dreamed of an unearthly love that would be "the sweet bondage which is freedom's self." Before he returned home he obtained a divorce, a move which shocked the orthodox Hsu family.

On his return to China in 1922, he discovered that China's freedom-seeking youth had leaped eagerly into the May Fourth Movement and its literary revolution. Fresh from Cambridge, Hsu joined them and, influenced by Shelley, Byron and Keats, wrote romantic poetry in which he melded English forms with Chinese imagery. His immediate success propelled him into the limelight, and in two years he became the spokesman for the younger generation advocating freedom and candor in thought and deed.

A member of the aristocracy, a pioneer in the new culture and a man of infinite charm, he was the natural choice for interpreter to the Nobel laureate Rabindranath Tagore when the famous poet made a lecture tour through China in 1924. Accompanying Tagore was his English emissary, Leonard Elmhirst, who struck up a friendship with Hsu that was to last until death intervened. The three toured the larger cities and universities, Tagore lecturing to the students and afterwards meeting with the faculties. Nanking, with its English-language colleges and missions, was especially eager to play host to the illustrious visitors.

Pearl and Hsu no doubt met in Nanking. As an English teacher she would certainly have attended Tagore's lecture. And it is not difficult to imagine Hsu's impact upon her, joyous in his own success and yet warmly responsive to others, while she was at her nadir, locked into a dead marriage with a hopelessly ill child. He must have represented everything she desired and could never have.

After the Nanking Incident, Hsu Chih-mo commuted between Shanghai and Peking, the leader in both cities of the literary set. As a fledgling author Pearl had a legitimate reason to meet with this visiting poet.

Hsu's international background and winning personality made him much in demand as a teacher and editor, and when he joined the Peking University faculty and the *Peking Evening News* his generous help to both students and writers made him almost a legend among his colleagues.

With this same devotion he threw himself into a love affair which became the talk of Peking and Shanghai. The girl was the incarnation of all his dreams. But like all well-born Chinese girls, she had been married off early by her parents, and the consequent tortures the lovers suffered during their enforced separations flooded their letters and diaries which, on publication, made them the romantic idols of their generation.

Sadly, however, once their marriage was consummated, Hsu found he had worshipped a figurine of clay. His perfect love was vain, selfish and empty-headed, and Hsu's ebullient spirits languished. Further, his wife's wanton expenditures for luxuries, including opium, forced him into a killing regimen of work. Four years later he was a changed man, writing miserably to Leonard Elmhirst in England that life in China had become intolerable: "My only hope is to get out."

Elmhirst, aware that Hsu's marriage had impoverished him, sent him passage money, and he sailed for England in July 1928, at almost the same time that the Lossing Bucks were returning to Nanking after their year in Shanghai.

At the time Pearl had told only Emma and Sara Burton of her relationship with Hsu. Years later, however, she felt free to reveal the affair and she wrote *Letter from Peking*, admitting it was her own story thinly disguised. It was depicted as a love returned and consummated: "It was in this house that we first consummated our eternal love. We were not married. I write it down. I have never told our heavenly secret to anyone, nor has he. I am sure he has not. He says he loves only me, whatever happens, and so he has not told. Say it may have been wrong, but I am glad now for what I chose to do. . . . Novels describe again and again the act of physical love between man and woman. I read these descriptions, wondering at their monotony and their dullness. The act of love can then be meaningless! I wonder at such degradation, and then I realize that it is degraded because the two who perform it are degraded. I thank the beloved who saved me from such desecration."

In 1925 she wrote *A Chinese Woman Speaks*, an emotional story about a girl loving a man across cultural barriers, and twice in her autobiographies reminisce about the young poet (using the spelling Hsu Tze-mo) who sat in her living room and talked for hours, "tall and classically beautiful, gesturing with hands graceful and strong and slender." The newspapers had dubbed him the Chinese Shelley and the Chinese Byron after his own favorite English poets, and she used those allusions in several of her novels. Twice he is the main character in a novel—a priest in *Pavilion of Women* and a professor in *Letter from Peking*—and under his own name he is a character in a novel who dies in the same way in which Hsu lost his own life. Obviously, she could not forget this man.

There is no tangible evidence that Hsu loved *her*. Indeed, when they met she was at her least attractive, overweight, enervated, careless of her looks. Possibly the emotion was all on her side—reason enough for keeping it hidden. It must be remembered that Pearl Buck was a romantic with a novelist's imagination, and after twenty-five years this version of the relationship may consist of nothing more than wish fulfillment.

No biographies of Hsu Chih-mo mention Pearl Buck, nor do his acquaintances admit knowledge of an affair. But, on the other hand, both parties were married, and as she was a missionary as well, it would have been natural to keep the affair a secret.

During those months of conflicting emotions, a curious change took place which Pearl wrote about to Emma: "For no special reason— it just happened—I find I've lost forty-five pounds!" It might have been the tension or perhaps she was repeating her feat at Randolph-Macon when she made herself over to win the approval she craved.

However, there is no reason to doubt that after she finished her novel, she wanted a professional opinion and approached Hsu Chih-mo. Or that he was the Chinese critic who, as she told her publisher later, opposed its being cut.

In any event, there were no further meetings in Shanghai. For in July 1928, with Hsu in England, she and Lossing were returning to Nanking. And so she went back to her roles as wife, mother, teacher, missionary and boardinghouse keeper—a desperately lonely woman.

They found Nanking, the new capital, rapidly being westernized into a city with electricity and telephones and movie theaters. Most of the missionary residences had been occupied by government officials, although the Bucks' house had sheltered troops and, at one point, a company of horses in Pearl's precious rose garden. Chinese friends took them in. And, to their great relief, they were cordially welcomed by most of the community. Particularly heartwarming was her reception by the university students. After the Incident they had gone to her house to salvage her books and while the manuscript left on a desk was never recovered, a box of typescript remained safe on a high shelf. Though glad to receive back this memorial to her mother, she attached to it no more than sentimental value.

To Emma she wrote of the present political situation: "It is all wonderfully interesting if one can keep a working sense of humor . . . take everything as part of a game." Chiang Kai-shek, fighting off warlords with one hand and Communists with the other, displayed more military vigor than statesmanship, seemingly oblivious to the mass of peasants who comprised the bulk of his people. "One cannot be wholly optimistic about the new order. In this new government the corruption of old times goes on. Men get jobs by pull and everybody squeezes all he dares. This enormously increased government expenditure has resulted in enormously increased taxes, and the people are groaning under it and reviling the government. . . . There is evidence of serious danger ahead, the danger of *real* revolution."

She and Lossing settled down to a collegiate routine superficially the same. Lossing, after several years of data analysis, had put together a mountain of charts, figures and, finally, conclusions on China's farm economy. Since his return from Cornell in 1925 the survey had been his chief preoccupation and by the fall of 1928 it was finished. Then, suddenly, he was faced with the question, how was it to be used?

With barely suppressed pride Lossing showed his mass of data to Dr. J. B. Condliffe, research secretary of the Institute for Pacific Relations, who was visiting Nanking, and Condliffe fulfilled the hope he had scarcely dared entertain by remarking, "This ought to be published," and a tentative commitment was worked out. In return Dr. Condliffe showed Lossing the U.S. Department of Agriculture's proposal for a study, to be undertaken in the United States, of the utilization of land and resources in China. When asked his opinion of the idea Lossing shot back, "Wouldn't it be better to study China's land utilization *in China?*"

Condliffe's acquiescence settled Lossing's career for several years. Groups of his students would visit China's eight regions gathering information in order to improve agricultural methods and also to acquaint the outside world with China's rural way of life.

The project, which would entail a trip to the United States for the whole Buck family, would take ten years from genesis to publication and would be recognized as the most comprehensive study of China's agronomy ever attempted. One volume would be a textbook explaining the other two, the second a series of large maps, each of a single district's soil condition, another featuring irrigation, climate, livestock, fertility and so on. The third volume contained statistics on the components illustrated. The impressive work ultimately became Lossing Buck's *Land Utilization in China*.

A Cornell member of Lossing's team, Ardron N. Lewis, explained the significance of the publication: "In the field of agriculture and agricultural policy, an idea will be held about a certain district, that its agricultural conditions are such-and-such, and the lawmakers will enact legislation based on that assumption. But if the assumption is wrong, untold damage may be done involving millions of people. However, if the economist knows the exact conditions he can formulate the most appropriate methods of dealing with the situation. That's the kind of knowledge that Lossing Buck contributed . . . it was a monumental achievement."

An American, well informed on China, agrees. "Even today, Lossing Buck's name is golden in China."

In January 1929, as Lossing's project got under way, Pearl wrote to Emma: "We may be going to America in June for four months. Lossing may be given a large sum of money for a certain project in research by the Rockefeller people and if he is, we will have to go home next summer for consultations . . ."

The trip to America turned into a fortunate event for Pearl. The political trends in China, exemplified by the March 24 Incident, had convinced her that a future for Carol in China was unthinkable. What if Lossing and she both died and left her alone? Noting that Carol responded to music, she tried that as a key to open her mind. Carol did pay attention, even using her fingers carefully. But then one day, touching the child's hands, she found them wet with perspiration. She was putting a cruel strain on her. "At that moment," she wrote, "my heart broke all over again." She must let her be just as she was.

She wrote to Emma: "The problem of Carol presses on me. I realize that I must leave her in some place where she can be trained to the highest of which she is capable, and my heart is wrenched in two at the thought. . . . The years do not make me resigned. Sometimes I can scarcely bear to look at other children . . . and see what she might have been. . . . Having Janice just *saves* me, and I continually marvel at my luck in finding her out of all the world. . . . We shall probably leave Carol when we come to America next summer."

In July they began the month-long trip and, upon arrival, made the rounds of various institutions. All proved disappointing. Some were attractive, even luxurious, but to Pearl's keen eye the emphasis seemed chiefly to be on keeping the children from making trouble or embarrassing the families. In one she was shocked to discover that older girls could be trained to hold a hand of cards, appearing to be playing bridge. After rejecting them all, they visited the Training School in Vineland, New Jersey.

The children of all ages seemed happy in the care of their attendants, who in turn were rewarded with trust and affection. Dr. Edward Johnstone, the director, greeted Pearl and Lossing and showed them around, answering their questions with candor. The grounds were obviously intended for play, a farm provided the boys with simple chores, and even the plumbing was designed for safety and comfort.

"We have just one rule here," the director explained, "the children must feel happy and loved. Praise them a lot is our motto. Pat them a lot—above the waist. Gently."

This, Pearl decided, was the end of her journey. But how to raise the fee, a thousand dollars a year? Two thousand dollars would be enough money to buy her two years free of worry in which to write. Somehow, somewhere, she must find a way.

Years later, in 1972, Pearl Buck was driving through New York City with a business associate. Passing a stately apartment house at One Lexington Avenue, she suddenly said, "Sometime I'll tell you of how a couple in that house helped to make possible my writing career." She never did explain to her companion, but later on she told it to a West Virginia newspaper: "I needed money desperately, and I went to the Mission Board and borrowed two thousand dollars. That was a great sum of money in those days." In return for the money she was asked to write an account of the missionary movement for children.

This transaction yielded Pearl Buck more than money. The members of the Mission Board were so impressed by her intelligence, sincerity and the urgency of her need that one member, the wife of the Editor of *The New York Times*, volunteered the necessary cash. But more than that, in Dr. and Mrs. John F. Finley, Jr., Pearl met two Americans who would become lifelong friends. Their home was at One Lexington Avenue.

Dr. Finley was a well-known figure in New York City. Before joining *The Times* he had been New York City's Commissioner of Education, and according to Harry Hansen, literary critic of the *New York World*, "a very dignified person who was always being asked to MC dinners. I always think of Finley in a frock coat . . ." Indeed, during Pearl's years as an after-dinner speaker Dr. Finley was Master of Ceremonies more often than anyone else. And Mrs. Finley seems to have been for Pearl a sort of mother-figure.

Their loan was based on nothing more substantial than Pearl's own personality, her job as a teacher, and a vaguely plotted story in her head—hardly security for a large sum of money.

Having deposited the loan and installed Carol in the Training School in New Jersey, Pearl had accomplished her objectives. So while Lossing finished his courses she visited a friend in Buffalo, and there a cable heralding a new life was delivered. In the confusion of the past year she had forgotten the stories mailed to agent David Lloyd, who did not have her present address. The cable, sent to Nanking, forwarded to New York and then Buffalo, read: "John Day offer Winds of Heaven subject certain changes ten percent royalty fifteen after five thousand advance payable on publication advise."

Pearl described that moment: "The news came on a morning when I was feeling very desolate at the prospect of a future separation from my child, and while it did not compensate, nevertheless it did brighten my life in its own way." Lloyd asked her to come to New York for a conference and, curiously calm, a few weeks later she met her agent, a tall, thin man with a small mustache and bushy eyebrows who, as her guide, would steer her through twenty-five years of furious literary activity.

He explained the terms of the cable. The request for changes was normal, as was possible dissatisfaction with the title. But the royalty schedule he considered unsatisfactory—ten percent of the book's price on the first five thousand copies sold and after that fifteen percent. The "ten percent to five thousand" clause was O.K. And the fifteen percent after five thousand *sounded* good, except that a first novel rarely reached a five thousand copy sale. Paying the advance *only on publication* was an irregular practice, possibly betraying a shaky condition in the firm.

Richard Walsh, John Day's president, Lloyd described as highly cultivated and charming, a Harvard graduate with impeccable taste. But the firm was only four years old and had not yet published a truly successful book. Indeed, John Day had been the last publisher on Lloyd's list, and he had only offered the manuscript there after all other publishers had turned it down. Having thus made clear this offer was the end of the line, Lloyd advised acceptance, and he escorted the author to the John Day office to meet its president.

Richard Walsh greeted them cordially. There had, he told them, been a great deal of argument over the novel because American readers were assumed to be uninterested in China, and the John Day staff had been evenly divided. Walsh had cast the deciding vote, less on the novel's merits than on the promise of a better one later. Pearl, properly humble, accepted his offer gratefully.

Walsh explained the changes he had in mind. The title *Winds of Heaven* might be improved upon. What about *East Wind: West Wind*? Also, though her prose style started out fresh, redolent of China, it later settled into a number of "Americanisms" and trite phrases. He had taken the liberty of making a few notes in the margin of the manuscript.

Carrying her novel home, she hurried to make the indicated changes and sent it back with a letter: "Dear Mr. Walsh, I am returning by this evening's post *East Wind: West Wind* (you see I have already learned to call it that!) Your suggestions are good. No suggestion is too meticulous for me to appreciate receiving. I want my work to be as perfect as possible and I appreciate much any help toward that end."

A contract was signed and Pearl became a professional author, a milestone which put her in a cheerful mood. There remained, however, the dreaded parting with her child. Lossing wished to spend Christmas with his parents, so she visited Emma White in the South, returning to New York for a final farewell.

Carol had accepted her new home with no signs of discomfort, so in early January the Bucks sailed for China. Pearl Buck was thirty-seven, with a new life about to unfold.

6

The publisher into whose hands Pearl had been placed must have been secretly as relieved as she at the merging of their fortunes. For so shaky was Richard Walsh's fledgling firm that his children had had to chip in with their Liberty bonds to keep it alive, a situation likely to unsettle a forty-two-year-old book publisher.

Born in Kansas of a family recently emigrated from England, he went from public schools to Harvard, graduating magna cum laude in 1907. There, blessed with an irrepressible sense of the ridiculous like his college-mate Robert Benchley, he wrote for the *Harvard Lampoon*, and the two remained fast friends, trading puns long into their middle years. From the *Lampoon* to journalism was a natural step and he entered the risky publishing world after working successively for the Boston Chamber of Commerce, an advertising agency and as an editorial writer for *Judge* and *The Woman's Home Companion*. As a freelance author he wrote a biography of Buffalo Bill and then for several years edited *Collier's* magazine.

By this time he had married Ruby Abbott and had three children, Natalie, Richard Jr., and Elizabeth, and a comfortable house in Pelham, a golfing suburb of New York City.

Having sampled various careers and found editing the most intriguing, he set his sights on becoming an independent publisher. In 1927 he learned that a firm named John Day, recently started by a small group to publish educational materials, was foundering and in need of cash. Drawing a deep breath and pooling all his disposable cash, including his children's government bonds, Walsh persuaded his friend, Earl Newsom, to join him. Together they began sorting out the current stock, primarily progressive education materials, and Newsom, considered one of New York's brightest public relations men, took on the task of promoting the name of John Day, a sixteenth-century printer famous for daring to print unpopular papers.

Newsom made known the firm's desire for manuscripts among literary agents and other sources of publishable manuscripts. David Lloyd had been conscientiously but wearily sending Pearl's manuscript to twenty-eight publishing houses. In submitting her work to the twenty-ninth, John Day, Lloyd described it to Walsh as "a direct yet delicate portrayal of the conflict between the old and the new in China," adding hopefully, "I think it may interest you." Seven weeks later he received Walsh's offer.

The relationship between agent, publisher and their client, Pearl Buck, unlike the more traditional one of polite wariness, was one of total respect and confidence (allowing, of course, for human frailties). Thus Walsh and Lloyd, already friends, had sent their author off to China trusting in their solicitude. Meanwhile Walsh and Newsom rolled up their sleeves and got to work in the nick of time. Christmas was upon them, and Pearl Buck's novel was the only likely-looking project the firm had in the house.

Pearl arrived home a woman torn between her loyalties. On one side was the exhilarating sale of *East Wind: West Wind* and the request for a juvenile book by the Mission Board, two reasons for modest optimism. On the other side was depression at a lengthy separation from her child. "The distance between America and China is too great," she wrote Grace. "Time is too long, too much can happen to a child who can never fully make any other know the small agonies of its heart." Grace, seeing Pearl tense and drawn, believed this year and the next two to be the hardest time of her sister's life. She assumed the separation from Carol to be the sole cause.

But she knew nothing about Hsu Chih-mo. In actuality, Hsu's shadow hung heavily over this period in Pearl Buck's life. How many meetings there were no one knows, but they could have been frequent, for both traveled often between Peking, Nanking and Shanghai on literary matters. Pearl, the author of various articles and stories, was often asked to speak, and Hsu taught courses in all three cities. And he was very much in evidence at the time of *A Chinese Woman Speaks* in 1925.

That story, developed later into the novel *East Wind: West Wind*, had been inspired by Pearl's fantasy of being Hsu's wife but in an article in *The Colophon* she actually involved him in its publication. After her great success with *The Good Earth*, the literary magazine invited her to relate the publication history of her first novel. She wrote that "a friend who was always urging me to write asked if I had not something to show him" and when she produced this story he told her to submit it for publication.

After arriving back home, she got out the *Wang Lung* manuscript, telling a neighbor, "I have to hurry up and earn a great deal of money as fast as I can." Later she wrote in *My Several Worlds*, "One morning I put the attic room in order . . . and faced the window in that Chinese house. That window and the landscape beyond still live in my heart. I see the green lawn, the bamboos against the compound wall, the crowded roofs of the city beyond, these encircled by the great city wall. Beyond that wall rose Purple Mountain. . . . At the desk one spring I sat morning after morning for three months writing my first real novel. My story had shaped itself firmly and swiftly from the events of my life and its energy was the anger I felt for the sake of the peasants and the common folk of China, whom I loved and admired.

"I had learned to love those peasants, so brave, so industrious, so cheerfully expecting no help from others. Long ago I had made up my mind to be their voice. . . . I chose the north country, and for the rich southern city, Nanking. My material was therefore close at hand and the people I knew as I knew myself. In three months I told their story, typing the manuscript twice."

Actually, Pearl Buck telescoped history for dramatic effect. What she wrote that spring was a rewrite of the Shanghai manuscript she had shown Margaret Thomson two years earlier. She reported this to David Lloyd. But in truth it may have been a third draft, for no one knew the subject matter of her first novel since that one was lost during the Nanking Incident. She told her publisher, "This book has been many years planned and pruned . . ."

"When it was finished," she admitted, "I felt very doubtful of its value, but to whom could I turn for judgment?" She never considered her husband. To ask her father seemed absurd. Her brother Edgar was currently in Nanking as a representative of the Milbank Memorial Fund's study on China's public health and Pearl was tempted to ask him to read it. But, she decided, "He had only a few days to spend with me. I had shyly mentioned that I had written a novel and he was kind as always, but I couldn't ask him to take his valuable time." She simply wrapped up the manuscript and sent it to Lloyd.

Having stolen time from her Mission Board obligation, she now set reluctantly to work on *The Young Revolutionist*. This would discharge $500 of the $2,000 debt, and she wrote it dutifully. Before it could be published by the Mission Press, however, *The Good Earth* had burst upon the reading public and the juvenile tract became an embarrassment to its author. Under an arrangement between the Mission Press and the John Day Company, a paperback edition was issued while John Day cautiously published a hardcover edition to fulfill Pearl's contract with the Board.

It was hoped that a frank acknowledgment of its origin might excuse its propagandist tone, and indeed, the critics showed remarkable respect. *The New York Times* commented: "*The Young Revolutionist* . . . is a story written with a purpose. . . . If it had been written without bias it might have been a very fine and moving novel. Even as it is . . . it is not without something of both power and beauty. Mrs. Buck writes beautifully."

Pearl had complained wistfully about the lack of helpful advice on her *Wang Lung* manuscript. Had Hsu Chih-mo been available when she first completed it, she would probably have turned to him, but by now he was totally involved with his wife's debts and his exhausting professional duties, commuting between Shanghai's Kuanghua University and Nanking's Central University, editing the *New Moon Monthly* and acting as trustee of the Sino-British Cultural Foundation.

His biographer Kai Yu-Hsi considered 1929 and 1930 his most difficult years (which is what Grace wrote of Pearl). Fading was his optimistic faith in man, his *joie de vivre*, though he still exhibited high spirits when he sought to inspire his students: "Nature contains an inexhaustible source for the nourishment, enlightenment and inspiration of each of us. . . . This temporary depression must not overcome our ideals . . ."

His biographers attributed his depression to a sudden awareness of China's political dangers, but more logically they blame his unhappy marriage. What part, if any, Pearl Buck may have played in Hsu's despondency will probably never be truly known. But the part he played in hers, childless and loveless, is indicated by what she did next.

The spring of 1930 had been a busy one. By May Pearl had finished and sent off *Wang Lung* and *The Young Revolutionist*. Then, suddenly at loose ends, the pent-up emotions of years swept over her, urging expression. "My mind could not rest after I had finished *The Good Earth*," she wrote later, "and almost immediately I began to write another novel, *The Mother*, in which I portrayed the life of a Chinese peasant woman. But more than that, I hoped it was the life of such a woman anywhere, who has been given no fulfillment except her own experience and understanding. . . . Yet . . . when I had finished *The Mother* I was far from pleased with it and I threw it into the waste basket beside my desk. There it lay and it was only chance that it was not thrown away permanently. The houseboy happened to be away for a few days and the basket was not emptied . . . and before the houseboy returned I had retrieved my manuscript to examine it again. . . . Eventually it was a book, although I put it away for several years first."

It is not hard to understand why she tried to destroy what she had written, for if ever a woman put on paper the agony of an animal in heat, this is it, poignant and pitiful. Pearl Buck's shock was overwhelming when she realized how much she had revealed. It would take her several years and residence on a different continent to disassociate herself from *The Mother* enough to take some pride in its authorship.

As a work of art it ranks high among her achievements. She has stated that Mrs. Lu was the model for the mother, but that character, the failed mother, the unfulfilled woman, could well be Pearl herself. When it was finally published, there were a few negative reviews but more that recognized the book's power and beauty.

In New York her publishers Richard Walsh and Earl Newsom were performing a minor miracle. Though nine months is the normal gestation period for a book, *East Wind: West Wind* was brought out in four months. In May Pearl, who had still received no money from John Day, wrote Emma: "*East Wind: West Wind* came out in April and has had . . . surprisingly good reviews—but of course reviews do not sell a book."

The *Saturday Review* assigned it for review to author Alice Tisdale Hobart, a resident of Nanking: "In the patriarchal home of China the relations of the sexes are so different from ours . . . that it seemed to me an impossibility for the Westerner . . . to know the mental and emotional reactions of the Chinese in the intimate relations of love and marriage." She acknowledged, however, that Pearl Buck had done just that remarkably well, sympathetically entering the mind of a young bride unable to win her husband's love due to the difference in their backgrounds.

After her long concentrated spell of writing, utterly submerging herself in her characters, Pearl finally came up for air and examined the real world around her. Chiang Kai-shek and his glamorous American-educated wife were lending glitter to the staid Nanking of old, but Pearl's classroom contacts informed her that his efforts to unify the country were being carried out with paranoidal severity. Young students often disappeared suddenly, victims of Chiang's reprisals against Communism.

At the same time he still fought the established warlords in the North. Of the two factions, he was more successful against the old bandits, who fought boldly, out in the open, than against the Communists, who stole weapons and supplies—and even dissident Kuomintang soldiers—from his own armies; who hid in the mountains and formed a network of small guerrilla outposts; and who, under direct attack, simply melted away. Chiang continued to chase Reds while a militant Japan loomed over him ready to pounce.

Pearl, reading accounts of the emerging young Communist, Mao Tse-tung, recognized in his use of military tactics a type of warfare portrayed in ancient Chinese fiction. In one novel, a tale of robbers and bandits, she was amused to discover Mao's entire strategy revealed.

To assuage her unbearable loneliness, she went back to her typewriter. "It was then," she wrote, "while my father was at Kuling with Grace and Lossing was buried in his agricultural survey, that I began my translation of the great Chinese novel *Shui Hu Chuan* which later I called *All Men Are Brothers*. . . . Four years I worked on the translation of that mighty book. . . . It was a profound experience, for though the book was written five centuries ago the pageant of Chinese life was still the same, and in the Communists, fleeing now into the Northwest, I saw the wild rebels and malcontents who had risen against governments in the old days of Empire."

The responsibility of entertaining visitors fell to the university faculty, and the Bucks' house, with its showplace garden, its unsurpassed cuisine and its stimulating conversation, generally attracted the VIPS who were passing through.

The eminent professor of Harvard's philosophy department and author of *The Meaning of God in Human Experience*, Ernest Hocking, was a member of an investigative commission appraising foreign missions for an interdenominational group of Protestant churches. Informed of his tour of inspection, Lossing and Pearl groaned. There had been a similar inquiry a few months before, when a group of conspicuously ill-informed persons had asked questions that betrayed a woefully superficial understanding of mission work. The Bucks were well aware that on such reports could ride not only their future work but their livelihoods as well.

Pearl planned a dinner for the Hockings in a mood of grimly suppressed resentment. Writing of their meeting later, she commented: "I remember his coming into the house like a strong wind, very vital and tall, extremely handsome, very blue eyes, very unselfconscious, full of confidence and knowing exactly what he wanted; talkative, humorous, a striking personality. His wife, who was the daughter of James Riley [O'Reilly] the Irish poet was just as striking in her way, though not as attractive as he because she did not have the brains or the looks that he had. He had a philosophical mind which of course attracted me at once. Hers was not philosophical so much as practical, yet it had a sort of Irish quality that was delightful. I remember with pleasure the evening they spent at our house. Then they went back to America and I thought no more of them."

Ernest Hocking, however, thought more of Pearl. He left the Buck house with the firm conviction that his remarkable hostess would end up somewhere other than Nanking and contribute something more than teaching.

Pearl labored over her translation of *Shui Hu Chuan* and wondered about the *Wang Lung* manuscript, which had reached Lloyd in June. Almost immediately Lloyd had sent it on to Walsh with the note: "I think you will agree that Mrs. Buck has done a very remarkable piece of work in this new Chinese novel of hers. I have now got it in shape to submit to you for first reading. I hope you are going to be as enthusiastic about it as we are here."

Walsh was more than enthusiastic and accepted the book at once on the same terms as before. Then, bowing to publishing protocol, he asked Lloyd's permission to write directly to his client: "Dear Mrs. Buck: I wish you were not so far away because I am afraid it is going to be impossible for me to express adequately in this letter our enthusiasm for *Wang Lung*. The beauty of style which attracted us to *East Wind: West Wind* is only one of its great merits. Your characters are drawn with such fidelity that the reader has no difficulty in forgetting that they are not of his own race and in sharing their emotions as human beings. . . . By your choice of incidents you have somehow succeeded in making us believe that we are seeing almost the whole of the life of the plain people of China in all its details, from birth to death. Over and above all this, I believe that you have written a book of permanent importance, one that will rank with the great novels of the soil.

"There are just three points I want to take up with you. One: the title. We feel that Wang Lung is quite impossible. The sound comes unpleasantly from the American tongue . . . and is subject to facetious parody, 'One lung,' for example, but also because of the immediate effect—that is, typing the book as Chinese. We have to present this book not as a story of Chinese life, but as a novel of the soil. The only title I have been able to think of is *The Good Earth.*

"Two: It seems to me that the latter part is rather prolonged, that you might do well to cut rather considerably.

"Three: date of publication. We should like to wait to see how fast the fiction market recovers from the present depression. We may also want to submit it to the Book of the Month and the Literary Guild. Furthermore I suspect that the delay will be helpful. As you know we got a very small advance sale on *East Wind*, but there is a very encouraging slow growth in its sale that will help to build up your reputation."

On September 9, Pearl, exhibiting remarkable composure, answered Walsh's letter: "My dear Mr. Walsh: I am of course very happy to receive your letter about my manuscript, as well as relieved. It is so hard to judge of one's own work, and while I felt I had put my feeling about China into the book I was not sure I had been successful in making others see what I saw.

"Now, about the points you mentioned: I like *The Good Earth* very much. Let us use it. As to cutting, my first impulse is against it. But this is purely personal and I want it to be right for the ones who will read it. Will you, therefore, send me a careful list of possible places of cutting. I do not wish any incidents to be out altogether for each one was planned to a particular end, but even on this point I should like to hear your suggestions."

She requested that Walsh have the proof reading done in his office, and the contractual details were left to Lloyd.

Though Margaret Thomson and Hsu Chih-mo had been unavailable for consultation when Pearl finished writing *Wang Lung*, the novel that became *The Good Earth*, when they returned she shared with them her news and sought their advice on the question of cuts. Two weeks later she had her answer for Walsh.

"I have at your suggestion reread again the manuscript of my book—shall we call it *The Good Earth?*—with the idea of making it shorter. . . . I have also given it to two of my friends to read—one Chinese, one English—and I have considerable confidence in their detached and literary criticism. . . . I gave them the book without comment except to say I wanted it shorter. . . . They felt there was no place to cut without breaking the chain of events, each dependent on the other. . . . It is a book, therefore, which I feel must be long for it portrays a long life—and more than that life, it portrays a family. . . . I am not at all sure I can promise any cuts. You see, this book has been many years planned and pruned many times. . . .

"In regard to the date of publication, I hope there need not be undue delay because I have quite clearly in my mind now my third novel and I shall begin writing it within the next few months. . . . My situation is this: I have purposely not written very early in my life, preferring to wait until I felt a certain maturity in myself. Added to this was a situation in my family that did not allow me my time free. That condition has now been removed. . . . Indeed, the plans for several new books are already quite clear in my mind. . . . I shall try to make each better than the last, and when I cannot, then I will write no more."

The mention of the years in which the book was planned and pruned supports the belief that its origin was the manuscript lost in the Nanking Incident.

Finally, she seems to feel that an explanation is indicated for her use of semi-Biblical prose. "In my mind the story spun itself in Chinese and I translated as I wrote. . . . I was not conscious of this as I wrote . . . but when I tried to rewrite it the people were all wrong. It was as if I had dragged them into a foreign house and they didn't know how to behave."

Following this letter she wrote one to Grace, who was in New York with her husband for a year's sabbatical study at Union Theological Seminary. She gets straight to her first priority: "I gather that Carol needs a new supply of toys. Next time you go to see her will you ask what she needs and get anything you can think of . . . three pairs of silk stockings . . . a little piano about three feet high I once saw. . . . Tell me what they cost and I'll try to rummage up the money. Please see that Carol has anything to give her pleasure. Also please buy something dainty and pretty for the girls who care for her." Then, almost as an afterthought, "My publishers sent me a personal letter about my second book which is perfectly astonishing . . . that 'you have written a book of permanent importance, one that will rank with the great novels of the soil' — . . . My breath was quite taken away. . . . Mr. Walsh is a hard, dry, conservative sort of middle-aged person, so I value this the more. It gives me a wonderful feeling of relief, for I feel I can write—I haven't been sure—and that I can provide for Carol's life and Janice's education as well as interpret some quality of China that I love. . . . I'm beginning to have visions of having enough money to do the things I want to do—care permanently for Carol, give you and Jess something I'd love to, give your boys little extra frills that missionary salaries don't provide. Funny how I don't want material goods any more, I don't feel I'd buy anything for the house if I had a million dollars!"

At last Pearl Buck's hopes that she could write had been officially confirmed. In October Walsh, the "hard, dry, conservative sort of middle-aged person" answered her September 9 letter. "What you say in your letter about future books excites me considerably. I feel confident that your writing is going to be increasingly successful. I only wish it were not going to be so long before you come to America." And, for a relieved author, he capitulated on all points: no cuts; the manuscript would be proof read in his office; and only changes such as cutting out "Americanisms" would be made.

Soon two cables arrived. The first read: "Good Earth March selection of Book of Month Club Warmest congratulations RJW." The second: "Please send photographs and biographical sketch." The first cable she answered calmly: "Of course it is very good news that the Book of the Month Club likes my book. I do not know exactly what it means since I do not belong to this club, but I looked up an advertisement of theirs in the *Atlantic Monthly* and see a very imposing list of names of well-known authors. Your second cablegram is more difficult. . . . I have engaged a Chinese photographer and perhaps he can do something. The biographical sketch is enclosed. I do not seem to find much in my life that you will find interesting. I would like to be known not for myself but for my books. The Chinese are very sensible about this; they take the artist as important only because of his art and are not interested in the personality of the artist."

She enclosed two photographs, one of herself and one with Janice.

In a follow-up letter from New York Earl Newsom explained the selection by the book club: "The Book of the Month will print from our plates from 30,000 to 50,000 copies for their subscribers. For this right they will pay us a royalty, your share of which will be $4000. I am writing your agent Mr. Lloyd today sending him our check for this amount. The effect of the adoption should not stop here, because the mere circulation of so many copies will bring in a larger sale through the book trade. Our first printing will be 10,000 copies and we are planning an extensive promotion and advertising campaign. . . . The Book of the Month Club must have a picture for the *BOMC News*, which goes to press on Monday. . . . Through *Asia Magazine* I found the address of your mother-in-law and she promised me a kodak picture, from which we can have a sketch made. Then we should like all biographical material you can jot down. We are going to be deluged for information and I hope you will not be too modest." He went on to assure her he would exercise good taste in the use of this material.

Considerably perturbed, Pearl answered Earl Newson: "I do not want to make selling the book more of a task than need be, but at the same time I really cannot endure personal publicity. Perhaps we can agree on a minimum satisfactory to us both. And I am grateful for your assurance of as little display of bad taste as possible."

Walsh, launching a promotion campaign, ordered ten thousand copies bound as the first edition, and in a pep talk to the sales staff reminded them, "We cannot afford to think for one moment that this is not going to be a bestseller."

Pearl wrote to Emma that she had just received her first real money, the $4000 book club money minus Lloyd's ten percent commission. "This success means most to me because it is the beginning of the sum needed for Carol's life annuity. If it had come earlier, or if my life had been different as regards Carol, I think I would have been wildly thrilled. As it is, nothing means overwhelmingly much. But I have learned to be quickly grateful for any success which will remove fear for Carol's care."

The Good Earth was published on March 2, 1931, and sold for $2.50 a copy. Walsh had received an advance copy of the *Sunday New York Tribune's* Book Section and at once mailed off to Pearl Buck their critic's influential review: "When Mrs. Buck's *East Wind: West Wind* appeared a year ago I wrote that it was the first mature novel in English dealing with China. Now with *The Good Earth* she is entitled to be counted a first-rate novelist. . . . This is China, China as it has never before been portrayed in fiction. *The Good Earth*, however, is much more than China. This is the elemental struggle of men with the soil anywhere, a struggle more stark and heavier with drama in China only because there men fight with the will alone, unaided by mechanical devices. . . .

"Wang Lung, peasant, takes unto himself a wife, slave girl to the house of the squire Hwang. He leads her through the city gate to his mud-walled house and without words they mate, mute because they are inarticulate and their feelings are too simple and dim for expression. They till the soil and beget, till and beget . . . their begetting differentiated from that of the animals only by the half-conscious grandeur of family and continuity of line. Then drought comes and settles on the land. Most of the peasants wait dumbly for death, but Wang Lung, of sterner stuff, leads his family to the South where by begging and by sweating as a riksha puller he manages to hold them together. Then by joining in the looting of a rich family they return to their own soil. . . .

"The earth flourishes and Wang Lung waxes, driven by his unappeasable hunger for land. . . . But as wealth comes he satisfies an equally pressing ambition, he sends his sons to school. And because it is also a mark of success he takes a concubine. His sons, learned in reading and writing, draw away from him. . . . He himself acquires ever more riches and with riches comes disillusionment. And egged on by his children he buys the house of the squire Hwang and himself becomes the squire. But he remains the peasant hungering for the soil, chagrined that his sons have no such attachment to the land. And he dies, while they plan to sell the land to become dandies."

The critic lauds the book's richness of detail and lyric beauty. "If there is some straining for effects of Biblical poesy, more often there is poignancy in the simple narrative. . . . Most of all there is verity. The undramatic horror of famine, the mute suffering of the peasant wife displaced by a flowerlike concubine, the primitive struggle for survival—these are the life of a race. Wang Lung is his people and his kind, but he is not only a Chinese and a peasant, he is an individual understandable apart from his race. . . . She has succeeded also in conveying a sense of the dignity of this life, however primitive it may be."

In the letter accompanying the review an ecstatic Walsh wrote, "There is a curious feeling about writing you at so great a distance. We sit here in the midst of a genuine whirl of excitement about your book and you the author are completely detached from it. I do not know whether you are fortunate or not. If you were here you would be subject to a distasteful round of interviews and teas and all of the worst features of the 'literary racket.' That would probably help the sale of the book, but it probably would not help your state of mind. On the whole I should guess that you, having the kind of spirit that you have, are best out of it. You are by way of making a considerable sum of money, and your name will be very widely known, and yet you will be free from the petty annoyance of success."

The still unflappable Pearl replied that it was "very interesting" to read the opinions of her work. "Of course I am pleased that my book is liked so far, and appreciate very much all you do for it. I am glad I am not in New York, however, I dislike whirls very much. . . . As I write I look on a scene of fields and hills, the farmers hoeing their beans in the sun, and I am satisfied to be here. . . ."

When a copy of the book arrived, she studied it carefully. "I love the blue cloth cover," she wrote on March 28. "One likes to see one's child properly dressed." She found only one typographical error: "'Cling like flees to a dog's back' should read fleas. . . ." (For collectors of first edition copies of *The Good Earth* this typo became known as the bench-mark of a genuine first edition copy.)

With understandable pride she yearned to show her book to someone. Relations with Lossing forebade interruption so she approached her father. After complimenting her on its appearance, he inquired when she had had time to write it. A few days later he handed it back, telling her he had glanced into it but had not felt equal to reading it.

"How much money do you think you will make from this book?" he wanted to know.

"Oh, about twenty thousand dollars," she replied.

"That's nice. That's a lot of money for a novel. But I'm afraid I can't undertake it."

The week after publication Walsh sent her a number of "extraordinary" reviews. The first edition was already sold out, and John Day was borrowing copies from the book club stock. His letter stated: "This leads me to a matter which I bring up with some hesitation. I am sure you have no idea of what we used to call the ethics of the publishing fraternity, but I believe you feel that we at John Day have done well enough with your books, and have a sense of responsibility for your reputation and your future, so that you would be unlikely to think of leaving us at this moment of success. But my duty to my associates and stockholders demands that I ask you to sign a contract for your next three books, which is the usual number in publishing contracts."

To which she replied, "I note your letter about a contract and will answer the points you raise as soon as I hear more fully from Mr. Lloyd. Needless to say, I have never found anything to criticize in my relationship to your company."

In May in a letter to Pearl, Emma chided her friend gently. Though she had read and liked her book a lot, she didn't think Pearl need have put in "quite so much of the coarse side of life" and that her friends had told her there were parts of it that made it unsuitable for high school libraries.

Pearl's lighthearted reply contrasted with the humble letters of a year before: "Emma dear, I appreciate your writing me frankly. You need never mind saying anything you like—you can't make me mad. I felt like giving you a good hard hug and laughing a little at the vision of you trying to make *The Good Earth* into a 'nice' book! For of course, you precious thing, it *isn't* a nice book! Your friends are perfectly right. . . . It *is* a coarse book from our standard. Wang Lung is in the Middle Ages; his class in China must be judged by those of Elizabethan times.

"This doesn't mean that I don't admire the common Chinese; I do. I like their matter-of-fact attitude toward all natural functions, I think it sane and wholesome. They provide for those things as they do for hunger and thirst and there's an end to it. . . . Some among the missionary group have minded the book very much. The first such criticism astonished me beyond measure . . . but when one writes of Wang Lung he must 'come true,' and I can only write as I see him. . . ." Strong sentiments for a missionary's wife, a woman whom Sara Burton had once criticized for eating peanuts on the street. Obviously, it was after meeting with Hsu Chih-mo and other young Chinese writers that she dared write with such candor.

"By the way," her letter to Emma continued, "Lossing's book *Chinese Farm Economy* is getting extremely favorable comment from the scientific group and excellent reviews, and I am proud of that. My reviews in England are excellent, too. I had even the honor of a poem in *Punch*—which is the Englishman's dream to achieve, I hear. Well, it's interesting in its way but I'd give it all away a hundred times for even a hope that Carol might be well."

In China the reviews varied widely. Some Chinese considered it "a marvel" that an American should have written such a "real and true-to-life story of the great Chinese masses" with such keenness and perception. There were enough like this to please Pearl and she wrote Walsh that "the Chinese are wise enough to appreciate the truth about themselves, having had the deepest experience of any race now in the world."

In other quarters, however, an uproar took place. Helen Foster Snow and her husband, Edgar Snow, author of *Red Star Over China*, had recently traveled as journalists through China. "When I first arrived in 1932," Helen Snow recalled, "*The Good Earth* had just come out. I was surprised to find how the young intellectuals hated it. . . . They would say, 'She ought not to write about all those horrible people; why doesn't she write about rich people, civilized people?' These Western-educated Chinese hated it because they didn't want foreigners to learn anything unpleasant about China; they were trying to hide the truth. I couldn't understand this point of view at first. But I learned that it was because some of them were dependent on foreigners, Westerners in Shanghai and other treaty ports or were under their protection or pay. They wanted them to have a good impression of China. Pearl Buck realized this and when she wrote *The Good Earth* she was actually trying to break through this tissue of lies and expose the real conditions, which they were covering up for political reasons."

A gentle rebuke was delivered by a reviewer who wrote: "Mrs. Buck's book is so moving and so 'actual' that I must note one point which seems to me slightly out of key. In the matter of childbearing the emphasis laid by Mrs. Buck on a child a year for every woman seems to me too great. Exceptions there probably are, but in a country where the poorer women suckle their children for three years or more a child a year is not the rule. Among the rich, one of the reasons given for concubinage is that excessive childbearing is too hard for a woman to endure—and children there must be. But what is a slight matter of overemphasis? It is ungrateful to mention it."

Walsh, like every publisher alert to the publicity value of controversy, asked Pearl to reply. She wrote: "I may merely say that the matter of childbearing is one on which endless discussion might go on, since reliable statistics are lacking. One argument given for concubinage is the one the reviewer gives. There are many others for frequent childbearing. In one place where I lived no woman who could afford it suckled her own child because she was afraid that might prevent bearing a child the next year and this was expected of her. Among the poorer class I should say that a child a year is not at all unusual. Prolonged suckling periods all too often do not prevent conception. It is true that this extreme frequency does not always last the whole period of childbearing, since the woman dies or a concubine is brought in or she has some illness, which stops the process. But where a man is too poor to have more than one wife and where this one is fertile by nature, it is the rule rather than the exception."

The missionary world pounced upon Pearl in a body. A member of the Foreign Board of Missions accused her of unmentionable depravity. "At first," Pearl confessed, "I was appalled by what I had unwittingly done." But after a certain amount of castigation, she said to herself, "What's all this about? I have only told the truth as I see it and no more can be done."

Through all the publishing activity her preoccupation with Carol never ceased. While the Yaukeys were in New York they made periodic visits to Vineland and reported back to Pearl. But after their return to China Emma White became Pearl's only link. *East Wind: West Wind*'s modest royalties were deposited directly into Carol's account, but the Book of the Month Club money provided a few extras, a week's visit to Vineland for Emma and a jaunt to New York afterward with Pearl's gratitude.

She was thankful also when Emma reported that Carol did not miss her. "It comforts me inexpressibly; I don't want her to even remember us if it makes her happier not to. . . . Emma, I can't tell you what it means to me to have someone like you. I do think faithfulness is the rarest quality in the world. . . . I love you, Emma, because truth and sincerity mean your very nature."

As predicted, soon after *The Good Earth*'s publication, queries began pouring into the John Day office about the author. Earl Newsom, despairing of any help from Pearl, put on the wire services a nationwide appeal for information. Several Randolph-Macon graduates responded, and Newsom was directed to Emma who notified Pearl.

Pearl wrote anxiously, "Emma, my dear, at John Day's request I wrote a short sketch of my life but I couldn't mention Carol. I am sore to the touch there and I cannot endure even the touch of sympathy. Silence is easiest for me, I suppose because I am not resigned and never can be. So make no mention of her and so spare me. Some day I shall write a novel that will be literally a study in sorrow and what it may do to a person."

By now her first novel *East Wind: West Wind* was selling under the impetus of her second. In July Walsh reported the first four month's sales of *The Good Earth* to be forty thousand copies, with an additional forty thousand by the Book of the Month Club, and he had just negotiated a contract for her next three novels. He described a special edition of *The Good Earth* which he and Lloyd were planning, and he ended his letter: "I cannot close without saying that my whole experience with you and your book has been just about the happiest and most wholly satisfactory I have ever had, not merely because it has proved financially successful but because I have been handling things of beauty and dealing with an author who is always considerate and understanding."

In her reply she called attention to the fact that the new contract contained a clause making it valid only if Richard Walsh was still head of the John Day Company. "It would be extremely distressing if I should become attached legally to a company whose ideas did not conform to my wishes." She included the news that her next novel was almost finished but suggested that he had better not announce it before reading it, "because it may be trash."

Walsh, in turn, was having second thoughts about the terms of the new contract. He had read Pearl Buck's short story, "The First Wife," in *Asia Magazine* and had immediately spotted a potential subject for a novel. And in *Country Home*, a farm journal, he had read an article on Chinese farming by Pearl and Lossing. More impressed daily by his author's versatility, he envisioned literary possibilities other than novels: history, biography, collections of stories and essays. He requested Pearl's agent to change the word "novels" in the contract to "books." Lloyd replied, "I think Mrs. Buck's novels are the meat of the cocoanut," but obliged by making the change.

In October the author sent her next novel to Lloyd and wrote to Walsh: "I should like it to be called *Sons*. However, if you feel it impossible I shall not be unreasonable. I am very distrustful of my own judgment." She added, somewhat apologetically, that she had two more novels clearly outlined in her head. "I have never told you, nor is this for publication—but there has been a family circumstance which has kept me bound for more than ten years. With this responsibility for someone quite helpless I had never any time of my own, and only last year was the bondage removed. But all these years these novels have been making themselves in my head and are there ready now to be put down. If the books come fairly rapidly, therefore, it is simply the putting into writing of material long pondered and revised. The actual writing of *The Good Earth* was less than two months. I explain this so that you will not feel me too quick in my books."

During the fall the John Day Company, along with all other publishers, received from the secretary of Columbia University the notice that nominations for the Pulitzer Prize to be awarded for "the best novel published during the year by an American author" should be sent to the Committee. John Day submitted three copies of *The Good Earth*.

Although 1931 was proving a good year professionally for Pearl Buck, for China it was disastrous. In July the Yangtse River Valley area received twenty-four inches of rain in two weeks, causing the worst flood in seventy years. The loss of life and property was staggering— farms along the river banks became lakes in which both livestock and humans drowned; higher acreage turned into isolated islands and marooned inhabitants starved to death. All communication was cut off except by boats, which plied the waters where dead bodies and garbage floated—the only water available for drinking, as the wells were under water.

Fourteen and a half million acres were inundated and twenty-five million people's lives were lost or left in ruins. Word of China's plight spread world-wide, and aviation hero Charles Lindbergh and his young navigator wife offered to survey the stricken area.

Nanking, situated on elevated ground, was to be the Lindberghs' base of operation and thousands of people, including Pearl Buck, gathered to greet them when their plane landed. Day after day they mapped the flooded countryside, spotting isolated villages where relief boats saved thousands of lives. Lossing's investigators, skilled surveyors, were also sent out in sampans and planes to locate the areas of greatest need.

Lossing and Pearl were invited to dinner with the famous American visitors, and Pearl described the evening to Emma: "Colonel Lindbergh is a typical Swede, rather uncouth, absorbed in his one object, knowing and caring for little else. He either talks aviation or is silent—but mostly talks aviation! He is youthful in his attitudes of mind and rather untutored, quite evidently opinionated, as who could not be who has received so much adulation? But I was not attracted at all.

"His wife I thought perfectly charming. She is very small, one of the smallest women I ever saw, and with a face that is increasingly pretty, because her prettiness is not obvious at first. She has lovely eyes and hair and a very winning simple manner. Both of them seem very young, but Lindbergh impresses one as the type of mind that will always be young because it is so limited to its own line, while she will probably unfold more and more, being, I fancy much the deeper of the two."

Like many novelists, canny Pearl used as her literary subject matter what crossed her path. Though she felt obligated to deny the fact, her 1941 novel, *Other Gods*, reflected her impression of Charles Lindbergh, and her book of stories, *The First Wife*, was based on the Yangtse Valley flood. Several of these stories, written to raise funds for China's Flood Relief, were sent gratis to American newspapers.

The year 1931 also brought Pearl a personal sorrow. She had spent most of her thirty-nine years with her father, the early ones in childish resentment, the middle in adolescent frustration, and the last in warm understanding. This summer he died. During the last two years, though continuing his work, he had grown increasingly frail. The Yaukeys, back from America, had taken him to Kuling for two happy months spent with old friends and Grace's children. Just before leaving, however, he was attacked by his old enemy, amoebic dysentery. The floods prevented Pearl from going to him.

"The last thing he did," Grace recalled, "he had me read some passages from the New Testament. Then he told me to write a check to the Seminary for a certain student he named. It was for thirty-one dollars, and it took almost every cent he had. That was the way it had always been—he'd eke out a little bit from his salary to help some Chinese."

After his death Grace wrote Pearl an account of the funeral, to which Pearl responded, "Grace, sometimes I think my sorrowing over Carol has just ruined me. It has been so heavy because I seemed to be carrying it all alone. My fear for her future provision has often been too heavy for me to control and has made me sad and depressed and impatient, when for Father's sake I wish I could have been different. At the time it seemed all I could do to exist, and Father was, as you know,

very silent and seemed not to understand, though I feel now he may
have understood more than I thought.

"How cruel it is that people can live together for years and because a
few words are never spoken, misunderstanding can go on. In reality
Father had the sweetness of pure goodness in him. If anyone ever lived
his faith, he did."

Grace herself reflected on this strange man who was her father. "I
don't think he was self-centered. He was just so centered on what he
felt was his calling, his mission in life. He just went his own way,
perfectly unconscious that he was bothering others."

Months later, when the roads again became passable, Pearl made the
journey to her father's grave. "It was on a hill top and I stayed for
hours, remembering his long and brilliant life, so little appreciated or
even understood by his fellow missionaries. There was something
symbolic in this lofty resting place, the noble mountains encircling and
the wind blowing the clouds down from the sky."

7

"I am somewhat confused and distracted at present," Pearl wrote Walsh in August, "on account of being beset by motion picture people and their various propositions. While gratifying in some ways they present many problems also, and I begrudge the time. I am however trying to keep my mind at leisure and I hope to send the new book to Mr. Lloyd not later than mid-August."

She described the film offers to her sister Grace. "Warner Brothers has gone up from ten thousand to thirty thousand, but I am standing by all my original conditions, having added a new one, to wit—it must pass the National Chinese Board of Censorship. I don't care about being *rich*; in this day and age it seems immoral. If I have enough for what I need I don't want a lot to worry about. And I don't want Janice to inherit money either."

In the same letter she related her first brush with publicity. She had remained adamant about making public appearances but now, to acknowledge her obligation to her publisher, she agreed to go to Shanghai.

"I rushed down for the day and gave my speech before the greatest mob of women I have ever seen. I was aghast and terrified. After the meeting tons of women came up. One gushing creature panted with maudlin sentimentality 'Oh, where is the hand that wrote *The Good Earth?*' It was so repulsive I replied coldly that I used a typewriter and two fingers. It was all very funny, but it is no life for me—publicity, I mean. In other words, I am just the same old thing."

Her extra activities required secretarial help and in the Nanking Mission office she found an attractive young American, Adeline Bucher, who not only handled Pearl's correspondence but cheerfully assisted with household affairs, even Janice's care.

Externally, Pearl Buck's life seemed to be remarkably successful, and she should have been, she knew, exuberantly happy. Instead she continued depressed and listless. The reason for her despondence could have been the tragic event which took place on November 19, 1931. The plane on which Hsu Chih-mo was a passenger struck the side of a fog-enshrouded mountain peak and went down in flames, killing everyone on board.

Stunned, Hsu's friends and students rushed into print with eulogies and accounts of his achievements, and Hu Shih wrote a full-scale memorial. Of all those who knew him, only Pearl Buck remained silent.

As the public memorials proliferated Hsu Chih-mo took on a romantic glow, becoming a cult figure. His wife made the most of the public attention, giving permission for publication of their passionate correspondence written during their courtship.

His well-deserved fame has proven enduring. Many Chinese living in America remembered his charm, his place in the youthful society of the late Twenties, and his genuine literary talent. Many of his exquisite poems and essays are available in English and at least one translation of his complete works exists.

During the fall of 1931 China's political situation rapidly deteriorated. Chiang Kai-shek had allowed his obsession with the Communist menace to blind him to the Japanese threat. His guiding principle, "Internal unification before external attack," left Japan free to move as it pleased. The Chinese Communists' argument, meanwhile, was winning over the peasants: "If Chiang would not fight the enemy, they would."

In September 1931, taking advantage of China's internal upheaval, Japan seized the Manchurian city of Mukden. Pearl wrote Emma in alarm: "This aggression of Japan! What this movement means no one knows. If the League of Nations can arbitrate it will be all right, but Japan is extremely belligerent and things are very tense here. . . . Last night the government students gathered around the Japanese consulate and yelled hideously, 'Down with Japan' for three hours."

Chiang, unable to muster the forces needed to confront Japan, appealed to the League of Nations for an investigation and to lodge a protest. But instead of withdrawing, in February 1932, Japan made a bolder move, deploying gunboats in the Yangtse River outside Nanking. "On Sunday night there was a slight fracas between a Chinese and a Japanese marine, and a volley of heavy guns began," Pearl wrote Grace, "It was about two A.M., bitter cold and dark; we had been warned to turn on no lights so we crawled out of bed and dressed in the dark. And I will confess I was simply terrified and shook like a leaf. Great searchlights began to play over the sky and we expected air bombs every minute, but the Chinese fort with great restraint did not answer, or else of course the city would have been blown to bits."

Chiang, foreseeing the possibility of panic in Nanking, asked the United States Consul to move the American women and children out of the city. A staff member quietly ordered the Bucks "not to broadcast what you are doing, just gather your things and slip out to Shanghai or Peking." Once more, along with their friends, the Bucks, fearful of an invasion, left their home.

Their sojourn lasted for several months while Japan organized the Chinese population in Manchuria into Manchukuo, a puppet state, and a desperate Chiang Kai-shek pressured the League to act. Pearl observed the deteriorating situation closely, even more convinced that China would not survive intact the combined problems of Japan and the Communists. "I only pray we can get out in time," she wrote Emma.

Upon arrival in Peking, Pearl settled seven-year-old Janice in a school the Thomsons and Burtons had organized, and after delivering her each morning, she set out to explore the city, absorbing its beauty in the sad knowledge she might never see it again. Part of her mind was concerned with events in America. Discussions regarding the film and dramatic rights to *The Good Earth* still hung fire. Meanwhile, $30,000 had been offered for the first serial rights, before book publication, for *Sons*. This sale, her publishers assured her, would help the book sales. "And it will make possible all I want to do for Carol," she wrote Grace, "including a gift to research into the matter of mental deficiency."

In her newly affluent state Pearl was thinking not only of Carol but of her sister. Luxuriating in the fabled beauty of Peking, she wrote to Grace, who also loved beauty but had fewer opportunities to enjoy it, offering her a house in Peking, rent-free, for a summer's vacation. But the vacation never materialized because Grace became pregnant. All

Pearl could do for her sister when the Bucks arrived back in America was to send her a large box of expensive clothes and money to cover the duty. It gave her pleasure, she insisted, for until now she had been "too dead poor" to buy luxuries for anyone.

The money was now pouring in. MGM had bid $50,000 for the film rights to *The Good Earth*, but the deal seemed so distant and impersonal that it brought her little sense of actual participation. "Shall I accept?" Lloyd cabled her. She cabled back "Yes." And the contract was signed.

In the meantime she indulged another long-time wish. Absalom's translation of the New Testament, the ogre from her childhood, had now become a sacred trust, and she had it printed in a handsome binding, perhaps in the same spirit of atonement that had inspired her mother's memorial.

In March a remarkable and unexpected windfall for *The Good Earth* occurred. During the past winter's disastrous flood Will Rogers, the famous cowboy and movie star, now a syndicated columnist and one of America's most beloved public figures, had been traveling in China. Having read Pearl's novel, he had attempted unsuccessfully to visit her in Nanking. The March 7, 1933, *New York Times* carried a three-inch front-page box under the headline: "Mr. Rogers Turns Book Critic and Highly Recommends One."

"Don't tell me we got people that can read and they haven't read Pearl Buck's great book on China, *The Good Earth*. It's not only the greatest book about a people ever written but the best book of our generation. Even in China, the Europeans and the Chinese say it's absolutely true, and there is few books written about people where they say it's good themselves. I had an engagement to fly up and meet her but it stormed that day and I missed the treat. So go get this and read it. It will keep you out of some devilment and learn you all about China, and you'll thank me. Yours, Will Rogers."

The following day all reading America stampeded to the bookstores, and Pearl credited Rogers with giving her novel its greatest push. She continued to credit him, even after *The Good Earth* received the Pulitzer Prize in May.

Freeman Lewis, then of the John Day Company and later vice president of both Pocket Books and Simon and Schuster, offered an observation on literary prizes in general: "They are very important to the author for his ego, and in terms of the Academy of Arts and Letters

Pearl Buck's parents, Carie and Absalom Sydenstricker, 1880.

Pearl's birthplace in Hillsboro, West Virginia.

Pearl, 1892.

Pearl holding her baby sister, Grace, 1900.

Left to right, Carie, Grace, and Pearl, 1909.

Helianthus

PEARL SYDENSTRICKER, A. B.
K Δ, AM SAM

CHINKIANG, CHINA

Philosophy

Member of Student Committee, 1911-12, 1912-13; Treasurer Class, 1912-13; Leader Student Volunteer Band, 1911-12, 1912-13, 1913-14; Treasurer Y. W. C. A., 1912-13; President Class, 1912-13; Commencement Debate, 1912-13; President of Franklin Literary Society, 1913-14; President Literary Club, 1913-14; President Senior Club, 1913-14; Senior Delegate World's Student Volunteer Conference, 1913-14.

"The Sky Pilot."

OLIVIA TALBOT, A. B.
Φ M

DANVILLE, VA.

History

Cheer Leader, 1910-11, 1911-12, 1913-14; Student Committee, 1913-14; *Tattler* Staff, 1913-14; Joke Editor HELIANTHUS, 1913-14.

"The Way to Hattyland."

Pearl's college yearbook, 1914. *(Courtesy Randolph-Macon Woman's College)*

Randolph-Macon Woman's College, 1910. *(Courtesy Randolph-Macon Woman's College)*

Pearl's wedding to Lossing Buck, May 30, 1917.

The Buck's missionary house, Nanking China.

Lossing Buck with daughter Carol, 1923.

Carol Buck, ten years later.

Pearl with adopted daughter Janice, 1930.

Lossing Buck, circa 1923.

Hsu Chih Mo, circa 1930.

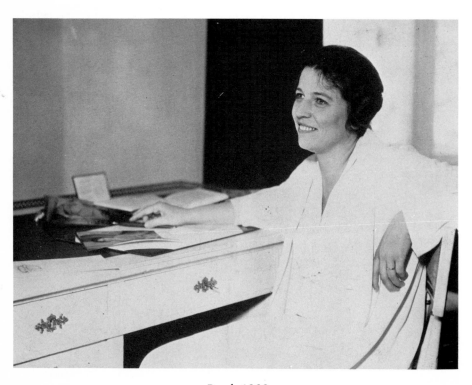

Pearl, 1933.

Pearl at the home of Edgar Snow near Peking, 1935. Left to right, Helen Snow, Pearl, H. J. Timperley, *Manchester Guardian* correspondent, unidentified friend, Richard Walsh.

Edgar Sydenstricker, Pearl's older brother, 1934. *(Courtesy Blackstone Studios)*

Mrs. Grace Sydenstricker Yaukey, 1940.

Richard J. Walsh, circa 1936.

Mr. and Mrs. Richard J. Walsh, 1938.

they may count. But prizes don't sell copies much. There's a discrepancy between best-selling authors and those who have high literary standing. Many of those are much over-rated. It's nice that they can have that kind of kudos instead of money. Actually, the word 'best-seller' is a phony nowadays. There's only one list that's accurate, the book jobber, Baker and Taylor. They make an actual copy count; most others are just estimates and opinions."

But, as Lewis observed, it's nice for the author. When John Day's cabled announcement reached Pearl, she rushed to write Grace: "You can imagine my astonishment. In the first place, I did not dream the book was eligible. I thought the scene must be laid in the U.S.A., and in the second place I did not dream it to be good enough."

There was also a great deal of bidding still taking place for the dramatic rights to *The Good Earth*, and playing it safe, Lloyd had chosen Owen Davis as the playwright. Author of two hundred plays, including a number of solid hits, Davis's name was considered surefire at the box office, and his talented son was engaged as his collaborator. The prestigious Theater Guild was chosen as producers; Davis's finished script was to be ready in June for a September start, and the play's gross receipts were to be split fifty-fifty between playwright and author.

To Pearl this phase in the life of her novel was proving more interesting. She sent a list of possible furnishings to the set designer and begged that the costumes not be stereotyped embroidered gowns and mandarin robes. Happily, Lossing Buck had decided to leave for his Ph.D. at Cornell that fall, so Pearl would be there and able to watch her novel take shape on the stage.

She begged her agent to keep the August 1 date of their arrival secret, explaining, "Frankly, we do not welcome social engagements with persons we do not know. I have been so amazed at the volume and quality of mail received that I am appalled lest such persons who now feel they can impose themselves upon me by letter may feel they can do so in person. I am not at all a social person by nature and must have my privacy."

Later, when Lloyd mailed Pearl a copy of the finished play, she wrote, "There are certain places my husband and I feel not in keeping with the Chinese character. Otherwise the writing is excellent and full of drama." She worried, however, about American actors portraying Orientals. "Chinese move more slowly, more smoothly, they are slower, quieter, except in anger, not jerky. I shall appreciate seeing some of the rehearsals and perhaps making suggestions."

She allowed herself a skittish moment with Grace. "Think of me having a play on in New York, old girl! Wouldn't it be fun to go together and see it? But I shan't go to the first night, I couldn't stand the suspense of people not liking it." Then she quickly checked her effusion. "In spite of all this fuss, the only realities in my life are what they have ever been—Carol and my own home here and you and yours—more remotely, Edgar. And then my very few intimate friends who are but two or three. All the rest seems external."

Pearl had written Walsh of their late July arrival, requesting him as well to guard their privacy. So, restraining a natural impulse to shout such news from the housetops, he released only carefully worded bulletins. But Edgar, not having been sworn to secrecy, innocently answered reporters' questions. It was all Walsh and Lloyd could do to plan a surreptitious arrival for the Bucks at an undisclosed spot.

Walsh wrote Pearl of his plan for a dinner welcoming them and asked for a list of friends to be invited. The Thomsons and the Reisners, now in America on furlough, were to be asked and Pearl especially wanted Dr. and Mrs. Finley present, for they had remained close since Mrs. Finley's fortuitous loan.

Their reception was to be a gala dinner in the Jade Room of the newly erected Waldorf Astoria Hotel. Two hundred of New York's most influential literary personages accepted invitations with flattering alacrity, and as July 19 approached Walsh prepared to drive to Montreal to meet the Bucks' train from Vancouver.

Lossing, Pearl, Janice and Miss Bucher plus a huge suitcase containing the *Shui Hu Chuan* manuscript arrived in Montreal, where Walsh outlined their program. While Miss Bucher took Janice on to Pleasant Valley, he would drive the Bucks to the Vermont home of Lee Simonson, the Theater Guild's set designer, for rest and consultations, and then whisk them secretly to the farm. After August 2, however, he confessed that procedures would have to be a bit different. A Waldorf suite had been booked, and since every New York newspaper and several magazines had demanded interviews, he had settled for a single mass interview on the morning of the dinner.

Dutifully Pearl acceded to everything. This arrangement gave them a few days in which to visit Carol, and they were relieved to find her seemingly unruffled by their sudden appearance, pleased to see them but content where she was. This being the test Pearl had awaited, she decided it was now time to set in motion certain business transactions.

When the Lindbergh baby was kidnapped in 1932, Pearl Buck had become fearful for the beautiful young Janice who was kept rigidly out of sight by Miss Bucher. And in Vineland strict secrecy was always maintained to protect Carol whenever Pearl visited. Now, the novelist called on the director of the Training School, Dr. Johnstone, and the following day his daughter made an entry in her diary: "Pearl Buck, who has a feeble-minded little daughter Carol at the Training School, has been looking the school over most carefully and gone over everything with Father. Her husband is just as fine as one could wish him to be, and though well known in his own field, he plays serenely and capably the more difficult role of the husband of a world-famous woman. Today she gave Father a check for $50,000, part of it for a cottage for Carol, part for research work. She says she wants to go on giving more as she earns more. She and he speak the same language and she wants to carry out his work."

The Carol Cottage was to be built specifically for her needs—a two-story brick bungalow with a bedroom and bath and enclosed porch, a kitchen, dining room and living room on the main floor, and rooms for several other girls and the house mother upstairs, with a well-equipped playground outside, including a wading pool.

Carol, though sadly deficient in most mental areas, appeared to be extraordinarily gifted in one. Music could evoke response. "Certain sounds," Grace reported, "could make her break into tears. She might say No, no, and stop you. Or she would just sit there and listen, weeping. Sad music generally . . . especially hymns, moved her. In time she acquired a great stack of records and a record player, and she could go down that pile of records and pull out the ones she wanted, no one knows how she knew. She'd listen to the music and hum right along with it—*in key* . . . carried away by it. She always liked *good* music best, could listen to a symphony for an hour."

Marian Gardner Craighill remembered Pearl telling her that there is supposed to be a narrow line between mental deficiency and genius; her daughter might have been a musical genius but fell just short on the wrong side of the line. "It was a consolation to Pearl," her friend believed. "She had hoped to give birth to geniuses. But at least she had that."

After visits with the Reisners and the David Lloyds during the Bucks' private period, came the purchase of a Buick and driving lessons with Clifford Buck, Lossing's brother now married and farming nearby. A quick shopping expedition for evening clothes, followed, and it was at last time for the Waldorf and the mass interview.

To Pearl and Lossing there seemed to be hundreds of searching eyes and questioning voices and hands scribbling down impressions. The *Herald Tribune*'s Ishbel Ross's response was typical: "A quiet, simple woman of reposeful manner, with coppery hair and a touch of flame in her blue-gray eyes, she is quite unmoved by the fame that caught her unawares in her missionary environment in Nanking. She was dusting in the attic overlooking the peartrees in her garden when a cable dispatch reached her announcing that she had won the Pulitzer Prize. She looked about for her husband. He wasn't in the house so she went on with her dusting. . . . 'It might have been thrilling when I was twenty,' she laughed. 'But after all I'm forty. You don't care much for that sort of thing when you're older. But I'm very happy that so many people liked my book.' . . . John Lossing Buck, head of the Department of Farm Management at Nanking University, sat beside his wife as they talked, a slim figure with brown hair, smoked glasses and a small reddish-blond moustache. He liked his wife's success, partly because it indicates the interest of Americans in China and the Chinese."

Walsh tactfully cleared out the reporters in time for Pearl and Lossing to get some rest, and finally escorted them to the Waldorf's Jade Room. Earl Newsom's wife remembered Pearl looking extremely pretty, her hair in a simple bun, pink-cheeked with excitement and wearing a blue lace gown to match her eyes.

On the whole the dinner was a substantial success, especially for its display of distinguished guests braving New York's August heat. Even Alexander Woollcott, the testy lord of New York's literary elite, came down from Vermont to write a piece for the *New Yorker* magazine, which perhaps owed its waspish tone to his having been seated, not at the head table but at number thirty-four with a group of Presbyterian missionaries. This *faux pas* turned out to have been an elfish prank perpetrated by a young John Day staff member.

Wollcott's piece ran, in part, as follows: "The dinner was held in the galled Jade Room. There, in Mrs. Buck's honor, on an evening of unbearable heat, some two hundred-odd people assembled docilely and in a state of acute discomfort stuffed themselves with expensive groceries, and then, in the ghastly tradition of such occasions, sat around on gold chairs and listened to speeches. All those were there who never miss such functions, from Dr. John Finley who does so much dining out on behalf of the *New York Times* that he must seldom have a chance at a snack at home, and that old reliable William Rose Benet, who responds automatically to every three-alarm invitation to a booksy dinner, to such unexpected *flaneurs* of the exotic as Rube Goldberg and Sidney Lenz, and of course the book critics. They were there in what is technically known as a body. . . . One could not help speculating on the thoughts of Consul-General Chang, who read . . . the briefest and most winning speech of the evening. . . . As he sat there slim, elegant and a trifle owlish . . . it must have seemed to him an uncouth and singularly inexpressive way for a people to exalt someone for an achievement of the spirit. I, myself, could not escape the impression that Mrs. Buck was also politely mystified. . . . Later she told us all that throughout the greater part of Chinese history, novelists had been regarded as such negligible creatures that they were ignored by their contemporaries and handed on nameless to posterity. One gathered she was beginning to think it a good idea. . . .

"It *was* interesting to see Mrs. Buck, inexpert as a speaker and obviously bewildered by the curious gentry around her, turn at last to that source from which all her strength had come. She read aloud a lovely old fabric of miraculously apposite Chinese prose . . . [For her speech Pearl had chosen the preface to *All Men Are Brothers*] in which the Thirteenth Century author asked, 'How can I know what those who come after me and read my book will think of it? I cannot even know what I myself, born into another incarnation, will think of it. I do not even know if I myself afterwards can even read this book. Why, therefore, should I care?" Mr. Woollcott, melted by her humility, finished his piece somewhat less sourly, noting that she had thereby "turned the evening at last into a great triumph." Unable to resist a final quip, he ended, "Then too, as some gross fellow said on leaving, 'It was a darned good dinner for a couple of Bucks.'"

From a publicity standpoint the dinner was a smashing success. Popular radio commentator Lowell Thomas, on his nightly newscast, gave *The Good Earth* a fortune's worth of free commercial time. "Not since Galsworthy has the American book world held such a gathering to do honor to a writer. Several hundred authors, editors, bankers, dramatists and rival publishers met . . . to welcome Pearl Buck from

China. World fame has come to this charming and exceedingly modest and soft-spoken American woman who is now interpreting China to the West through the wizardry of her pen."

During all this enthusiastic recognition Pearl managed to polish the translation and work on her next novel and keep to her tight schedule. A record of one hectic week-end survived:

"Thursday, August 17. Lunch, Colony Club with Miss Gertrude Lane, Editor of *Woman's Home Companion*, accompanied by R. W.

August 17, 2:00 P.M. Drake de Kay at Hotel Lexington to prepare radio interview.

August 17, 4:00 P.M. Arnold Genthe for photographs.

August 17, 6:00 P.M. Dinner, R. W., Mr. and Mrs. Buck.

Friday, August 18. 10:30 A.M. Mrs. Buck to studio of Edward Steichen for photographs arranged by Crowninshield of *Vanity Fair*.

August 18, 1:00 P.M. Lunch with Mr. Rubin of MGM.

August 18, 2:30 P.M. Lee Simonson, to go to Chinatown to see tailors about costumes.

Saturday, August 19, A.M. *Christian Science Monitor* reporter.

August 19, 1:00 P.M. Dr. and Mrs. John Finley and members of *New York Times* staff, at lunch.

August 19, 3:00 P.M. Drake de Kay to studio for rehearsal of radio interview.

Sunday, August 20, Evening. R. W. and Rimington call at Hotel Lexington to take Mrs. Buck to radio studio at 6:30.

P. S. Movietone News wishes interview if time can be found."

Richard Walsh must have been the happiest publisher in New York. His background had prepared him for the enjoyable task of caring for literary treasure, the know-how in public relations to present a product in its most favorable light and, more importantly, the sensitivity to do it with dignity and taste.

Pearl Buck, ill at ease in the swirl of attention, was each day more grateful for Walsh's steady guidance. After a lifetime of privacy and uncomfortable amid such clamor, she escaped to the Buck farm whenever possible. At times, however, the celebrity game had to be played, and with Walsh's support she participated in it with growing skill.

8

Among the welter of invitations and requests for speeches Walsh received daily and forwarded to Pearl were a number from the boards of foreign missions throughout the United States asking the now famous author for an appropriate statement. Having for years pondered the subject of mission work and arrived at certain conclusions, Pearl agreed to take time from her third novel to share them.

While remembering her days as a raw young missionary and her angry frustration at the depraved Nanhsuchou heathens who had resisted being saved, she realized how far she had come during the last fifteen years. Here was an opportunity to present her more mature thoughts, and she agreed to speak before a group of mission leaders. She labored over her speech for several weeks, admitting to Margaret Thomson that it might upset some of her audience, though she would "try not to be too offensive. I'll be hugely relieved when it's over," she confessed.

The day of the luncheon found her dry-mouthed and sick with apprehension. "I supposed the affair would be a private lunch in a private room," she wrote many years later. "To my horror . . . it was arranged in the huge ballroom of the Hotel Astor and tickets had been sold to literally hundreds of people. Page-boys in the lobby were shouting 'This way to the Pearl Buck luncheon.'

"I thought, Oh, what shall I do, because my speech is not for the public. It's for a chosen few of the mission board. Yet I didn't know what else to say except what I had prepared very carefully. . . . I sat at an immensely long head table with the chief of the Board and other important religious persons. Well, I had to give that speech and I got up and gave it."

Throwing aside tact, she tackled head-on the problems of waning financial support for missions, asking not only why the decline, but *should* they be supported at all? She told her rapt audience that having been a missionary all her adult life, she now entertained mixed feeling about her calling. "I have heard [the missionary] criticized in the bitterest terms and I have sometimes agreed with that criticism. I have seen the missionary narrow, uncharitable, unappreciative, ignorant. I have seen him so filled with arrogance in his own beliefs, so sure that all truth was with him and him only that my heart has knelt with a humbler one before the throne of Buddha rather than before the God of that missionary. I have seen missionaries . . . scornful of any civilization except their own, so harsh in their judgment upon each other, so coarse and insensitive among a sensitive and cultivated people that my heart has fairly bled with shame.

"I can never have done with my apologies to the Chinese people that in the name of a gentle Christ we have sent such people to them . . . ignorant . . . mediocre . . . arrogant . . . superstitious. I have heard a missionary say 'Of course I tell them their ancestors are in hell. If I did not believe that . . . I would not be here.' There are still these missionaries."

She accused the mission boards of sending their second best over-seas, "preachers who would have bored you beyond endurance . . . young men and women just out of college who knew nothing and did not even know they knew nothing. . . . How dared you send so many of these little men and women?" The better ones, she declared, often found themselves obliged to leave the service, so hampered by the criteria of membership rolls and statistics.

Of course, she admitted, they were not all second-best. "Wherever there was a sincere Christian . . . I found a good man in the accepted sense of the word, honest, morally decent." She reassured her audience that she would not wish to see the figure of Christ pass from the earth; only to see that His work was fairly done. The missionary, she stated, must go to fill a need. Not to represent a creed. "This shifts the emphasis from preaching *to* a people to sharing a life *with* them . . . the only possible basis for missionaries. It gives us besides a test of our own worth. Before we can share anything with benefit we must have tried it ourselves. . . . So let the spirit of Christ be manifested by a mode of life rather than by preaching."

She looked around the enormous ballroom. "I am here speaking as one of you," she told them. "By birth and ancestry, I am an American, and by choice and belief I am a Christian. But by the years of my life, by sympathy and feeling, I am Chinese. So let me say to you what many Chinese have said to me, 'Come to us no more in arrogance of spirit. Come as brothers and fellow men. Let us see in you how your religion works. Preach to us no more, but share with us that better and more abundant life which your Christ lived. Give us your best or nothing.'"

She finished to total silence. Describing the reaction later she wrote: "It was appalling. I felt as if I were alone in the middle of the Sahara. . . . But I sat up straight and looked calm—I hope. Then clapping began and I had a very great ovation. Evidently there were many people there who agreed with me, but I can't say the people at the head table joined in. I left it rather abruptly, knowing I had done something devastating."

A noisy and emotional hubbub erupted when she finished. Cries of outrage were mixed with those of praise. The Board members rose from their seats, some bewildered, some angry, and began milling about. Standing alone, Pearl saw to her great relief Richard Walsh pushing through the crowd. Smiling reassurance he squeezed her arm protectively and she felt a wave of gratitude and comfort. It was something entirely new in her experience.

That afternoon and the next day were spent on the phone. *The Literary Digest* and *Time* requested copies of the speech. Dr. Finley wanted it for a *Times* editorial and *Harper's Magazine* for an article which she was to edit. When Walsh heard Pearl groan at the latest demand, he took the manuscript from her. "Let me do it for you," he offered.

Next day she wrote him: "Dear Mr. Walsh: I did not think until after I had left you yesterday afternoon, how very selfish it was of me to leave the editing of that long speech upon you. I cannot excuse myself—it seemed suddenly at that moment a relief not to see the thing again.

"At no time while I was with you either could I put into spoken words what it meant to me to have you come straight after the speech and let me see your understanding. While I was talking the strangest and most horrible feeling of loneliness swept over me, so that twice I could scarcely go on. Afterwards I felt cut off from everyone and utterly spent. So perhaps you can see how I appreciate your understanding of what it meant for me to open the door I had never opened before, and that in the presence of so many. I hated it very much, and yet I had to do it. I am greatly grateful.

"But your quick appreciation is only part of your whole attitude which I value more than I shall ever tell you. I am coming to see that the ideal relation between a publisher and the writer whose life-stuff he considers worth presenting to the world is a very delicate and important one. It is of the utmost importance to me that I happened upon a man like you rather than upon another sort. I can see that had you not been what you are, I might have been dwarfed in my work in all sorts of imperceptible ways. As it is, I feel stimulated to do my very best. Sympathy and understanding appreciation are so delightful—I am not used to them—and it is for me wonderful—I mean, so far as my work is concerned. I have not since my mother died years ago lived among people who considered such things of importance or who understood my supreme interest in writing.

"But you must not let me impose on your sympathy, which I value so much, and take on yourself tasks I ought to do myself. You have won my warm regard."

The breakdown of Pearl's reserve seems to have opened another kind of door. Both Walsh and she, business associates, had apparently maintained an appropriate distance, but this revelation of feminine vulnerability had produced a new and potent effect. Both adults knew the perils of unorthodox relationships. Pearl presumably was still smarting from the painful episode with Hsu Chih-mo, and Walsh, according to publishing associates, had been involved in an extramarital relationship of unknown intensity. However, Walsh's family ties were close and affectionate as Pearl's had never been.

Small and blonde, Ruby Walsh played golf with her husband and entertained his friends, a popular matron in their suburban community. His three children took summer trips with their parents and were included in their Sunday evening "literary suppers." Walsh brought home the excitement and glamour of his bookman's world and to them he was someone quite special. "We kids felt slightly superior to the unfortunate people without our advantages," Natalie, Walsh's elder daughter, recalled. "That traditional teenage rebellion was not our stuff, we were terribly proud of our parents and showed them off to our peers. Dad was a real family man. When we kids were older and went off to Vassar and Harvard it was one of our few house rules that the first night home on vacations was a family night, no matter what else was going on. He was very sensitive, a very loving person, and quite sentimental about all of us."

Therefore, the advent of Pearl Buck in his life resembled a stone being thrown into a placid pool. According to Freeman Lewis, "Richard Walsh was a real charmer, gentle, kindly, talented, but not a driving kind of person. He needed somebody who was, the way he had needed Earl Newsom." Pearl Buck, on the other hand, despite her soft light voice and outward composure, was, in truth, a noiseless humming dynamo. She once wrote: "I learned early to live all I wished, and as I wished, but always silently."

Their correspondence, Walsh's written from his office, Pearl's from Pleasant Valley or Ithaca, though properly formal, revealed two people, at first unconsciously, gravitating toward each other. During her first weeks in New York, Walsh as her editor and publisher observed the usual amenities, taking his important author out to fine restaurants, later with his wife and both Bucks, and finally inviting them for weekends with their daughter, Janice.

And Pearl and Ruby often lunched together while Lossing and Walsh discussed tax matters with lawyers. Gradually, however, the friendship was becoming something more. Though John Day published other important authors, notably Franklin D. Roosevelt with *Looking Forward*, acquiring Pearl S. Buck was like introducing an eagle into a cage of canaries; inevitably the atmosphere changed. Her dislike of attending business functions alone, and Lossing's boredom at such functions, threw her together with Walsh. Numerous working hours had to be spent over the *Shui Hu Chuan* manuscript, and as the John Day office was small and crowded, her hotel suite was the logical alternative. Further, she still had many things to observe about New York life, and the theater and after-theater suppers all contributed to her education.

She learned fast and accepted unhesitatingly. By fall she had made her plans for the following summer: when Lossing's Ph.D. year was completed, they would return to China by way of Europe. To avoid the hot Nanking summer, they planned to visit the British Isles and France, and Lossing could also undertake some agricultural research in Germany. In September, she wrote Walsh, "You had better think seriously of going to England with us next summer."

As her publisher, Walsh was naturally drawn into her orbit, and found himself deeply embroiled in the theatrical production of *The Good Earth*. Pearl had eagerly attended the first rehearsals, watching director Philip Moeller manipulate his actors, admirous of the molding of form out of shapeless substance. The world of theater was a brand new experience, and the immediacy of the medium, human response rather than written words, took her breath away. She spent every free moment at rehearsals.

During the play's out-of-town opening she reluctantly stuck to her work in Ithaca, but Walsh went to Philadelphia. "It was a qualified success," he reported. "Alla Nazimova was extraordinary as O-lan but Larrimore and Travers were weary and showed it. . . . There were some laughs at the wrong places, and it needed a lot more work."

Later Larrimore was dismissed and Claude Rains replaced him as Wang Lung. "Owen Davis says 'tell Mrs. Buck it's been a tough fight but we will win it.' . . . Business is building. . . . It will be all right."

Pearl arrived in New York for the pre-opening rituals. An *Evening Post* interview quoted her, "This play experience had turned out a pleasant surprise. The book I wrote has taken on a new life of its own . . . a life beyond my conception . . . in an art foreign to me but which I appreciate." When asked if she planned to write a play herself she laughed; she had never thought in terms of the theater and she wouldn't know how to start. And at the moment she had a novel to finish.

The Good Earth opened at the Guild Theater in New York on November 14: direction by Philip Moeller, sets by Lee Simonson, script by Owen Davis and Owen Davis, Jr., with Alla Nazimova, Claude Rains, Henry Travers, Sidney Greenstreet, Jessie Ralph, an additional cast of twenty-five and a crowd of extras. The *New York Times*'s dean of critics, Brooks Atkinson, was unimpressed. "Those who have been wondering how *The Good Earth* could be translated into a play have their answer now. . . . It cannot. . . . Uncharitable as it may be to say so, it is a complete failure on the stage. . . . How could it be otherwise? For part of the novel's somber magic grows out of the Old Testament style of the writing and the basis of it the peasants' passion for the land, which cannot be represented on the stage. . . . Here and there the Davises, father and son, have managed to indicate that the story is a great circle, in which peasant supercedes top dog and falls heir to the top dog's vices. But precious little of the novel's spirit has been preserved. Claude Rains is quite on the surface in his early scenes but when Wang Lung becomes more like a gentleman Mr. Rains is more suitable. And as O-lan, the slave wife, Nazimova has in the early scenes an interior image of the dumb clumsy peasant that goes straight to the heart of the magnificent character. But in the latter half her acting subsides into torturesome grimaces and her speaking becomes a series of primordial sounds. . . . It is hard to forgive the other players. . . . In the exact proportion that *The Good Earth* is a good and excellent novel it is an empty play."

There were other, more charitable reviews, and for a while simple curiosity brought in business. Pearl was not greatly upset; after all, the failure was not in her novel. And at this time other important concerns demanded her attention. *Sons* had recently been published.

Cannily, Walsh had not offered *Sons* to the Book of the Month Club. Pearl's name alone, he predicted, should pack the coffers and the same number of bookstore sales would yield $14,000 against the BOMC's $5000 guarantee. And he guessed correctly. *Sons'* advance sales were phenomenal. "Nothing like it ever in the book business for some years," Walsh caroled. Hopefully remembering Will Rogers's Midas touch, he sent the cowboy actor copy number 59 of the first edition with a personally inscribed message from the author.

Pearl had offered *Sons* to the world, she told Emma, "with great trepidation, because when a book has touched people's sentimental spots as *The Good Earth* has, no second book can be loved as well." Fearful of a less than perfect rendition of her material, she may have unwittingly been preparing herself for a letdown.

For years she had pondered the changes in her beloved China as ancient society gave way to modern ways. Each phase took shape in one of her novels: *East Wind: West Wind* depicted life bounded by century-old rules, and Pearl, identifying with its tradition-bound heroine, had written it as a sort of catharsis.

The first novel had dealt with the fifteen percent of the population consisting of upper class Chinese. *The Mother* and *The Good Earth* represented the remaining eighty-five percent, peasants whom Pearl had known in Nanhsuchou. There now remained only the new urban population, the product of the 1911 Revolution. Replacing the scholars, once China's leaders, were the wealthy squires, tradesmen and warlords. To personify each Pearl had chosen the three sons of the peasant Wang Lung, and for this novel the warlord known as the Tiger served as protagonist.

In a broad sense the protagonist is actually the good earth itself, and the greedy sons, by selling their land for cash, prove themselves unworthy of it. The warlord, buying an army in order to found a dynasty, finds the earth foiling him when his only son, rejecting conquest, reverts to the land. The strongest contender is not necessarily the winner.

The book's thesis appeared sound, but its multitude of weak descriptive passages failed to bring it to life, and though most critics were respectful, others considered many incidents incredible, and author James T. Farrell deplored its needless melodrama.

Conditioned to unadulterated praise up to now, Pearl Buck was crushed and in a *Saturday Evening Post* article attempted to strike back at her critics by describing the actual idiosyncrasies of warlords she had known personally.

The criticisms notwithstanding, *Sons* did rack up phenomenal sales, and the distinguished General John J. Pershing deemed it a better novel than *The Good Earth*. Certainly its sales helped Pearl's finances. Carol's care had swallowed up *The Good Earth* income. "But," Pearl wrote Emma, "on the strength of *Sons* I have felt I ought to go off salary since missions are so hard up." And she wrote Grace joyously, "I have achieved my heart's desire—self-supporting! You know what that means to me, old girl!"

Following Pearl's speech at the Astor Hotel, she was asked to review a book, the *Laymen's Inquiry Report*. When she read the complete title, *The Report of the Appraisal Commission of the Laymen's Foreign Mission Inquiry*, Edited by W. E. Hocking, a light had flashed on— W. E. Hocking was the philosophy professor from Harvard who had dined with Lossing and her in Nanking a year before, impressing them with his candor and common sense. The two-year study, undertaken by laymen of seven Protestant denominations, had been sponsored by John D. Rockefeller, Jr. In summary, it found that:

Christianity, as a religion, must no longer regard all other religions as inferior.

It must instead make common cause with the others in combatting the new materialism of Marx and Lenin.

It must no longer teach hope for heaven through a dread of hell, but rather promote heaven here on earth.

It must accept that the "heathen Chinese" is not a lost soul burning in hell because he knows not Christ, but is indeed himself one of God's children.

It must recognize that the Western countries have no corner on salvation and that all countries alike are God's kingdom.

Finally, missionaries themselves tend to be narrow, arrogant and limited in outlook and must raise their standards in order to be worthy of their calling.

Pearl read the report with an excitement bordering on exultation. Here was a group of fearless, clear-headed men and women saying exactly what *she* thought, and she immediately sent off a letter of congratulations to W. E. Hocking, the editor.

A similar congratulatory letter from Hocking crossed hers in the mail in which he praised her speech. Both were equally cordial, initiating a long friendship.

After the exhausting furor over her Foreign Missions speech, Walsh suggested that for her own peace Pearl should refrain from further involvements for a while. Heartily she agreed, and there followed a peaceful hiatus for two weeks. The invitations to speak increased, however; the public wished to see and hear this firebrand in person, and finally it was decided Pearl would be under exclusive contract to John Day for all speaking engagements.

Pearl also sought Walsh's advice about honorary degrees. He answered: "My inclination is for you not to accept an honorary degree unless you have reason to know that institute is genuinely interested in you, except from any institution large and important enough not to have any ulterior motive—that is, Randolph-Macon, Vassar, Bryn Mawr, something like that. If I may I should like to suggest the *tone* in which you write them, in order to prevent the wrong kind of publicity should you refuse."

One day, Walsh, leafing through the mail, came upon an invitation from *Opportunity Magazine*, at an address in Harlem. Elmer Carter, the editor, declared himself to be a great admirer of Pearl Buck and hoped she would come to tea with him and a group of Negro women who would value the opportunity of meeting her. In spite of their mutual resolution that she should rest, Walsh forwarded the letter to Pearl with a note: "I am in favor of your accepting this invitation, not only because it would be interesting for you but also there are not enough people who give practical encouragement to the aspirations of the Negroes. I don't know quite enough about *Opportunity* and Elmer Carter; however I shall make inquiries and write you again."

In his next letter to Pearl, Walsh reported that Elmer Carter, after reading *The Good Earth*, had decided that anyone who could write such a book must understand the question of race. For him Pearl's viewpoint was "no sugar-coated philanthropy, it was basic under-standing." Eagerly Pearl accepted.

On December 11 she and Walsh went to Harlem where they were introduced to a group of business women, teachers, housewives, trained nurses and other professionals. They spoke to the author of their exclusion from the mainstream of American life, and Pearl, in response, described her own experiences as a member of a minority group in China and her keen sympathy with the problems of other minorities. It was an illuminating afternoon, but she became even more impassioned about the situation of the Negroes after attending a Harlem exhibit of paintings by Negroes. "What I saw," she wrote, "confounded me. The paintings were of unimagined horrors. I saw sad dark faces . . . dead bodies swinging from trees . . . charred remains of houses and tragic children. I saw slum streets and poverty-stricken people and patient ignorant faces. Of the educated Negro men and women in the crowd there I demanded an explanation. What I saw they had lived . . . prejudice and segregation and denial of opportunity. And lynching."

Up to now America had always represented, for Pearl Buck, a heaven where all was clean and good. Other nationalities might act cruelly, might despise those of another color, but not Americans. Stunned, she went on, "my heart filled up. . . . I found myself speaking to a group of people, white as well as colored. . . . I tried to tell them that unless we Americans fulfilled our destiny, unless we practiced the great princi-ples of human equality upon which our nation was based . . . we would one day have to suffer for the sins of white men everywhere in the world, we would have to bear the punishment of Asia upon the white man. And so that we might prove our difference from those white men whom we are not, we must begin here and now, by actions to our own citizens who were not white, that we and they were one, that all were Americans alike, the citizens of a great nation . . ."

From that time on she read everything she could find on the Negro. "I made up my mind," she stated, "that if I ever returned to America to live, I would make these people my first concern."

Sara Burton, then living in America, recalled, "Many people didn't realize all the things Pearl did in her quiet way in New York. She spoke to me one day at great length about black women and said she was doing things on the quiet so no one would know about it and distort it.

She had them come to her apartment one or two at a time so it wouldn't get into the papers. She was talking to them about trying to better their conditions, getting more women to try to do what a few advanced ones were doing—push harder, demand more in education and jobs, to do it all legally and legitimately so there would be no backlash."

Pearl contributed several articles to *Opportunity Magazine.* On May 3 at a dinner in New York given for her by the Opportunity Group of the New School for Social Research she made a notable speech. "I have come," she told her mostly black audience, "to feel as much a part of your people as one human being can feel part of another. And I think I comprehend some of your problems. Let me," she suggested, "for a while be of your blood and race and try to think as one of you. We are here in a white man's country, brought here for their service, and we have not received as good training as they had had. This is a fact and we have to face it. . . . We are not foreigners here, we are Americans, but sometimes we are afraid we are not really as good as the white man because we cannot forget our fathers were slaves." She agreed that it was natural to be angry and bitter against white people, but also against each other for letting the white man lord it over the black. "We can never become accustomed to the slights," she observed.

She referred with pride to those Negroes who had become successful artists, authors and inventors, thus achieving equality in the creative world, and a kind of tranquility through the serene consciousness of their own worth, oblivious to what others thought or said. "We have two problems," she told her audience. "One is the actual fact of being discriminated against. That fact can be dealt with by fostering every Negro who achieves something, by encouraging and helping gifted children, employing Negro doctors and lawyers and workers, fighting for equal education . . . these are weapons to foster achievement. But the more serious problem is within ourselves. We must believe in ourselves. . . . I must as a Negro believe in my own race or I can never get anyone else to do so. And we must equally believe in each other, to keep up our morale."

She was not advocating passive resignation but positive aggression by people who quietly dare to do what they think is right, dare tranquilly to be their own true selves. "So," she ended her speech, "let us work together . . . see that our children learn to overlook slights and see larger issues. I am convinced that one race is not superior to another, only individuals are superior."

During the winter of 1933 Pearl was only vaguely aware of what the newspapers referred to as the Great Depression. Commuting between the insulated corner of Ithaca where she wrote all day and the celebrity world of New York City where she attended an average of three social functions a day (so pursued by the public she often had to switch hotels), she was afforded little contact with the real world.

She joined the prestigious Woman's Cosmopolitan Club where she met women architects, bankers, explorers, opera singers, actresses and philanthropists, but none who were not well-to-do. The New York theater was aglow with notable plays which she saw from the most expensive seats. And if she failed to notice the apple sellers on the street corners, it was no doubt because poverty was a natural scene on every street in China.

Furthermore, her own financial situation did not suffer, since her magazine articles and stories continued to bring thousands of dollars, filling in nicely the gaps between quarterly book royalties.

After the inauguration of President Franklin D. Roosevelt and his closure of the banks she first became acutely aware of America's dilemma. She woke, she wrote, "on a clear bright morning full of the day's engagements and pleasures and went for a walk. And there, gathered about the shut doors of a bank, was a mass of silent anxious people."

Her publisher, however, was keenly aware of the country's dire economic situation. True, he had *The Good Earth* still a best-seller, and President Roosevelt's *Looking Forward*, with its prestige value. But after six months the sales of *Sons* were slowing down, and worse, the only new Pearl Buck book was *Shui Hu Chuan*. Certainly a prestigious work, this one's enormous length and its esoteric nature made it a publishing risk, yet Walsh dared not refuse to publish it after the years Pearl had put into it.

In two volumes, *All Men Are Brothers* was received with flattering respect by a number of New York critics. But best qualified to pass judgment was a Chinese scholar and author barely known in America in the early thirties though destined for future fame. Lin Yutang wrote in *The China Critic*: "I consider this translation of a great Chinese novel by Pearl Buck into English as one of the most beautiful presents she can give on behalf of China to the Western world." Previous translations, he continued, failed to present the English reader with a Chinese novel as a Chinese reader would savor it.

Lin's praise would help the sales somewhat, but this book would never be a best-seller. Since apparently anything by Pearl S. Buck was sure to sell, Walsh now gathered her early short stories into a book, *The First Wife*, and announced it for June. But short story collections were a stop-gap at best. And after that, what had he?

The third volume in Pearl Buck's *The Good Earth* trilogy was progressing slowly. Social demands had taken their toll on her literary concentration; and some of Lossing's studies, especially French, had required her help. She had nothing currently to offer her publisher. As an afterthought, however, she mentioned a short piece she had written years before, but she was not anxious to show to anyone.

Pursuing this frail lead, Walsh persuaded her to let him read it and with some reluctance, she did so. Walsh's enthusiastic response surprised and delighted her, and the manuscript of *The Mother* went into production for January 1934 publication.

Even with Pearl Buck's considerable contributions the John Day Company faced major monetary problems. Long before President Roosevelt's enforced Bank Holiday and the national moratorium, most U.S. businesses were retrenching financially, holding onto their cash. With customers not buying books, bookstores were not paying publishers nor publishers paying authors. On March 18 Walsh wrote Pearl's agent explaining why he had not sent the $6000 due the author on March 15. Citing the government's extension of the income tax deadline from March 15 to March 31, Walsh asked Lloyd for the same sixteen days' grace period. He had explained the situation to Pearl and she was agreeable, so Lloyd agreed also. By diligent scrimping Walsh met the March 31 deadline thus gaining a breathing spell.

However, by June 15 the cash flow situation worsened, and Walsh asked A. G. Glidden, Lloyd's partner, for the same extension. On June 26 he sent a check for half the royalty payment. "Collections have not yet caught up," he wrote, "but I am hoping that the $3000 balance can be sent as other collections come in." They did arrive; once again he gained a grace period, and the crisis finally resolved.

With the end of Lossing's year at Cornell and their return to China approaching, Pearl's involvement in the Negro cause was requiring numerous meetings and out-of-town speaking trips. And occasional weekends with Janice spent at the Walsh home made a pleasant change from hotel life. Often when Pearl traveled with Walsh as escort and manager, Janice remained behind in Ruby Walsh's care. But on these occasions the child, bewildered by the erratic pattern of her life, developed eating and sleeping problems.

In all these events Ruby Walsh, the mother of children whose memories of her are admiring and affectionate but vague, remains a shadowy figure. Literary agent Nannine Joseph, who had known Walsh for many years, remembered her as "a gentle, sheltered little woman, quiet without being wishy-washy. She was always just crazy about Dick. She said Yes to anything he suggested."

Ruby's daughter Natalie described her mother as "a lovely lady, a tiny undemonstrative New Englander full of energy and quite a musician, but she didn't show her feelings. Up to when she died I never knew what went on inside her head. A difficult person to know." Whenever a new element entered her life Ruby Walsh accepted it stoically—even the plan Pearl had broached to Walsh the previous September that he and Ruby accompany the Bucks to Europe on their way back to China.

Every day it seemed Pearl Buck became more deeply Walsh's concern. In March she wrote him (using the term of address that prevailed in all their correspondence) "Dear Mr. Walsh: We were speaking a few days ago about my original manuscripts and where they should be kept and in what custody, and I realized that your office would be the safest place but I would not want them to belong to a company. I want all those manuscripts you now have, and all those I shall send you in the future, to belong to you personally, to be kept by you and disposed of as you see fit, as your private and personal property. Sincerely, Pearl S. Buck."

Responding to her request, he stated that he was deeply moved and accepted the manuscripts in the capacity of custodian, who would at some future date dispose of them according to her wishes.

And when a sudden, distressing event occurred Pearl turned not to Lossing, but to Walsh for advice. A long distance call came on April 18 from the *New York Post* to the apartment in Ithaca asking for Mrs. Buck's comment on a report, published in the morning papers, to the effect that she was about to be tried for heresy unless she stated that she believed that all Chinese before the advent of Christian missionaries were eternally damned.

Stunned, Pearl listened while the reporter explained that she was accused of having said that a great many Presbyterians believed, herself among them, that the doctrines of infant damnation and predestination, fundamental to the Calvinist creed, were impossible for an enlightened person to accept and represented an attitude of cruelty rather than religion.

At that point Pearl broke in, telling the reporter to call back in an hour, and hung up. Fortunately, she found Walsh in his office, and he immediately told her not to take any further calls. In the meantime he would investigate the report and get back to her.

The two-week brouhaha that hit the front pages of New York's newspapers contributed to Pearl's already growing disaffection with organized religion. Within the Presbyterian Church were three well-defined factions, the Fundamentalists or Conservatives, the Liberals and the Centrists. Far over on the Fundamentalist side stood the Reverend J. Gresham Machen, professor at the Westminster Theological Seminary of Philadelphia, who had demanded of the Church's General Assembly that Mrs. J. Lossing Buck not only be tried for heresy but that the entire Mission Board be dismissed for its extreme liberalism in electing the kind of persons presently on their books.

In his charge Dr. Machen quoted from the *Harper's Magazine* article, "Is There a Case for Foreign Missions," in which Pearl had referred to the doctrine that the heathen races were damned without knowledge of the Gospel as "a magic religion from which superstition" the Chinese should be protected.

He also quoted from an article in the May issue of *Cosmopolitan* in which she discussed her belief that Jesus Christ "was not truly believed in even by those who profess to be his followers. . . . He who is most simple and unafraid, how can men who are not simple and who are full of little fears or some great fear truly believe in Him? . . . Except in places of formal worship one seldom hears Christ's name and there He is not to be found for me." But she added that "His simple spirit, harmonious with the universe, is with us still if we will give ourselves up to it. There is no magic needed, no creeds, nothing except the pondering on Him simply, the simple joining of ourselves with that greatest simplicity. . . . Here is the unifying force, the Christ against the evil in this world. Therefore, by His simplicity, in His fearlessness, in His truth, Christ stands to me unique and unsurpassed, His spirit my solution."

And she had questioned, "What if He never lived? What of that? Whether He had a body or not, whether He had a time to be born in history and a time to die as other men have is of no matter now;

perhaps it never was of any matter. What lives today is not the ephemeral body of flesh and bone. If once it lived, then well enough. If not, then well too."

Such statements and beliefs, Dr. Machen asserted, made Mrs. Buck unfit to hold the post of missionary. The secretary of the Board of Foreign Missions declared that the Board could never sanction departure from the Church's doctrine, adding his hope that Mrs. Buck would clarify such statements.

After several long-distance discussions, Pearl and Walsh decided that she should counter the attacks with a single, simple statement. The next time the phone rang and a reporter asked if she intended to recant her previous stand, she replied, "I shall not make a martyr of myself, nor shall I engage in any controversy to justify my position. I shall hold to the article in *Harper's*, for it is my credo on missions and I cannot explain it away. No notice has been given me of any impending action and I have nothing further to say."

In the face of an impasse the Board sent Pearl a friendly note contending, "This is no inquisition," and inviting her to New York on Monday to talk the matter over. Lossing answered their call inquiring if she could be expected, informing them that she could not possibly come on such short notice. "I am unable to say . . . whether she will be willing to talk the matter over at all or whether she will let her clearly stated and published views . . . talk for her. It is not a pressing decision, for she will not be in New York until next Friday at the earliest."

The possibility of Pearl's refusing their invitation had not occurred to the Reverend Cleland MacAfree, a junior secretary. With newspaper reporters buzzing around him, he stated, "If she can say that her beliefs are consistent with the Presbyterian Church Creed, that will be an end to the matter."

At their next meeting, the Board discussed its next move, as well as, with some severity, the actions of Dr. Machen who by his public charge against the Mission Board had caused them extreme embarrassment, affecting the standing of fifteen hundred missionaries. "His attack was unfair and unfortunate," the press was told. "It is too bad, for we wanted to do the whole thing in a fair, Christian way, and we did not desire this publicity."

Again Pearl had asked Walsh to act on her behalf. She wished to send a letter of resignation, but Walsh, schooled in the subtleties of public relations, met with the secretary and worked out a terse statement free of any possible interpretation that Pearl had resigned under fire. The press, kept at bay for a week or more, were finally handed a release. It read: "After various friendly conversations and without appearing before the Board, Mrs. J. Lossing Buck has requested that she be permitted to retire from active connection with the Presbyterian Board of Foreign Missions, and at a meeting Monday the Board accepted her resignation with regret."

A separate statement was circulated that Lossing Buck's connection with the Mission remained unaffected. There were a few further rumblings as the storm subsided, and the main residue was Pearl's abiding suspicion of all men with the title Reverend attached to their name.

Happier events were to follow. In March, William Lyons Phelps, dean of English professors, at Yale, had invited Pearl to visit him. Accompanied by Walsh she made the trip to New Haven where Phelps informed her that Yale wished to honor her with a Master of Arts degree. In June, wearing cap and gown, she listened to Dean Phelps's accolade, which described her as "the ablest living interpreter of the Chinese character. The stage Chinaman is no nearer the truth than the stage Irishman or the stage college professor. . . . Mrs. Buck represents the Chinese as human beings with a shade of that quiet pessimism that follows acceptance of unwelcome conditions. She loves them and their country. In view of Yale's long and close affiliation with China it is especially fitting that she should become one of us."

Even more heartwarming was her visit to Randolph-Macon to deliver a commencement speech. In a stunning new outfit (bought, no doubt, with the amused memory of her first appearance there twenty-three years before) she greeted her former colleagues in a gay mood. Former classmates Annie Kate Gilbert, Emma Edmunds White and Rey Parker admired her beauty (which was by now quite remarkable), and the Am Sams and Kappa Deltas marveled at her poise. "She was," the Bulletin reported, "constantly surrounded but always the quietest person in the crowd. She talked, but to individuals, not to the group as a whole. Her voice is low and charming, and one hangs on her words, as much for the sound of the voice as for what she is saying. . . . Again and again she commented on the beauty of the college."

Before leaving, Pearl wrote a sizable check for Alumnae Association back dues. "I never sent in anything before," she admitted, "because I never have had any money before."

Her speech was delivered eloquently in her exquisite voice. She told the senior class that they had great responsibilities, as well as great privileges—the privilege of good birth, plus an education for life. But they must share it, or it would mean less than nothing. She cautioned them against a sense of superiority because of those privileges for, she said, they came from the accident of birth. She spoke feelingly of humility and service.

Her plea was addressed to all such privileged young women everywhere, for she had become appalled at the life of ease led by the American woman, her general apathy toward challenge, her emphasis on fashion, her lack of interest in her changing world.

A member of that 1930s group, reminiscing many years later, remarked, "She reminded me of Margaret Mead and her stand about life. If we'd known the word at that time we would have labeled her a liberated woman too." Pearl had thought her role as a missionary was finished. Actually, it had only just begun.

9

There were one or two matters for Pearl to wind up before leaving the United States. Fond of Lossing's family and their Pleasant Valley farm, she enjoyed lavishing her new wealth on them. Lossing's brother Clifford described the new chimney on his house and the exterior paint job, white with green shutters. "I started to thank Lossing," he recalled, "but he said 'Don't thank me, thank Pearl.' I must say, when Pearl got rich she didn't get grand, and she was very generous."

Lossing's parents received a new radio, a row of shrubbery around the house and a suite of furniture. A porch was built off one room and a wall demolished to make one large room of two. A portrait of Pearl painted the past winter was hung over the mantelpiece and a fine old bedstead refinished. Just before leaving she bought the farm, deeding it to her in-laws for the remainder of their lives, and took out a five thousand dollar annuity for each. (She told Emma later she had given Lossing the same annuity.)

She traveled to West Virginia for a farewell visit with Emma, and there, unburdening herself, she asked her old friend for advice. Emma, the wife of a small-town missionary, suddenly found herself confronted with Pearl's overwhelming problems—divorce, a second marriage, even the unspoken hint of adultery. Pearl no doubt described the ever-widening gulf of incompatibility with Lossing. Certainly Emma could sympathize, but she found it impossible to encourage her friend's actions. Without scolding or criticizing, she simply counseled against foolhardiness, stressing the sanctity of her vows. And indeed her counsel had its effect, for Pearl went home committed to the *status quo.*

There is evidence during this trying period that both Pearl and Walsh were uncertain of themselves. Pearl's suggestion the past fall that the Walshes join their European trip, plus her appropriation of Walsh's time and attention, suggested that she was the prime mover in their relationship, and an intimate friend observed that Walsh had expressed to Pearl pity for his first wife. "She is so delicate; she has been protected so much that she will suffer to a greater degree than you could ever suffer, because you are so strong. We must consider her."

"To the contrary," Pearl had retorted, "she can suffer only to her capacity. Her capacity is small and so she will suffer little, while I, with my large capacity, can suffer enormously. If you are so worried about how she will suffer you had better stay married to her! I shall go back to China."

On the other hand, she had told Emma that Walsh had proposed marriage many times, first during the past winter, when she had refused him and then several times thereafter.

After a final visit to Carol and one to Cornell where Lossing received his Ph.D. the Buck party drove to Montreal for an inconspicuous departure. Richard and Ruby Walsh joined them on board the *Empress of Britain* bound for Liverpool. Lossing had recruited for his Land Utilization project a young Ph.D. in economics, Ardron Lewis, who would sail third class on a slower boat to meet them in London.

There they all regrouped. After installing Janice and Miss Bucher in a London flat, Lossing and Pearl drove through Britain, returning to London where Lossing joined Ardron Lewis and a friend for a lively three weeks of sightseeing while Pearl went to Stockholm with the Walshes. In Sweden they ran into a covey of touring writers, among them Marc Connelly, Louis Bromfield, Edna Ferber, Russell Crouse, Donald Ogden Stewart and Philip Barry. Marc Connelly took a snapshot of the distinguished group; Pearl is visible but neither of the Walshes.

At summer's end they all met in Paris. The Walshes sailed home and the rest packed themselves into a Buick for a trip across Europe to Venice. Lossing drove while Lewis navigated, and the three females squeezed themselves into the back seat. Those few days proved to be tense. "Mrs. Buck was definitely *not thin*," Lewis reported, "and Miss Bucher was a good size as well. The main trouble was the restlessness of little Janice cramped in between two ponderous women, and there was something of a disciplinary problem there. Nobody actually *slapped* anybody, it was only a matter of threats, but there was talk of throwing her out over the Corniche cliffs. I'm sure she knew there was no real danger. Anyway, we survived."

Along the way more tension bubbled to the surface, and in Nice Pearl finally expressed her feelings. Lossing's account of the scene was typically crisp: "Nice is where Pearl gave me the news. After dinner she asked for a separation. I was prepared, I'd seen it going on, they were pretty brazen about it. I *cared*, of course. But it's foolish to protest, that only makes things worse. So we went on to Venice in the morning and sailed for home."

On September 17, 1933, aboard the *S.S. Conte Rosso* Pearl wrote Emma, "What the future holds I do not know, for nothing is decided except that I am going back to China and let life itself decide what to do. One thing complicates the situation unbearably, and it is that, feeling as I do for Richard, I cannot have any physical relations at home. It has always been hard but now frankly if I am to live in the same house with Lossing I cannot go on with *that*. I simply can't stand it—it's a violation of all that is best in me. I have told him how I feel and why, hard but inevitable.

"Emma, do you think it possible to go on like this year after year? It's a day-to-day, hard, impossible relationship—possible when one doesn't love anyone, because one can try to think of work, duties, children—but utterly impossible when one has met the congenial and responsive mate. Nevertheless I'm trying to make a fair trial and so is Richard. . . .

"I've never suffered like this before. I once loved someone—I told you, you remember—but I beat that down year after year. But it was no such love as this and no such man as Richard. . . . Nevertheless here are Richard and I loving each other more than ever, and trying to try out staying apart. I make no promises for the future. . . . I don't think the results you prophesy for Lossing would necessarily be true. Anyway, he has insurance enough that I have bought for him, an annuity and the farm. His parents both have annuities I bought for them, so he need never work at all and still have enough to live on. . . . I have done everything for Carol, have made provisions for Janice, have helped him in his work—everything I have known to do I have done, for no return in joy, companionship—nothing. It is hard to think of all this and deny

Richard. Think of it humanly, Emma, not as a preacher's wife. . . . If I decide to go with him nothing else will count. Things are far more urgent with me than they were in June. Emma, I am quite desperate these days."

When the ship reached Shanghai Pearl found a note from Mrs. Selskar Dunn, former Broadway star Carroll McComas, and wife of the head of the Rockefeller Foundation, whom she had met in New York. The invitation was to dine with friends, the staff of the English language weekly, *The China Critic*, managed by westernized Chinese. At the dinner Pearl met Lin Yutang, a mission school graduate and political essayist noted for his witty and irreverent barbs at Chiang Kai-shek. Pearl, captivated by his vivid personality and learning that he was writing a book about the Chinese, alerted Walsh in New York.

At the same time that she had sailed east to China, Walsh and Ruby had traveled west to New York. (Ruby had apparently been with them constantly, so the proposals of marriage in Paris, Stockholm, Venice and London, which Pearl recounted, must have been difficult to manage.)

During Pearl's and Walsh's separation the correspondence in the John Day files has become the only record of their movements. A letter from Pearl in London asked Walsh to see Lloyd about stopping distribution of *The Young Revolutionist* which, to her great embarrassment, was being sold as a new novel. There was also a report on surprisingly good advance sales of *All Men Are Brothers*, the *New Yorker* and Owen Lattimore having reviewed it favorably, and hopes that the two-volume giant might some day actually pay its own way.

Walsh's letter also noted that "the *Asia Magazine* matter was settled up yesterday and I start as editor on Monday. . . . The Elmhirsts spoke again last night of their appreciation of your interest in *Asia*, and you know how much I shall count upon your suggestions, the more the better."

The friendship begun between Leonard Elmhirst and Hsu Chih-mo on Tagore's tour had flowered. Elmhirst had married the widow of Willard Straight, a former U.S. Consul in Peking and the founder of *Asia Magazine*, whom he met through Hsu Chih-mo's literary group in Peking. On Straight's death his widow had taken over the management of the magazine and after her marriage to Elmhirst they had edited it together. Pearl, a contributor for years, knew Elmhirst well, and now that the magazine needed a new editor, who better than Pearl's editor, Richard Walsh?

Walsh needed a second job, for the publication of *All Men Are Brothers* had proven costly. Pearl stepped in and bought three hundred sets of the book for friends and influential outsiders. "This is extremely generous of Mrs. Buck," Walsh wrote Lloyd's partner, A. G. Glidden. "It represents not only her desire to compensate us . . . but to give it a good start. . . . This will mean a deduction of $1200 from the royalty we will owe you the end of this month."

Even with the deduction, however, Walsh could not make the royalty payment on time. On October 3 Glidden wrote him stiffly, "It will be no surprise to you if I say I do not like it." And Walsh answered miserably, "You cannot feel worse than I do. . . . Imagine my embarrassment having to hold up not only this royalty but that of President Roosevelt. . . . People are slow in paying what they owe but it is only temporary. I can meet the royalty payment within the current month."

A few days later he wrote Glidden again, "I quite understand that you will have to write Mrs. Buck about this. In fact I have sent Miss Bucher copies of my letters to you so she already understands the situation. Both Mr. and Mrs. Buck are aware of the economic situation here . . . and I know they have full confidence in our integrity."

"Integrity is not, to my mind, the same thing as credit," Glidden replied, "which is a purely practical matter and not always in our control. . . . I hope nothing will ever give you a wrong impression of my high regard for you and confidence in your organization."

By October 30 Walsh had scraped together the full $2700 owed and sent it on to Glidden. In apologizing for the delay he promised to try to send the next quarterly payment *before* the due date, but Glidden was not impressed, regarding royalties, like premiums, due on the contractual date.

Back in China, Pearl, having been notified by Walsh of his difficulties, wrote him her understanding of his problem and willingness to cooperate, her only inconvenience being an income tax payment of $5000 due on December 1, 1933. Would he let her know in time to raise the money elsewhere if necessary? Within a few days, however, the check had arrived accompanied by Walsh's apologies.

On December 15 he was also pleased to hear the news that the filming of *The Good Earth* was progressing, since the film should stimulate book sales, and he reported that advance sales for *The Mother* were "perfectly extraordinary." Their correspondence revealed next the information that he was to join her in China in January, the office to be run by his capable assistant, Critchell Rimington.

Before Walsh left New York he entrusted his secretary with a document and letter to be filed. Whether Pearl was aware of their existence is not known. The document read: "Statement. Together with special regulations concerning the distribution etc., of prizes by the Nobel Foundation by the Swedish Academy in Stockholm, given by His Gracious Majesty, King of Sweden and Norway at the Palace at Stockholm, 29th day of June 1900." Attached were several pages of regulations and requirements for nomination, including the names of supporting sponsors and their qualifications.

The accompanying letter was from the president of Randolph-Macon Women's College to Walsh, reporting that, as requested, the president had written the Committee in Stockholm proposing that Pearl S. Buck be awarded the Nobel Prize for literature.

Pearl's last letter to Walsh had assured him that her new manuscript should be ready for him when he arrived in China—good news indeed, for he was desperate for a profitable novel. But when Pearl and Lossing reached Nanking in the fall, she had been too upset to write anything of importance and the novel had languished while she filled her time writing short stories. Restoring the garden to its erstwhile glory was a good cure for depression and the request from the North China Union College for a lecture on the Chinese novel provided an incentive for engrossing research. (Years later the resultant manuscript was to come in handy when a scholarly dissertation was needed on short notice.)

Of the old group only the Thomsons were back in Nanking and Pearl kept to herself, but Lin Yutang and his wife Hong in nearby Shanghai supplied new stimulation. This happily married couple and their three daughters maintained a household where wit and scholarship reigned. Lin was eager for publication in America and Pearl had promised him an introduction to Walsh.

Meanwhile, external problems haunted her. China's fate seemed to her hopeless for while Chiang told his people that his brand of Nationalism was their salvation he permitted Japan's aggressions to continue unchecked. The peasants, too disorganized to block Japan's incursions, were afraid to move since the intellectuals interpreted any peasants' unrest as communistic, and ordered them executed. Pearl, observing, and reading constantly, finally reached the conclusion that for her China had no future. Lossing, however, entertained no such qualms. He intended to stay with his all-absorbing work, for which he was gaining an international reputation.

When Lossing and his associate, A. B. Lewis, reached Shanghai in October 1933, they discovered China in the midst of a depression of its own, reeling from unemployment and bankruptcy. Suspecting that China's economy, based on the silver standard as opposed to the West's gold, was suffering from the world-wide rise in the value of silver and its consequent lower prices, Lossing set Lewis and a committee to work on a bulletin. This was published by Nanking University and later expanded into a book.

When Chiang Kai-shek read the book, he summoned his committee chairman at one A.M. to a meeting that included Madame Chiang and her brother-in-law Kung informing them that China was going off the silver standard. As a result China's depression eased somewhat and Lossing's status rose sharply in the Nationalists' esteem.

A few months later Lossing learned that Richard Walsh was expected in China. With his characteristic compliance, he collected a few soil specialists and went for an exploratory trip to Tibet via flat car and camel-back.

In January 1934, Walsh, with a new Leica camera to take photographs for *Asia Magazine*, sailed for China. Pearl met him with the news that, leaving Janice with Miss Bucher, they must go to Grace and Jesse in Yoyong. On the way she prepared him for a distressing situation. A year or so before, when Grace's third pregnancy became known, Pearl had felt that, in view of the extremely primitive conditions in the area, Grace should go to a city hospital for sophisticated care. But the Yaukeys, attempting to live their lives by the Christianity they taught, refused to accept special privileges and Grace chose the care of a young Chinese doctor.

Her delivery was a long and agonizing ordeal, during which the baby, in a transverse position with which the young doctor was not familiar, suffered injuries in the nerves at the back of her head. As long as she lived, the Yaukey's daughter Anne would be completely helpless.

Pearl likewise had prepared her sister for Walsh, and Grace recalled a conversation with him. "He was pacing around on the upstairs porch and he said, 'I want you to know that I've made up my mind to marry Pearl and I hope you agree.'

"I said, 'I don't know that it matters whether I agree or not.'

"He said, 'Well, I'd like you to think it was the right thing.'

"I said, 'I don't know whether it's the right thing or not but it's your decision anyway, not mine.'"

Jesse Yaukey added, "You see, our first impression of him was very much of a *city* person, maybe too sophisticated for backwoods missionaries. He wore tweeds and smoked a pipe, that sort of thing. A square peg as far as we were concerned."

"The whole time they were there," Grace confessed, "there wasn't the usual sisterly feeling. Pearl thought I wasn't going to understand. And actually I wasn't sure about him, not till I came to America and got to know him." But the sisterly bond survived the initial shock of the news, all was well, and Pearl and he continued south to Indo-China and India.

Their trip was an exploration Pearl had planned to make before leaving the Far East. She wrote later to Emma about it, omitting certain facts and details: "I had a chance to go to India this winter— way paid—with a group of writers and editors. It was too quick a trip and I hate traveling with a group. But still it was very interesting and valuable. India was the poorest and most wretched country I have ever seen, the climate is fearful and the religion the most vile and enslaving one can imagine. In spite of all this, however, I felt it a serious indictment against my much-admired English—you know I love England—that although they have ruled the country for 150 years they have done practically nothing for the people. There are almost no schools, ninety percent of the people illiterate, and there have been almost no agricultural improvements or any thought taken of how to provide more food for the people, who are nearly all half-starved. Danger certainly lies ahead in India for the English. The Indians openly say they are only waiting for another war before they revolt."

While Pearl and Walsh were sightseeing in India, Lossing Buck was discussing his problems with Grace and Jesse Yaukey. By an odd coincidence, as he sailed north to see them on a Yangtse river boat he had sailed past another boat heading south and had seen Pearl and Walsh on deck. "He came to Toyong to see me," Jesse related. "I remember our trekking it out together in the country. . . . Lossing felt very alien to the literary world she was moving into, inferior to her in abilities. He was very cut up . . . her wanting to leave him . . . and didn't know what to do. You see, I think he loved her very much, loved and admired her. I told him I thought it was a mere infatuation and that she'd get over it and come back to him."

Several weeks later Pearl wrote to Emma: "I am on my way to the Peking University Medical College to see the doctors about Anne before I sail for America, because I want to see specialists there about whether or not Grace should bring her home at once. If the child lives it means thousands of dollars necessary. . . . It is Carol all over again, Emma, as far as I am concerned, and I must buckle down and make as much money as I can. You may see many more potboilers now! As to my writing, Emma dear, I don't mind what you say of it if you don't mind if I go on writing as I can. I am definitely now planning to stop writing about China and do more and more experimentation with white people stories."

The mention of potboilers apparently referred to a comment of Emma's on one of Pearl's stories which Emma felt had contained an unflattering portrait of Lossing. She warned her friend about hurting people's feelings. Pearl had replied firmly, "On my own work I must be my own judge. I shall write about anybody and everybody—myself too. Lossing's type is so average that if I never write about anybody like him I shall be hard put to it. . . . Time and again, if you continue to read my stories, you will find people whom you think you recognize. Sometimes you will be right, sometimes wrong but always I shall write as I please, about whom I please. . . .

"Don't judge me more than you can help, Emma, I am doing the best I can. It is so easy to judge people when one is happy and one's children are well and doing well. I envy you. Yet I have to deal as best I can with my own life. At least I am not changed toward you—only *very* overburdened—so many people depending on me financially.

"I am getting a list of specialists to see in America about Anne, and the minute I get there and get Janice in a camp I shall get to work on Anne. Training and massage and so forth may help, although how much I do not know. But it is obvious it will be another case of many thousands. . . ."

During their trip together Pearl had introduced Walsh and Lin Yutang to their mutual benefit. Lin, in turn, recommended to Walsh two promising young writers, Edgar Snow who was teaching journalism at Peking's Yen Ching University and his wife Helen Foster who taught English classes. Currently studying Mandarin Chinese, the couple planned to translate modern Chinese literature and introduce the new Literary Movement to the West. Helen Foster Snow later recalled their meeting with Pearl Buck and Richard Walsh. "We had a tiny house five miles from the city and they came by taxi early in the morning and stayed till late that night.

"At first sight Pearl Buck looked like a Pennsylvania farm wife. I loved her at once. She was large and matronly, not tall though she gave that impression, and she had a sweet shy smile and was friendly and outgoing. And I noticed she blushed very easily. Her hair was plainly drawn back and her skin was fair, without make-up. The remarkable feature was her eyes, a kind of changeable blue-green, clear and intelligent and very bright. Her mouth was cut in her face like a gash, uneven and not well-defined, but she had a most lovely speaking voice.

"Although the first impression was of a dowdy missionary, actually she was very expensively dressed—a handsome blue crêpe de chine, and very elegant silk stockings, which were rare in China due to import duties on silk. We had two greyhounds on a leash and we walked them all over, though she had on high-heeled shoes and the ground was rough.

"Richard Walsh too was very attractive, not much taller than she but very witty and sophisticated, and it seemed strange, somehow, for him to be mixed up with a missionary, they didn't seem to have anything in common.

"We liked them right away and got along perfectly. They were very formal in manner with each other but you couldn't miss a certain lovely atmosphere of two people who were terribly happy and productive together. I felt sure something had just happened—they had just decided to get married or something. She was simply glowing, and he was also very alive and happy. He kept saying things like—she was not only a great novelist but a great scholar as well, and they were bringing out this great translation of hers.

"We talked fascinatedly all day, because everything Edgar and I were doing was just what they wanted to know about, what was going on in China among the new writers. . . . Edgar and I felt that the best way to get at understanding the Chinese mind was to translate what they wrote *for each other*, and later Richard published many of our things in *Asia* and with John Day. Actually it was he who introduced Asian writing to the West. *Asia Magazine* had a big influence in its small way.

"Well, we had a wonderful day together. Pearl had a real 'folk' quality, a housewife quality. It was this which endeared her to women readers. She was a real woman, and she could communicate with other women, that's what made her a best-seller. Meeting her and talking with her, you got this impression of a human famale—a *woman*, not a *non-man*. Today many professional women who have had to sacrifice their lives for their work want you to call them *persons*. She'd never have had that notion. She was successful as a woman as well as a writer, and it's that combination that's the secret of her life and career."

After their time with the Snows, Pearl and Walsh set off in different directions, he north to Manchuria while Pearl consulted the doctors about Anne and then prepared for her voyage to America. What had transpired before their meeting with the Snows that lifted Pearl's and Walsh's spirits so markedly is not known. Perhaps it was simply their happiness in being together. Pearl had declared that she still had not decided on a second marriage and that when she left Nanking, she was not sure it would be for good. But even while assuring her friend Emma that she intended to stay with her husband, she wrote: "But the friendship with Richard goes on, deep and steady and true. He had done for me what no other person in the world had. I can never be grateful enough to him or repay him."

On May 30, 1934, accompanied by Miss Bucher and Janice, Pearl Buck rejoined Richard Walsh on the *Empress of Russia* and they sailed for Vancouver.

10

When Richard Walsh stepped off the ship in Vancouver, he was surprised to find Critchell Rimington waiting for him. The young executive was the bearer of bad news. According to the firm's accountants, John Day was bankrupt. Walsh was to return to New York immediately.

Earl Newsom having left John Day some time before, it fell to young Rimington to oversee the publication of *The Mother*. Earlier Walsh had sent on from China the manuscript of Pearl Buck's new novel, *A House Divided*, and Rimington had watched over its early stages as well. Advance copies of *The Mother*, due out shortly, had garnered fine reviews and sales orders looked healthy. An optimistic John Day had been happily anticipating another *The Good Earth*. Instead, sales suddenly dived, leaving the company with no money to pay authors their royalties.

Rimington had appealed to Pearl's agent for an extension of credit, and because of high hopes for President Roosevelt's upcoming book *On Our Way*, Lloyd acquiesced. But the faded hopes for *The Mother* knocked the publisher's plans awry and Rimington had hurried to Vancouver.

Forty years later Richard Walsh's son, Dick, reminisced about that trying period. "My father refused to accept a state of bankruptcy. Instead he pared everything to the bone. The office staff was let go except himself and a secretary. He raised all he could on his own life insurance and so on, put everything in the business, mortgaged his house, got people to hold off on bills; and the firm that did the company's printing accepted John Day stock in lieu of cash. Eventually, as he told me always with pride, he paid off every cent."

The question arises, how could Walsh afford an expensive trip to China under such precarious circumstances? Presumably, as *Asia Magazine*'s new editor he was financed by the Elmhirsts. He had planned a fine photographic spread for the magazine, but it was discovered upon his return that through a technical mishap every film in his new camera was blank. It was an unhappy home-coming.

Walsh yearned for his good friend Newsom's return to the fold, but by then Newsom was running his own flourishing business. And Walsh's Chinese junket had not sat well in Pelham. "The visit to China," Mrs. Newsom remembered, "was unbeknownst to Earl—at least the purpose. It was a heartbreaker, because the Walshes were apparently still living on Cliff Avenue in Pelham. He took a room in town after that and I don't know how much longer Ruby lived there. Some time, I think.

"She was the most pathetic-looking little thing, a little dainty person, quiet and shy and with a heart of gold. We were torn by the whole thing."

On her return, Pearl lost no time in regrets or self-doubts. Rolling up her sleeves, she took stock of her priorities. While Miss Bucher moved her into a penthouse apartment in the East Fifties overlooking the East River she visited Carol briefly and found her well and happy in her own house. But Dr. Johnstone was failing physically and so as a member of the school board she inaugurated a search for a new director.

Next, putting Janice in a camp near the Bucks' farm, she turned to the question of doctors for Grace's daughter. Consulting three Boston specialists, she wrote Grace advising her to bring Anne to America the following year. Meanwhile, she sent explicit instructions for the baby's care and daily exercise. She had found a child in the hospital who resembled her niece and commissioned a film to be made illustrating the recommended exercises.

Her brother, Edgar Sydenstricker, in spite of Pearl's warning that his new love interest, a young girl, would prove no better for him than his first wife, married her anyway. Pearl, smothering her misgivings, visited the newlyeds, for Edgar, though much older than his sister, was still, in an odd way, one of her responsibilities.

Finally, with most family problems solved, Pearl made out her will leaving everything equally to Janice, Anne and Carol, with the Training School the eventual beneficiary. Then, with her personal matters in order, she turned to her professional life.

Obviously John Day had to be saved. Walsh, facing overdue bills as well as the payment of authors' royalties, was desperate for cash. Pearl authorized him to withhold her royalties while continuing to pay her agent his commission, and agreed simply to draw out money as she required it. And, aware that a publishing house without editors was like a boxer without fists, she joined the John Day Company as an "advisory editor." When the news broke of this famous author's adoption of an old English publishing tradition literary agents began to submit manuscripts again. Walsh insisted on a token salary of $1000 a year and arranged with Reynal and Hitchcock, a publishing firm with a full staff, to see to the production, promotion and distribution of John Day books.

Meanwhile, in Yoyong, the Yaukeys had also arrived at a decisive point in their lives. Their district now being a battleground for various warlords' attacks, they were ready to heed Pearl's advice to bring their handicapped daughter to the United States.

Pearl realized that her brother-in-law, with no experience except in mission work, might be difficult to place during the current depression, but she had plans for Grace, who had written several articles for *Asia Magazine*. Together Walsh and she would make a writer out of her. Cornelia Spencer would be a dignified *non de plume*.

While striving to help John Day stay afloat financially, she remembered the old cardboard box containing the memorial she had written after her mother's death. It had been intended for Carie's grandchild to read when she grew up, but Carol would never read it. She located the cardboard box and offered it to Walsh.

The moment he read its contents Walsh knew he had the next book by Pearl S. Buck. Some minor editing was required, but his firm jubilantly announced *The Exile* for publication in January 1935.

This, however, did not supply immediate cash. So Pearl, *The Exile* manuscript in hand, approached Gertrude Lane, editor of *The Woman's Home Companion* and a personal friend. She spoke frankly. If Mrs. Lane liked the book would she do the best she could for it financially? Unhesitatingly, the *Companion*'s editor offered her magazine's highest payment, $25,000. Pearl immediately channeled the cash through John Day and the company was saved. Then, relaxing a bit, she turned to her own work schedule.

Planned were a novelette, a play and several short stories. An "American novel" was in its beginning stages, but this was a long-term project and would have to alternate with the threatened "potboilers" she had mentioned to Emma. Her days were now spent writing, reading manuscripts, meeting with Walsh, and granting an occasional interview.

At forty-two she was handsome, serene, well-dressed, and surrounded by beautiful things, presenting to a reporter a woman "slimmer, more vital, self-confident and prettier than last year." Her desire, she said, was to live quietly, unnoticed, and to study her fellow-Americans and then write about them.

She attended the theater a great deal because she planned to write a drama on a social theme. Otherwise she seldom went out, writing daily from nine to one and devoting her afternoons to other business. She gave no lectures and accepted no speaking dates unrelated to business, concentrating totally on a heavy writing schedule.

Pearl, blessed with instant concentration, could indeed move easily from one literary project to another, and so, aside from work done out of necessity, she was finally indulging herself in a long-dreamed-of pleasure. Ever since *The Good Earth* she had been mesmerized by the theater, first as an observer and then, at the director Philip Moeller's urging, as a hopeful playwright. In the summer of 1934 she took the plunge and typed out the words, Act One, Scene One.

Three months later she wrote to Emma, "My play is about finished. Thursday evening I read it to a group of critical listeners, friends who will be nice enough to tell the truth. If it passes muster I send it to the Theater Guild. It's all a great gamble, this life of mine!" Six weeks later, baffled by a dismaying silence, she was still waiting to hear.

She was also worried about selling her stories in depressed times. *Cosmopolitan Magazine* had been buying her work but she hoped for other magazine sales as well. "It is not easy," she observed, "to get good prices *and* good magazines."

Ten days later came a rejection from the Theater Guild. "I decided the play was not good enough," she wrote Emma bravely. "I have started writing a better one. . . ." Thus began, confidently at first and then with less assurance, a life-long quest, time after time seized with a brilliant idea and then seeing it fade into a mist.

Helen Foster Snow had a theory about Pearl Buck as a playwright. "Plays are dialogue, and Pearl didn't know how to talk to people. She'd been a missionary living with a dull man—a nice man but a stick—and she'd never really talked to anybody much. That's why people who have lived in China a long time find it difficult to fit in here. Americans don't know what to say to you, they ask a few questions about chop suey.... Pearl had never heard Americans talk among themselves. Her years at Randolph-Macon didn't count, they were just like gabbling kids there. Then, coming here already famous, she was treated as an authority, someone way *up there*, who had to be talked to solemnly about important issues. I don't believe she ever had a friend she talked to just on an ordinary basis."

Apart from the ups and downs of her play writing, all went well. *Cosmopolitan* bought the novelette instantly, for it was vintage Buck, written, as she hinted to Emma, from her heart and mind. The heroine has her own successful career and the man who loves her wants to marry her, but she is afraid. The only marriage she knows well is her parents', and they are a bored and bad-tempered couple, mother a nag, father a stubborn, impractical failure.

The girl tells her sweetheart, "I don't want a man as a provider, someone to cook and sweep for. But I do want *you*. I need *you*, for my working partner, my mate, my particular friend—my lover."

When he promises her their marriage will be that and more, she confesses, "I don't believe any love can stand the strain of everyday life—washing and being tired and having colds in the head. I prefer to do those necessary things in solitude." Shocked, he insists she does not love him. The heroine then asks him to become her lover. When he protests that his love is greater than that, she argues, "We aren't children. We belong in a great modern city where we can do what we like. You have friends who, quote, live in sin and you don't think less of them. It would be our lovely and precious secret." At the story's end they plan to live together for six months. "After that, we can see— marry—or go on that way. Or part."

Pearl often declared that she was ahead of her time, and certainly the story's philosophy seems more of the Eighties than the Thirties. She did not, however, voice such controversial ideas to everyone. To Grace, as to Emma, she wrote guardedly when expressing her enjoyment at living alone. "I like it enormously, so much that I am rather frightened at myself. I feel as though I had come out of prison. I'm quite conscious of Lossing's good qualities, but I am suddenly grown awfully tired inside, exhausted with trying to find topics of conversation, the strain of living with a heavy and inelastic mind. I just have to get myself in hand again, which doubtless I will and so be able to go on with him. But

I shan't hurry myself. I may not come back to China until a year from now, if I feel I need the time."

While legally still Lossing's wife she was actually moving toward freedom. On the theory that she could more easily make up her mind where she belonged if she had a base in America as well as China, she and Walsh explored New England and New York State. But only among the rolling hills and stone farmhouses of the Pennsylvania Dutch country did she feel at home. Furthermore this area was near Carol's Vineland School.

In her romantic fantasies she envisioned an old house beside a brook surrounded by trees and acres of land, with deep fireplaces and wide chimneys, the sea nearby and all conveniently near New York. And after a fortuitous glimpse at a real estate broker's photograph and a drive to Perkasie, she actually found it, making a down payment on the spot. The house, with three bedrooms and an attic and cellar, had stood empty for seventeen years after sheltering farmers for nearly a hundred, and was overgrown with weeds and briars. Her $4100 were only the first of thousands that would be spent for electricity, running water, bathrooms, and its forty-eight acres. Gradually it expanded as a new kitchen, a new wing and an office and greenhouse were added. Later there would be six baths and eighteen rooms as well as the huge barn. Flowerbeds proliferated and acres multiplied until there were several hundred planted with thousands of trees. Pearl's old house was finally a complete working farm.

Before any work was done Pearl brought Janice to Perkasie to see if she approved. Janice had had a good summer at camp, but she was still small and much too thin and still had difficulty eating. Sponsored by Richard Walsh, she was slated to attend Brearley School in New York City and it was hoped that country living would fill her out.

Pearl, beginning to feel America taking hold of her, suggested that her brother Edgar move to the stone house down the road. Edgar, with a bad heart and loath to see a doctor, was gaining national recognition with his population studies, making his scholarly mark on America much like Lossing Buck's on China. As an economist and the first public health statistician in the United States Public Health Service, Edgar Sydenstricker had broadened his early concern with sanitation, pure water and disease control to include personal health education and preventive health measures, and was working to increase their availability to the public.

With Dr. B. S. Warren he had written a report proposing "health insurance, not just sickness insurance" thus anticipating debates that would persist for the next half century. And an early house-to-house investigation of pellagra among South Carolina cotton mill families — one of the first to identify the behavior of a disease among the population—ascertained that the disease was due to nutritional deficiency rather than contagion, a landmark study which also resulted in international acclaim.

Edgar's work in monitoring and evaluating public health conditions took him to the League of Nations in Geneva where he founded the international "epidemiological" service which still serves the world. Thus after years spent analyzing illnesses and their relationship to the environment, both social and economic, Edgar wrote his esteemed book, *Health and Environment*, proving that an unfavorable environment (i.e., poverty) was conducive to illness. And as the depression worsened, he increased his pressure for public financial assistance. As a direct result, in early 1934 President Roosevelt's Committee on Economic Security appointed him to draft a proposal for public health insurance. He and representatives of the medical, dental, hospital and nursing professions drew up recommendations for an Economic Security Bill which was presented to Congress and ultimately became the Social Security Act of 1935.

Pearl, worried over her brother's haggard looks and exhaustion, impulsively bought the house down the road for him, hoping that the peace of Perkasie would ease his obsession with his work and the strain of a failing marriage.

That fall Pearl sublet a small house in the quiet New York area of Murray Hill from Malvina Hoffman, the sculptor. It contained a ground floor studio and back garden, and its upper floors provided comfortable living quarters for Pearl, Janice and the housekeeper. And in a living room notable for its enormous couch smothered in vari-colored cushions, Pearl and Walsh happily met and talked. She was able to laugh as she had never done before. His quirky wit stimulated her rusty sense of humor and she learned, much to her own amazement, to be frivolous and on occasion even undignified.

It was here that Pearl Buck considered her future, alternately accepting and rejecting Walsh's proposals of marriage. "The more I thought of going back to China and to my old life there the more impossible I realized it was," she wrote. "The missionary group at the University was rather narrow and I knew I had to step out into the world even if I had to do it alone." But with the purchase of two houses her decision was actually already made.

The idea of divorce and remarriage was repugnant. Like the girl in her story she had her own life, her own success, and moreover, her children. Her first marriage had been no recommendation for matrimony, nor had her mother's as she remembered it. There was, too, the stigma of divorce, shocking to her friends, and even worse, to her public. Scandal, she well knew, had wrecked many a career.

Perturbed, she sought a woman's advice. Schoolmate Annie Kate Gilbert remembered a conversation with Pearl. "We'd been to a Randolph-Macon alumnae meeting . . . and she told me about Carol at Vineland. Then in her usual quiet way she asked what I thought the effect of a divorce would have on her career. I said frankly I thought if she did it in an unobtrusive way it would raise no uproar and probably have no effect on the acceptance of her writings."

David Lloyd's wife agreed. "West Virginia society, of course, would be down on you, even say terrible things. But actually it might even build your sales."

Still undecided, she was suddenly jolted by learning that Lossing, summoned by the Treasury Department, would be arriving in October. She wrote Margaret Thomson, "The Treasury is spending money like water and calling in great numbers of people who go to Washington and sit around for nothing, and then it dismisses them almost before they get here. I dread the experience and the disappointment I am afraid is in store for Lossing."

Secretary of the Treasury Henry Morgenthau, considering a congressional proposal to purchase huge quantities of China's silver, and having learned of the study *Silver and Prices in China*, made under Lossing's supervision, had sent for him as an advisor. In Washington he was given the use of a large room in the Treasury building in which to display his charts for the President, and it was here Pearl visited him.

Describing the occasion half a lifetime later, Lossing reported with some satisfaction, "She was obviously deeply impressed and perhaps annoyed to find me in one of the best rooms in the Treasury. It was clear she didn't think me worthy of such accommodations." She had come to ask him for a divorce. He had offered no objections, but when Pearl suggested that he go to Reno, Lossing refused to commit himself. The issue was therefore left hanging, since Lossing would be in Washington for an indefinite period.

For Pearl and Walsh, the timing of a divorce was important. A

House Divided, the new novel, was due out in January 1935, and it was crucial to avoid any unpleasant publicity at that time.

Pearl Buck's *The Good Earth* had featured the farmer and *Sons* the warlord. *A House Divided* presented the new Chinese student, educated in the West. The hero is a youth with a heart divided, loving the East but drawn to the West, and unable to commit himself to either. As a protagonist he is vacillating and vague.

Wang Yuan is the son of Wang the Tiger and the grandson of farmer Wang Lung. He has tried to be the soldier his father wished him to be but he moves instead into big city political life, falling half-heartedly into the Revolution. Prison, escape to a foreign land and years at a large university make him neither a real Chinese patriot nor a real American agriculturist. Finally he retires to China where his inability to commit himself will leave him an eternal spectator.

Unfortunately, the style so effective in *The Good Earth* seems here a mere affectation. Places without names, events unanchored in time leave the reader floating in a formless void. *The New York Times'* John Chamberlain considered the book "a weak and disappointing close to the trilogy."

As a synthesis of China's twentieth-century evolution, however, her trilogy is historically matchless. In this the least successful third volume, written while Pearl Buck was shaking off one allegiance and seeking security in another, can also be discerned her own spiritual dilemma.

To help promote the book, Pearl eased cautiously out of her retirement, though most invitations to speak were declined by Walsh, as her manager, with a gracious form letter. Among the few she did accept was one from the Women's Advisory Council of the National Conference of Christians and Jews, thus reflecting her continuing concern with race relations. Another was the twenty-first anniversary celebration of the birth control movement, where Margaret Sanger, its founder, spoke on the fighting days of the past. Pearl spoke hopefully on congressional legislation in the future, her participation reflecting Edgar Sydenstricker's revelations of the effect of poverty on health and the implied effect of too many children on the American family's budget.

For the most part, however, Pearl kept to herself. To Emma she wrote, "Edgar has developed a serious heart condition and I have been with him every moment I could. Then getting the little farm near Carol fixed up and arranging to live there, and my work, and Carol, and Janice—and the unutterable strain of Lossing's presence—everything has just about ended me."

The worst strain, of course, was the one unmentioned—making up her mind. She never specified whether it was some particular consideration or just "the inconvenience of not being married in our society," as she expressed it. At all events, she had decided to "get the legalities over with for it was the only practical way to live." Once again she pressed Lossing for his cooperation.

Lossing had never mentioned their marital rift to his family and Pearl had maintained the pleasant relationship with her in-laws. Indeed, on March 14 Mrs. Buck had gone to Vassar to hear Pearl speak on "The Creative Mind at Work" and had duly noted it in her diary, adding that "the building was filled." When Lossing appeared alone, he broke the news to his family.

He had already discussed his situation with Secretary Morgenthau and now Lossing's brother Clifford echoed the Morgenthau edict: "Since it is time soon for you to go back to China and get on with your job, let *her* go off to Reno and get the divorce."

Apparently Pearl did not visit the Buck farm again, for her name appears no more in Mrs. Buck's diary. But in a final action on April 12 she filed a deed in the local courthouse returning the Pleasant Valley farm to Vincent M. and Grace T. Buck "with love and affection." And the annuities bestowed on them earlier by their daughter-in-law were also left intact.

Pearl wrote to Emma: "Strictly confidentially, I am starting for Reno next week. I *hate* it, but it is the only thing, get it over quickly as possible. I am giving Lossing the furniture in both the Chinese house and Dutchess County farmhouse and will help him some financially if necessary. He will have good homes at both ends of the world. I will help him in his work and do all I can—ask nothing of him for myself and the children, only ask, that is, not to have to live with him. He has never seen nor understood anything. . . .

"I'm desperately tired these days, must pull through and be ready for Grace in July. Dick and I will be married in June in some obscure little town at a county clerk's desk."

On June 12 the headline in *The New York Times* read: PEARL BUCK WEDS AFTER RENO DIVORCE. IS MARRIED TO RICHARD J. WALSH, HER PUBLISHER, SOON AFTER WIFE DIVORCES HIM.

TWO WOMEN WERE FRIENDS, LIVED TOGETHER IN NEVADA CITY. NOVELIST AND FIRST HUSBAND WERE MISSIONARIES.

"Reno, Nevada, June 11, Special to the N. Y. *Times.* Pearl S. Buck, the novelist whose book *The Good Earth* won the Pulitzer Prize, divorced her Presbyterian mission husband, John Lossing Buck, this afternoon and soon afterward married her publisher, Richard J. Walsh, of New York, former husband of her close friend, Mrs. Ruby Abbott Walsh. The wedding ceremony was performed by the Reverend R. C. Thompson, Dean of Men at the University of Nevada, a few minutes after Mrs. Walsh had obtained her divorce. The novelist and Mrs. Walsh had lived together while they were establishing residence here and they retained the same lawyer.

TWO DIVORCES IN TWENTY-FIVE MINUTES

"Mrs. Buck and Mrs. Walsh gave their testimony at private hearings before Judge Thomas F. Moran. It was understood that Mrs. Buck charged incompatibility and that Mrs. Walsh charged cruelty. Mrs. Buck's case required twenty minutes, but Mrs. Walsh's occupied only five. Two hours after Mrs. Buck obtained her freedom Mr. Walsh, who arrived this afternoon unobserved, obtained a wedding license. After the ceremony the novelist, who is the mother of a son 15, and of a daughter, 10, [sic] by her first marriage, declined to be interviewed. She and her new husband left here immediately but did not divulge their destination.

"The bride smoked nervously before and after the divorce proceedings. She wore a white summer dress, a cape and a blue straw hat. Mrs. Walsh planned to leave Reno tonight for New York. The Walshes were married September 26, 1928. They have a son, Richard J. Walsh, Jr., a daughter Mrs. Robert Coltman and a daughter, Elizabeth, 17. A property and custody agreement was signed by them on May 6."

On the same day the *New York Mirror*, a tabloid newspaper, announced, *Reno Unsets Ruby and Pearl Buck Is Walsh's Gem* while the *New York News* commented, *Divorce Without Passion.* "A new high in modern divorce methods has been marked by a woman who after twenty-seven years of marriage agreed not only to give up her husband to a prettier rival but lived on friendly terms during the six weeks both were establishing divorce residences in Nevada. But there were tears in her eyes when the gray-haired little woman, Ruby Abbott Walsh, moved with determined step into Washoe County Courthouse in Reno to charge her forty-nine-year-old husband, Richard Walsh, the New

York publisher, with cruelty 'I can neither forgive nor condone.' And she fled by the rear entrance five minutes after the divorce court had granted her petition, not waiting to see Pearl S. Buck, also newly freed, meet Walsh at the court house door and hurry away, radiant and flushed, to a second marriage.

"Her husband and her friend had fallen in love. For six months and more Mrs. Walsh faced the inevitable and acquiesced quietly. She knew her husband and friend had fallen in love, a love deeper and more demanding than the passions of youth. There was nothing she could do about it. So when the time arranged set the wheels in motion Mrs. Walsh agreed that she and Mrs. Buck might as well go through the divorce together. 'Mrs. Walsh,' her friends say, 'has seen with amazing clarity this true life plot so similar to the pieces of fiction Pearl Buck has written.' In the spirit that she could do more harm than good by standing in her husband's way, Mrs. Walsh agreed to a divorce. Their property and custody agreement was signed last May 6, and what was more natural than that both of these friends live together during those six weeks of Reno residence?"

After the brief ceremony the Walshes drove from Reno to Lake Tahoe. On the way out of town, followed by reporters, Walsh, making a wrong turn, found himself at the Reno Zoo, where according to one humorist, "the happy couple ended up at the monkey house."

After a few days relaxation at Lake Tahoe they returned to New York where they were met by piles of scorching newspapers and intrusive reporters who sent them fleeing to the country. There they shut off the phone. One local reporter, Lester Trauch of the nearby *Doylestown Intelligencer*, managed to reach them, and he recalled Pearl being "terribly upset, really rubbed raw by the furor. It was in papers all over the East about how she and the first wife went West together. She couldn't understand the fuss. . . . I was surprised that Richard Walsh hadn't realized how it would look, specially to local unsophisticated people. They were not used to actors and writers—it was before the day when Bucks County had a big colony of artists from New York and Philadelphia, and she stood out like a sore thumb. She and Walsh just went into hiding for a long time. There was a road ran through her property and pretty soon she even had the road moved so people couldn't drive by and peek in the windows."

Among her friends who reacted with understanding to the affair was Margaret Thomson. Pearl wrote to her gratefully, "I appreciate so much your kindness. . . . I am really happy, it seems to me for the first time in my life, and so I am at peace. It is all like a dream come true—companionship in the perfectest meaning. Nothing anybody can say or do can ever hurt me any more. I do not need to grasp at little straws of friendship and companionship any more—bitter compensations that were always so disappointing. I have a real home at last. And I am not afraid of anything."

And to Margaret Bear, a missionary friend, she confided, "For the first time in my life I can look *up* to my husband and feel he's my equal or above."

Other old friends, like Sara Burton and Marian Craighill, did their best to remain neutral. Sara Burton avoided any discussion of the affair by pleading she had not read the papers and knew nothing about it.

Marian Craighill found the subject "a little ticklish" to talk about. Their southern Presbyterian friends had vowed to cut Pearl dead on sight, but the liberal Marian listened sympathetically. "She told me of how Dick Walsh and his former wife had grown apart, that the reason Mrs. Walsh didn't want a divorce was because she didn't like life as a divorcee, not because she loved Dick. She said she accompanied Mrs. Walsh to Reno at her request because Mrs. Walsh was too timid to travel alone. And she said that Lossing had asked to be released from his marriage because he was in love with someone else—who turned him down," the first—and last—reference to that piece of information.

David Lloyd's daughter, Andrea, an assistant in his office, recalled a luncheon where Pearl told her Walsh had a bad heart. "'But,' she had said, 'it had nothing to do with me. It was the strain of living with his first wife.' I guess she didn't want any responsibility for that."

Pearl wrote Margaret Thomson that she was prepared for criticism from the missionary ranks, but she had been stunned at the harshness of some of the attacks. As a result, having been booked since the previous fall to speak at the Virginia University Institute of Public Affairs, she offered to let them cancel her appearance. They replied warmly, "This is an Institute of Public Affairs, not of private affairs," which delighted her and gave her new heart.

On the morning of Pearl's lecture the other speakers on the agenda found their lecture halls deserted while hers was jammed. Her subject, a comparison of the Chinese and the Americans, had, by accident or design, a few points to make. "We two nations are extraordinarily alike," she declared. "What differences there are exist because our forefathers came from small, compressed countries with hard religious convictions. We are now in a transition period, the Puritanic ideal giving way not to lower but to more humane ideals. And while the 'sense of sin' is typical of the Puritanic residue, the Chinese, born without it, lives in tune with his environment, afflicted with no sense of inborn personal unworthiness conflicting with his natural impulses."

As she spoke one of her former classmates recalled that Walsh sat on the edge of the platform "gazing adoringly and giving her moral support." Her reception that day provided them both with a sense of exoneration that eased somewhat their future public appearances together. Another reassuring event was the news of an increase in the sales of books by Pearl S. Buck.

One jarring leftover from the divorce remained which Pearl could never quite forget. At the May 6 alimony settlement, the judge had granted Ruby Walsh $4800 annually from Walsh's $25,000 yearly income. She now lived in a one-room apartment in Tudor City, a housing development in New York City, and spent her summers in the Maine house. The Walsh's third child, sixteen-year-old Betty, was still in high school with college looming ahead. It is not clear whether the $4800 was to cover schooling as well as living expenses, but if it was, Ruby would not find her new life an easy one. Pearl, however, was vastly irritated. Cheerfully lavish with her own dependents, Ruby's alimony seemed to her "outrageous."

During her mother's sojourn in Reno Janice had been boarded in a home near the Training School. "It was," she recalled, "the happiest time of my childhood. . . . It's funny but that was the first place I felt I really belonged. I knew these people were different, but I was used to Carol so they weren't strange to me. . . . When Mother and Uncle Dick got back from Reno she said 'Uncle Dick is your Daddy now, I want you to call him Daddy.' It was kind of sudden but I had had so much turmoil in my life I was afraid of being sent away again, so I tried very hard to please and I went right from Uncle Dick to Daddy without ever making a slip."

Later when she attended boarding school in Plainfield, New Jersey, her eating problems miraculously disappeared and within six months she had become a tall, healthy young girl.

The problems of Pearl's niece, Anne, did not evaporate quite so easily. The Yaukeys arrived soon after the Walsh's wedding with their two sons, eight and ten, and two-year-old Anne. Edgar Sydenstricker had found work for Jesse in Fall River, Massachusetts, Pearl had found a camp for the two boys, and Grace took Anne to Boston for tests. These again gave no hope and it was suggested that she be placed in a foster home.

"They said she wouldn't know the difference," Grace explained, "but she did recognize us, Jesse especially. So we kept her. She lived two more years and all that time I couldn't leave the house. So Pearl and Dick pushed and pulled me into writing. She got me work at home writing an article on China and Japan for *Compton's Encyclopedia*. Later they suggested a book on the three Soong sisters, my first published book. Then they stimulated me to write other books for John Day. And finally I struggled onto my own feet and wrote for other publishers."

Until Anne's death Pearl faithfully replenished "Anne's fund," a supply of cash for baby-sitters which Grace always declined and Pearl insisted on. "I love you all so much," Pearl wrote her sister, "and value the feeling of family and relationship and the way we all share in each other's lives, that I simply can't keep from sharing as far as I am able."

11

After *A House Divided* failed to match the success of *Sons*, which in turn had failed to match that of *The Good Earth*, Pearl's confidence in her writing talent began to sag. The public remained as interested in her personality as ever, and the women's magazines devoured her less prestigious work. But being revered by the public was, for her, not enough. Until the esoteric literary journals began considering her important and profound, she would feel cheated. "I want everything," she once confessed, only half in jest.

She had always understood that the years of anger and bitterness had to be exorcised before she could be truly at peace. "Someday," she had written Emma, "I shall put into a book the wickedness of a marriage without love, the evil that comes from it." Somerset Maugham's great novel *Of Human Bondage* had been such a literary catharsis, and similarly her book had to be written in order to quiet her own soul.

Under a flimsy camouflage she set it, not in China, but in Middle-hope, Pennsylvania. The heroine is named Joan, a college student, her parents are a puritanical minister and his long-suffering wife, and there is a younger sister and her missionary husband. An oafish farmer, to whom Joan is married, and his acidulous parents, are based harshly on the Buck family. The early part of the novel is more bitter than moving, but the core, the tragedy of their retarded child, is heartbreakingly honest, some of her finest writing in this genre.

The couple separate and the wife adopts two children. Then suddenly the story changes pace with the entry of an aviator, married but wavering in his loyalties. From there on the writing loses all verity. The explanation came only years later.

The change came when Pearl had to go to Reno. When trying to return to it afterwards she found her mind a blank, unable to end her story. Thus John Day, with all publishing commitments made, had no book.

Frantic for a substitute, she recalled that in *The Exile*, she had painted her father as an unkind and selfish bigot. Now, having come to love him, she took the same married couple and with her warmer memories produced in *Fighting Angel*, an engaging and magnificent protagonist.

In January *The Exile* was published to ecstatic reviews, and the promise of its royalties lifted the tension. She was, however, making expensive alterations on the house and furnishing an apartment in town, as well as paying Anne's medical bills, so her need for money was great. She resorted to writing serials strictly for magazine sale, *Now and Forever* being such a story, quickly sold and as quickly forgotten. Finally, in October 1936, all pressure was lifted. The Book of the Month selected both *The Exile* and *Fighting Angel* as a dual offering and the money poured in.

After the success of *The Exile* Pearl had returned to the unfinished novel and added a stagy and contrived ending with the vacillating aviator feeling obligated to his weak wife but finally choosing the strong woman, with implications of marriage.

Some time before she had said jokingly to her husband, "Could you bear it if you saw yourself in a novel—not you as you are, of course, but bits of you?" His answer had been, "Take anything I have to give." Now, however, when she handed him the completed manuscript of *The Time Is Noon* he was taken aback. The depiction of the weak-willed aviator-husband must have been a shock. But the manuscript presented other problems as well. The portraits of Lossing and his parents would be devastating to the innocent Bucks. And the revelation of the retarded child would render useless all the care taken to conceal Carol's existence.

Mechanically he went through with the editing and initial production, then with Pearl's permission he gave the galley proofs to their close friend Dorothy Canfield Fisher. Wise in publishing matters, she was asked if it should be published and without hesitation her answer was no. *The Time Is Noon* was far too personal.

Exercising Confucian self-control Pearl said nothing. The galleys were shelved, and the official word went out that during that period Pearl Buck had been too busy to write another novel.

She did, however, put her feelings into a private journal no one knew she was keeping. She expressed shock at Walsh's rejection of her work, a sense of having given her deepest self and been rejected. Years later she admitted feeling that their perfect union of souls had been shattered and in that disillusionment she had withdrawn into herself.

This was a "dark period," when she felt her husband's love had failed her. Slowly anger gathered, not altogether at her husband but at what she interpreted as the situation of women in a man's world. Unconsciously rebellion crystallized and became a conscious urge, a determination to waken women to the wrongs carelessly done them.

In 1936 to attend the yearly Bach Festival, Pearl and Walsh drove to Bethlehem, Pennsylvania. Pearl had arrived, her mind in a turmoil. Was she, she asked herself, to restrict her work to impersonal subjects, fearful of hurting people, wounding their egos? Sitting on the grassy hillside, listening to the grandeur of Bach's oratorio with its three hundred voices, her spirits were lifted and she felt suddenly strong. In a wave of exhalation she determined to be herself, to forge ahead in the manner she saw fit, write as she chose to write, do what to her seemed right and good. Hers was a proud heart, hers an indomitable spirit. Later she said that this was a turning point in her life.

This Proud Heart became her next novel. Defiantly challenging her husband and the critics, she chose herself for the protagonist. Boldly she painted her heroine as she saw herself in her own mirror.

Susan Gaylord, talented and intelligent, is a sculptor married to her kind but ineffectual childhood sweetheart. A natural artist, she is discovered by a famous sculptor but will only agree to leave her children to study in Paris after her husband dies suddenly. Her mentor, Barnes, acknowledges she is a genius, "even though she is a woman," and introduces her to his Paris salon. An American student falls in love with her, and Susan, for the first time emotionally aroused, marries him and returns to New York and a studio there.

Blake Kinnaird, her wealthy playboy husband, has seduced her with his sensuality and luxurious way of life. But when her work wins public acclaim, his love for her fades, and he turns to another woman. Anguished, but still in love, Susan analyzes the situation until she understands her true problem. She had wanted everything—to be a good wife and mother and to have her work as well. And when she met Blake she also wanted love. But she realizes his defection is inevitable because she is "too big, too much for him to cope with," and furthermore, this is how life is to be. "She will be too much for any one person and none will ever be able to fulfill her altogether. But she will still have the one indispensable, her work, and no matter how she may grieve for love in the night, in the morning she will get up and go to work and then she will not grieve."

This Proud Heart, so obviously frank about the author, lent itself to gentle ridicule. The critic for the *Saturday Review of Literature* observed, "*This Proud Heart* is a good story, well put together and fast moving. The heroine is a sculptress and to be perfectly frank, I thought her tiresome. . . . Mrs. Buck likes fine women. This is her first attempt to do a novel with American characters, but O-lan (*The Good Earth*) was a fine woman of China victimized by the Oriental attitude toward women. Susan Gaylord is a fine woman to the cracking point of credulity . . . physically and morally stronger, more sensitive, more talented than any of her family. Her enormous capability, whether with pies or with statues . . . alienates her from other women. But she is not embittered by it. She knows that loneliness is the curse of creative genius. . . . Susan has no sense of humor. Neither does Pearl Buck. But she does know what things twist a woman's heart through sleepless nights and she is far too skillful and sophisticated to mistake bathos for sentiment."

Overdone or not, Pearl Buck's message to the women of the Thirties was clear: "This is what it is like to be a brilliant woman in a world of men." She was a leader calling out her troops, and the mail that poured in after publication of *This Proud Heart* proved that the women in her audience were listening.

The Book of the Month Club's dual selection of *The Exile* and *Fighting Angel* had been, Pearl Buck wrote, "the best thing that could happen to me professionally," for it acknowledged her non-fiction, which she had never regarded as her forte. Writing fiction was for her sheer joy—"Like being God," she once commented—while writing non-fiction represented human labor.

In a *Chicago Tribune* article she explained the difference: "In fiction the writer may choose whatever characters he wills out of the whole world and his imagination, and make them what he likes. But in writing biography the writer is given his materials. He has to portray a creature of a known nature, who has lived in a certain known way in a known time. The writer, thus limited, has only the freedom of how he shall use or arrange these facts. . . . He has no right, for instance, to suppress any facts whatever . . . because all of those facts have significance. Of course he must eliminate, but it must be only duplication which he avoids. He must choose every salient incident and speech, everything which reveals a new aspect of his subject's nature. Sometimes those facts seem contradictory but he cannot suppress any of them for in that very contradictoriness may lie still further truth."

The review of *The Exile* was featured in the most envied spot in the book reviewing field, the prestigious front page of *The New York Times Book Review* with the headline, "Pearl Buck's Portrait of Her Mother Is Richly Human Record." Other reviewers agreed, Lewis Gannett in the *Herald Tribune*: "Pearl Buck's most profoundly felt book, more moving, I think, than any of her books," and Hershel Brickell: "One of those rare books that 'if cut would bleed.'"

Fighting Angel also earned a front page review in *The New York Times*: "Intensely interesting story laid against an intensely interesting background. . . . She has done what she did in *The Exile*, has drawn a portrait of far more than personal vividness . . . touched problems as deep as all humanity."

Among the reviews for her books were a few harsh ones, criticism of the "unchristianly behavior" among the missionaries in *Fighting Angel*, which she took very hard. Others felt that in *The Exile* Pearl Buck had been unkind to her father. She reacted angrily in letters to her friends: "I have had a great many letters from people who appreciate the characters of my parents and saw what I felt, that they were too great to need sentimentality. . . . I couldn't be my father's daughter if I cared what people say. For myself, I feel I have made them a monument. . . . If I'd glossed them over and idealized them they would not have come to life. . . . My father lived ten years in my home and told me—precious memory!—that they were the happiest years of his life. I have no patience with nonsense like the anger of a few missionaries over what I wrote of my own parents."

Warming to the subject of criticism, she wrote Emma: "The thing I fight against . . . is that thing of 'You're wrong and I'm right.' None of us has the absolute truth for every human creature. Each soul *must* struggle, must have the *freedom* to struggle for its own truth. I'd fight, I'd die, go to prison, to preserve that liberty for you, for me, for everybody. It's my only creed. . . . Don't think I don't get plenty of criticism to keep me from conceit. I do, so much that it rolls off me as praise does too, like water from the proverbial duck. I don't give a penny for either praise or blame, I see what I want to do, it's right for me, and nothing makes me waver."

Early in 1936 Pearl had written a retrospective letter to Margaret Thomson: "Christmas of 1935 was the happiest I have ever had. Janice and Richard said the same thing. We spent it quietly in our little old stone house in the Pennsylvania countryside, and we had snow . . . and our trees lighted and wreaths on the doors and windows and inside such warmth of love and understanding as I have never known.

"The day before we had spent with Carol, and the day after we came to New York, had a big family dinner with Dick's nice children and darling mother and with my own brother and sister. It was all quite perfect. Carol is better than I have ever seen her. If Dick were not quite perfect anyway, his attitude toward Carol would make him so in my eyes. She might be his own child. For the first time all the problem of her life is shared with me. She is very fond of him and has been very well, no more spasms since I came to this country, curiously enough.

"Grace's little Anne has been through the medical mill. Verdict, no hope for recovery. . . . Grace and Jess have been wonderful but it has been bitterly hard. . . . Janice is happily in school and you would not know her, she is nearly as tall as I am and almost *fat*! She goes to camp in the summer and this year we have her in an excellent private school in the country. She sleeps in the school the two nights we are in town but we pick her up on the way to and fro; she swims beautifully and rides horseback like a young Indian and is prettier every day . . . loves America desperately and never wants to go back to China.

"Dick and I are adopting two boys soon—as soon as they are well on their bottles and full of their various modern inoculations. We both love children and are starting off with two boys with no promises as to where we shall end. I can scarcely wait for them. Names Richard Stulting and John Stulting Walsh. Lots of my friends think this is insane but one is so often thought mad that it is not worth heeding, and it is foolish to count the cost when one really wants to do something."

The idea of adoption was not Pearl's alone as her friends had believed. Before their marriage Walsh had begged Pearl to stay with him during the summer, "Don't go off the way some wives do." And a neighbor opined that "he wanted to keep her close, keep her attention. If she had children she'd be responsible to them, to him. She was a big new public attraction and I think he foresaw her being away from him a lot. He really wanted to have a family with her. His own were all grown and she couldn't have any children normally, so they'd do it this way. There already was a grown Richard John Walsh, Jr., but their first baby boy was named Richard Stulting Walsh. They were really sort of starting over from scratch."

Another neighbor described that period in their lives: "They hadn't any local social life; they thought the locals were gawkers and peeping toms. Friends from New York came down, Chinese people, the Yaukeys and Edgar and Phyllis, his wife and her mother-in-law, Mrs. Walsh—she loved her very much. . . . But they wanted children to make their lives complete."

Janice was tactfully consulted before the adoption and with her approval they went to the well-known Cradle in Chicago, and in February 1936 became the parents of "lively enchanting little boys, one month old and born only two days apart."

In the beginning both new parents took complete charge of the babies' care. Pearl reported to Grace that Walsh was wonderfully handy and quick "only he won't change their pants. . . . They are a bit strenuous at times for middle-aged parents but they give a new impetus to life." An advocate of three-generation homes, Pearl begged Walsh's mother to make her home with them, and when the independent old lady declined she was genuinely disappointed.

Visiting in July, an amused Emma White watched the babies being bathed out of doors, sprayed with soapy water as they lay on a sheet of oilcloth. Transported weekly between the Pennsylvania farm and the new apartment at 480 Park Avenue (on the eighteenth floor, with three terraces), they traveled in market baskets with Walsh stopping along the way at a Howard Johnson to have their milk bottles warmed.

The following year they adopted two more babies, a boy named for Edgar and a girl, Jean, a name used by Pearl when traveling incognito as Mrs. Jean Comfort Walsh. A young registered nurse, Miss Kay, was put in full charge five days a week. She had her own suite in the apartment and was treated like a daughter, and she and Esther, the cook, traveled with the family. When a famous guest came to tea, Pearl invited Miss Kay in to show off the children and meet the celebrity.

About this time Pearl also hired Mrs. Loris, a hearty mid-European who for twenty-five years would cook and clean and mother the children when Pearl was otherwise engaged.

Taking care of the children sometimes fell to Janice. Pearl wrote to Grace, "Janice is a great help. And she is really wonderful about the babies . . . feeds them, dresses them, changes them. She is so lovely and so unfailingly tender and patient that it is beautiful to see. I feel lucky to have her adolescence no more stormy than it had been so far. . . . I was thinking about my good fortune in life—by sheer force of obstinacy to have collected these beautiful children. And Dick, aiding and abetting me, has made it possible. . . . Of course, there is no one like him for largeness of spirit. He always says Go ahead to anything I want to do and helps me do it, never fearful or holding back and always standing by me."

In 1936 Grace's family life was not as serene as her sister's. In Fall River the Yaukeys were struggling with their daughter Anne's illness and Jesse's career problems. Grace, who would always be Pearl's "little sister," had matured into a wise and lovely woman. Pearl, always maternal toward her sister, now had a friend and companion. Her letters contained suggestions for stories, checks for furnishing the house, for clothes, or a second-hand car to give Grace some freedom. There would be a long letter of encouragement about a story she and Dick "like very *very* much and will try to sell to Viking." And eventually with the death of Anne, Grace was at last released from that time-consuming burden.

At this period Pearl's brother Edgar lived within waving distance across a field and stream from the Walshes. Though miserable in his second marriage and childless by his present wife, still he had a magic touch with children and was warmly intrigued by his sister's new brood. For some months his health had been failing and Pearl begged him to consult a doctor. He protested that he had no time. And then suddenly, without warning, he died in March 1936.

Pearl wrote Grace, "I valued him so . . . was so proud of him and admired him so much. . . . Dick has been wonderful about everything, so understanding and quiet and efficient. . . . In spite of everything I am *happy* . . . at the core of my life. I am so lucky to have found this love so late in my life."

12

Her introduction to Lin Yutang had proven fortunate for Pearl. After the immense success of his *My Country and My People*, he was writing another book and had been persuaded to visit the United States. In September 1936 the five members of the Lin family arrived, in Chinese fashion heaping gifts upon Pearl and Walsh—a model of a junk for Walsh, a Chinese dress, a jade pin, a silk scarf for Janice, and, for Pearl, a Cantonese tea set, fine China tea, silk pajamas, a warm dressing jacket and rich brocade.

They had left behind in China not only friends jealous of the Lins' new-found prosperity but relatives clamoring for assistance. Lin's articles critical of Chiang had placed him in some danger, so they had pulled up stakes, leaving behind all their furniture but transporting, at great expense, a complete library of books.

Alighting at the Walshes' farm the couple left their three daughters in their care while they went house-hunting in Princeton. After being turned down several times they found a pleasant house, only to find their lease broken when the owner, the wife of a university professor, learned of their race. A furious Pearl shot off a five-page letter to the landlady on the subject of racial prejudice and to Grace one raging, "I *loathe* the American woman!" Finally the Lins settled in a New York apartment where they could comfortably meld with the city's multi-racial atmosphere.

Pearl and Lin had immediately brought each other up to date on their various projects, and she shared with him her enthusiasm for writing plays. Helen Hayes's recent hit *Victoria Regina* had inspired her to take up the craft again after her previous disappointments, which she brushed off as "excellent practice." She had a new idea, a revolutionary theory about Jewish settlers in China which she felt would make a powerful drama.

During the Bolshevik Revolution in Russia thousands of Jews had escaped to China and, born traders like the Chinese, were welcomed. The Chinese had even intermarried with them. Pearl explored the theory that when the Jews found no opposition they couldn't endure the bland atmosphere and within a decade or so moved on, their inherent nature being such that persecution stimulated them to achievement.

Excited by her premise, she invited Lin to collaborate and, as excited as she, he agreed. Night and day they worked together on *Flight into China* by dividing the scenes between them, and in a month Lin's contribution was finished.

Pearl considered Lin's scenes a keen disappointment. After a good opening the rest seemed slipshod and unexciting, and she was becoming disenchanted with collaboration. "I'm too individualistic," she decided. "Perhaps I demand too much, too high a standard." But they continued their work.

A month later the play was finished, and Lin showed it confidentially to George Jean Nathan, critic and essayist, who found it unworthy of both their names. With that professional assessment, the collaboration collapsed.

Immediately Pearl got out an earlier half-completed play. If that one was no good, she told herself sternly, she would get on with her next novel. "I don't know," she complained, "why so many people think the writer's life is an easy one."

After his fling at play writing, Lin sensibly completed his own book, *The Importance of Living*, which Walsh and Pearl considered even better than his first, and when it was published, the American book reading public agreed. The Book of the Month Club chose it and for the first time in several years Pearl relaxed, the John Day Company at last financially out of the woods. She described Lin as "the greatest person I have ever met."

Prior to the Lins' arrival in New York they had visited Hollywood, where they were shown an early cut of the film of *The Good Earth*. Lin

Yutang pronounced it excellent, but the studio feared it would never open. The recent death of Irving Thalberg, the production head of MGM, was only the latest in a series of catastrophes. The cameraman sent to photograph background scenes in China had found his activities consistently blocked, even his studio burned down. In despair he returned to Hollywood declaring that evil forces were at work against the film. Later it was learned that the forces were made up of members of the Nationalist party who wished to prevent the filming of poverty, insisting instead that the streets be swept and the peasants wear clean garments and flowers in their hair.

The film itself seemed jinxed. Two million feet of film, footage shot in China, was contaminated by acid, only twelve minutes of which ever reached the screen. Panic ensued when Thalberg's successor, standing in front of his fireplace, was nearly killed by a falling painting which missed his head by inches.

Nevertheless *The Good Earth* opened on February 2, 1937, with abundant glory for all involved. Paul Muni and Luise Rainer starred, he giving an honest performance but remaining an American, while Luise Rainer's role as O-lan, which was to win her her second Oscar, seemed to Pearl Buck so miraculously right that she declared she must be Chinese.

The ending of the book had been changed to provide a locust plague for its stunning climax, and Pearl watching from her gallery seat was delighted by the result. How far from this night she reflected, were those early days writing the novel, when only Mrs. Finley's loan had made its completion possible. Wonder and gratitude filled her heart.

The year 1937 was full of drama for Pearl. Just before *The Good Earth* premiere, she had seen a play starring Katharine Cornell, often called the Theater's First Lady—certainly its most glamorous with her dark eyes, high cheekbones, full sensuous mouth and rich voice. Playing a Malaysian princess in Oriental make-up she had so impressed Pearl that she sent her a note: "You will not remember me but I met you once backstage with Thornton Wilder at the Belasco. What I want to say now is that I have long been wanting to write a play about the last Chinese Empress. I saw you some weeks ago in *Wingless Victory* and immediately the very next day began to write the play. It is called *The Empress*, and I would greatly like to send it to you when it is finished, to find out if you can see yourself, as I can see you, in the part of that great and dramatic Chinese woman. May I send it to you? Yours in great admiration . . ."

Katharine Cornell's cordial reply was that she had always been fascinated by the Old Buddha and was eager to read the play.

Pearl, hurrying to finish the first draft, had faith that after five tries she had at last achieved a real play. She wrote Grace, "I may not still have quite the hang of it, but I'll get it or die."

On March 12 Cornell telephoned that she was thrilled with the play and would show it to her husband, Guthrie McClintic, the prominent producer and director who always directed her plays.

Shortly thereafter the McClintics and the Walshes met for lunch at 480 Park Avenue to discuss the play. Cornell, Pearl reported later to Grace, liked it as it stood, but McClintic had a few suggestions for changes. The only drawback was that Miss Cornell, tired after a winter with *Wingless Victory*, was hesitant about appearing as another Oriental so soon. Pearl told the couple she would be happy to hold the play for her convenience.

McClintic's changes having been duly incorporated, Pearl sent them the revised version, assuring Miss Cornell she wasn't pressing for an answer but unfortunately she could not concentrate on other work while decisions were hanging fire. If Miss Cornell could indicate whether she wanted the play no matter how far in the future, she would be content. By the way, she added, did Miss Cornell know that Alfred Lunt and Lynn Fontanne were looking for a play with a Chinese theme?

Not to be pushed into a corner, Miss Cornell replied cautiously that she had not yet been able to read the changes but still loved the play, and Mr. McClintic was impressed with Miss Buck's speed in making the proposed changes. However, she did want to be honest; she couldn't use the play for at least eighteen months. If Miss Buck could accept that date, would she name her terms? Otherwise, she didn't want to prevent the Lunts from having it.

Contrary to standard theatrical practice Pearl was dealing directly with her producers rather than through her agent, but Lloyd had long since let his energetic client have her head. During *The Empress* discussions Pearl had mentioned her other play, *Flight into China* so now she sent that one to McClintic as well.

On April 17, only four days after submitting *Flight* Pearl wrote

Grace jubilantly that Katharine Cornell had "definitely accepted" *The Empress*, and contracts were to be signed that very day. Moreover McClintic was negotiating for *Flight* as well. "It's a grand start in the play business, and I am fairly stunned with my good fortune. *Flight* will come next fall but *The Empress* probably not until 1938. . . . Of course both may be flops but the chances are excellent."

This twin dramatic truimph was quickly announced to the press. And riding high, Pearl sent Cornell still a third play to consider, *Shadows Marching*. This however failed to arouse any excitement, and she then countered with a fourth, *The Crystal Heart*, which Miss Cornell thought might do, "with some changes."

By now the two women had become occasional visitors in each other's homes, and Pearl thought she detected friction in the McClintic's Beekman Place residence. Could it be that McClintic was jealous of his more famous wife? Pearl remarked to Grace on how few people really loved a successful person. "I have been, not hurt, for I am past that, but interested to see how few of my friends can really feel pleasure over my two plays."

In July Pearl sent Cornell a somewhat expanded version of *Crystal Heart* and asked for a decision. A month later, still waiting, she exploded to Grace, "Theatrical people are the most whimsical and unreliable in the world—all enthusiasm one moment and perfect blankness the next. They've almost made me want to give up the play business altogether."

In September she sent Katharine Cornell still another version of *Crystal Heart* and shortly thereafter heard from the actress from Europe: "I have read and reread your *Crystal Heart* with care. I love it. But I have reservations." She went on to analyze the characters' interrelationships, wondering whether they were interesting enough to be the subject of a great play. "I am looking for something more, a contemporary theme but one as dramatic as *The Empress*'s life. Perhaps I am asking for the impossible in a modern play; perhaps we are too close to the events, to get something universal. I can and have played parts that are not great, but the modern woman that I want to play must have a great universal theme . . . something of a larger scope than the *Crystal Heart* gives me. I think if I could talk to you I could perhaps make it clearer, but it boils down to this—I don't feel it is a great enough play for you to have written about the modern woman."

Pearl accepted this blow resolutely, replying, "I quite understand your point of view. I have not as yet seen any modern woman whom I consider great, and for the present at least I don't see a play about any great modern woman. One of the major disappointments of my present life is that women, at least in America, seem to me so fragmentary and to have made so little of their unparalleled opportunities. Each one seems to limit herself to her own little groove and there seems nothing universal about them beyond the few rather trite though always important universalities such as love for their husbands, enduring unhappy situations, motherhood, etc. But even at that it seems they are not very great. So I shall have to wait a while before I can see just where in the modern life it is possible for a woman to be great. She has so much less chance really to do anything in American civilization than she has in some others." She closed her letter almost absent-mindedly, but then took it up again.

"P.S. Your letter has set me thinking very hard. Why *are not* modern women great? Why aren't their lives dramatic? What about Mme. Curie? No, she wasn't great, after all. Sometime let's talk about it. I do so appreciate your letter."

Pearl had often admitted to Grace that she felt their parents' missionary blood flowing stongly in her veins. That instinct to teach, to reform, was as natural as breathing, and she had already followed it in relation to the problems of the American Negro. She had grown up in China with a picture of Americans as just, virtuous, strong and merciful, and when finally in America she witnessed inequities she had thought a word to someone in authority would bring about justice. Though slightly disillusioned over the years, still she dreamed of perfecting the imperfect. In 1931 at a luncheon party, she had exploded with exasperation at the "selfish, ignorant, self-indulgent American woman of wealth and privilege." And increasingly commencement invitations from women's colleges called forth from Pearl Buck an exhortation to do and to dare. "You women," she told them, "are the hope of civilization. It is you who will shape and form the future of this country and it is for you to make the world you want."

Nor did she stop at merely cheer-leading. She became the coach sternly whipping her team on. "Everywhere about me I see things which women should do and have not done. Even the housekeeping instincts which are peculiarly a woman's should not end with the walls of her own home, and her love of children should not be expressed merely for her own. The nation is hers too, but she has not claimed it.

The education of women should somehow include this obvious well-proved fact, that privilege must express itself in a greater development or it is a curse to the individual who is privileged."

The solution, propounded in both her writings and the interviews she gave, was *work*. "Of privilege women have had plenty, and yet most of them have been denied the one great blessing of man's life, the necessity to go out into the world and earn his bread directly. . . . By this privilege man has been compelled to put forth his utmost effort, whetting his brain and sharpening his ambition. There is no way of progress for women except the way that men have gone, the one supreme privilege which will really make them free."

Warming to her subject, she turned on the men, declaring them to be slaves of tradition drugged by their unchecked privilege to own, to use and to abuse their women. They have resisted every step taken by women toward education and independence. Even after granting them an education, they have frustrated their professional practices, and she gave as examples the woman doctor who cannot find a hospital internship "because patients won't trust themselves to a woman," or "the executive secretary who does the boss's work but never becomes the boss because people don't like working for a woman."

Lashing out in her feminine zeal, she was equally critical of the woman who sided with the man, detailing to her audiences the struggles of pioneers Elizabeth Cady Stanton, Lucretia Mott and Susan B. Anthony, who were forced to fight for equality not only males but their own sex. "The real obstacle to women's development" she wrote in a *Harper's Magazine* article, "is the women who don't want to *think*, who prefer life in a mental vacuum. They pull each other down, instead of standing beside them in a kind of sisterhood."

Her crusade was not without its perils. "My *Harper's* article is bringing down roars of thunder about my head," she admitted to Grace. But she also stated stoutly, "I am going to go on being a gadfly," adding ruefully, "I'll probably end up with all my books being boycotted by women."

Twenty years later she would wistfully declare, "Greatness always carries with it a curse. The gods and men combine against the great to bring them down."

By this time Pearl's career as a public speaker was flourishing. On the podium she presented the picture of a stately woman, seeming taller than she actually was due to her regal bearing. Her melodious voice made her seem younger than her years, and her lack of make-up and a simple coiffure gave her an unpretentious look.

The demands for speeches fell into three categories, Musts, Nevers and Perhaps. On the Musts list were the Vineland Training School, race relations and international relations groups and women's rights activists. The Nevers were made up of labor and political organizations, garden clubs (and other seemingly "frivolous" groups), book autographing parties, church groups and chambers of commerce. In the Perhaps category were the catch-all invitations such as college commencements, literary and cultural organizations, Bucks County libraries, and so on.

For the Vineland School she truly extended herself, responding to all requests and on occasion producing a prize speaker such as Eleanor Roosevelt. She and Walsh expected of any group asking for a speech that it benefit either the world-at-large or herself. If the world, then she would help if she could, if otherwise there must be something in it for herself. Her attitude here was entirely pragmatic. She once heard a committee co-worker complain that some petitioners were "trying to make use of us."

"Of course they are," Pearl Buck snapped. "And we'll make use of them. That's what makes the world go round."

At her installation into the American Academy of Arts and Letters she spoke of her gratitude for America's welcome to her, an unknown, saying, "I am constrained by my own experience to believe that only complete lack of merit prevents a writer from generous recognition here. And I am further persuaded because I now see for myself the eagerness with which all young talent is searched for, encouraged and developed." Her gentle message thus also managed to convey to budding authors that they could expect a sympathetic reception at John Day.

Furthermore, she had learned from her publicity-oriented husband that startling and controversial statements often became next morning's headlines. To her it was "jolting the audience." To others it was "stealing the show."

During 1937 the flow of speaking invitations intensified as China flooded the news. Chiang Kai-shek and his Nationalist government seemed to have more or less contained the Communist threat. In the large coastal cities the populace was gradually adopting western ideas and technology in road building, transportation and taxation. But unfortunately the peasants, who made up eighty-five percent of China's population, inherited only taxation.

Chiang, unaware of the peasants' growing alienation, had steadily fought the Communists, in 1934 erecting a chain of pillboxes and fortresses joined like a noose around the Reds' stronghold in Kiangsu Province. But the encircled 100,000 Communists slipped the noose one October night and began a six-thousand-mile walk to Yenan, Shensi Province. Across plains and mountains and rivers ninety thousand men made their famous Long March, only twenty or thirty thousand reaching their goal. These still continued their guerrilla warfare and Chiang sent young Marshal Chang to contain them as far from the central government as possible.

Meanwhile China's real enemy, Japan, was making inroads, so in 1935 the Communists initiated a startling move. They proposed that Chiang and the young Marshal Chang join forces with them and all fight Japan together. This Chiang hotly refused to do, while Marshal Chang approved the plan. Chiang went to the Marshal's headquarters to discuss a new anti-Communist stratagem. They quarreled; Chiang walked out, and the Marshal's troops took him captive, demanding cooperation under threat of death.

This bold action electrified the world. A panic-stricken Mme. Chiang flew to Sian to arrange a truce under which, in return for Chiang's life, he would agree to the joining of forces. This he did, and upon his release and return to Nanking, he was hailed as a hero by the relieved populace. However, he had agreed only under duress, half-heartedly, and it soon became evident that China's civil war was far from over.

Japan, meanwhile, staged an "incident" at Marco Polo Bridge in which a confrontation took place between several Japanese and Chinese over the whereabouts of a single Japanese soldier. Deliberately blown up out of proportion, the incident resulted in the Japanese marching on to Peiping.

Overseas the world watched worriedly, for Japan was an important market for international trade and the West, while clucking its disapproval, continued to sell the Japanese its scrap iron.

Thus, immune from western interference, Japan proceeded with its invasion while the Chinese retreated in defeat. Bombings by the Japanese sent them even farther into the hinterlands and left their countryside scorched and flooded. Nanking fell in December 1937 and Canton shortly thereafter. The Nationalists, their coastal cities gone, moved the capital to the inland city of Chungking, which became the capital of Free China. Chiang Kai-shek was still nominally China's leader, but the Communists, with increasing peasant support, were now being called "agrarian revolutionaries," hailed as the country's hope for reform.

Sick at heart Pearl Buck watched these developments, all too aware of the corruption in Nanking and the stupidity that had placed China in this position. Though her heart was unconditionally with the country she hesitated to be wooed into taking sides and for the present she would only watch.

During this period Pearl was suffering a depression stemming from more than China's perilous situation. Her brother's death, Grace's frequent absences with her husband, and particularly the suppression of her novel *The Time Is Noon*, which had left an indelible scar, all together culminated in a frightening sense of inadequacy in her work.

Further, after *The Good Earth* none of her Chinese novels had approached its success with either the critics or the public. She considered *The Exile* and *Fighting Angel* to be successful flukes, impossible to duplicate. *This Proud Heart*, even with its multitude of women fans, had been treated badly by the critics.

Bothering her most of all, she admitted only to herself, was her failure to conquer the technique of writing plays. Her only recourse at this point, she decided, would be a return to her area of confidence, the novel.

Even here, after two failures with the American scene, she was forced to return to the Chinese, so halfheartedly, she took the theme of *A House Divided*, the young westernized Chinese at war with his times. But she found it hard going, lacking the self-propelling confidence of her earlier work. And her various responsibilities nagged at her—a house, an apartment, servants, children, and a husband who, though loving and faithful, still was dependent on her for the main source of his income.

Of course, Grace—at a distance—could be complained to, and her old friend Emma was there, as loyal as ever but so far removed from Pearl's problems that correspondence had become cumbersome. There were no other intimate friends; these days she saw only those people involved in her work or a project or a cause.

When Grace's Anne died suddenly, unattended, she wrote, "You must not blame yourself. . . . you were absolutely perfect in your care and patience and love. . . . But I know how you feel. . . . I think when one has been through a special and irremediable sorrow such as you and I have one remains always at certain points close to tears."

And then suddenly, there was November 10. Pearl had been working after breakfast in her old blue velvet dressing gown when Miss Bucher burst in to announce, "You've won the Nobel Prize!"

Her instant reaction was disbelief. "I don't believe it. That's ridiculous." And her first public statement, "It should have gone to Theodore Dreiser."

The rest of the day consisted of transatlantic telephone calls, whirlwind discussions on how to handle the publicity, and an interview at the John Day office where she answered the reporters' first question, "What are you going to do with all that money?" with "I'll be giving a lot of it to the government."

Another reporter asked her to speak the Chinese words for the phrase, "I don't believe it." When they printed it incorrectly, Lowell Thomas broadcast it incorrectly that night on the air.

The papers prominently featured the fact that Pearl Buck was the first American woman to win the Nobel Prize. The international writers' organization, the Pen Club, felt obligated to celebrate with a dinner, and Sinclair Lewis, a former laureate, made the introductory speech.

While they talked privately after the dinner, Lewis advised her to enjoy her triumph to the hilt, for it was the greatest moment in a writer's life, and he knew from experience some of what she would now go through. People would talk to her, he confided, as if *The Good Earth* were the only book she had ever written, as they had done to him about *Main Street*.

Other writers were frank in commenting on her award. Robert Frost had remarked, "If *she* can get it anybody can," and years later William Faulkner would be quoted: "I don't want it. I'd rather be in the company of Sherwood Anderson and Theodore Dreiser [who had not got it] than S. Lewis and Mrs. China-hand Buck." Henry Seidel Canby of the *Saturday Review of Literature* declared, "The Swedish Academy's standards are high but evidently they are flexible, otherwise it would be difficult to account for the recent award. . . ." And even Theodore Dreiser with whom she had corresponded and who, Pearl had said in her press statement, should have been given the award, abruptly stopped writing to her. She observed that there seemed to be anger that a woman, and a woman who had spent much of her life in China, should be given the award as an American. Inwardly the barbs went deep.

The month before the presentation ceremonies in Sweden was partially spent in shopping sprees—five evening gowns, all with trains, were selected as well as long white gloves and other appropriate clothing. Walsh was required to wear white tie and tails and Betty Walsh, his teenage daughter, who was also invited, wore her first evening gown.

Meanwhile Pearl had to ready her next Chinese novel, *The Patriot*, for the copy editor, write her monthly *Asia Magazine* column, and polish her acceptance speech for which she used her Peiping Union paper on the Chinese novel written in 1933.

They would be gone nearly a month, so Pearl put Mrs. Loris, the cook, and the governess, Miss Kay, in charge of household affairs. Only two questions remained unanswered—the time of arrival of Grace's new baby and whether Pearl's new front tooth inlay would hold out for the duration of the trip.

Upon landing in England, Pearl recognized the atmosphere of approaching war. The stench of Adolf Hitler was pervasive, and she knew that the English were preparing for a stand-off. Interviewed in Copenhagen on the future of China, she stated that a strong central government was its only hope for peace but that Chiang had lost his chance by ignoring the peasantry. As her remarks were widely circulated by the press, China's Nationalist representative boycotted the Nobel ceremony.

As Sinclair Lewis had prophesied, this was her greatest moment. In Stockholm's mid-winter darkness the city blazed with lights and she and Enrico Fermi, the Italian physicist destined one day for international fame, as the two Nobel recipients were overwhelmed with attention. A handsome young attaché with a detailed, printed schedule guided Pearl through the four days, paying special attention to the presentation ceremony and the tricky exercise of curtseying to the King and returning to her seat walking backwards.

The ceremony, held in a huge concert hall decorated with flags and greenery, was appropriately magnificent. Academy members and the royal family, in full formal dress, were seated on a wise platform when

Pearl and Fermi entered, heralded by a blare of trumpets. The speeches, delivered in Swedish, enumerated the laureates' achievements, and Pearl, who had seen an advance translation, was gratified that each of her books was cited separately (except *This Proud Heart*, which the committee said had been published too late for inclusion). The presentation itself required a long walk across the platform, a curtsey, and the acceptance, with handshake and compliments, of a large book (her citation), a gold medal in a box, and an envelope containing the check. Backing away thus encumbered while avoiding her own train necessitated supreme concentration, but she made it to her seat without looking back, and the tense audience burst into applause.

Dinner for a thousand guests followed in the Gold Room where Pearl sat between the Crown Prince and his son, and across from the King and two elderly Princesses. The following day Pearl delivered her hour-long lecture on the Chinese novel before the Academy. In between the principal events were scattered luncheons, teas, a traditional mid-winter fiesta, and a dinner hosted by the Swedish-American Society.

Finally, exhausted but as stimulated as Lewis had promised, the Walshes sailed for home. Remembering that Sinclair Lewis had told her she might someday come to hate the very name of *The Good Earth*, still Pearl read and reread the comforting words of the Nobel citation: "For rich and genuine epic description of Chinese peasant life and for biographical masterpieces."

On shipboard the thought of seeing Janice and the babies put Pearl in a playful mood and she set down her reactions to ocean travel, "Seasick Rhymes for Janice from Mother. Illustrated by Daddy."

> The ocean looks so very nice
> But really that's its chiefest vice.
> It's very wicked of a saint
> To go and act as if it ain't.
>
> The only thing 'twixt me and Sweden
> Is that the ocean is betweeden.
> I think that all the Nobel prizes
> Should wait until the ocean dryses.
>
> Oh say what you like about the sea,
> Say it's as blue as blue can be,

Say this, say that, say such-and-such of it,
The fact remains there is too much of it.

Publicity subsequently sent out by John Day gently emphasized that
the prize had been given for the body of her work. So persistently did
this publishing phrase crop up that bookstore salesmen reported lady
fans coming in to ask for "Pearl Buck's new book, *The Body of Her
Work*."

In a *New York Times* interview Pearl stated that "the award came as
a tremendous surprise." Indeed, it is unlikely that Walsh told her of
having started the promotion four years before, and if he heard rumors
later he would mercifully keep it from her. For, as well as a business
partner he was a loving husband, and as her fame increased he accepted
second place with humor and grace, thereby maintaining successfully a
difficult relationship that might have destroyed many marriages.

Historically the Nobel Prize connotes greatness, and its recipients
must surely feel the effect of its luster upon themselves. Pearl Buck
was peculiarly constituted to do so, for she had long been pondering
such matters.

When the spectacular success of *The Good Earth* endowed her with
sudden power she had used it to inspirit and support both the Negro as
a race and Woman as a sex, thereby calling down upon herself thun-
ders from outraged whites and indignant husbands. The commotion, a
shock at first, had brought out all the fighter in her, and when
Katharine Cornell called for a play about a great woman her mind
immediately leaped to the thought of a woman fighting greatly for a
great cause . . . what would she be like? Was there such a woman
somewhere? Who, perhaps, might she be?

The Nobel Prize was given, according to the citation, for her greatness as a writer. But every day she became less the writer and more the
woman driven by her nagging sense of responsibility for the world at
large. As the years passed her efforts would tend ever more toward the
role she wanted most; and at the end, when catastrophe struck, this
sense of herself would be her comfort and shield.

13

Although a segment of the public seriously questioned the Swedish Academy's choice of Pearl Buck as recipient of the Nobel Prize in literature, both she and her publishers were happy in thinking the award was bestowed on the entire body of her work. Most people, however, disregarding the wording of the citation, did assume it was for *The Good Earth* alone.

The decisive factor in the Academy's judgment according to Anders Osterling, Permanent Secretary of the Swedish Academy and Chairman of the Nobel Committee on Literature, "was, above all, the admirable biographies of her parents, the missionary pair in China, two volumes which seemed to deserve classic rank and to possess the required prospects for permanent interest. In addition her novels of Chinese peasant life have properly made a place for themselves by virtue of the authority, wealth of detail and rare insight with which they describe a region that is little known and rarely accessible to Western readers. But as literary works of art the two biographies remain incomparable with anything else in Pearl Buck's earlier or later production."

Time Magazine, however, suggested an ancillary reason: "As critics realized on second thought, the Nobel Prize went to Pearl Buck only partly for *The Good Earth*. The democratic-minded Swedish Academy was also giving an accolade to Pearl Buck's sympathy for the Chinese common people. The influence of her writing far transcends its importance as literature. . . . And a further impetus came from her interviews and articles attacking dictatorship."

In the midst of all the controversy, Pearl told friends, "It gave me back my confidence, which I had lost, and I never lost it again."

Her Nobel Prize did not, however, affect the opinions of the major literary journals, a fact recognized by Malcolm Cowley in the *New Republic*. "Her book had not been discovered in the orthodox manner. A really good novel was supposed to be turned up by the younger critics who act as scouts for the rest, and afterwards this reputation spreads from the center in widening rings to the public. Pearl Buck had reversed that order and only William Lyons Phelps praised it at the beginning, and in those circles his praise was the kiss of Judas."

The thousands of adoring readers who kept her books at the top of the best-seller lists never suspected that their adulation had been a reversal in procedure. Pearl Buck was America's most translated author (eventually in sixty-nine different languages), and even in Nationalist China, a country eager to suppress the fact that most Chinese were poor, dirty and ignorant, seven different translations were eagerly gobbled up.

Her views on the craft of writing were now widely studied. Aside from her two Master's degrees, one earned, and the other honorary, she had had vast experience as a teacher. In *The Mind at Work* she analyzes the ingredients necessary to a novelist: on the one hand an organizational mind that delights in order and pattern (i.e., the mathematician, the bridge-player, the crossword puzzle addict) and on the other, a heterogeneous creative mind which creates its own materials and conditions (i.e., explorers, painters, some master criminals, actors, religious fanatics, poets, and, of course, writers). Among this maverick group the novelist carries his materials within himself—the powers of observation, emotion, imagination, and expression.

Having been seized with the inspiration for a piece of work, the writer calls first on his powers of observation, the people, things and places stored in his memory. These powers of observation are a gift he was born with, instinctive and ever-active like breathing. The world, all humanity, provide his fertile grounds. All humanity means all humans, good and bad, beautiful and repulsive. The writer must be receptive without prejudice. All are part of life and life is his material.

She warns against note-taking. The novelist must not be a spectator, but plunge in and live with his material, comprehending by experiencing from within. Such feeling is another essential ingredient, the power of *emotion*. By forgetting himself in his involvement, the novelist becomes a part of what he observes. But he must retain his sense of balance, never distorting the truth to prove a point. If he does he becomes a mere propagandist delivering messages instead of depicting reality.

Thus through observation and involvement he acquires his basic material. Now called into play is the third ingredient, imagination, which must take the raw material and create plots and incidents, pushing characters into situations even beyond his own experience. But again, he must be careful to keep his imagination within the story's boundaries.

Lastly the novelist, having observed and absorbed his material and breathed life into it, still faces the task of giving it appropriate expression. Expression embraces two forms, the skeletal structure and the language. Combined they are *the style*, clothing appropriate to the individual body. Structure may be carefully planned, either a group of characters for whom suitable action must be invented, or a special situation in which characters must act out a suitable plot.

As for the language, its effective use requires an inner ear not unlike a musician's. Each word possesses an individual character like a note of music, and rightly choosing it the writer can be a poet, a wit or a demagogue, making his sentence murmur, leap or flow.

And behind all of these necessary components and motivating the whole lies the *need to create*, the energy that drives an author. Using his gifts to the highest pitch he experiences the rapture of a god.

Pearl's own style resembled that of the chameleon in its gift for accommodation. Unlike some writers, who worked in a single style, their trademark, Pearl Buck suited hers to her material, and for the most part was successful. She had written five novels about the Chinese. *The Good Earth* with its slow-moving dignity combined the poetry of the King James Bible with a literal translation from the Chinese. Carl Van Doren found its style "fluent and flexible; simple in idiom and cadence, like a realistic pastoral or a humane saga." Phyllis Bentley spoke of her "grave, quiet biblical speech, full of dignity, in which without ever raising her voice she is able to render both the deepest and the lightest emotions."

Paul A. Doyle in his study of the author pointed out the simplicity of *The Good Earth*, its concreteness, its stress on long serpentine sentences, parallelism, balance and repetition of words as characteristic usages. He commends her style for avoiding purple passages despite the poetical overtones.

In *The Mother* Doyle finds the same semi-biblical prose, now less rich, poetic and varied and possessing an economy which, though lyrical, can become at times somewhat monotonous. Yet the book as a whole, to his mind, achieves an effect of deep emotion severely controlled.

In a radical departure, Pearl Buck's two biographies are examples of straight exposition. Some of the author's missionary friends considered *The Exile* an over-sentimentalization of Carie, lacking the rigidity and sternness of the real woman. They felt too that Carie's life had not been quite the martyrdom depicted. A sad, remorseful daughter had written the memorial and while Doyle finds the style too flowery, with too romantic an emphasis on hardships bravely borne, still the mother's character is sympathetically drawn and the reader remembers her vividly.

Most critics considered *Fighting Angel* a more nearly perfect accomplishment. Henry Seidel Canby summed up both biographies as "unquestionably the best studies ever done of the unique personal traits developed by the missionary fervor of the 19th century, which some day will be recognized as a very important part of the social history of Western civilization in that departed epoch."

Doyle found fault with *Fighting Angel* only in its lack of illustrative incidents, lauding its simple, factual style and narration which makes totally comprehensible the author's change of attitude from a childhood resentment to a mature understanding and deep affection.

Pearl Buck's pronouncement that *Sons* was her favorite Chinese novel could be more a show of maternal loyalty than objective judgment. For the background is less absorbing and the characterizations less convincing. The biblical style, carried over from *The Good Earth*, seems less appropriate to the martial content which is so historically accurate that it could serve as a textbook for students of Chinese history.

A House Divided, the third in the trilogy, is even more historically evocative. An accurate picture of the disoriented young Chinese of the Twenties, vacillating between the old China and the new, the book is itself a structure divided against itself. On one side is the social history that formed her subject matter, on the other the novel's form, the mythological folk style inherited from the two former volumes. In combining the two she produced a book which like its hero is weak and ineffectual.

This Proud Heart, which mercifully escaped the scrutiny of the

Swedish Academy, is a downward step from the excellence of Pearl Buck's earlier books in its style. Studded with clichés and repetitions, lacking in variety and telling imagery, it remains curiously reminiscent of the radio serials, popular in the Thirties.

During the late Thirties Pearl Buck continued to express her theories on writing in speeches and interviews, and her sharply nanalytical views generally made good copy. In an interview in the *Providence Bulletin* she warned writers against isolating themselves in an ivory tower. But her dialogue in *This Proud Heart* suggests that if she had left her own ivory tower and listened more to Americans, that novel would have been more convincing.

Other literary inconsistencies appear between her theories and her practices. In her lectures she claimed that she planned her books so carefully that she knew the last word before the first was written, yet with *The Time Is Noon*, the manuscript was all but finished before the ending occurred to her.

She was vehement in warning young writers against being "mere hacks writing drivel to please the magazine editors," yet she too wrote eagerly for them, declaring that "any publication bought by three million people is a perfect place to reach those who don't read books." In the same spirit she came to the defense of potboilers, lightly claiming that, after all, *The Good Earth* had been the biggest potboiler of all time.

In choosing their subject matter she suggested that writers avoid "such transient stuff as front-page news" and choose instead the timeless aspects of life, specifically denouncing the didactic novel. Art may teach a lesson, she stated, if it describes life in all its wholeness, but writing a novel solely to push a political point or teach a moral lesson is to play down one part of the truth to play up another, thus turning a work of art into a sermon. Yet, as Pearl Buck's point of view changed, she would often sermonize. To Pearl Buck it seemed all rules, even her own, were made to be broken.

Shortly after the announcement of the Nobel Prize, Katharine Cornell had sent Pearl Buck a gracious note of congratulations. Hearing from the actress after a long silence opened up new possibilities. Months had passed since all the false starts on *The Empress* and Pearl wrote Cornell, "It is now a year since I put *The Empress* into your hands and, as I remember, we agreed then that at the end of a year we would talk about it again." She inquired about Cornell's present plans and Cornell replied that she was still hesitant to play another Oriental so soon.

This suggested to Pearl a door still slightly ajar, so she asked if Cornell had any objection to *The Empress* being published to establish priority, since it was rumored another play about the Empress was making the rounds. Cornell's reply was so polite but indifferent, that she then approached Helen Hayes. Hayes, an unlikely Tzu Hsi, failed to see herself in the part but helpfully suggested: "This role cries aloud for Katharine Cornell. Why don't you try her?"

In a last desperate grasp at a vanishing dream, Pearl wrote Cornell pleading for some kind of future commitment. None came and she finally gave up thinking all lost.

Cornell, however, had mentioned *The Empress* to Mary Kennedy. This poet, actress, novelist, and playwright was a friend of Lin Yutang's and asked him for an introduction to Pearl Buck. Given the play to read, she found the love story powerful, the atmosphere fascinating, and some of the blank verse beautiful. There were too many characters (fifty-one plus extras) and too many scenes (ten sets) but if Mrs. Buck were interested, they might go over it together and sharpen it a bit.

Several months of energetic play-doctoring followed. Kennedy, who was chairman of the Cosmopolitan Club's drama committee, suggested an all-star play-reading for the club's membership, thus providing not only entertainment but an opportunity to get a look at the play in performance. She then enlisted another member of the club, the eminent actress and monologist, Cornelia Otis Skinner, to play Tzu Hsi recalled the event: "Mary Kennedy got the idea very strongly that I should do a reading of Pearl Buck's new play, all very hush-hush. Kit Cornell had had it two years without doing anything with it. No wonder; it was a very bad play in my opinion.

"Anyway, Vincent Price, hardly a Chinese type, was to play the Empress's lover, Jane Wyatt the discarded wife and Margalo Gilmore, a dazzling blonde, was also in it. We met at my house and it took four mortal hours to read through, literally. Afterwards, when all the other actors left, Margalo and I looked at each other and said, 'We can't do this, we've got to cut it.' We had told Mary we were going to, and she'd said all right, so I got a blue pencil and Margalo got a red one. We cut mercilessly—the Boxer Rebellion, the First World War. We cut out the downfall of whatever dynasty the Empress was in, and we got it down to a workable length.

"Mary had been to China and she had a lot of beautiful embroidered coats, and at the performance we got dressed up in them and sat around before little low tables reading from scripts.

"We had cut it down from four hours to an hour and a half. But one trouble was we only had four scripts, also we had to share them. Vincent Price and I shared one, and one of us being quite short-sighted and the other very long, we had to keep the script politely seesawing back and forth to each other's sight level. It wasn't easy.

"I suppose you'd say the performance went well. At any rate, it *went*. The ladies and a few sheepish husbands followed our efforts with gratifying attention and according to one ecstatic lady it was a *succès fou*.

"Mrs Buck, a fellow member, sat in the front row center and listened with a completely deadpan expression. It was glaringly apparent that she didn't a bit like the cavalier way we had cut her play, and all of us carefully avoided meeting her eye. After the performance she was very cold and distant, and about two weeks later I got a typewritten letter, 'Dear Miss Skinner: Thank you very much for taking part in the reading of my play *The Empress*, on such-and-such date at the Cosmopolitan Club. Sincerely, Pearl S. Buck.' The others never got a word." (Ten years later Skinner would write an hilarious account of the event, "Actors Will Do Anything," for the *New Yorker Magazine*.)

Cheerful Mary Kennedy did not allow Cornelia Skinner's lack of enthusiasm to dampen her enthusiasm for *The Empress*, and the rewrite continued, Kennedy offering each new version to her wealthy friends in and around the theater. Bayard Veiller, John Golden, Alfred Lunt and Lynn Fontanne and Dorothy Whitney Elmhirst, among others, read it respectfully, declining to become backers. At last the battered script came home to rest.

But one last hope remained—the possibility of a movie, and Walsh sent it off to Myron Selznick's theatrical agency on the West Coast. The agent's response to Walsh is the most astute diagnosis of the play's weakness. "I have read the play and I am going to present it to Hollywood, but I doubt it is the type of thing Hollywood would do. I enjoyed reading it. However, we in show business have an expression which seems to cover it—namely, it is 'good *reading* writing,' that is, it is well written but doesn't seem to have the possibilities to *play*. You might tell Mrs. Buck that this is the fault most novelists have when they turn to playwriting—their plays just refuse to play."

This apparently was the demise of *The Empress* as drama. But Pearl

Buck, never one to waste good research, put Tzu Hsi aside only temporarily.

In the meantime, despite the West Coast agent's opinion, she had no intention of giving up play writing. If other people could write plays that *played*, so could she.

As the fate of her play *Flight into China* was still hanging fire, she invited Guthrie McClintic to the apartment. He still insisted heartily that his interest in the play was hampered only by the egos of various stars who would like to appear in it but were unwilling to share star billing. Almost a year later the newspapers announced that McClintic planned a production. After two more months Pearl inquired discreetly about progress and was informed that the Jewish backers who were approached had objected to the theme of the play. After this her connection with Guthrie McClintic ended.

But there was one final gasp. The following year, *Flight into China* achieved production when a young actress with a rich and indulgent father wanted to star in a play, and Lee Strasberg, the drama coach, wanted a play to produce. It was tried out at a playhouse in Millburn, New Jersey, and ran for two weeks to "mixed notices."

Later it would reappear in another incarnation when Pearl Buck told the same story about the Jews in China in her novel *Peony*. There was no Jewish protest over the novel. Indeed, it caused no stir at all, for it is one of Pearl Buck's least successful novels about China.

During the visit to Sweden Pearl was already researching the novel that was to follow *The Patriot*'s publication in March of 1939. She was also steadily turning out articles and stories and at least one serial a year to meet the household's increasing expenses. New wings were added to the house and new pools and gardens to the grounds as her concept of the good life enlarged. Furthermore, with the education of her five adopted children looming over the next twenty years, she asked her old Kuling friend, Dean Kelsey, now a New York insurance broker, to buy each of them a $10,000 annuity. Each would be given his or hers on reaching twenty-one after which they would all be on their own.

This expensive life style was almost entirely Pearl's responsibility. Though Walsh remained president of the John Day Company and editor of *Asia Magazine*, his publishing firm was still largely dependent on Pearl Buck's literary output and the magazine had never been a profitable operation. Furthermore, he still made alimony payments.

For some years his blood pressure had been a source of worry. So now the Walshes decided to ask Richard's son Dick, employed by a Buffalo newspaper, to join John Day as an editor. This would enable Walsh and Pearl to move their offices to the country and simply maintain a pied-a-terre in New York City for an occasional night in town.

This move entailed further changes. Walsh's daughter, Natalie, after attending Vassar and the Katherine Gibbs secretarial school, moved with her husband Bob Coltman to a house near the Walshes and Natalie became her stepmother's secretary. Pearl wrote Emma, "I have let Miss Bucher go for several long-standing reasons and have my stepdaughter working for me."

Pearl had brought Miss Bucher from Nanking in 1932 and apparently after eight years the young woman had thought her position permanent. Nannine Joseph, the New York literary agent, recalled Miss Bucher's surprise and dismay at the manner of her dismissal. She had, she told Miss Joseph, been ill in the hospital and when Pearl Buck visited her, she had said to her, "I can't come again unless you move to a private room." Obediently, she had moved into a private room which she thought would be her employer's responsibility, but she was subsequently billed for it and then dismissed.

A friend had once asked Pearl Buck, after remarking that she seemed to handle her life so well, "With all the problems you have, how do you do it?" Pearl had answered, "When I'm faced with a problem I do everything I can to solve it. If I can't solve it I put it out of my mind—close it off completely." No doubt the Confucian influence— with emotions under perfect control.

In beleaguered China, the Japanese offensive continued to sap the strength of Chiang's resistance and he was forced farther and farther inland, making a final stand in Chungking. Even within his Nationalist party control was shaky, some members wanting to adopt the Communists' guerrilla tactics, others favoring compromise with Japan. Chiang leaned toward compromise, meanwhile closely observing events in Europe where war with Germany was brewing. If the United States became involved there, China would somehow become involved as well and thus, in an ultimate victory, would share in the spoils. Meanwhile, the United States continued to declare its neutrality.

Pearl Buck realized how slim America's neutral stance really was and hoped only that when war did come China's plight would not be altogether overlooked. Her fame had irreversibly linked her name with China and she was besieged with questions and pleas for advice. She did what she could, leading "Stop Japan" rallies and joining the causes that seemed effective.

Summer usually brought an exodus of Walshes to the beach. They now owned, aside from a cottage on the Jersey shore, an abandoned Coast Guard house consisting of one cavernous room for the boats and a dormitory upstairs. It was a primitive existence, with second-hand furniture and cots under mosquito nets, and the children relished the lack of rules. But these rural retreats brought no relief in July and August for Pearl's hay fever. Consequently this summer they decided to vacation on Martha's Vineyard, the tiny island off the coast of Massachusetts.

On July 18 Pearl wrote Emma, "This is a heavenly spot and we are taking our vacation here with all the children.... Janice chose not to go to camp this year and is working regular hours and getting a small salary as second nurse.... Dick and I work hard all morning on Lin Yutang's new book *Moment in Peking*, and play hard all afternoon. Lin's book is perfectly magnificent, though it needs a great deal of work as all his stuff does, but it is going to be a wonderful picture of upper-class Chinese life. I think it ranks with Tolstoy's *War and Peace*. Every other novel about China fades before it."

The Lins had traveled to Europe earlier that year but finding the threat of war unbearable returned to New York. "They are living with the utmost simplicity," Pearl wrote Marian Craighill. "He has to support many relatives in war-torn areas—twenty-two, the last I heard." Shortly after this letter the Book of the Month Club took *Moment in Peking*, thus providing financial relief for the Lins and their twenty-two relatives.

In July tension in Europe increased as the Hitler-Stalin pact insured Russian neutrality in the face of the Fuehrer's plans.

"How well I remember the day war began in Europe," Pearl Buck wrote. "We had taken a house in Martha's Vineyard that summer, a comfortable place next door to Katharine Cornell's beautiful place on the bay.... I was at work upon my novel *Other Gods*.... One morning, however, unable to work ... I joined the children on the beach earlier than usual. A few minutes later I saw my husband hurrying down the dunes. It was to tell me the fearful news from the radio, that war had been declared in Europe.

"It seemed impossible in spite of certainty. The sun shone upon the calm sea and upon the smooth white sands. Our two babies, hand in hand, were running up and down the beach in the shallow water, while the two little boys dug for sand crabs. Upon this scene in spite of all its grace and calm the war broke that day and we knew, my husband and I, that our life would never be the same again, for war would change our country and our people. It would change, indeed, the whole world."

Hitler, unleashed by the Russo-German pact, invaded Poland on September 1, and on September 3 England and France declared war against Germany. That fall, while Russia and Germany carved up Poland, Britain rearmed in frantic haste and France shuddered behind its Maginot Line, a French version of China's Great Wall.

In June of 1940 Pearl and Walsh, forcing themselves to carry on normally, set out for a trip to the Midwest. Kansas was Walsh's home state, and Pearl, familiar only with New York's polyglot population, yearned to see "real America." Meanwhile they kept tuned to President Roosevelt's addresses to the nation, knowing they were being warned of a possible American war.

However ardently they both opposed intervention, as the months passed they sensed the gradual change in the country and even in themselves. Pearl Buck had her own priorities. Using her considerable influence, she founded the China Emergency Relief Committee headed by Eleanor Roosevelt to raise money for medical supplies. Lin Yutang, Luise Rainer and others broadcast appeals and a message from Madame Chiang Kai-shek was aired in which she enumerated the needs of the Chinese people. When this committee with its roster of powerful names became a fashionable cause, Pearl withdrew, leaving it to run on its own momentum.

One day she received a call from Edgar and Helen Snow, with whom she and Walsh had spent a delightful day in Peking some years before. They were looking for a house in the country, and the Walshes invited them to Bucks County to consider local possibilities. The Snows had recently left China where they had organized the uprooted workers into cooperatives to combat famine, and here they were eloquent in alerting America to China's plight.

On December 7, 1941, the Walshes had been attending a birthday party when two teenage boys who had been listening to a football game on the car's radio, rushed in shouting, "The Japs have bombed Pearl Harbor!"

Typically, Pearl Buck's first thought was of Chiang Kai-shek—how relieved he would be at last. And her second was of Eleanor Roosevelt, who served her husband as another pair of eyes and ears. Apologizing for her presumptuousness, Pearl wrote Mrs. Roosevelt that, as a loyal citizen, she could not resist sending a warning "to those shaping the country's course."

She reminded the wife of the President that in all Oriental peoples resided a deep sense that the white man was the common enemy of all Asiatics, Chinese as well as Japanese, and a hard solidarity would now burgeon among them. In her five-page letter she warned that in India, China and Japan the likelihood was great of a common front against the whites. America must not count on cooperation from any Asiatic country, for all were too racially embittered. She hoped that the United States, as a conciliatory gesture, would repeal the insulting law discriminating against Chinese immigration, since this would represent acceptance of their equality.

Both Pearl Buck and Lin Yutang watched with concern the bond developing between Roosevelt and Churchill, which seemed to them to portend a discriminatory concentration on the war in Europe. Fearing that not only China but India would be forgotten in the thrust of the war aims and their post-war settlement, Lin Yutang labeled the Churchill-Roosevelt relationship "the costliest friendship of history."

Pearl Buck never knew how much weight her words carried in high places, but certainly the President's wife appeared to listen to them, and before a projected trip to China Mrs. Roosevelt asked her for advice. Pearl sent a long, detailed letter describing the country's political factions, listing Chinese tastes, customs, and prejudices, even cautionary advice about eating local foods, and proffering the names of residents whom she might find helpful.

Though never offered a political appointment by Washington, Pearl Buck's name was twice introduced as a possible candidate for high office—once for Congress by the citizens of Bucks County and once for Ambassador to China by Clifton Fadiman in *New Yorker Magazine*. Both times Walsh hastened to quash such talk. "Mrs. Walsh feels she could be much more useful doing her own work in her own way," he told her supporters.

Had she been a professional politician she could hardly have found herself with a fuller schedule of chicken lunches followed by speeches. The following organizations comprised a cross-section of her activities: American Committee for Democracy and Freedom; Provisional Committee Toward a Democratic Peace; Unemployment Insurance Appeal Board, Department of Labor; Committee for American Democracy; Coordinator of Inter-American Affairs; Committee on Friendly Relations among Foreign Students; Federal Union; Council Against Intolerance in America; Foreign Policy Association; American Civil Liberties Union; American Committee for Christian Refugees; Quaker Hostel in Harlem; Intercultural Education Workshop; Institute of Pacific Relations; American Scandinavian Center; Henry George School of Social Service; Howard University; Community Services, Office of War Information; Japanese-American Committee for Democracy (in connection with which she wrote: "I have read yesterday's paper and am sorry the Chinese Consul General objected to the march of the Japanese Americans against internment of Nisei. He is a friend of ours and I shall tell him we think less of the Chinese who take such a stand.").

Although she belonged to all of the above organizations, Pearl Buck was in no way a pushover for program organizers. Her husband carefully screened all such invitations to join, as he explained to a friend requesting his wife's support: "Pearl occupies a rather unique place today which enables her to speak out boldly on public questions. She has successfully been kept aloof from any one group and from any one ideology, and it is in the public interest that she should stay so. In deciding whether she should appear at a meeting the really important thing is, who would be the other speakers. I am inclined to ask that you obtain most of these and let me see the list before deciding whether Pearl Buck is to be included. This is no more than we have asked of other cases. For twelve years now I have tried to guard the position Pearl Buck holds, so that her public usefulness will not be impaired by letting her be picketed or pigeon-holded. Just now it seems very important that her attitude on India and China and on race relations, which is unchangeable, does not appear to be anti-British, and that she does not drive wedges between us and our allies. . . ."

On the first day of January 1941, Pearl wrote a retrospective letter to Grace. "I have never felt better in my life than I do now. But I fret sometimes over the years between twenty-five and thirty-five, which were largely wasted. What was I doing in those years? And why didn't I get to work? I see now that I was in a queer submerged state. It was like living in a solitary cell, nothing and no one came in and I seemed unable to communicate with anyone. Whether it was that missionary environment I cannot tell. But remembering it I have the feelings of one having spent part of his life in jail. . . . I am in good shape physically and have myself trained to hard work and long hours and responsibilities. My mind is at its sharpest and best and I am really myself."

The many facets of her well-organized life ran smoothly. The house was managed by the mid-European with salty good sense and hard-headed devotion, Mrs. Loris. Nurses and governesses appeared as required, but by now the children were growing big enough to care for themselves. Walsh oversaw every phase of his wife's work but the writing, which she did in longhand, sometimes revising but sometimes leaving even that to his care. For recreation she had her studio where she sculpted the children's heads in clay, and a piano—and later an organ—with which to indulge her passion for Chopin and Beethoven.

Still feeling a responsibility to protect the interests of the East against the pull of the West, she formed the East and West Association on the theory that, since international relations were rooted in one country's instinctive feelings about another, its citizens should be better informed about each other. To this end the Association sent representatives of both cultures to visit the other's country. For eight years Americans traveled to China, and Asians came to the United States, their expenses funded by membership dues, grants and often privately by Pearl S. Buck whose speaking fees now ranged from $500 to $1200. The writers and lecturers and others spent several days at different colleges and schools, mingling with American students; an American Information Service was provided to answer questions about the foreign countries, their customs, their literature and art, and young Chinese were trained in American factories and technical schools on industrial scholarships.

A fifteen-week course, Peoples East and West, was given in New York City and other large cities, and in many areas teachers who attended were given credit by the Boards of Education. A series of thirteen lectures was broadcast by NBC on local stations which reached an audience of fifteen million. Theatrical artists, musicians and dancers, both Chinese and American, were sent out on an exchange basis to perform for their opposite numbers in China and the United States.

For the Asians who came to the States Pearl Buck had one simple admonition: "You have nothing to teach, nothing to preach. All you have to do is be the best citizen of your country that you can, to represent what you would like Americans to think about your country." The same advice was given to the Americans traveling overseas.

An important adjunct to the East and West Association was *Asia Magazine* which never had been a money-maker and had been subsidized for years by Leonard Elmhirst and his wife. When Pearl and Walsh took it over new money to back it was sought and several times nearly found, only to be frightened off by rumors of war. Pearl Buck contributed book reviews and a monthly column; segments of her books were often included, and for a 1943 issue she tried a new venture in novel writing. Resembling a journal more than a novel, *The Promise*, appearing each month, chronicled the fortunes of fictional characters caught up in war in the East. And to help the magazine stay afloat she turned over to it full publication rights to the book, not only to provide news and views about the East but to support the magazine staff, some of whom were elderly and highly specialized.

In 1946 despite all her efforts, the magazine folded. It was later combined with two other magazines, reappearing as *United Nations World* with Richard Walsh as the chairman of its editorial board.

After the war the temper of America's thinking began to change and the East and West Association came under attack from Senator Joseph McCarthy. There were accusations of Communist infiltration among the Chinese exchange performers and while the Association never knowingly offended, it was impossible to police private thoughts. McCarthy's rumors cost the group memberships and patronage and it finally disbanded.

Pearl Buck had conceived the East and West Association on a grand scale, with handsomely furnished quarters adjoining the John Day offices. Among the large staff were Fay Glover, a Black, and Tsuta Lombard, who was half-Japanese. Fay Glover remembered the warm atmosphere that pervaded the offices. "After I'd been there a while I developed an ulcer. Pearl Buck heard about it and said one day, 'I'd like you to see a friend of mine, a Chinese doctor. . . . He put me on a strict diet that went on for about a year. I wasn't making much money and I worried about the cost, because I went to him regularly for a check-up and he only sent me one bill. Years later I found out she'd told him to send me one bill for about thirty dollars so I wouldn't wonder, and she paid the rest all that time. And when one of her books hit the Book of the Month she gave the whole staff a week's salary as a bonus. That was typical. We all loved Pearl Buck very much."

Tsuta Ohata Lombard, a graduate of Columbia University, and a Phi Beta Kappa, possessed a fine singing voice and had joined the East and West group as a concert singer. She later worked for the John Day Company. Efficient, imaginative and loyal, Tsuta came nearer than almost anyone in supplying a missing element in Pearl Buck's world— genuine friendship. When she was asked who her close friends were, Pearl's usual response was "I have none." True, as a board member of the Vineland Training School she met regularly with other members. But they were all unhappy, shrinking parents like herself, special people bonded by a fraternity of sorrow. She had found a certain comfort in these meetings because there she could talk freely in a sharing companionship.

Gradually she had ventured a little out of her shell, making a few neighborhood appearances on behalf of the Training School. Otherwise her life was divided between her public work and that of family and home. Lin Yutang and his family were an exception. Walsh considered Lin his closest friend, and Lin's wife Hong became Pearl's. Stocky, amusing, Lin Hong was the traditional Chinese wife, feigning subservience to her husband while going serenely her own way.

Yutang, slender, moon-faced and witty, was a philosopher who lacked the pomposity of the professional thinker and managed to establish a gay and breezy relationship with Pearl.

In 1940 the Lins, suffering deep feelings of guilt over living luxuriously in America while their country was being torn apart, had departed in a shower of publicity for the war zone. Their arrival in Chungking at Chiang's camp coincided with a heavy bombing and they endured three months of air raids. Finally, unable to contribute anything useful to the cause, they came home.

Their hasty return demanded of Walsh, as Lin's representative, a logical explanation which proved hard to devise. Pearl had sincerely admired the Lins and this was her first disappointment in their friendship.

Some years later she used the Lin family's hegira to China as the basis for her novel *Kinfolk*. By then the friendship had soured a little and some readers have found in its pages an amusing but not altogether flattering portrait of Lin. In 1948, appointed to UNESCO, he moved with his family to Paris. The final split occurred when Dick Walsh, Jr., on the advice of his accountant, deducted a larger withholding tax from Lin's royalties than Lin thought justified. In 1955 Pearl Buck wrote to Dick, "Lin is a fascinating character. I'm glad he is on the other side of the world."

Aside from the Lins, her children and her husband, a constant in Pearl Buck's life was her care for her sister. Grace, encouraged by Pearl, had written a biography of the three Soong sisters and, also at Pearl's suggestion, a Chinese novel. This, voted one of the best first novels of the season, was honored at a Book and Author luncheon which Pearl Buck attended. She wrote Grace later, "You looked lovely and I was proud to be your sister, for it was an Occasion, something with a very precious flavor and different from anything I ever had. I am so glad this recognition came just when it did, for I know it was what you needed. Now it is something to build solidly for your work to come."

In 1943, however, a rift between the sisters occurred which lasted for five years. The Yaukeys, disillusioned by the evangelical life, had left their China mission station, finally becoming Quakers. After Pearl's unhappy experience with the foreign missions organized religion became anathema to her, and she had found it difficult to accept her sister's new religious affiliation. When America went to war and the Yaukeys as Quakers remained pacifists, Pearl Buck advocated America's military policies, and years of estrangement followed. For both it was a painful break. Finally, however, the sisters were reconciled.

Her causes. Her home. Her work. Pearl Buck admitted that these three things mattered most in her life and in that ascending order. She could have given up the causes, perhaps even the home, but work was the essence of her life. Ideas for stories, characters based on unique personalities, incidents to be developed—all were grist to her literary mill continuously grinding out its rich harvest.

The war years, quantitatively, were her most productive. There were numerous speeches, monthly columns for *Asia Magazine*, evaluations of manuscripts for the John Day Company; light fiction and articles for the women's and other magazines and long, weekly letters to Grace—and ten novels: *The Patriot* (1939), *Other Gods* (1940), *Dragon Seed* (1942), *The Promise* (1943), *Portrait of a Marriage* (1945), *The Townsman* (1945), *Pavilion of Women* (1946), *The Angry Wife* (1947), *Peony* (1948), *Kinfolk* (1949). Nor had she totally put aside her interest in writing plays.

A few of the novels were important contributions, others unmemorable. Some were based on a personal incident, others were simply written to obtain money.

Three, *The Patriot*, *Dragon Seed* and *The Promise*, were set against a background of the Sino-Japanese war. *The Patriot*, in Malcolm Cowley's opinion, was a re-write of *A House Divided*, and he advised Pearl Buck, half-seriously, to destroy the earlier book, re-name the characters and publish the new one as the third volume in *The Good Earth* trilogy. A young Chinese, unable to commit himself to his country's needs, chooses Japan as a convenient home until he becomes aware of Japanese atrocities, when he finally takes his place in China's defense. It is a finer novel than *A House Divided* and, as a book club selection, provided money at a difficult time.

Dragon Seed, about peasants Ling Tan and his family who live outside Nanking, describes their response to the Japanese invasion, the air raids and the brutal destruction of the city, the rape and torture. Generally regarded as one of the author's best books, it was enormously successful, again a Book of the Month selection and a film starring Katharine Hepburn and Aline MacMahon. The style used in *The Good Earth* details the horrors of war with an understatement more telling than dramatics. The Ling women are especially well defined, relieving the horror of many scenes with a humor not always present in Pearl Buck's work.

At the end, however, the author falls into a familiar trap. Once quoted as having been bored with the writing of *Dragon Seed*, when her hero's fate seems unresolved she hastily introduces an heroic American-educated Chinese girl to make a convenient match.

As these novels of war were written amidst the emotion-laden events themselves, they did not escape a taint of propaganda, but both *The Patriot* and *Dragon Seed* deserved their success.

The Promise, which followed *Dragon Seed*, dealt with the same family but did not fare as well. Written month by month as the actual events unfolded, it tells of the unkept promise of the white Allied armies to the yellow forces of China. The whites, retreating from Burma, had asked Chiang Kai-shek for help and he had responded with his best divisions. In a desperate stand the Chinese held back the enemy while the white men retreated across a bridge. But when the Chinese attempted to follow, the bridge had been destroyed. This account of stupidity and betrayal comprises a sorry tale.

As an indictment of the racial attitudes that led British and American generals to sacrifice their Chinese allies, *The Promise* could not, under wartime conditions, have been pleasant reading. In his review Christopher Morley wrote, "All the more because it is so skillfully told this is a painful story," and he hoped it was not altogether true. That sales were not encouraging is not surprising, and indeed it had taken courage to publish it at all. It was the last of Pearl S. Buck's war novels.

These three war novels were published between 1939 and 1943, but another novel written earlier had been sandwiched in after *The Patriot.* Following *This Proud Heart* Pearl, still hoping to strike a rich American vein, had tried a different theme. Harking back to the evening spent in Nanking with Charles and Anne Lindbergh, she had given considerable thought to the hero-worship syndrome. Linking it up with her own tumultuous but bewildering reception in 1932, she transmuted the handsome young flyer into Bert Holm, a mountain climber, and the transatlantic flight into the conquest of a Tibetan peak. In *Other Gods*, based on the Lindbergh experience, she delivered an unflattering but fascinating analysis of the effect of hero worship on a susceptible personality.

Various aspects of hero worship are studied—the hero's blind acceptance of the public's exalted view of him; the precariousness of hero-status if he makes a misstep; and the resulting plunge into disgrace. She also notes the rewarding effects of praise. Bert Holm, who had been guilty of minor defects, reacts to the public's expectations of him by acting like the gentleman they consider him to be. The book is of interest because of its sharp psychological probings. But, curiously, it lacks the reality of her Chinese novels, probably because of the conditions under which it was written.

During this period of financial pressure, Pearl Buck was driven to writing less than her best and *Other Gods* had been written first as a serial for *Good Housekeeping* in 1938. Later she expanded it for book publication, but without improving on its original magazine style. She seems to have recognized this as a mistake, for she wrote to Grace, "It is one of the novels which reviewers will blithely call a potboiler, not comprehending how far from that it is or how much feeling and thinking have gone into it. It seems to me that whatever one does, one dies at the hands of critics. Other professionals pursue their professions without having to support a parasitic group who make their bread and butter off the work done by others." Her bitterness was excessive; the critics were actually quite kind, but many felt it far from her best.

Undaunted, she tried again. After the three Chinese novels, *The*

Patriot, *Dragon Seed* and *The Promise*, she returned hopefully to the American idiom. By this time her beloved brother Edgar had been dead nearly ten years and she mourned and puzzled over the tragedy of a brilliant man always unfulfilled. She recalled that he had always felt inferior in his father's eyes and that his two marriages, both failures, had exacerbated his unhappiness. So, pondering all possible alternatives, in *Portrait of a Marriage*, she pictured the kind of marriage she believed he should have made.

The hero, young William Benton, oppressed by his wealthy, aristocratic family, is interested only in living in the country and painting. He meets a beautiful, uneducated farm girl with a loving disposition and marries her. The marriage is a success because the unlettered girl is content that he is handsome and ardent, and he is satisfied that she is healthy and amenable—such an unlikely combination of elements that the probability of their melding satisfactorily is unconvincing.

During these years John Day collected many of Pearl Buck's speeches and essays in a series of Talk Books. The earliest, published in 1942, was *American Unity and Asia* which contained seven speeches, four of which were thoughtful, passionate arguments against race discrimination, not only black-white but Nisei-American, Indian-British, and Chinese-white. She made the point that race hatred jeopardized victory in the war because racial democracy was essential for armed victory in the field and to the permanent freedom for which the war was being fought. Eleanor Roosevelt reviewed it, calling it "a very important book."

In another of the Talk Books, *What America Means to Me*, the theme is the same: "If we want victory in war we must practice democracy in our race relations." And in two post-war books, *American Argument* and *Friend to Friend*, she discusses the same subject with the wife of famous Negro artist, Paul Robeson, and with Carlos Romulo, the Philippine Ambassador to the United States. Both candidly, but without rancor, discuss America's alliances with colonial powers and explain the colored races' distrust of whites.

In *Talk about Russia* Pearl Buck and a Russian woman, married to a *Time Magazine* correspondent, discuss Russian and American customs and activities, comparing their advantages and disadvantages. The book was hailed by some as "the only objective book yet written about Russia," while others saw it as subtle Communist propaganda. This was neither the first nor the last time Pearl S. Buck was to run afoul of this label.

14

In 1945 Aline MacMahon, the celebrated film and Broadway actress, fell in love with a Pearl Buck story in *Asia Magazine*. Ten years before she had been cast briefly as O-lan in the film of *The Good Earth* only to be supplanted by Luise Rainer.

For some time she had wanted to produce a play and had now discovered a story that cried out to be dramatized. *"With My Daughter's Indian Family"* dealt with a young Indian scientist, his western wife and the girl's mother who lives with them in India. "I loved the story, they were three lovely people, and I was dying to play the mother," Aline MacMahon remembered. "I wrote to *Asia Magazine* to get an option on the play and picture rights, thinking I'd ask Maxwell Anderson to dramatize it. Instead Dick Walsh wrote back that his wife Pearl Buck would like to do it. I never dreamed of such a thing and of course it was irresistible.

"We set up a lunch. He and she came, and I took my husband. She was in a garnet red tweed suit with a matching sort of slouch hat. She was an impressive lady of size, quite open and very interested. My husband was quite a distinguished man, a town planner and architect, and she seemed interested in us and asked how I came to be investing in a play for myself. I explained that I had had so many wonderful breaks in life and was so happily married, and it seemed to be a nice next challenge. So we decided to go ahead.

"Pearl Buck was always *most* agreeable, there were never any problems, never a word. She would come to my apartment, she'd have a cup of tea with me and we'd talk about the most recent version of the play

. . . never any arguments. She sometimes took notes, and she'd go off and then—it seemed to me twenty-four hours later—she'd be back. She said if she was interested she'd write indefinitely, day or night, or both. It was like a juggernaut, it simply *poured* out of her.

"I'd been engaged as artist in residence at Stanford University and I thought we might try out the script there if we ever got one. I asked her if she'd come out and sit in on rehearsals because I knew she'd get an idea of theater that way, but she didn't have the time, she was doing too many other things.

"So we tried it out. The critics had a few kind words for it but they all agreed it just *wasn't a play*. When I came back I showed her the notices and she said, 'Oh yes, I see what they mean,' and she went back and wrote practically three new acts, and it was no better than before. But she wouldn't give up. So, trying to be nice, I thought of asking Moss Hart—he's absolutely the best in the world—to try to help her.

"He tried. We had about three conferences. And then finally, somewhat to my surprise, he said right out, 'Miss Buck, if I were a Nobel Prize novelist I don't think I'd try to write for the theater.'

"So that was that. The problem with her was she didn't really *listen* when you tried to tell her. There's a difference between *listening* and *hearing*. And she wouldn't take the time to learn. I gave her the chance. Had she come to Stanford and spent a month watching rehearsals the director could have said, 'You see what's missing here . . . what doesn't work there.' She could have worked with the actors and learned the way stage speech differs from eye speech. She'd have learned about *tension*, the things that make an audience sit up and listen and laugh and be concerned. That's all the things you don't have in the written novel. Well, that was the end. Miss Buck was very nice . . . I felt sorry for her. She tried so hard."

For a number of years Pearl Buck, trying hard to "write American," was both bewildered and distressed at her failure. She studied the bestseller lists angrily. "Think of that book of Dale Carnegie on influencing people selling and selling!" she had stormed to Grace, "Or a *Gone with the Wind* being considered a *great* novel!"

She and Walsh pondered the current market place and it may be that the success of *Gone with the Wind*, a regional novel about the America of a past era, stuck in their minds. At any rate in early 1940 they drove to Kansas purportedly to look up Walsh's birth certificate and visit his remaining relatives. They visited his Uncle John, now eighty-seven, who, at fifteen, had arrived from England with Walsh's mother and their parents. Pearl admired the sweet serenity of the old gentleman and listened for hours to his reminiscences of the early days in Kansas.

And the countryside attracted her—endless flat farmland like that of Nanhsuchou, and an enormous sky reaching down to the low horizon. "I could live here happily," she confessed, as she collected facts and scenes and anecdotes for a novel.

Pearl blamed her readers for their rejection of her American books— "their determination, sometimes loving, sometimes critical, to insist that there must be no other me than the one they had always known . . . the Asian one. . . ." If she wanted to embrace new worlds, she decided she must break free of that prejudice, and she chose a pseudonym, John Sedges, because "men have fewer handicaps in our society." And no one, *no one*, was to know of the plot.

The Townsman by John Sedges is the story of an immigrant family arriving in Kansas in the 1860s and the fifteen-year-old who became not the predictable gold miner, cattle baron or cowboy but, instead, a school teacher and town planner. These pioneers face blizzards, droughts, floods and tornados, but Jonathan (Uncle John) remains with the town when the rest of his family move westward, and as he grows the town steadily grows and prospers too.

Exciting without being melodramatic, peopled with credible characters, *The Townsman* achieved a richly deserved success. Pearl Buck had followed Margaret Mitchell's trail-blazer into a time and place just foreign enough not to require familiarity with contemporary speech and mores. Only at the end the author cannot refrain from repeating her peculiar failing, the introduction of a sudden romance to tie up loose ends.

A few critics speculated accurately on the author's real name and one or two found the novel dull and ponderous. But William McFee, who had ridiculed Pearl Buck's recent novels, on the front page of the *Chicago Tribune*'s Book Week dubbed it "A Regional Novel in the Best Sense of the Word, a Dynamic and Absorbing Portrait." And equally satisfying, the Literary Guild sent it out as its monthly selection (the editor having demanded to know the author's identity but promising to keep it secret).

The John Sedges ruse reassured Pearl about her writing. It also provided her with an alter ego permitting John Sedges to establish his own audience without poaching on Pearl S. Buck's preserves. Thus *The*

Townsman was published only six months before *Portrait of a Marriage.*

Pearl Buck's 1946 novel was considered one of her best, not only Chinese but subtly autobiographical. In *Pavilion of Women* she deserted peasant life for the luxurious household of an ancient aristocratic family untouched by western culture. Madame Wu, head of the sixty-member household, at forty, anxious to free herself from childbearing, buys a pretty peasant girl to replace her in her husband's bed. A brilliant woman, though illiterate, Madame Wu has her sons taught by an Italian priest, gaining an education of her own by listening in on the tutoring sessions.

Father Andre, though deeply spiritual, has been defrocked for providing the people with humanitarian services instead of ritualistic exercises. It is this philosophy, however, that brings Madame Wu under his spell. She is gradually made aware of her own selfish and cruel life, and she discovers that she is in love with him—she, a married woman and he a foreign priest.

After going to the aid of a stranger who is being assaulted, Andre is killed. Mourning him Madame Wu becomes convinced that his spirit is closer to her than it could ever have been in life. She lives now only to carry on his good works, positive that he and she, though separated by worldly barriers, will meet in the hereafter. Her new happiness and fulfillment are evident in the last lines of the novel: "Yes, she now believed that when her body died her soul would go on. Gods she did not worship and faith she had none, but love she had and forever. Love alone had awakened her sleeping soul and made it deathless.

"She knew she was immortal."

Even through a thick veil of fictional symbolism a good deal can be discerned about Pearl Buck. The spirit of the poet Hsu Chih-mo is still apparently very much in her thoughts fifteen years after his death. A teacher whom she revered—a man from whom she was barred by racial difference, marriage, and finally death—is present in this novel. Even his name, Chi-mo, is bestowed upon one of Madame Wu's sons, and the son's death mirrors that of the real Hsu Chih-mo.

Pavilion of Women became one of Pearl Buck's most popular novels, a Literary Guild selection, and her second biggest seller after *The Good Earth.* It is colorfully written in a modified and graceful *Good Earth* style. Some critics were put off by the "sentimentality" of Madame Wu's conversion, and some Chinese experts regarded the novel as a westernized picture of Chinese life, in that a "soul" in China is simply a ghost and love is irrelevant or nonexistent in marriage.

Unfortunately, the author's usually fertile imagination failed her again toward the end as she introduced a brand new character and a series of unbelievable coincidences to wind up her story. Nevertheless, *Pavilion of Women* reestablished her immense popularity.

After *Pavilion of Women* Pearl Buck decided to rest and let John Sedges take over. Within a year *The Angry Wife* appeared. Undistinguished except for its intriguing title, it is, in reality, a textbook tale of racial intolerance after the Civil War. Two white brothers on opposite sides in the fighting represent the Southern and Northern positions on racial questions. But they, and the beautiful mulatto sisters with whom they are romantically involved are mere symbols rather than flesh and blood characters.

Eight months after publication of *The Angry Wife* Pearl Buck revamped her research for *Flight into China* into fictional form. *Peony* could not be labeled a failure, since even the author's lesser works could be depended on to sell thirty-five or forty thousand copies, but neither was it a blockbuster.

Her next novel was *Kinfolk*, clearly modeled from life. While Dr. Liang is not an actual portrayal of Lin Yutang, it could conceivably be called a very good caricature. Sterling North, the *New York Post* critic, wrote, "In one of the most devastating portrayals in modern fiction, Pearl Buck has gently boiled in oil Dr. Liang ... who makes his living by lecturing ... upon the celestial wisdom of Confucius. The principal action takes place in New York, Shanghai, Peking, and Dr. Liang's native village. All four of his American-born children for varying reasons return to a China they have never seen and about which they know little save the roseate fiction spun by their escapist father. Two of the children find their calling as teacher and doctor in their ancestral village where they meet one of Pearl Buck's most richly drawn characters, old Uncle Tao, with his belly and belches and tumor preserved in a glass jar.

"Pearl Buck," North went on, "has seldom before achieved satire. Most of her books have been notably lacking in humor. But with *Kinfolk* she has reached a new peak of instructive entertainment which balances romantic story-telling and social significance with sly malice toward the ancient enemy, the male sex."

Even during this prolific writing period Pearl Buck's interest in China never waned, and she was acutely aware of that country's vulnerability.

After Japan's defeat in 1945, the Communists hurried to fill the vacuum by seizing Manchuria and occupying Northeast China. And now the two Chinese factions carried on their own private war for control of their ravaged country.

American sentiment was strongly in favor of the anti-Communist Chiang and their support of him continued. But he became the loser and finally, in January 1949, the formation of the Central People's Government of the People's Republic of China was announced to the world. As the Communists swarmed into his headquarters, Chiang, poised for flight, took off for Taiwan. There were now two Chinas, each claiming vociferously to be the only one.

Subsidized by Moscow the Chinese Communists began a program of land reform, breaking up estates and confiscating private properties. British investments, worth $800 million, as well as American holdings, were seized and nationalized. "Foreign devils" were driven from the land; international relationships were severed, and mainland China, as a nation, turned its back on the world.

In 1944 the United States had sent four young members of the State Department to China to assess the new leader, Mao Tse-tung, as a possible partner. John Peyton Davies, John Stuart Service, Raymond Ludden and John Emmerson visited Mao and Chou En-lai in their cave houses in Yenan, observing their guerrilla tactics at the same time they broadcast weather information for the U.S. planes bombing Japan. Impressed by their Communist hosts' efficiency, they advised the United States to cooperate with them.

President Roosevelt then sent General Patrick Hurley to negotiate a truce between Chiang and Mao and to authorize a United States treaty with both. Hurley wanted Chiang as Commander of the combined forces, but the four diplomats, possessing first-hand knowledge, recommended Mao, with the result that Truman, having taken over the reins after Roosevelt's death, asked Hurley's advice. Hurley was convinced the young diplomats, tainted by contact with the Communists, were probably Communists themselves.

After Chiang had fled to Taiwan in 1949 and America had "lost" China to the Reds, the four diplomats, along with Owen Lattimore and others who had explained the facts on the current China as they knew them, were remembered as having backed the enemy, accused of disloyalty and subversion and dismissed in disgrace. Stirred up largely by the "Free China" lobby, the Red scare, sponsored by Senator Joseph McCarthy, infiltrated America.

Pearl Buck tried to do what she could. An early admirer of Chiang Kai-shek, she had later come to recognize his weaknesses. And she considered the United States' support of Taiwan a shortsighted policy; Mainland China, Communist or not, was still the home of millions of Chinese, and only ill could come if the United States turned its back on them.

In articles and speeches she begged America to keep the channels open to the Chinese people. Trade with the Communists was, she insisted, the best hope of reaching and influencing them. Thus by making the Chinese government dependent on American rather than Russian trade, friendly feelings could conceivably penetrate the propaganda.

"Britain," she observed, "follows this policy. But we Americans think that recognizing a government means approving it, which is straining at gnats and swallowing camels. The new government will be driven to providing the necessities of life to its people and they will get them where they can." Citing a new railroad being built between Russia and China, she warned, "It is now Russia who will supply these necessities. So our only hope is that Russia will show her evil side to China and will thus arouse resentment in the Chinese people."

For her common-sense views Pearl Buck received her share of martyrdom. She had, she now learned, first raised the eyebrows of a few Red-baiters in 1943. At the request of Roger Baldwin of the American Civil Liberties Union, of which she was a vice-chairman, she had testified before a California Senate Committee against the United States' confiscation of Nisei-owned farmlands. Six years later the California Un-American Activities Committee under its Chairman Republican Senator Tunney solemnly presented to the news syndicates a list of dangerous persons who as Red appeasers had for a long time been following the Communist party line.

Dated June 8, 1949, Sacramento, California, the item ran on the front pages of a number of newspapers. Headlined over photographs of Fredric March and Florence Eldridge the list contained the following names: Larry Adler, Pearl S. Buck, Charles Chaplin, Norman Corwin, Bartley Crum, Helen Gahagan Douglas, Paul Draper, John Garfield, Florence Eldridge, John Huston, Danny Kaye, Gene Kelly, Ring Lardner, Jr., John Howard Lawson, Canada Lee, Dr. Thomas Mann, Fredric March, Burgess Meredith, Clifford Odets, Dorothy Parker, Larry Parks, Gregory Peck, Vincent Price, Paul Robeson, Edward G.

Robinson, O. John Boggs, Artie Shaw, Frank Sinatra, Gale Sonder-gard, Lionel Stander, Donald Ogden Stewart, Orson Welles, Katharine Hepburn, Dashiell Hammett, Lena Horne, Langston Hughes, plus others less well known.

Pearl Buck's reply was swift and stinging: "I want to do more than merely deny that I am or have ever been sympathetic to Communism. I am anti-Communist to the last drop of my blood. As a loyal and enthusiastic American I say that the present activities of a few Ameri-cans are making our country a laughing stock for the whole world. Other peoples are amazed. They are asking if we are a nation of fools, with this silly, wholesale accusation now being made against random persons high and low. I hope this folly has now mounted to such fantastic heights that it may stir healthy-minded Americans to rise up and put a stop to it."

Her hopes were not immediately granted. For several years whiffs of the same bad odor floated across her path—a cancellation of a speech at a high school or an editorial in a vigorously virtuous newspaper—but undeterred, she gained the eventual satisfaction of seeing the accused persons publicly vindicated and some U.S. senators relieved of their offices.

By the year 1949 Pearl Buck could bring her daughter Carol home for an occasional visit without the usual heartache. "I have lost all sense of my own flesh," she told a friend. "I feel toward her as tenderly as ever but I am no longer torn—just resigned, I suppose. Agony has become static. I will not allow it to move in me."

She had often had Carol visit the Walsh home, but the Vineland staff reported her always disturbed and difficult after the bustle of the large family, so eventually her mother bought a small isolated house on the Jersey shore and took her there to be alone with her, apparently unable to accept defeat. Finally, she gave even that up. But she con-tinued pouring money into research wherever it was being carried out.

Also in 1949 she forced herself to undertake something unthinkable up to this point. At the Training School she heard of a case even more heartbreaking than her own—a young couple, having adopted a baby girl, later learned she was retarded but, still loving her, kept her for life. "Pearl was tremendously impressed," said a woman who knew her well, "I never saw her more moved—here were two really heroic people. I think this made her realize how much one was helped by knowing about others with the same trouble. It may have been what inspired her to write about hers."

At any rate, Pearl quietly and without fanfare wrote the article, "The Child Who Never Grew" and submitted it to the Goulds, editors of the *Ladies Home Journal.*

Its publication there caused a sensation. In opening the door on herself she opened the door for thousands of other suffering parents. Letters poured in describing her readers' problems and their relief at realizing they were not alone. So many requests for reprints arrived that the article was eventually published in book form with all royalties going to the Vineland Training School.

Some months after publication the John Day Company received a letter from a training school in Michigan. "We have received by parcel post a copy of *The Child Who Never Grew* with a card inside reading 'from Carol.' We did not order this book. Will you check your mailing list and advise us to whom we should send it?"

On checking, the company came across a letter from Mrs. Sam McMeekin of Louisville, Kentucky. Enclosed was a check, a list of mental institutions and the request that a copy of the book be sent anonymously to every institution on the list.

Research into Carol's disease had been in progress for some years and finally, many years later, Pearl would be able to write to Emma: "Let me tell you that Carol is very much alive and in fact is unusually well. The eczema which plagues her life seems to have abated for some reason. While I am speaking of her, I must tell you that we have at last discovered what makes her condition. She has phenylketonuria, (PKU). This is an inherited inability to absorb essential proteins. Its presence is discovered through the urine. It is not present in my side of the family, for we have all had tests made. Her father has two normal children, and I suppose that there must be a recessive gene somewhere in my side so that the result is something like the Rh factor. Carol seemed entirely normal at birth and for several months thereafter. This is usual in such a case, for the doctors say that the mother's elements protect the child for the first months after birth. In Carol's case I noticed changes about the sixth month, or rather my mother did.

"If the cause had been discovered in time, she could have been given injections of concentrated proteins and would have grown up entirely normal, although the injections would have had to be continued throughout her life. But after a year, it is too late. Doctors are now trying to get hospitals to make these tests on babies after the first few months in order to prevent brain damage."

After the magazine article and book appeared Pearl became accustomed to finding young couples on her doorstep holding a retarded child by the hand. This was an intrusion the busy author never resented; she asked them in, brought out toys kept especially for the purpose, and sat and talked quietly with the parents. Always they said it helped to talk with someone who understood.

About this time Pearl Buck embraced another cause. She described her new interest in a magazine article, "From time to time during the fifteen years I have lived in this farmhouse . . . I have received letters from unknown persons asking me to find somehow a place for a certain little homeless child . . . perhaps some Asian family who might be willing to adopt the child." She instinctively sensed that it would be a child of mixed blood, Asian and American, whom neither whites nor blacks would adopt. At Christmastime 1948, a letter arrived from an adoption agency mentioning the fifteen-month-old child of an American missionary daughter and a young East Indian. The girl's family had brought her to America but insisted on putting her son out for adoption. The agency, unable to place the child and aware of Pearl Buck's stand on racial matters, wrote to ask her help.

"We had thought our family was finished," Pearl wrote. "But I read the letter to the children. It said that unless we could find an adoptive home for the child he would be placed in a Negro orphanage. 'What shall we do?' I asked the children. . . . 'What shall we do?' I asked the father of the family.

"'It doesn't seem right to let him go to that orphanage,' he said. 'We must do whatever we think right.'

"Our smallest child, a blue-eyed brown-haired daughter, crept into my room one night. 'Mother, we will have to take that baby or I won't have a good time this Christmas,' she said."

David arrived, brought one night by strangers and Pearl undressed him and put him into a cot brought down from the attic and sat beside a child so frightened he could not cry.

Perhaps because of her acceptance of David, a second child arrived during that same Christmas. In a nearby hospital a child had been born to a Chinese surgeon and an American nurse. "I knew my husband and I were too old to take infants," Pearl told a friend, "so I called adoption agencies and told them of these two beautiful children. Everywhere I was faced with the same answer, they could not place these children because they could not match parents. I was indignant so I started my own agency."

Thus out of Pearl Buck's anger and frustration Welcome House came into existence. And that was the Christmas that served as the model for Pearl Buck's Christmas story, *Nineteen Stockings by the Chimney Piece*, the Christmas when the four adolescents were still at home, there was no war and all was well.

After the decision to keep the babies, she realized she had a battle on her hands she could not wage alone. Her one friend in the area, other than the farmers and tradespeople, was Margaret Fischer, the wife of Kermit Fischer, a Philadelphia industrialist. The Fischers had two adopted children whom the Walsh children played with at school, and Pearl knew Margaret to be an experienced organizer well versed in social work, both volunteer and professional.

"Margaret," she told her friend, "I can't sleep at night for thinking about these half-American babies being born here in the United States and nobody doing anything about them. Social work agencies can't place them because they don't fit into any neat pigeon-hole and I want to know what's going to happen to them."

Pearl and Margaret had already discussed the harm done children placed in temporary foster homes and moved again and again. "We decided," Mrs. Fischer said, "that something better must be found. That, really, was the genesis of Welcome House—to give the babies a permanent foster home with two parents and sisters and brothers, a real family relationship.

"First of all we had to sell our husbands on helping us. Both men refused. Richard contended he and Pearl were too old to start such a project but Pearl persisted. She said, 'Margaret, you work on Kermit and I'll work on Dick.' So she invited us to a cosy dinner and turned on the charm. She said, 'Kermit, you're world-minded. You're starting a business in different parts of the world all the time and it'll be good for relationships of Americans with the East.' And she said to Dick, 'I've chosen you two men because you have a world outlook. Kermit and Margaret are younger than you and I, they have the energy, and I know that together we four can make it.' So the men gave in."

Margaret Fischer recognized that social work demanded a board of directors. The Fischers knew the David Burpees of Burpee's Seeds fame who lived in Doylestown, and Lois Burpee was a missionary's daughter with energy, ideas and a social conscience. Margaret Fischer invited the Burpees to join them.

Pearl thought of Oscar Hammerstein, who had an estate nearby. Hammerstein, well-known lyricist and producer of *Oklahoma* and other successful musicals and known as one of the best-loved men on Broadway, was also active in the Authors League where Pearl Buck had met him.

"Out of the blue," Dorothy Hammerstein recalled, "Pearl Buck invited us over for dinner. She brought out this handsome little half-Indian boy she wanted to get adopted. At first Oscar thought she wanted us to take him and he thought we had enough children already, but she only wanted us to help. So we went along."

Also among the new recruits was a minister whose book John Day had published, and so with Dr. and Mrs. Frederick Stamm, Welcome House had a board of directors and was ready to function.

At first Pearl visualized a warm and motherly woman to run it, but Mrs. Fischer advocated a typical home set-up—the husband going off to work, the wife staying home with the children. And not too many children, never more than nine. A house was bought near the Walsh farm with a mortgage and a Mennonite couple was found. Lloyd Yoder, a schoolteacher, and Viola, his pleasant wife, had two sons nearly old enough to leave home, so the set-up seemed perfect. "The whole thing," Mrs. Fischer recalled, "seemed almost preordained."

In April the house was formally opened with two baby boys in residence, one Eurasian, the other Chinese. "Our own children are good with them," Pearl told a friend, "and it has been a fine thing to have them—it's decentralized the children, so to speak."

Welcome House was incorporated in the Court of Common Pleas in Bucks County, Pennsylvania, and a social worker engaged to oversee its operation. By the end of 1949 six children of mixed blood lived there, and as time went on more children arrived, some older.

"Then we had another baby," Margaret Fischer remembered, "one we had no place for. Pearl was speaking one night to a group of people in Bucks County and she said, 'Isn't there anybody in this audience willing to take a lovely baby with yellow skin and slanting eyes?' Afterwards a young Presbyterian minister came forward and said they would love to take him but he was fresh out of theological seminary and didn't know if they could support it. They were so right for this baby that contrary to all good social work practice the group subsidized them, fifteen dollars a week.

"We had to raise money, of course, so we had small fund-raising affairs and started a thrift shop in Doylestown and people were coming forward with contributions. Some big names came on the board, Judge and Mrs. Biester, and the Burpees and the James Micheners, and of course the Hammersteins.

"All the board worked very hard raising money. Pearl Buck went around speaking and Dorothy Hammerstein gave a tremendous fashion show and gala on the lawn of their beautiful place. There was a prize and raffle, and Jane Pickens sang and Kitty Carlisle modeled the clothes.

"Kermit even got his employees interested. It was very touching, Kermit and I always exchanged Christmas cards with every employee—about a thousand—and at Christmas we found money and checks in lots of the cards.

"Pearl was a wonder. It took her a lot of time writing thank you notes for contributions. But you know, this was the first time she had ever moved out among the neighbors. Everyone had always thought she was very stand-offish, but I think she really enjoyed this. It was her sort-of coming out into the community."

After *The Ladies Home Journal* published Pearl Buck's article in December 1950 about the arrival of the children, adoption agencies wrote to offer children. Parents also began to ask for children. Many wrote, "We have always wanted to do something meaningful with our lives. Perhaps this is it."

"But," Lois Burpee stated, "we were amateurs, and state laws were very strict. They had always insisted a child had to match the adopting couple in religion and race and appearance—blue eyes for blue-eyed parents, and so on—and the final decision whether you can have a child or not rests with a judge, who may have very prejudiced notions. Pearl went to the mat over those laws. She distrusted social workers, said they like to play God, often holding back a child on some technicality just to keep themselves in work.

"When these crowds of babies began appearing, needing homes, we all worked very hard. Pearl and Kermit Fischer, and sometimes Pearl and I, went to the State Welfare Department in Harrisburg to try to get ourselves accredited. She did most of the brainwork. She is a great student, she studies whatever she goes into, so she got a directory of foundations that give grants, found out their particular interest and that way raised money.

"One of our constant worries always was paying off the mortgage on the Yoder house, but a nice thing happened. Oscar Hammerstein was president of Welcome House, and on his sixtieth birthday Richard Rodgers, the composer who had worked on so many shows with Oscar, celebrated it by paying off the Welcome House mortgage."

"Welcome House has prospered through the years," said Margaret Fischer, "because we were careful to obey all the laws. When more children came than our own homes could take we found other homes and sent them directly there after our social worker, along with Pearl or Mrs. Biester or someone, had investigated the place. Serving the public this way we had to meet many legal requirements and sometimes Pearl got pretty impatient. But she was always diplomatic with lawmakers, and I can say now that adoption laws nowadays are considerably more liberal in this country directly because of her.

"We had started, of course, with Asian-American children born in this country. Then when we enlarged our charter we were empowered to place half-black children as well as Asian-Americans. So then we were really serving the whole community."

In 1949, after the inauguration of Welcome House, to get away from the ragweed pollen, Pearl and Walsh drove to New England. A book on maple sugaring published by John Day had excited Pearl's curiosity and its author, Scott Nearing, had invited them to visit him in Vermont.

The beauty of the green hills, much like the mountains of Kuling, and the sparkling pure air, gave Pearl more than a pleasant weekend to mill over. Here, she thought, might her three adolescent boys find plenty of useful and harmless ways to keep busy during the summers. She bought several acres of land at two dollars an acre.

They made their plans for the following summer. The boys would build a stone and cement house under the supervision of a local man, Richard Gregg. Three miles in from the road along a path favored by bears, they would build a structure of stone, laying floors and setting windows, meanwhile camping out in an old schoolhouse. There would be two weeks of roughing it, alternating with one week at home for decent food and a bath.

The following year, impressed with the results, Pearl bought a second old house with wide acreage nearer the road and installed running water and a kerosene stove.

Janice, now an independent young woman, visited the campers, remarking afterwards, "Mother was really a pretty good sport. The first summer she had pumped water by hand and cooked in a fireplace. She had done it all herself long before and thought kids should know how to survive without conveniences." In time both houses were furnished with the basic amenities, but a pleasant sense of the simple life lingered on.

Three months was not too long to stay in the beneficial atmosphere of Jamaica, Vermont, but soon Pearl's work demanded the attention of a local secretary, and an inquiry led her to a young couple who had recently settled nearby. Jackie Breen, doing her housework one hot afternoon, looked out her window to see a long black chauffeur-driven limousine. "This very impressive couple walked up the driveway," she recalled. "She was rather portly, and the husband was very youthful looking—he had a crew cut and it gave him a kind of flair." Somewhat nervously, she invited them in.

George and Jackie Breen had left Connecticut with their children to homestead on their sugar-maple property. He had practical outdoor experience, and his wife secretarial skills. By the end of their visit George had become Pearl Buck's general estate manager and Jackie her secretary.

Later Pearl bought still more acres on a mountain facing famous Stratton Mountain. This was to be her lifetime retreat from crowds and hay fever, and she laid out the plans for her dream house. It was to be high on the side of the mountain in an open space with its back nestled into the earth and windows on three sides. "You are crazy, ma'am," the builder said of the site selected. But the house went up as she planned, with a road slashed through the woods and huge logs cut for the beams. Jackie Breen supervised the decorating according to Pearl's instructions, every detail from the size of the fireplace stones to the color of the walls.

In a quarterly newsletter written and mimeographed by the young Bucks with some help from their elders, appeared an essay entitled "Our Vermont House," a portion of which read: "As most of the family knows, we have been building a house in Vermont for three years and it is now completed. It is one mile from the road. The walk in is quiet and runs along a stream, good for drinking if you get dry. The house itself is built of stone. It is forty-nine feet by twelve feet with a wing for a bathroom and an office. The big room is a kitchen, a bedroom and a living room. This room's walls are old barn siding.

weathered silver. The roof, which comes to a point, is of Nature's own coloring, a beautiful brown. There are two big fireplaces, one at each end. The fireplace at the east end has a crane for cooking. We have visitors from old Mother Nature, some friendly, but some of Nature's hoodlums hang around this neck of the woods, such as bear, lynx, wildcats and porcupines."

Whether the Buck children's literary parents hoped for second-generation authors is unclear, but both Pearl Buck and Walsh believed writing could be taught. Pearl, always patient and generous with young writers, gave a course in novel writing at Columbia University in the hope of discovering literary talent. And she and Walsh made several scouting trips for authors throughout the East and Midwest. (It was, after all, on just such a trip south that Macmillan's editor Harold Latham was given the manuscript of *Gone with the Wind*.) In 1951, while Pearl Buck lectured on "Chinese Cultural Civilization," Walsh interviewed students of creative writing and managers of bookstores.

Even Pearl Buck once had enrolled in a writing course. Approached by the government to write a few scripts for broadcasts to China, she had taken Erik Barnouw's well-known course at Columbia University.

"Out of the blue (it may have been 1941 or 1942) I received a phone call asking me to have lunch at the *Asia Magazine* office with Pearl Buck and her husband, Richard Walsh," Barnouw wrote in a letter. "It was in a small private dining room. After minimal preliminary, she said she would like to enroll in my class on radio writing. Would this be possible? I was flabbergasted and said it would, yes. (By the way, I had never met her before this.)

"She hoped she could attend the class without it creating a special fuss. It was decided she would register as Mrs. R. Walsh and hope for the best. She did enroll and attended regularly and punctiliously. She usually entered just before class time, wearing a hat that came down over her eyes somewhat, and promptly went to a seat near the rear. She handed in work on schedule. I don't believe I discussed any of her work in class, but wrote a page or two of comment on everything she turned in. The comments, as you may guess, were usually of a technical nature, relating to the medium. The following week (somewhat to my embarrassment) she would hand in a revision marked *corrected copy*. She was probably the most punctilious student I ever had."

This effort was two-pronged—to prepare herself for anything new that came along, and to keep the channels open between budding writers and John Day. Pearl Buck was unfailingly quick to spot unrecognized talent. The half-Japanese singer, Mary Tsuta Ohata Lombard, had been asked to do secretarial work for Pearl after the East and West Association was dissolved. Her first day on the job, she wrote her employer a memo: MTL-PSB: "I told Mr. Walsh today that, at the risk of making some wild suggestions, I should like to jot down ideas that come to me for possible books, articles, etc., as I think of them, then if they seem at all feasible I would be glad to do any of the legwork, research, correspondence, et al., necessary to explore further the possibilities. First, of course, I am making it my business to brief myself on every article you have written in the last five years or so."

The following day Tsuta sent to Pearl Buck, in Perkasie, another memo describing an exploratory meeting with the Lloyd agency people:

"(A) In re *Come My Beloved*. I detected in the Lloyds a genuine enthusiasm and interest. Difficulties in serialization of novels were carefully explained to me.

(B) In re Article on G.I. babies in Japan, which is now in *Look*'s hands, they feel it depends on the turn of political events. They think publicity breaking now should create demand for your article.

(C) In re television: I gather cost alone is not the stumbling block in finding sponsors. The old cry with which I know you are familiar, 'Pearl Buck has been associated in the public mind with the Far East and right now that is not good for TV appeal.' This shows how uninformed sponsors are. Meanwhile perhaps another type of TV should be the entering move.

(D) Article for *Rotarian*. You might consider an article on the contrast between East and West minds. They might take one on Welcome House if no fund-raising pitch."

Tsuta evaluated the general situation at the Lloyd office: "Some aspects of their thinking I like very much such as their policy of playing hard-to-get in the magazine field, never appearing over-anxious. I suppose this would be easier if you weren't so prolific as well as being in the top class. I believe however that regular, persistent nagging, which I could do gracefully, would help. I was glad to have them suggest that I meet with them regularly. Weekly conferences would not be amiss."

A later memo from Tsuta read: "I discussed with Miss Lloyd the subject of non-fiction articles. I think it's most important once in a while, without taking away too much time from your valuable fiction writing, for you to get in your licks in the molding of public opinion.

"Idea for John Day book: A book with two distinguished scientists, one in the physical science and one in the biological, to clarify the issues to laymen. You could handle it brilliantly. It would be such a service to a scientist to have you put into human terms the problems about which he is usually inarticulate."

After this evidence of Tsuta's initiative and drive, she was officially designated as Pearl's personal representative. She did indeed run interference in countless personal affairs, even minute ones: "Note re your luncheon date. Don't forget that this is St. Patrick's Day. The streets will be jammed. Better plan just to walk from the office to the Harvard Club, only a block away, rather than to try to go by taxi."

Pearl S. Buck came to lean on Tsuta gratefully, although perhaps unwisely rejecting one of Tsuta's ideas for promotion: "Oct 2, 1954, PSB to Tsuta: I have watched the Dave Garroway Today show and I have decided it is not worth doing. He is now featuring a monkey named J. Fred Muggs. While the monkey is very clever indeed, still I am not sure he adds dignity to the program. Besides, I am not convinced that television sells books. Those morning programs are not looked at by serious people. Dave Garroway just fills up time which nobody else wants."

Tsuta's anxiety about taking Pearl's time away from her fiction-writing proved to be groundless. Between 1949 and 1953 Pearl Buck turned out seven books, one non-fiction, *The Child Who Never Grew*, and six novels, three by John Sedges and three under her own name, *Kinfolk, God's Men* and *The Hidden Flower*.

The Sedges fiction, which she called her "summer novels," were not in the class of the original Sedges book *The Townsman. The Long Love* is about a "completely happy marriage," a simple tale which Fanny Butcher of the *Chicago Tribune* described as a "rare, sweet, gentle, tender book."

In *Bright Procession* Stephen Worth, the son of a minister, is drawn to the less sanctified calling of public relations but still finds, in the end, that he must follow the star of his minister father.

Voices in the House is a short, lightweight novel about the inner life of a good man. He is bewildered by the tough younger generation, but before the story ends he has achieved a kind of compromise between middle age and youth.

During the war Pearl had also written a number of articles for the *New York Times Magazine*, some at the editor's specific request, others because he had once told Walsh, "If Mrs. Walsh has any cosmic things on her mind we should like to hear about them." In response to the latter suggestion the April 28, 1943, issue of the magazine featured a piece, "We Need Most of All the World View," subtitled "Let America Take the Lead in World Action in Terms of Supplying World Needs."

In the article the author attacked her country head-on. "We are at this moment the most hated and the most feared of all nations"— feared because of the dropping of the bomb, and hated "because we are rich and well-fed while most of the world is starving, and also because of Americans touring or stationed abroad who rape and loot and show off our wealth." She reminded her readers of the Asian countries' former reverence for George Washington and Abraham Lincoln and their belief in American idealism, and she mourned their disappointment, looking at the "world leadership America assumes simply because the war had left her rich and strong while they were left in ruins." She cited the atmosphere in Washington wherein a government dignitary, when approached by an Indian official for food for his country, refused it on the grounds that India, after all, was not "in the war-devastated zone." This warm-hearted gentleman stated, "Even a dog lover has to decide which puppies he will keep." Is this, she asked, the best world leadership has to offer?

What the world needed, she felt, was a leadership able to offer not just sporadic charity but cooperation capable of preventing revolutions, a world leadership of administrations displaying supra-national orientation. Only under that kind of wise direction could countries be supplied with the two most important necessities, food and oil.

Starvation, she said, was already recognized as a present fact. On the other hand, oil, though plentiful in 1943, had the potential for a world crisis as the demand increased in the future. "America," she warned, "with its greedy overconsumption, must start considering the rest of the world before it is too late."

Unfortunately the book in which she expressed these thoughts was not well enough written to prove as memorably influential as an *Uncle Tom's Cabin*. *God's Men* sold well, as all her books continued to do, and almost by habit was taken by a book club, but the critics were baffled. They agreed on the importance of her message, but the heavy-handed presentation of it put them off. Like a medieval morality play the characters tended to arrive on stage labeled Greed and Hypocrisy, Vision and Strength.

Evil is represented by a ruthlessly ambitious missionary's son and modeled with remarkable exactitude on Pearl's famous contemporary in the news-magazine field, while Good supposedly represents the Los Angeles restaurateur, president of "Meals for Millions" who instituted a program that produced nourishing food costing only three cents a meal. The novel does contain wonderful scenes of the two boys' childhood in China, but as adults the magazine magnate and the crusading philanthropist are tightly drawn, their dialogue artificial and many incidents transparently contrived.

The Hidden Flower by Pearl Buck is the story of a Japanese girl and an American soldier who marry in a Buddhist ceremony before going to his home in Virginia. There his parents oppose the union, viewing "miscegenation" as a family disgrace, and when it is discovered that Virginia's laws actually forbid such marriages the young man's love for his wife is severely tested.

Finding herself pregnant, the girl leaves without telling her husband and when the baby is born, she puts him up for adoption. A woman doctor, single and compassionate, takes the child for her own. With the upbeat ending Pearl Buck makes a touching plea for all such "world children."

Reviewing the novel critic Elizabeth Janeway commented on what she saw as Pearl S. Buck's reduced standing in the literary community. Her kind of optimism and moral conviction, plus her concern with average people in average situations was deemed declasse in the worlds of fellow writers such as William Faulkner and Paul Bowles. Janeway was very much aware in 1952 that Pearl Buck's support was derived mainly from the middle-class woman in her millions, the woman whom H. L. Mencken had called an idiot. But Janeway had a good word for her. "She is not an idiot. If our mores are changing in the direction of tolerance; if our knowledge of the world is broadening, it is she who is accepting the change. It is vital to communicate with this woman, for if literature had first of all the duty of reflecting life truly (I don't mean photographically), it has the second duty of presenting this reflection to as large an audience as possible. For twenty years Miss Buck has done this. It is an excellent thing that she continues to do it so well."

But book critics derived only what they saw revealed in an author's work. They did not speculate on Pearl Buck's literary reputation had her publisher shown less complacency or if he had insisted on higher standards of literary performance—or if he had rejected stereotyped characterizations and plots and contrived solutions—publishing only the best of which she was capable.

On the other hand, however, if Pearl Buck had perfected only the books of real importance, she would have earned less money with which to support her other projects. It is interesting to speculate on which, given a choice, she would have chosen.

15

In the ten years since Pearl had written the *New York Times* article exhorting the United States to develop a world consciousness she had mellowed in her view of her country. In 1953, writing in *My Several Worlds*, she observed, "The advance in our national thinking since the end of the Second World War should pacify and encourage even the most exacting and loving of critics. In spite of mistakes I see the American spirit reaching new levels of common sense and enlightenment. We are already beginning to give up our destructive prejudices in color, creed and nationality, and we are no longer so boastfully sure that we can lead the world.

"We are not empire builders. How important this fact is no American who has not lived in Asia can appreciate. It goes against our conscience, which is a very tender part of the American spirit. I am therefore hopeful; in spite of dismaying contradictions I feel the controlling spirit of our people generous, decent and sane."

In this mood she finished *My Several Worlds*, the book about her life. Shortly thereafter the whole family set off on a trip they had long dreamed of and planned. Along with their luggage, each member took pads and pencils to make notes for their Green Hills Farm newsletter. Those signed R. J. W. were featured on the front page.

"On August 10 we set out for the longest family trip we have ever taken. There were seven of us in the car, with Mr. Ottinger driving. On top of the car, in racks, was most of our luggage. In the trunk were a refrigerator, a Coleman stove (operated by the boys), a folding table for picnic use, and lots of food, which we replenished by daily stops at supermarkets. PSW cooked hot meals including breakfasts, and she and Jean washed dishes each evening, when we stopped at motels. One of the strong impressions of the trip is the excellence of the motels, many of them new or improved this year. By telephoning ahead we invariably had a stopping place reserved, and never once did they fail us, even when on one occasion we rolled in at nearly midnight. (Here we had telegraphed ahead with a deposit of ten dollars.)

"We made high speed, beginning on the Pennsylvania Turnpike, across Ohio, Indiana, Illinois, Iowa and South Dakota. As we drew near to the Rocky Mountains we realized that we had planned too long and too fast a trip. Arrived in Sheridan, Wyoming, we revised our route and schedule. Being so near to Yellowstone Park and the Continental Divide, we sent the children and Mr. Ottinger on in the car, while PSW and I settled down for a rest. We hope to have in this issue an article by one of the children on Old Faithful and other features of Yellowstone."

He continued his account of a week at the IXL Ranch after which they drove home via Montana, Wisconsin, Michigan and then back to Vermont. "We stayed in Vermont for two more weeks. There was no hay fever there at all which means that in the future years it will be our annual refuge at this season."

While in Sheridan, Wyoming, however, Richard Walsh's physical condition began to worry the family. "Such a little blow it had seemed at the time," Pearl wrote later. "No more than a mild heat stroke, we thought. It had been a comfortable and happy time, all of us in a big air-conditioned car driven by our tried and true chauffeur. 'The trip will be good for him,' our family doctor had said, 'if he does not do the driving.'

"So it had seemed until that sunny day. The next day we were to go on to Yellowstone. Instead he and I stayed at the pleasant IXL Ranch House while the children went on and came back and we all went home, still thinking it was nothing, but that we had better go home. The Sheridan doctor had not been quite sure it was a heat stroke. Later we knew it was not. But he seemed as well as ever, as vigorous, still carrying on his busy life in the New York offices and in the country office at home."

After a series of check-ups in New York, Walsh was put on decoagulants. One side of his face had become somewhat drawn and his speech a little slurred, but after two weeks he seemed back to normal. Then the sight in one eye began to fail, a blow because it interfered with his reading. Month after month, slowly his health deteriorated, but he never complained, patiently sorry to give so much trouble.

At times he seemed better but then would slip back. Pearl watched over him carefully and Tsuta and Dick, Jr., were always alert for a call. In the summer of 1954 the Vermont house was completed. They had planned to spend the summer there but now feared being out of touch with the doctors for too long.

One weekend, however, they did drive up, having alerted the Breens, who had worked frantically to get everything ready. Ottinger drove them in the big limousine and at the appointed hour the four met at Mountain Haunt.

"We had been over at the house working since early morning," Jackie Breen recollected, "and we only just got the last decorating detail done half an hour before they were due. We rushed home and showered and got on our Sunday clothes. It was a beautiful day and we got back just before they arrived. When they got there we were shocked, Mr. Walsh was quite incapacitated and she had to help him through the doorway. They walked in and she looked around. She took a deep breath and let it out and said, 'It's *just* what I wanted.'"

That week-end, according to a letter Pearl wrote Emma the following November, was the only trip they took that fall. "In answer to your question . . . my new book is *My Several Worlds*. The book I am working on now is a novel about the old Empress Dowager. After that I rather imagine I shall turn to American subjects, but I am not sure.

"Welcome House is developing now into an adoption agency for American children, that is, children born in the United States but of Asian or part Asian ancestry. We have only the two houses—five children in one house and eight in the other. We can get all our babies adopted. We have a real waiting list of parents, I am glad to say. We always need money, however, and if you can ever influence anyone to send us some for this work I shall be grateful. We have placed about one hundred children. It is a great comfort to me to see them going into good homes.

"Dick was very ill this summer but he is now better. I was not able to go away for hay fever except over one weekend and was quite miserable. I hope we can manage better another year."

Pearl Buck's Welcome House had become an accredited agency for children of mixed blood born in the United States. But she was now distressingly aware of the thousands of abandoned children of American G.I.'s, wandering the streets of Japan and Korea—waifs with black hair and blue eyes or red hair and Oriental features, children with no families, no schooling and no hope. Author James Michener, returning from a trip to Asia, confirmed that there were thousands, homeless and officially nonexistent.

In 1925 Pearl had heard of a Japanese woman, the daughter of a wealthy Japanese industrialist, whose fortune had been confiscated but who had opened a home to receive the deserted children. On learning that Mrs. Miki Sawada was expected to arrive shortly in America to raise funds, Pearl asked to be notified of her arrival.

Miki Sawada remembered their first meeting. The Consul General of Japan told her that "Miss Pearlbuck" was waiting to see her. Pearl sent her car and chauffeur, and she spent the night in Perkasie. James Michener arrived after dinner, and they talked until two A.M. Mrs. Sawada told them the U.S. Army would not discuss the G.I. children, but that she had set up a school for the children, having received vocational training in England. She admitted being much impressed with Miss Pearlbuck, "very strong-minded woman, maybe stubborn like me."

Every year after that she returned. Many people she had known before the war now lived in the United States and they supported the school financially. This small, intense, humorous Miki Sawada kept Pearl informed on Asia's abandoned children, periodically flitting in and out on her fund-raising tours, always like "Miss Pearlbuck" stubborn and strong-minded. The two became fast friends.

Pearl's Welcome House had proved that Americans would eagerly adopt Amerasian babies born in America. So, Pearl asked, why not the thousands born in Asia of American fathers? Immigration laws, however, forbade their entering to the United States. The solution to the problem therefore would be to change the laws, a miracle not to be accomplished overnight. But if all means available were utilized— letters to congressmen, visits to senators, speeches to the public—it could come about.

Pearl Buck had already brought one G.I. baby into the country under her own auspices. Not long after the world began to consider adopting Amerasian children, an official of Howard University made an appeal to Pearl. He knew of a three-year-old child in Germany, the daughter of a Negro officer, the only dark-skinned child in the town, who was suffering cruelly from the taunts of the other children. Her German mother sadly agreed to send her some place where she would be less conspicuous.

This case did not fit Welcome House's charter and regretfully Pearl had to say no. But she could not forget a lonely child being jeered at for being the wrong color. This, she realized, was the very thing she had fought so long, and in her large house full of Caucasian children, all carefully selected, she unwittingly had practiced race discrimination.

She reconsidered. She was no longer young, but she and her husband were apparently healthy (this was two years before Walsh's health failed), and the other children were not always at home. So, in 1951, when she was fifty-nine and Walsh sixty-seven, they watched at the airport as a small, mulatto five-year-old walked down the steps of the plane clutching a ragged doll.

Young Henriette proved as strong-minded and stubborn as the white woman who took her home, speaking not a word of English and for many weeks refusing to become a member of the family. Rebellious and tense, rejecting friendly overtures, at Christmas, presented with a new doll, she accepted it in silence. Then while Pearl watched, the child took the clothes off the new doll, undressed her old one, the new clothes on it and threw the new doll away.

Gradually, Pearl's and her family's patience paid off, and they won the child's trust. She grew into a beautiful girl with a gracious personality. Years later, Pearl remarked, "Henriette is more like me than any of the others."

Henriette's memory of Walsh is a hazy one. As she grew older, he grew frailer, and she had little contact with a man who could scarcely speak. Much too young to be a companion for the other Buck children, she became an exquisite little loner whom Pearl taught to play chess and found to be an avid listener to adult conversation.

For Pearl these became the years of watching her husband decline, years of having to handle unfamiliar business matters and making difficult decisions alone, of inviting other escorts to affairs or else staying at home. No longer would there be Walsh's welcoming smile and outstretched hands for the ritual of receiving her new manuscript, or the gallant announcement, "This is a big day. I thank you."

"He is sweet and uncomplaining," she told a friend, "but the old sharing of thought and communication is gone. We sit in the same room and it is worse than if I were physically alone. . . . I went to see Carol last Friday and tried as usual to satisfy that childish heart in its need for love and communication. And then I came home to find my poor dear . . . waiting patiently for me. So different, so different . . ."

What lay ahead was all unkown. Janice, now twenty-eight, was working as an occupational therapist in an institution. The four teen-agers, with their own problems, were monumentally bored with Pearl's. Henriette, though companionable, was still a child. And Grace, the perfect companion, was accessible only by long distance.

There was of course much to do for Walsh. A male nurse was found and later a companion; still later a couple and round-the-clock nurses. Pearl read to him by the hour, Colette and Proust by preference, and he had the Talking Books. But for Pearl herself there was a strange emptiness.

She came to dread the evenings. Years ago during the Lindbergh kidnaping scare, she had developed an exaggerated distrust of strangers, so that now there was no close friend or neighbor to share a lonely evening when she was too tired for work and not tired enough for sleep.

When her business took her to New York, with no Walsh beside her, the apartment was equally desolate. So Pearl, being Pearl, decided to do something about it.

She had always played the piano, not well but with pleasure. Tsuta, now a treasured fixture in her life, had an Austrian accompanist of whom she was very fond, and happily Pearl arranged for piano lessons.

"She was a wonderful pupil," Alexander Itkis remembered, "obe-dient like I seldom saw somebody, always took two hour lessons, was never tired. She made *me* sometimes tired. At the beginning she didn't know very much, but after two years she played Chopin, and Beetho-ven's sonatas. Not the brilliant things, not the technique, but good."

Later she took up French, which she had studied in school. She met a young Parisienne, Eve Eshleman, to whom she confessed, "My French is getting as rusty as my Chinese. Would you mind if we had French conversation?" And they met weekly after dinner at Green Hills Farm.

Without Walsh to handle her public relations, she assumed that job as well. An extraordinarily handsome woman, with her hair piled high or worn low on her neck, she knew the power of her own beauty. From dodging photographers, she had graduated to seeking them out; the famous photographer Yousup Karsh was invited to Perkasie for a

sitting, and she ordered Tsuta to make an appointment with Editta
Scherman, another photographer, "in time for her exhibition in
March."

A co-worker reminisced affectionately, "She knew she was wonderfully photogenic, and she was an impossible ham. She absolutely
sensed whenever there was a camera around and you could see her
bracing for it. She always knew how to make a good picture."

Walsh's poor health had not in any way interrupted the steady flow
of her literary output. On their trip through Montana and Wyoming
she had collected notes along the route for the forthcoming *My Several
Worlds*, and within a week of their return a new novel was published.
Come My Beloved, though carelessly written, was important because
of its subject matter. The title suggests a love story, but its plot
examines through a four-generation family of missionaries the varying
motives and manifestations of missionary zeal.

Weary of Chinese background, she has shifted her locale to India
but otherwise the situation between the races is the same. David
MacArd, a wealthy, brash industrialist of the Andrew Carnegie-John
D. Rockefeller school, hungry for the kudos of good works, travels in
India where he is shocked by the filth, poverty and superstition. He
plans an immense seminary to substitute Christianity for paganism
and destroy the idols, close the temples and stimulate the people to
productive employment.

His son David, only passively interested before, suddenly opts for
the missionary life himself, which shocks his practical father into
dropping the entire enterprise. David, however, builds a huge theological seminary with his late mother's money. Living a life of ascetic
devotion he supports a faculty and student body of Christianized
Indians with the purpose of modernizing India with western
advantages.

His son Ted, after a Harvard education, returns to India. Exposed to
the saintly but dynamic simplicity of Gandhi he experiences a sudden
blinding illumination, and goes to live and teach in a primitive village.
Through prayer, precept and practice he regenerates first the village
and then the countryside, a missionary so sincere that he has reached a
completely effectual way of life through love for humanity.

The fourth generation is represented by Ted's daughter who has
grown up as an Indian among Indians. She falls in love with a young

Indian doctor and wants to marry him. But here the dynasty's religion collapses. Even the saintly Ted suddenly becomes aware of racial differences and, unable to override his unconsciously nurtured prejudice, drags his daughter off to America to escape the calamity of miscegenation.

Pearl explained her book to a correspondent: "I wanted to express my faith that one cannot achieve real religion unless one is willing to yield every last prejudice. The three men each had a noble idea but could not quite give up his prejudices. Thus I think that Christianity has never achieved its real potential because Christians have not been able to obey the principles expressed by its founder Jesus Christ."

In the novel she paid tribute to her familiar concern for race relations; but there are other facets that set the book apart despite its poor presentation. This is her first novel about missionaries, which, considering her background, is surprising; and its final episode with the missionary's daughter in love with an Indian doctor is a throwback to the first Welcome House baby.

Even more intriguing, however, is Ted's illuminated vision of the God-directed life; the writing has a ring of extraordinary conviction as if the author had either steeped herself in books such as William James's *Varieties of Religious Experience* or had at some time such an experience herself. If the latter is true, some of her later writings then become more comprehensible.

Come My Beloved had been finished a year before her husband's stroke, and Pearl had by then nearly finished *My Several Worlds*, which was published the following year to unqualified hosannas. As a commentary on her life it is enthralling, indeed even inspiring with its benign view of the world and the breadth of its scope. As an autobiography, however, it is needlessly, even irritatingly selective. Lossing Buck's name is never mentioned; to account for her child she acknowledges her husband as "the man in the house." Many of Pearl's friends were indignant at her treatment of this remarkable man, and this pretense of a solitary existence creates the illusion of a monolithic woman considerably larger than life performing, unassisted, miracles of achievement. On the whole, however, it is a portrait of courage, deserving of its enormous success.

Having met, in 1938 at the Nobel celebrations, Italian scientist Enrico Fermi, who had won the Prize for his work in nuclear physics,

Pearl had found herself fascinated by their few conversations. Back home she began the collection of books on nuclear physics that by 1952 filled the shelves in her library.

When Tsuta became Pearl Buck's assistant what had been a one-woman operation burgeoned into a well-run assembly line. Pearl had always planned her literary schedule several projects in advance, but now her plans became formalized. First on the line was the novelization of *The Empress*, which she had finally given up as a play.

Looking ahead, Tsuta had noted Pearl's library on nuclear physics, and she introduced the subject in a memo to which Pearl replied: "The idea of a book interpreting an atomic scientist and his problems to today's public is certainly fascinating." She would need to get substantial cooperation from an expert and asked Tsuta to begin a file on scientists and their activities in the field. Meanwhile she tackled the Empress Tzu Hsi.

This novel was a natural for Pearl S. Buck. With a firm background in Chinese history and lore only needing a little brushing up for the wider scope of a novel and with a heroine as stubborn and strong-minded as herself, writing it must have proven easy. In record time she produced a stunning pageant of color and action, with a love story highlighted by the conflict between passion and ambition. Highly readable as a novel, it is nevertheless suspect as history, for the cruelties and murders, the greed and self-indulgence are glossed over, achieving a heroine possible to admire and even understand.

Thousands did so. *Imperial Woman*, her forty-fifth volume, became one of her greatest literary successes. It also seemed a natural for the screen, and for several years there were nibbles and options from Hollywood and once even a full treatment. But a final sale was never made, and Tzu Hsi's glittering career remained unfilmed.

For some reason Pearl Buck's books seemed susceptible to that fate. Though her popularity, augmented by book club selections, was near the all-time record for any author, her only films were *The Good Earth*, *Dragon Seed* and *China Sky*, this last a minor effort written for a film director and quickly forgotten.

One other book brought in big option money but was never filmed, the next project on her schedule, *Letter from Peking*. A short, deeply emotional novel, it reveals happy memories. Formerly married to a university professor in Peking who is half-Chinese, the heroine now lives in Vermont with her Eurasian son. She and her son had been sent to the United States when the Communists overran China, but as a

Chinese subject responsible for his institution, the husband had remained at his post. Her love for him never wavers even when he writes
that, though he will love her until death, he is forced by the Communists to marry a Chinese woman.

At the novel's end she learns that he did indeed love her until death,
having been shot by the Communists while trying to escape to
America.

A secondary plot concerns the racial difficulties encountered by the
part-Chinese son in a small New England community, but the story of
the star-crossed lovers is the main thread. Pearl revealed publicly that
the love story was from her own life, and there is in it a hushed
tenderness making it seem totally credible.

After *Imperial Woman* and *Letter from Peking*, Pearl approached
her next work. Tsuta had collected a mountain of physics material and
Pearl turned to it with relish. In the meantime, a bout of play-writing
fever attacked her once again.

It started with "Omnibus," the prestigious Ford Foundation television show appearing on CBS. Though earlier Pearl had turned up her
nose at television's power to sell books, by 1954 Tsuta and Walsh were
convinced otherwise. Tsuta had been pushing Pearl gently toward the
CBS producers, and when *My Several Worlds* was published, she and
Walsh were delighted to sell a segment of it to TV with Pearl as the
narrator.

While CBS was preparing an adaptation the director assigned to the
show asked for a consultation. Soon afterwards, the young director
and his pregnant wife drove to Green Hills Farm. Both were Polish-
born, the wife young and pretty, the husband courteous and solicitous
of Pearl's every wish. Tad Danielewski had had theater experience in
Poland and Germany with the Allied Occupation Forces and then
trained for the theater in England and the United States. After the war
he had taught and coached at various colleges, and in New York finally
landed on the fringes of the big time. His assignment on "Omnibus"
was a big step toward the center.

My Several Worlds was televised in May 1954. During rehearsals
Pearl felt relaxed and happy, favorably impressed by Danielewski's
handling of the program. "But then," she wrote, "on the final day the
program manager came bustling in and barked out a few orders. 'It's
not commercial,' he snapped and abruptly changed it so that all that
was graceful and beautiful was removed.

"Tad Danielewski was terrifyingly disappointed, crushed. I sympathized with him, so after the performance I looked for him. He was standing with his face to the wall and saying nothing. I could see he was furiously angry but it was no use to say anything. I tried to console him."

Danielewski later left CBS to join NBC's Department of Program Development. Remembering Pearl Buck's cordiality, he wrote to her in June 1955, asking for an interview. At their meeting he told her he hoped to work out an idea for a program, perhaps an adaptation of a story, and she agreed delightedly. At their third meeting Pearl mentioned that her assistant, Tsuta Lombard, was a singer with operatic ambitions. Sensing an opportunity to please Pearl Buck, Danielewski offered Tsuta an audition at NBC, but, conscientiously separating her business and personal lives, Tsuta declined.

In August Pearl, forced to the Mountain Haunt retreat by hay fever, invited Danielewski, his wife Silvia and their poodle to stay in one of the smaller houses. Silvia's visits ceased with the birth of their son, but Danielewski continued the consultations and finally *The Big Wave*, a story about a tidal wave in Japan, was chosen for television.

Pearl wrote the adaptation and after its broadcast she happily admitted, "My reward was the newspaper headline, 'Pearl Buck Television Show a Masterpiece.' This was a new field and I enjoyed succeeding in it." Later Pearl adapted *The Enemy* for the Robert Montgomery show with Danielewski directing, and again there were rave reviews for all. A management shake-up at NBC, however, resulted in Danielewski's departure and the end of Pearl Buck's connection with the network.

The director–author affiliation continued, for Danielewski had noted Pearl's fascination with the dramatic form and saw thereby a way to fulfill a dream of his own. He told her he had always wanted to produce a play. Had she written one he could bring to Broadway?

Had she indeed! Enchanted, she described the play about an atomic scientist. Danielewski considered the idea timely and dramatic, and the two again found themselves locked in a collaborative effort.

Pearl and Danielewski decided the play needed revisions, that it should tackle head-on the burning questions of whether the bomb should have been dropped and whether such a technological development was essential to mankind. For this they decided additional first-hand information was necessary—not only the reasoning of the men who assembled the bomb and the way it was put together, but the scientists themselves. None of the experts lived in the New York area so introductions were sought. For one Nobel laureate to meet another was not difficult to arrange, and the lesser-known personages were even more accessible. Dr. Arthur Compton, a Nobel Prize winner for his work in nuclear physics, was the scientist who had headed the bomb project during the war, and he consented to introduce Pearl to his co-workers.

Travel presented more of a problem. By now Walsh was completely house-bound. He gave his blessing to Pearl's ventures, but she was still a missionary's daughter with a strong sense of responsibility and so far had never left him by himself. But it was a matter of priorities. With her enormous expenses she had to think first of earning a living, and so she compromised by hiring others to take her place at home. At various times there were a nurse, a college teacher who stood in as a parent for Henriette and a companion for Walsh; at other times a couple came in. The house still functioned smoothly while its mistress moved out into the world.

There were trips to Los Alamos, Oak Ridge, the University of Chicago, Argonne Laboratories, Washington University in St. Louis where Compton headed the physics department—all interspersed between various other activities.

Dick Walsh, Jr., though acting editor of John Day, lived in a suburb far from Bucks County and rarely saw his stepmother except occasionally in the office. Since her research was for a play rather than a novel, it was of no interest to the publisher professionally; consequently he knew little of her travels. He did remember Pearl talking about Compton. "There were correspondence and phone calls. I think she visited him in New Mexico and other nuclear installations gathering material. He may have even guided her research."

Later Pearl Buck did her own reminiscing: "I was writing about scientists, especially about one who had to decide whether to drop the atom bomb. I had visited a number of atomic installations, among them Los Alamos. We left Albuquerque after breakfast one desert-bright summer morning and after a motor trip we climbed into an aircraft slightly larger than a bathtub and floated up the mountain to this installation to hear the story of the atomic bomb that was made there."

"We" of course included Tad Danielewski. Pearl, at this time an overweight sixty-three, suddenly found herself accompanied by a slim, active young man carefully attentive to the comfort and safety of his celebrated charge. She was on an exhilarating adventure never before attempted by any woman in history, briefed daily, entertained and venerated by army generals and presidents of giant chemical corporations. Her college friend Annie Kate Gilbert had once observed, "Pearl always had to have a man in her life." Certainly this must have been a heady period in her life.

Pearl had often discussed with Arthur Compton the morality involved in dropping the atomic bomb, and he stated his reasoning. "We in that laboratory were the only persons in the world who could prepare that weapon before the Nazis had it. If we had not done our part the world would be exposed to the mercy of the Nazis. Further, even though Germany had surrendered, continued fighting would kill millions more." Even so, nagging at her was the question "Couldn't a *sample* bomb dropped on some uninhabited island have frightened Japan into surrender before all that slaughter?" Compton told her it had been considered but that Japan, thus given advance notice, could have knocked out the U.S. installation.

So, satisfied from a moral standpoint, and now possessing a unique inside view into the making of history, Pearl returned home to rewrite her play, respectful and admiring of the scientific mind.

Interviewed in May 1959 by book reviewer John Barkham, she stated, "For years scientists have fascinated me. Some of them feel a responsibility for the things they do as scientists; others feel only that they must pursue knowledge wherever it may lead, leaving to others the responsibility for putting that knowledge to best use. My belief is that we cannot afford to curb the scientist, especially the theoretician. He must be encouraged to go on with all his strength and genius. It is the duty of others to make the wisest use of what he discovers or creates."

This is the gist of what Pearl wanted to put into her play, alerting mankind to *its* responsibility. It was an abstract thesis difficult to translate into human terms, therefore she sought to express it in symbolism. When it was completed, Danielewski tried it out on New York's theatrical producers. None were impressed.

Their negative reaction prompted Pearl and Danielewski to enlist the aid of an old theatrical acquaintance for some practical guidance. Gertrude Macy had been Katharine Cornell's general manager for many years, steering her productions through casting, rehearsals and the run of the plays. On her own she had produced several successful plays, including *I Am a Camera* and two musicals, *One for the Money* and *Two for the Show*. She knew her way around the theater, and Pearl invited her to lunch.

"Miss Buck invited me to lunch several times," Gertrude Macy recalled. "Danielewski always was with her, but I recall she always paid the check. I got the feeling she was backing him, making contacts and setting everything up. He wanted to get a theater and put on a production, and I think they were wanting me to be their general manager, the way I had done for Kit Cornell. She said she and he could raise all the money necessary. He was going to be the over-all director, do the casting and everything, yet she said to me, 'Tad wants to ask you how you go about producing a play, about theaters and all those technical things.' He'd done some college plays and studied somewhere, but it looked to me that he'd just latched onto someone with money and though I'd have been proud to be associated with Miss Buck I felt he really didn't know enough to produce a play. I just said I was busy with other things."

Discouragement met them on every hand and Pearl was once again harried by the frustrations of the theatrical business, plus the fact that time was passing. The John Day Company was impatiently awaiting a new Pearl Buck manuscript and for two years she had given them none. One was badly needed. So, with her mind still steeped in nuclear physics she took the bomb story and rewrote it as a book.

In some ways the novel form was more suited to her thesis, for no symbolism was needed; she could relate the bomb's history in realistic terms, using technical language and actual people to present the basic theme, the responsibility of man to use his new powers for the good of mankind. So while she and Danielewski continued to pursue the elusive stage production of *Desert Incident* the new novel *Command the Morning* came into being.

For the novel she found it necessary to travel for more research, and guilt pricked her. Jackie Breen said, "You mustn't feel you've got to sacrifice your whole life, you're already doing everything for Mr. Walsh you possibly could." So Pearl assuaged her guilt by employing a college teacher to stay with Walsh and help Henriette with her math.

Sara Rowe remembered that Pearl and Danielewski were still working on the play. "He came to the house very often with his poodle and to Vermont. She liked him. She always had a soft spot for strangers in

America. She had strange—shall I say, 'loyalties.' I think he thought he was a brilliant young man.

"They kept working and working on the play. I must have listened to seventeen versions of it, she would read them to whoever was around. They were trying to cut it, it ran about three hours and a half.

"After I'd been there about two years . . . Mr. Walsh had reached the point where he really needed a nurse. I would see about his meals; sometimes in Vermont I would go over from the small house to see if he was ready for his dinner and Mrs. Walsh would be working with Mr. Danielewski. She would consider my coming over sort of an invasion of her privacy with him. It was time for me to go."

During these years the Green Hills Farm house, empty save for Walsh, Henriette and the servants, suddenly had a new occupant. Miki Sawada, always in close touch with Pearl, wrote her about a six-year-old child, half Japanese, half Negro, who was desperately in need of a home. "Dear Miss Pearlbuck, I remember, don't you have a little room over the kitchen? Can you take in a poor little girl who needs it?"

Pearl did have a little room over the kitchen, and soon Chieko arrived, and later Johanna and Teresa, all via Mrs. Sawada. The house was again filled with feminine voices.

Asked why her sister felt constrained to take these children, Grace replied, "I think she had created something of an image for herself. And she had the house and the space. When a human case was presented to her, she just couldn't *not* respond."

Pearl considered them all her daughters, but there was one whom she loved in a different way. In October 1957, Mary Tsuta Ohata Lombard married her stepson, Richard Walsh, Jr., each having obtained a divorce, and this daughter was very special indeed. To Dick she said, "There may be some finer person in the world than Tsuta, but if so I have never met one."

Happily at this time she found another woman of the same caliber. Her faithful agent David Lloyd had died in 1956. Long ago she had ceased paying Lloyd a commission on the books published by John Day, specifically the American hard-cover publication rights. But Lloyd still represented her plays, films, magazine pieces, and all the foreign rights.

Foreign rights in Pearl Buck's case were extraordinarily remunerative. According to Lloyd's figures at that time, her books were translated into more foreign languages and sold in more foreign countries

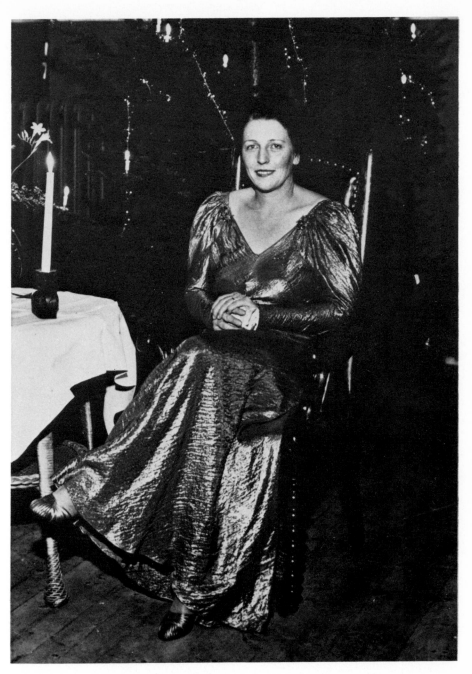

Pearl in Sweden, 1938, to receive the Nobel Prize.

Pearl with the first two children taken at Welcome House, 1948.

Pearl and Richard, 1950. *(Courtesy William A Smith)*

Pearl with Oscar Hammerstein, 1949.

Pearl with John Anderson and Tad Danielewski in India,
1963.

John, in turban, Pearl, and Tad during the making of their film, India, 1963.

Danielewski and Pearl being greeted by Jawaharlal Nehru, 1963.

Pearl, with John Anderson, giving autographs to Indian children, 1963.

Pearl accompanied by Ted Harris, December, 1965.

Theodore F. Harris, 1968. *(Courtesy Clara Sipprell)*

William Earnest Hocking, circa 1960. *(Courtesy Pach Bros., N.Y.)*

Pearl as guest on the NBC special made in conjunction with President Nixon's trip to China, 1972. *(Courtesy NBC)*

than those of any living American author. These were the royalties that provided the major portion of her wealth. Thus, representing Pearl S. Buck's literary output throughout the world was not unlike running a huge international conglomerate. "The labor attached to it was terrific," said Andrea, Lloyd's daughter and assistant. "From big countries the money just poured in effortlessly. But the small countries were different. You'd sell a book to some small country and your troubles were just beginning. I remember I sold a book to a publisher in Burma, three thousand copies of one of the little Talk Books, and we corresponded back and forth, negotiating, and finally I sent them a contract for forty dollars. They wrote back, Oh dear, we'd love to have it but forty dollars is what a teacher here earns in a year. So I reduced it to four dollars, and there were more contracts and more letters. But you do it because it's another country opened up and every country adds to her prestige and market value, so you do it. That's what an agent's for."

This was the job Pearl must now entrust to another agent, an especially important job now that Walsh's health was failing. The selection was vital, and Walsh chose the one he considered the best, the Harold Ober office. Ivan von Aux handled their books and Dorothy Olding the magazines, and Walsh invited them and Tsuta to lunch at the Barclay Hotel. Everyone chatted amiably, and when the check arrived Pearl drew forth an enormous roll of one dollar bills. "These," she said as she peeled off a small pile, "I got from selling off my pine trees."

Dorothy Olding remembered the hat Pearl Buck wore that day, blue to match her eyes, "the most compelling eyes I've ever seen." There was another luncheon at the Harvard Club when Pearl asked Dorothy questions about her childhood. "I found myself telling my whole life story, which is something you don't do with authors. I never had before. But it was that pull of her eyes, and that warmth and that interest. She just wanted to know what sort of person she was dealing with. She was a very warm person, and at the same time very formal. She never called me anything but Miss Olding, and when she slipped up one day and said 'Dorothy,' quickly she turned to me and said, 'I beg your pardon, my dear.' I was pleased, but she apologized. Her Chinese upbringing, I suppose."

The new agent-client relationship began in April 1956. Dorothy Olding wrote her, "I am very proud to be offering my first Pearl S.

Buck story to the *Ladies Home Journal* today, and very happy that our association has now begun."

However, this first story, "The Crucifixion," was rejected by the *Journal* and several other magazines as well. When Miss Olding reported the disappointing news in some embarrassment, Pearl wrote, "Thank you so much for your work with Crucifixion. Every now and again I seem to write a story, usually one that means a good deal to me, that cannot find publication. Do not be discouraged if it doesn't, for I shall not be."

"That was like her," Miss Olding said. "She was very appreciative of what you tried to do for her." Their harmonious association continued until Pearl Buck's death.

Another business relationship at that time proved equally fortunate. The Authors Guild (the book writer's division of the parent Authors League, of which the Dramatists Guild, and at that time the Radio Writers Guild, were also parts) was experiencing some difficulties between the Authors and the more solvent Dramatists Guild. Someone with a prestigious name was needed in the subtle tug-of-war. Luise Sillcox, the legendary executive secretary, nagged and wheedled Pearl Buck to enter the fray and she finally agreed to become president.

Peter Heggie, Sillcox's successor, observed, "Pearl Buck's leadership during this time was very important to the Guild. She had good executive ability, would come in and spend an hour or two before the luncheon meeting and go over the points to be discussed. Her grasp was really great and the way she conducted the meetings made her a great chairlady. It was all very technical—finances, contracts, legislation for authors, court cases, copyrights and the increase in postal rates—legal matters that took a lawyer as well. But her name helped tremendously, especially with all the Washington stuff."

Heggie summed up her contribution: "Until she became president the Guild was in the doldrums. Then her very visibility, plus Rex Stout's work as membership chairman, and John Hersey's as book contract chairman, they all made the membership increase. That brought in more dues, and as our bankroll doubled we could hire more help. So then the Guild became more effective, it really began to mean something. Pearl Buck gave it momentum. She had the affection of the people she worked with and I would say that her being a part of the team was of really great value to all authors."

16

Early in 1959 Grace Yaukey, living in Washington, D.C., received a surprise visit from Tsuta, who had come down from New York expressly to see her. Tsuta, devoted to Pearl, and since her marriage to Dick Walsh, Jr., deeply involved with the John Day Company, had come to ask Grace's help in a private matter of the greatest urgency.

Distressingly, Tsuta said, Pearl Buck had become the source of gossip. Items were appearing in the gossip columns, rumors about the author and a young man and the twenty-five-year difference in their ages. Considering Pearl Buck's public image, one of almost regal dignity, such gossip was disquieting to Dick, Jr., and herself and would prove most upsetting to Walsh if he heard it. Could Grace, her closest and dearest relative, do something?

Grace, miles away and not privy to her sister's private life, felt powerless to intervene. She knew of Pearl's business affiliation with Tad Danielewski; she knew he was considered an attractive and likable young man, well-educated and well-mannered, all of which would naturally appeal to her sister. She also knew Pearl's long-standing interest in the theater and assumed that to be the bond between them. She had often seen Pearl take an interest in someone with a special talent who needed to be encouraged—indeed, hadn't Pearl done that for *her* with her own writing career?

As for Danielewski's escorting Pearl in the evening, Grace was aware of a young Chinese painter, Chen Chi, with whom Pearl attended the opera now that Walsh was incapacitated. There was nothing clandestine there. Could this be the same?

Hardly; Tad Danielewski was married. And it was bruited about that
Pearl had given him a great deal of money. Even more importantly, she
was investing her time in writing plays rather than novels, a worrisome
factor to John Day. Grace, though understanding and sympathetic,
still felt there was nothing she could do.

Later Tsuta tried again, asking Grace to meet her in Philadelphia.
She and Dick were even more worried now, for they believed Pearl to be
emotionally involved. By this time Grace understood more fully Tsuta's concern, for on a visit with her sister, Pearl had suddenly turned to
ask seriously, "Grace, do you think a person of my age could really fall
in love again?"

Taken by surprise, Grace had answered, "Oh, I suppose it's possible." Thinking it over later, she said, "I believe there was a sort of
infatuation. Whether it was just mental, I don't know, but it was
certainly an infatuation. As a matter of fact, I think she herself was
surprised that she could be so affected by this young person."

Friends and acquaintances were equally concerned. To stave off
loneliness, Pearl had proposed that she and Tsuta and Dick take an
apartment in New York together, and one night, a friend recalled, "we
all went to a concert at Carnegie Hall. Afterwards as we walked
downstairs I took her arm the way I would my mother's. Later Tsuta
told me she didn't at all like the implication she was getting old. She
was very vain, you know, she was trying to relive her youth. Even Mr.
Itkis, her music teacher, told me he would take her to the movies and
she would act sort of kittenish and flirty, like a teenager with a boy
friend."

Itkis, asked if she had flirted with him, hooted. "With *me*? Never! I
was too old. She thought the young men had younger brains and she
could get more out of them than from an old man like me."

One of Pearl's adopted daughters recalled watching Pearl during
Danielewski's visits to Green Hills Farm. "Tad was often there but he
was always very decorous. I don't recall his trying to push her to invest
in his interests or to direct her life. This was toward the end of my
father's life, when she had no intellectual companionship at home. We
kids were all too young and the older set were off doing their own
thing. We felt two ways about Danielewski. He and his first wife Silvia
were both pursuing their own careers independently and he was a sort
of presence in the house."

In Vermont, however, Pearl seemed to have found a confidante with whom she could talk freely. Jackie Breen, the lively young woman who acted as her summer secretary, was a warm and admiring companion and to her Pearl presented her new persona.

"Mrs. Walsh was very lonely. . . . Danielewski used to come up and visit. He was very attentive and would bring her flowers and so on. She thought very highly of him, and at those times she seemed to get more alive and vibrant. I found her a very lusty woman with great sexuality. I remember when we were talking about a mutual friend in his seventies and she asked if I thought he was still sexually active. I was then in my thirties, so to me anybody in his seventies was over the hill. 'Oh,' I said, 'I don't think so, he's seventy or over.' Meaning it was about impossible.

"'*Well*,' she said, sort of archly, 'you'd be *surprised*,' a little bit irate that I would imagine anybody at seventy would be finished. She was nearly seventy at the time.

"Another time I remarked that I'd seen a movie about *The Three Faces of Eve* and she turned slyly and said, 'Only three?' She had said once that no one man could satisfy her, and I'm sure that she needed more than one. She had a heart big enough to include three men at one time, I'm positive of it. And as for that one young man, I think she was really in love with him. When he was around she *preened* herself. She *glowed*."

Thus while still caring for Walsh, now part of her fading past, she had apparently moved on to a live present, embracing new outlets for her energy. "It's all the same thing," she told Jackie Breen. "Whether you write a book or wash the floors or make love or paint a picture, the source is all the same—energy, the most important thing for living your life. I know a singer who is very careful never to have intercourse the night before she sings because it affects her voice—it drains off her energy."

Writing a play and watching it come to life on a stage was the specific form upon which her energy ached to expend itself. She had waited twenty years since the aborted *Flight into China* production in New Jersey and had meanwhile had other plays rejected. Now she had found not only a director who admired her plays but seemed to be wholly dedicated to her personally.

Tad and she had discussed forming a production company to produce her plays and had named it Stratton Productions after the beautiful mountain seen from her Vermont windows. In 1958 the company became a reality, with a three-room office located in the heart of the theater district. There was stationery with Pearl's and his name upon it, a bank account and an assistant to help him in the office. (Also, for tax purposes, stationery for Stratton Productions at 277 Park Avenue, her apartment.)

The publication of *Imperial Woman* and the film sale of *Letter from Peking* made money reasonably plentiful and the initial costs of the new venture had not alarmed her. But after being warned of a possible overcall for funds, she turned to a member of the Vineland School Board, Morris Feld, who owned a carpet shampooing business, and he became co-producer of *A Desert Incident*.

Jeanette Kamins, a woman with theatrical experience, was hired as Danielewski's production assistant. She had been told to help with the casting, but actually there was little of that to do. "Tad told me he had promised his wife the lead," she confided, "and Paul Roebling came with the show. Paul was a rich young actor, a descendant of the Roebling who built the Brooklyn Bridge, and I think he had put in maybe twenty-five thousand. His part called for an Englishman from Cambridge and he had gone to England and spent a month there picking up the correct accent.

"While the show was in rehearsal Miss Buck often came in the office like the Queen Mother with her chauffeur waiting downstairs. She didn't socialize with anyone very much, not even the leading actors. She wasn't snobbish, she was just famous and rich and didn't bother.

"In the office I heard her and Tad talking about her business affairs, not only about the play but other things. He seemed to be sort of her manager; she'd get requests for adaptations of her works and ask him for advice. I don't think she knew much about money—except how to make it.

"Tad was a little afraid of her, always trying to be on his best behavior. She was somebody he had to cater to, his meal ticket, his whole career really. During rehearsals I used to sit with her and talk while Tad was directing and I got the impression she didn't know much about play writing. There were lots of changes made in the script every day, things taken out and put back in next day. Towards the end there was a great deal of confusion. Finally Tad said, 'Well, when we open out of town I'll get a better idea of how it plays.'"

At the end of February the company, Sheppard Strudwick, Cameron Prud'homme, Silvia Daneel and Paul Roebling, along with the set designed by Howard Bey, entrained for New Haven. There, for twenty-one performances, they endured the breaking in process with its accompanying tortures. Sheppard Strudwick described those weeks: "When I first read the play I knew it wasn't well written, but I respected what it had to say and I thought it might be fixed up in rehearsals, that Danielewski might be able to help her with it. Tad's a great promoter but he didn't have the professional know-how to help her with the play.

"I was sorry, too. One day during rehearsals I had lunch with Miss Buck and she told me she had been writing plays all her life and that this production was *the* great adventure of her life."

On March 24, 1959 (coincidentally the thirty-second anniversary of another adventurous day in Pearl Buck's life, the Nanking Incident) *A Desert Incident* opened in New York. "The opening night was one of the most painful experiences I ever went through," Strudwick confessed. But they all got through it somehow, slogging along despite an overwhelmingly depressing atmosphere. Everyone had been invited afterwards to a party at Pearl's apartment, the cast plus Arthur Compton, Chen Chi, the John Day staff, Pearl's agents and a few friends. They picked at a lavish supper while waiting tensely for the radio review and then the morning papers, and while no one was hopeful, not even the most pessimistic had foreseen the massacre by the critics.

Brooks Atkinson of the *Times*, noted for his gentle spirit, acknowledged Pearl's good intentions and the bravery of the actors, but otherwise deplored the play. Richard Watts headlined his review "Further Evidence of Atomic Horror," incorporating the phrase, "probably the worst and certainly the most pretentious play of the season."

Coleman of *The Mirror* headed his review, "Desert Is Cure for Insomnia," also labeling it "Worst play of the season . . . ridiculous, confused and disastrous," meanwhile congratulating the actors for their "valor under devastating fire." All the critics reacted identically, their reviews exuding a kind of animosity at having been so ill-used.

The party turned into a wake. Dorothy Olding recalled, "You looked around and everybody had disappeared. They didn't want to be there to see the holocaust."

Suddenly Pearl began to rail at the power of the press. "She was like a colossus being torn down," Robert Hill, an editor at John Day, remembered. "And there was not a thing she could do about it."

Paul Roebling, the only cast member absent because he had hosted a party of his own, had fared somewhat better with the critics than his colleagues, and he called Pearl the next day to sympathize. "When I talked to her her only cry was, 'What can we *do*? What can anybody do about people that criticize plays this way?'"

The shock of public ridicule had cut to the bone. But she held her head high and in a few days she dismissed her attackers with a gesture of calm superiority. "In writing the play," she told the press, "I took too much for granted in assuming that the critics would possess the necessary background in science and anthropology to grasp its meaning. They didn't, and must have found it very confusing. I'm afraid I wrote it without sufficient thought for the audience and the critics."

Pearl and Danielewski must have condoled with each other over the crassness of the public. She never admitted failure and she rejected sympathy as readily as she had rejected advice. Oscar Hammerstein, who loved her deeply, had read the play and would have liked to warn her against wasting her money; his son, who had worked in television with Danielewski and had read the play, deemed it "stiff, awkward, untheatrical and DOOMED." He too would have cautioned her. But all doubts were greeted with the author's response: "Mr. Danielewski is a brilliant young man. I know star quality when I see it."

Ignoring failure, Pearl and Danielewski soon moved on to a new enterprise, a different kind of challenge, and Stratton Productions' press agent sent out the following release: "Pearl Buck leaves for a European business trip Wednesday, September 2, with her partner in Stratton Productions, Tad Danielewski. Miss Buck will visit the Scandinavian capitals, Paris, Rome and London. She will deliver the major address before the World Convention of the Red Cross in Oslo on September 5, negotiate for the sale of foreign rights to her current best-selling novel *Command the Morning*, and discuss the forthcoming film version of another of her novels, *Imperial Woman*. Plans are also afoot to present Miss Buck's play, *A Desert Incident* in London and in Germany this season."

In London she and Danielewski were invited to visit famous Rockingham Castle where its eerie quality inspired them to make fresh creative plans; Pearl would write a mystery novel and Danielewski would film it. The resultant novel, *Death in the Castle*, was finally published many years later, but the film was never made. At least, however, the two partners enjoyed their European jaunt with its attendant crowds and public acclamation.

Pearl Buck, the novelist, had now allowed two years to pass without producing a new book. In 1958 she had announced to the newspapers a fact already suspected within the trade, that John Sedges was Pearl S. Buck. And what looked like a creative dry spell had been filled with her intensive research into nuclear physics for her play. Finally, however, John Day had reclaimed her from the theater by announcing that her novel *Command the Morning* about the atom bomb would be published in July.

Conscious of the obligations of a Nobel laureate who was also one of the world's most widely read authors, she was doubly conscious of the power of the written word. So, discarding the symbolism of *Desert Incident* in the book she made her plea for world sanity in straightforward terms.

The unrelenting earnestness of her plea, however, seemed to intimidate the fiction writer. The *New York Times* summed up the problem: "The intention of the author is obviously and most honorably serious, yet this is a poor novel. . . . If any of its broadly concerned scientist-types had been individually characterized . . . if all of them had been seen as persons rather than as their caricatures, this might have been a fine novel. As it stands, *Command the Morning* remains a bland and dull scenario."

The general concurrence of the critics that the novel's intent was honorable but that it failed to achieve a high standard of entertainment must have been deeply disappointing. But Pearl Buck never gave up easily. And finally she was able to make her point. *The American Weekly*, a periodical which reached as many people each week as her play and novel combined might have reached in a year, asked for a Christmas story. She later gave her account of the request: "I am frankly sentimental about Christmas. I said I would write a story, and it grew out of my interest in nuclear scientists as human beings. The magazine gave its entire issue to the story and afterwards reprinted it in a small book." Thus by having her message printed in a third medium, that of the magazine, she finally reached an audience of twenty million readers.

As far as is known, Danielewski was not a party to the magazine piece as he was to *Death in the Castle*, where the contract gave him a share in the book's royalties. For his help on *Command the Morning* Pearl wanted him to be acknowledged in some way so she told Dick Walsh that "without *much* help from Tad, not in the writing but in the research and approach preparatory to the actual writing, this book would not have come to life. I find I'd feel uncomfortable without some sort of acknowledgment, so I have compromised on a sort of double acknowledgment to him and also to the scientists from us both."

The following dedication appeared in the front of the book: "To Tad Danielewski, who joins me in appreciation and gratitude to the many scientists who so generously shared with us their time and their experience."

After their initial affiliation Pearl had drawn Danielewski more and more into her affairs. She did not become discouraged when Stratton Productions' first offering failed so spectacularly. But when the total output of disastrous ventures over the years is assessed, it is easy to question what kept them going.

Actually *Desert Incident* had not been their initial offering in the theater. When Danielewski first asked her for a play to produce, Pearl had disinterred the *Indian Family* script and contradicting both Moss Hart and Aline MacMahon, he had declared it worthy of production. Pearl and he finally decided on a musical version, for Pearl was enchanted by musical· comedies, determined some day to write an entire show, including the music. Together they turned the *Indian Family* into a libretto.

After failing to sell the libretto they interrupted work on it to turn to the long research in physics which resulted in *Desert Incident* and *Command the Morning*. Meanwhile, the libretto managed to find a producer who went ahead independently, mounting an opulent production under the title, *Christine*. With Maureen O'Hara as its star, *Christine* opened in New York City in May 1960 and closed after twelve performances.

Following this disaster, Stratton Productions hurried to their next project. Danielewski proposed to use the NBC-TV adaptation of *The Big Wave* as the basis for a film. So Stratton Productions, in association with a Japanese company, spent months in Japan filming on location. The finished picture was shown to executives at Allied Artists in December 1962. Neither Allied Artists nor any other distributors wanted to handle the film and its only recorded performance was at a private screening in Bucks County for Pearl's friends.

Hard on the heels of the Japanese film came another in India. Pearl Buck's close association with Jawaharlal Nehru and his sister, Madame Pandit, gave Danielewski and herself special entree. They arranged a co-production deal with one of India's largest film companies whereby the Indians put up a million dollars and Pearl Buck fifty thousand. *The Guide*, starring their top male and female stars, opened at the Lincoln Arts Theater in 1964 and ran for two weeks.

Such dogged and unrewarded persistence suggests that standard success—good notices and full houses—was not the sole motivation that kept Stratton Productions going. For Danielewski there were subsidized showcases for himself as librettist and director and producer. For Pearl there was the adventure of the theater itself. And something else as well.

Behind her lay her aging publisher and a quiet marriage with its established way of life; before her lay youth, adventure, the stage. And love. Being Pearl Buck she had to reach out for them all.

Paul Roebling may have caught a glimpse of the rationale for her persistence. A few months after the demise of *Desert Incident*, Roebling invited Pearl to dinner. That morning while dressing he had made up his mind to propose to his girl, and during dinner he confided his exciting news to Pearl Buck, at which point the conversation took on a more than normally personal atmosphere.

"We'd been discussing Betty Friedan," he recalled, "and the feminine mystique. She said, 'I don't think there's any such thing.'

"I said, 'But you're a feminist, aren't you?'

"She said, 'Oh no, I'm not a feminist. I'm just a worker.' I knew what she meant. My own mother, who was the first lady bank president in the world, doesn't consider herself a feminist either. And then she said, 'Why do you want to spend an evening with an old woman like me when you're about to propose to your young fiancee?'

"I said, 'Well, she is out doing a show. I invited you and I think this is great fun. You and the proposal make it twice as memorable an evening.'

"That was the point when she said such a strange thing to me. She talked on a little bit, I don't remember what, and then . . .

"'You know the most awful thing a man does to a woman? It's to withdraw his love, physically and emotionally—and *stay with her*. This is the awful thing we can't overcome.'

"I thought, 'What is she telling me?' What a thwarted existence this was exposing. It came like a cry from her soul and it was totally unexpected. I just said, 'Yes, it must be awful. And it would be just as awful if it happened to a man. He is just as vulnerable.'

"At the time I had no idea who she was talking about. Even now, I'm not quite sure. If it was Danielewski, I could hardly believe it. I didn't see the slightest mystery in their relationship, it seemed more relaxed than if they had been lovers. Of course he was courtly to her, she was always the queen. But it was like he was a boy who was working with a great lady who took him places he'd never get to otherwise, and he met von Braun and Compton and people with money and prestige. He was terribly respectful. And yet he insisted on working with her. I guess it *was* sort of an unusual relationship. She was a woman of great mystery and when she came out with this thing about a man withdrawing his love and yet staying with her—and the question 'how does a woman overcome such a thing?'—I was very embarrassed. I didn't know what she was talking about."

No one can know for certain. But the following handwritten poem, dated 1958, was found among her papers:

> The heart, it seems, can never know its age.
> I would have said that at this stage
> I'd never love again.
> Yet here it is—the pain,
> The ecstasy, the joy.
> Against you I employ
> My whole will to hide
> Truth I have denied.

Behind all the theatrical fiascos was the irresistible drive of a strong-minded woman who had discovered that if one had to pay for attention and love, still it made it all worth while, and Pearl Buck strained to hold onto whatever ecstasy remained.

Tad Danielewski's presence had not been known to the *Christine* producers during the five years they had awaited a workable libretto from Pearl. She had told the press she was "learning about musical comedy writing" with the veteran librettist, Frank Loesser, but he later bowed out under the pressure of other plans. Charles Peck was called in as co-author, which so outraged Pearl that she threatened to sue if Peck's name was not removed, disclosing that from the start in 1955 or 1956 Danielewski had been her co-author. She further demanded that Danielewski be given public recognition and reimbursed by the producers for his expenses past and present. There was a great deal of squabbling over the division of profits, but *Christine*'s sudden demise automatically resolved that conflict.

When asked "how often she would try if, God forbid, *Christine* should be treated as roughly by the press as *Desert Incident*," she had replied gaily, "Again and again." And she was as good as her word; after *Christine*'s brief run, she and Danielewski, with no time to lick their wounds or mourn, dashed on to their next project.

Danielewski appeared to be tireless. While *Christine* had been going through its out-of-town tryout he had been directing an Off-Broadway production of something called *Brouhaha*, which ran just long enough for *The New York Times* to give it a scathing review; simultaneously he was negotiating for *The Big Wave* movie in Japan, all this in 1960. Sheppard Strudwick's observation seemed reasonable: "Tad was great as a promoter, but somehow his projects didn't have a way of coming through." With all that activity there was always hope; Pearl Buck hated stodginess, and by now the publishing world had lost its zest.

There was nothing stodgy about Stratton Productions. The tie-up between Allied Artists in America and the Toho Film Company in Japan for *The Big Wave* movie as previously presented on NBC-TV had about it a can't-miss quality. Danielewski was to direct in tandem with a Japanese producer while Pearl's presence would lend prestige and support. Actually she was also there because she was suffering the malaise of jealousy, and justified or not, was suspicious and unhappy. Dorothy Olding received word that Pearl was there to prevent any American-Japanese incidents that might roil international relations.

The production moved along despite two major crises. After altercations between American and Japanese authorities, Danielewski threatened to resign if his Japanese counterpart were not removed. "There can only be one director," he declared. "It is I—or it is not I." Pearl arranged for Danielewski to be the sole director.

The other crisis occurred when Pearl answered her phone early one morning to hear: "The United States calling. Pennsylvania. Stand by." It was Pearl's daughter. "Mother, I have something to tell you."

Pearl already knew. Her husband, Richard Walsh, was dead. "I'll come home at once. Tonight."

The operator downstairs overheard the conversation, and soon everyone knew. There was no plane out until midnight, so Pearl called Miki Sawada, who invited her and Danielewski to her house outside Tokyo for the day. This was the site of her famous orphanage where she had erected a number of small buildings on the grounds, and she showed Pearl around to see the 148 children in residence. At midnight Pearl left for home.

On the plane she fought a gnawing sense of guilt at being absent when Walsh died, repeating to herself the doctor's advice: "Go. He won't know if you are here or not." But back at home, she sensed that there were those who blamed her for being absent.

Calm and dry-eyed, she nodded approval of the simple funeral arrangements; Walsh's family and children would be there with Grace the only outsider. There would be no formal religious ceremony, for he was an avowed atheist, and the closed casket was placed in the wide living room.

"At the ceremony," Grace recalled, "Pearl and I went through the courtyard into that room. And we all gathered around the casket. At that moment she gave one indication of almost breaking down, just the way she caught her breath. But that was all."

The service consisted of a few non-denominational readings and was conducted by Dr. Frederick Stamm, whom Walsh had liked as a man and genially tolerated as a minister. The family then made the four-hour drive to the Walsh plot in New Rochelle, New York. Afterwards they all had dinner and drove back. Emotions were held in check. But the daughter who had phoned Pearl was bitter. "She thought," Grace reported, "that Pearl should not have got involved in those things with Tad while her father was ill, that she abandoned him when he was dying."

That afternoon Pearl went upstairs to Walsh's room to stare out at the half-finished porch she had planned for him so that he could be carried out into the sunshine and see the willows waving in the wind. According to her conscience, she had done her best.

There were adjustments to be made now, both internal and external. With Walsh and his attendants gone, she took the three girls, Henriette, Chieko and Johanna, to Vermont for the summer. Hundreds of sympathy letters awaited her acknowledgment and, punctilious in such matters, she took time to answer them. Then she tried to get on with her own writing. But her mind kept straying back to Japan, and finally she returned. Just to be there was for her the main thing, just to be there and observe.

Back in Japan her fame caught up with her. A prestigious women's magazine in Korea had heard of her proximity and invited her to visit

Seoul. Miki Sawada was also invited, and they decided to travel together.

Before they left Tokyo, they agreed to travel lightly. Mrs. Sawada would pack two suits, one long and one short dress for evening and afternoon. Pearl agreed to do the same. "But," Mrs. Sawada laughed, "she's such a coquette, she loves beautiful dresses . . . and there I see outside her door ten pairs of shoes to be polished. And she had a closet full of dresses."

The Koreans were generous with their invitations, and Pearl, Mrs. Sawada remembered, was soon "drowned in kim chee," which upset her stomach. But they met innumerable homeless children, and later they would meet even more.

The time spent in Japan was not a happy period for Pearl. At one point she felt it necessary to discharge an attractive secretary by telegram; at another she paid off an employee whose feelings had been hurt, but she doggedly stayed for the entire filming.

That winter while Danielewski was editing *The Big Wave*, they gave a number of publicity interviews on its behalf. While he promoted their Indian film Pearl decided to write a book about her widowhood.

A Bridge for Passing is brave and touching in its account of her trip to Japan and Walsh's death. It looks back with affection on their life together, on his foibles and his talents. "He loved me and with him I lived in freedom. I was never afraid to speak . . . to come, to go, to withdraw into solitude . . ." she wrote. "Neither did it occur to me to want him changed. I loved him, so why try to change him?"

They had enjoyed their frequent arguments, with only one subject taboo, life after death. "He believed that all life ended with death while my position was that one cannot decide without facts.

" 'We know nothing of the future,' he said, 'I shan't fool myself or let myself be fooled.'

"But not knowing doesn't mean there is nothing to be known.

" 'Whatever there is,' he said, 'I shall know in due time—or rather *not* know, for I shall cease to be.' "

In *A Bridge for Passing* she described her deep grief and how after long months of meditation she rose above it. And she also wrote: "I was beginning to understand the relativity of time to space and speed. What a miracle, that Einstein was born in coincidence with the practical experience of jets and rockets in space! My mind, unable as yet to face the profound change in my own life, explored the meaning of eternity, time without beginning and without end. Whatever exists now has always existed and always will, the universal and eternal law being only that of *change*. . . .

"'Mass is interchangeable with Energy.' This sentence, so simply written, resulted in the awakening of my own mind to the new age. It was more than an awakening of the mind. It was the conversion of my soul, the clarification of my spirit, the unification of my whole being. I had a new conception of death, a new approach to life."

Mass can become energy. Mass is potential energy even while it is mass. Pondering this statement and projecting it beyond those words, she had to accept that her husband *as mass* was not lost but had simply changed into something less visible. . . . *Invisible but still present.*

This opened up a vista of infinite possibilities, events that would be called miracles if they had not yet happened. But, as Arthur Compton had pointed out, many "miracles" had already happened—talking across oceans, outdistancing sound, seeing through solids—and were not called miracles because man had discovered how to do them. Which led to the hope—the possibility—of other "impossible" miracles.

Compton believed, with a scientist's caution, "An examination of the evidence seems to support the view that there is *no* very close correspondence between brain activity and consciousness. It seems that our thinking is partially divorced from brains, a conclusion that suggests though it does not prove the possibility of consciousness after death."

Corroboration of this idea came from another equally qualified source, William Ernest Hocking, the eminent philosopher who had dined with the Bucks in Nanking and then written her after the controversial 1932 Foreign Missions speech. Their paths had crossed again during the war. Both, ever watchful of events in China, had even dreamed briefly of maneuvering a rapprochement between China and the Communists. They shared a deep concern for India's struggle for independence, and he and Mrs. Hocking had dined with the Richard Walshes when the East and West Association held meetings in Boston.

In 1960 it was not surprising that Hocking, whose wife had died five years earlier, should be sensitive to news of Pearl's loss. A deeply religious man, he had long pondered the question of immortality, putting his conclusions into a book, *Thoughts on Death and Life* (later incorporated into the larger *The Meaning of Immortality in Human*

Experience) and he sent Pearl a copy in the hope it might contain something to sustain her.

It did indeed have the effect of corroborating the scientific views of Compton and others, lending them the added authority of philosophy. Hocking states his position unequivocably: "The peace that comes to the dying is not that of terminus; it is—as I interpret it—the peace of *handing-on*, and of reverting to origins with the felt opening of a perspective more profoundly valid."

Here he is referring to the natural death of the aged; but to him even the premature death of youth only sharpens the conviction that this unfulfilled selfhood deserves a fulfillment which human life has not granted. This expectation of fulfillment in turn is justified, in his philosophy, by his firm conviction of the existence of an indestructible and therefore eternally creating and maintaining God.

Pearl, her beliefs strengthened by the best minds she knew, ended *A Bridge for Passing* on a hopefully positive note.

"I have a stopping place in New York, that city of wonder and grief. He and I always kept a place there. He needed it for his work and his spirit, and I have continued our tradition. It is not the place we shared for so many years. Within the confines of our old apartment I could not escape the torture of memory." She went on to describe the rental of a new apartment after one hasty inspection at night, unaware of the surroundings except that there was a school across the street.

She continued, "The choice was haphazard, I would have said, a chance thing. But I am beginning to believe that there is no such thing as pure chance in this world. . . . When I was a child and often reluctant to do my duty, my father used to say to me firmly but gently, 'If you will not do it because it is right, then do it for the greater Glory of God.'

I did not once see the apartment while it was being decorated. When all was finished, I opened the door and went straight to the big window . . . and facing me, across the building, under the eaves and along the roof, I saw these words carved in huge stone letters: AD MAIOREM DEI GLORIAM.

"They face me now as I write. 'To the greater glory of God!' What does it mean, this voice from the grave, my father's grave? He lies buried on a mountaintop in the very heart of a China lost to me. I am here and alive and thousands of miles away. Are we in communication, he and I through my father? It is not possible.

"How dare I say it is not? Some day we shall know. What day? That day, perhaps, when saints and scientists unite to make a total search for truth. It is the saints, the believers, who should have the courage to urge the scientists to help them discover whether the spirit continues its life of energy when the mass we call body ceases to be the container. Faith supplies the hypothesis, but only science can provide the computer for verification. The unbeliever will never pursue the search. He is already static, a pillar of salt, forever looking backward.

"There are no miracles, of that I am sure. If one walks on water and heals the sick and raises the dead to life again, it is not a matter of magic but a matter of knowing how to do it. There is no supernatural; there is only the supremely natural, the purely scientific. Science and religion, religion and science, put it as I may, they are two sides of the same glass, through which we see darkly until these two, focusing together, reveal the truth.

"On the day when the message comes through from over the far horizon where dwells 'that great majority,' the dead, the proof will reach us, not as a host of angels in the sky but as a wave-length recorded in a laboratory, a wave-length as indisputable and personal as the fingerprint belonging to someone whose body is dust. Then the scientist, recognizing the wave-length, will exclaim, 'But that's someone I know! I took his wave-length before he died.' And he will compare his record with the wave-length just recorded and will know that at last a device, a machine, is able to receive a message dreamed of for centuries, the message of the continuing individual existence, which we call the immortality of the soul.

"Or perhaps it will not be a scientist who receives, but a woman, waiting at a window open to the sky."

17

In reviewing *A Bridge for Passing* Edward Weeks, editor of *The Atlantic Monthly*, commented on the contrast between Pearl Buck's busy days on the movie set and her lonely nights in her empty hotel room, noting how she "finds consolation in reliving her happiness with her editor," adding prophetically, "This book will be a touchstone for those made desolate by sorrow, and in writing it Mrs. Buck lifts our spirits as she revives her own."

Doubtless it did lift many spirits and doubtless the author would have been sincerely pleased, but at the same time, in view of her present attachment, she must have been aware of a certain anomaly.

In any case, others were. Danielewski's assistant, a young midwesterner, John Anderson, who saw them together daily, was no less devoted to Pearl Buck for understanding her motives. "She didn't write *A Bridge for Passing* out of a deep searching for religious meaning to Mr. Walsh's death," he said. "Sometimes she wrote things simply because they were appropriate to the situation or the times. When she wrote that book she was actually hotly in love with Danielewski. I know. I saw them together. She wrote it because it was a timely subject and it would be read by every hot-loving American woman and would bring in lots of dollars."

Even if she had wanted to be totally honest, she could in no way admit that her mourning had been done years before and that now there was someone else. Convention would not permit it. Her public and her friends expected her to perform the rituals of mourning.

Pearl Buck was also a writer, and a writer prudently uses the material at hand. So she made the best of her situation. Widowhood was one of life's great common denominators shared by a host of her readers, who would expect a profound and comforting statement. So she returned to her married life, dwelt on its early joys, re-suffered through its dreadful years, extracting from them the philosophy her scientific studies had taught her.

Were her readers as well-informed as John Anderson, they might well have been outraged. But what she now wrote *had* been the truth once, and surely that truth was worth telling.

Thus, having freed herself from the past, she put it firmly away and returned to the present, and she and Danielewski traveled to India to film *The Guide*, a trip which included a visit with the Dalai Lama for two *Ladies Home Journal* articles.

In New York Danielewski had been conducting a workshop loosely affiliated with the Academy of Television Arts and Sciences. Danielewski, who had made something of a name as a teacher, was described in a *Herald Tribune* interview as "Polish, blondish, slight, almost thin, very sure of himself and razor-sharp. No nonsense in conversation, speaks his mind softly and patiently but presumably could bite your head off. It is noticeable that the assembled actors in his class listen spell-bound to his comments."

When the acting classes were interrupted by his trips to India, John Anderson, the young midwesterner with theatrical ambitions, held down the office. Meanwhile Pearl found in Anderson a mine of useful information. Despite her own houseful of teenagers, her knowledge of the younger generation was oddly meager and there seems to have been among the Buck children and their mother very little free-and-easy socializing.

Dawn Akins, a visitor at Perkasie, remembered sitting on the grass by the pool eating a watermelon and competing with Pearl's daughters in a seed-spitting contest. An outraged Pearl ordered them to their knees to retrieve every seed and stood waiting until all of them were removed.

John Anderson, beyond such adolescent horseplay, found himself invited to Perkasie for weekends where Pearl made a special point of discussing the strange ways of the young. He recalled, "She would ask the significance of things men said or did, asking about love mores of the Sixties and acting shocked about living together without being married . . . or a man making an 'improper proposal' to a lady right after meeting her." Later he was to discover much of what he had said in print.

Anderson's office work included assisting Danielewski in his workshop. He remembered a pretty girl from Main Line Philadelphia who auditioned for the class. Accepted, she attended regularly, and after they became friends she invited him to her home for a weekend. Mentioning this to Danielewski he became aware of a look of displeasure which put him on his guard. He decided against accepting the invitation, and from then on, putting two and two together became for him a daily exercise in self-protection. He had seen Pearl Buck with Danielewski and he sensed the situation to be charged with crosscurrents dangerous for an ambitious young man.

The past summer Pearl had bought a guest cottage near Mountain Haunt where Danielewski had been the main guest and all had seemed serene between them. In the fall, when the drama workshop was reactivated, Anderson helped backstage, and one night the class put on a performance in which Danielewski's wife Silvia played the lead. Afterwards Anderson saw her go home alone, and having noticed a certain frigidity between husband and wife, he was not surprised. What did surprise him was that half an hour later, after he had closed the theater, he saw Danielewski and the girl from Philadelphia emerge laughing from another exit and run across the street hand in hand. He decided from then on to keep his mouth shut and know nothing whatever about anything.

Shortly after this decision, while rummaging through a file cabinet in the office, he came across a packet of letters in Pearl's hand. A single glance told him they did not concern business matters.

Later that fall Danielewski moved out of the Park Avenue apartment into a smaller one alone, and there were rumors of a divorce. At the same time Anderson noticed a subtle change in Pearl Buck. Whereas formerly she had been tense and unhappy, now she was cheerful, relaxed, "almost," he recalled, "sort of smug. I couldn't help thinking that she believed Mr. Danielewski was going to marry her. She seemed to have a new sort of self-confidence." (His intuition proved remarkably accurate. Ten years later Pearl confessed to a woman friend that she had expected to marry Tad Danielewski "but then something happened to prevent it.") Anderson felt vaguely sorry for her, realizing that she was unaware of the girl from Philadelphia.

February 16, 1963, was to be departure day for India and Pearl, Danielewski and Anderson were making preparations. One morning while Anderson was working in the outer office, he heard Danielewski on the inner phone calling Pearl at her apartment. He was saying, "We have a change of schedule and plans. John isn't going. I'm in need of him here in the office. Instead I'm taking an American actress who will play the bit part of the reporter and be my assistant."

It was difficult not to listen. "Miss Buck must have asked, 'What are you talking about, you can't do that,' because he began arguing, saying yes he could, and I guess she slammed down the phone. Anyway, in a few minutes *my* phone rang and it was Miss Buck. She said, 'John, go to an outside phone and call me.'

"I made some excuse to Mr. Danielewski and went out and called her. She said, 'Who's the girl?' I sort of stumbled, 'What do you mean?' and she said, 'Don't play games. I just found out Mr. Danielewski wants to take an American actress and leave you here. Who is she?'

"I saw I was caught, so I said, 'Well, her name is Priscilla Decatur, that's her stage name. She's from a Main Line Philadelphia family, related to the Duponts, and she's been in the workshop we've been conducting all winter.'

"She said, 'Well, don't worry, she's not going. Or there will be no production at all.'

"So that's all I know. If it came to a break my loyalty was to her, so I went to India and Priscilla didn't. But he resented me every time he looked at me, because I was there and she wasn't. It was a very painful time. There was all this strife and Miss Buck almost came home several times."

Throughout the strife Pearl, being Pearl Buck, would not, could not give up. It was her money and her power that kept Danielewski in work. But he possessed power too, and the three months in India alternated between icy demeanor and serenity.

Pearl, ever the worker, even on the set occasionally helping actors with their English, did research for the new novel to be titled *Mandala*. Danielewski, keeping up a barrage of correspondence with New York, was impatient to get home and there were problems with the Indian director. Dev Anand, the male star, whose own company had millions at stake, was equally disturbed, and at times the entire production seemed threatened. Once or twice it fell to Anderson as the only bi-partisan employee to mediate through his Indian counterpart.

Pearl's letters to Grace at this time revealed more than she actually wrote. "I got the feeling," Grace admitted, "that she was sitting alone in her hotel room while the rest of the troup—younger people—were out somewhere else. There was nothing personal about Tad in the letters, but I think she cared for him a great deal and was very lonely."

Pearl spent much of her time with Anderson, who stayed by her side whenever he was not needed on the set. "I only got out alone to sightsee a few times," he recalled, "and even so, when I got back people in the lobby would rush up yelling, 'Madame's looking for you, where have you been?' She'd be almost in a panic."

That panic could strike often, and at any time. Several years later she described such a moment, though minimizing it. "I had been in India for months," she wrote, "making with others the film *The Guide.* . . . One day the filming was over and it was time to go home. I wondered what would take the place of those months of working and living in so vivid a country. . . . I lay on my bed, supposedly resting but my mind was not at rest. I thought 'What next?' How to answer the question? I reflected on what I had not yet done of all I want to do."

Suspecting that there might soon be a vast change in her life, she feared she might be the loser. And she had to find ways to fill the emptiness that loomed ahead.

She mentioned trivialities. "I wanted to renew my French. And yes, I wanted to learn how to dance and do it well. I like to do things well, I have a passion for excellence." But these ambitions were surely not uppermost in her mind that day.

Their departure from India came in great haste, almost like an extraneous decision of Danielewski's, and part of the film remained uncompleted. Everyone wondered why. The explanation, however, seems to have come some weeks later in New York. Enigmatically Pearl wrote in her diary, "On this day, after a telephone call which resolved my heart, I burned in the fireplace of my office a handful of letters, all short, which I had written over the years to one I loved. I burned them because they were dreams never to be fulfilled and therefore they recorded nothing. Now in the fireplace there is only a small pile of ashes. This is as it must be, and perhaps as it should be. But many hours of my life lie wasted there, and some of my deepest feelings. And the one to whom the letters were written does not know what has been lost."

But, as always, she carried her head high, and still conducted business at Stratton Productions. Not until a year later did the sad story finally come to its end.

Her mind had long ago faced the fact that Tad Danielewski might return to the companionship of his own generation. His engagement to a woman his own age, the actress from Philadelphia, was proof of that. But apparently even the wedding invitation in June 1964 could not quench the nagging hope that Danielewski and she could still have some kind of relationship. She chose John Anderson to take her to the wedding, for by now she was totally at ease with him. "With her nothing ever really came to an end until the wedding," Anderson reported. "Then she gave up; she really gave up then. There was a kind of resignation in her—almost like heaving a sigh of relief, saying this is the end at last, the struggle's over.

"I sat with her at the ceremony. It was lovely, a garden wedding with a tent and orchestra and Priscilla in her grandmother's wedding dress. It was like a movie."

Paul Roebling was their best man. He had not seen Danielewski since the days of *Desert Incident* but Danielewski had asked him and he consented. "I was practically born at a Philadelphia wedding," he says, "and he needed someone presentable. I said to myself, 'Well, he did me a favor once, gave me a good part, so I'll do him a favor now.'"

Pearl managed to sit through the ceremony, though she had been given a seat on the aisle where the couple would pass on their way out. Later, beside the bride's father at the wedding banquet, she felt her strength begin to fail her and she suddenly asked Anderson to take her home.

"I think she couldn't stand seeing Tad acting like a happy bride-groom any longer, so we left and a few of us went to Bookbinder's for dinner. Afterwards Miss Buck and I went back to the farm. I think she didn't want to be alone.

"She wanted to walk down to the old summer house by the brook where she and Richard had once been so happy having picnics with the children. We didn't talk about—things. But I was so attuned to her by this time that I knew what she was thinking. And right in that little clearing she paused and turned to me and said out of a clear sky, 'Did you notice that look on Tad's face when we looked at each other? What did it mean?'

"I knew what she *hoped* it meant, that he was telling her he still loved her and was only marrying Priscilla for convenience. I couldn't tell her it was that, it wouldn't have been true or fair, but that was what he wanted *her* to *think* he was saying. He was throwing her a crumb, keeping all the doors open. So I just said, 'You know what it meant,' and let her think what she wanted. And she took a little breath—like a sigh of relief, as if that was what she hoped. And as we walked on she seemed to be happier somehow, sort of more at ease."

Whatever the message Pearl inferred from the look, she bore the new bridegroom no grudge. She continued to support Stratton Productions for a year or so, even doubling Danielewski's salary after his marriage and presenting the couple with a combined business and honeymoon trip around the world.

Years later, when someone spoke disparagingly of her former partner, she snapped, "Tad Danielewski was nothing but a blessing to me. We traveled over half the world together, he saved me many lonely hours, and we made two beautiful motion pictures together. We had unforgettable experiences that some stupid people are not even capable of understanding."

Since Pearl Buck did most things on a larger than life scale, it is not strange that in the year 1961 while she was writing lovingly of one man and clinging in despair to another, at the same time she was genuinely in love with a third.

Jackie Breen often remarked that Pearl Buck had a heart big enough to include three men at once. Each time the involvement was sincere, and each man involved brought out a different side of the multi-faceted woman.

William Ernest Hocking, despite his vast accomplishments in the academic world, was called by *Time Magazine* "The People's Philosopher." Both an idealist and a pragmatist, he was a professor at Harvard, Yale and UCLA, Gifford Lecturer at Edinburgh (one of philosophy's most prestigious appointments), and consultant to governments and financiers. He was still, as one colleague put it, "a man who thought more with his heart than with his head." It was this contrast that made him so approachable, with an almost playful sense of humor.

The book he had sent Pearl in 1960, *Thoughts on Death and Life*, written after his wife's death, had touched Pearl deeply. She had written to thank him and at his request driven from Vermont to his home in New Hampshire.

"I remember well that August day when I reached his house and saw him after a period of years," she wrote later. "He was then over eighty but he looked twenty years younger, and very vigorous . . . his eyes were as blue as ever, his step as strong. . . . I remember the feeling of recognition that passed between us, we had so much in common. "I spent the afternoon that day. But after that he began to write me regularly. . . . I wrote back. . . . It was like a new friendship. We began really to know each other. . . . In a way I had a companionship with him that I have never had with anyone else."

Since she was seldom in Vermont and he no longer drove a car, remaining on his mountain-top farm in the company of a housekeeper or his children, letters were their all-important means of communication. The earliest letter to survive was written during the winter of 1961, when their relationship had become very special to each. In the meantime they had met in New York at meetings of the Academy of Arts and Letters. Hocking had asked for her picture, and she sent a photograph of herself gazing at a small Chinese figure taken by a friend in Vermont. Hocking wrote back in delight on January 9, 1962: "O my dearest. It is here, saying what one hardly believes a photo-portrait can say—the spirit with which you regard that being—seeking, understanding, loving, evoking whatever is real in it. It is a treasure. . . . It makes one see why, in the heavenly aspects of human life, the woman is so essential—more than the father-god of the human race.

"A silly suggestion—but I don't mind being silly with you—it reminds me of Rembrandt's historic contemplative bust of Homer. . . . I don't know what it is you are looking at, but it too will come alive. I love you. Ernest."

Pearl's answer was written a few days after she had seen him.

Jamaica, Vt. Sept. 11, 1962
"My dearest. I cannot sleep tonight without telling you what you already know, that these few days with you have brought me into a new stage of being. . . . I have such an inexpressible consciousness of rest and release and confidence in knowing that we know and understand

each other completely. I *respect* you and have always looked up to you.
. . . And now to the respect and admiration is added—the immeasurable. Thank you from heart's height and depth for every moment of
these past days, for the good talk with you. I do love to listen when you
talk, and you take so amiably my questions and comments and open
another window for me to look through. . . . I think of the moment
when you suddenly changed our lives by asking me a question. That
was on our first evening, and I admire you so much for courageously
asking. . . . And then today, just before I left, you set the seal upon all
that had gone before. How deeply happy and grateful I am, dear love!
> "I love you. Pearl.
> "P.S. If this sounds like a love letter—*well, it is!*"

Pearl wrote again after another weekend spent with Hocking.

> Nov. 2, 1962

"My Ernest, my best beloved;
"It was happiness to be with you in the quiet of Mountain Haunt. I
hold the special memory of that evening when you opened your heart
to me—a treasure, a jewel in time, which I shall never forget. And on
the way home—darling, you are right about the clasp of a hand, so
warm, so reassuring. Thank you, thank you, my dearest, for every
memory."

She refers to an abstruse discussion they had had and goes on with
touching humility and pathos to reveal a life-long struggle. "I wish I
might have been your pupil long ago . . . that we had met when we were
younger. But it is entirely possible that I might not have been ready for
you as I am now, for it is not easy to cope with a temperament, an
imagination, even a talent, if you will, such as God and ancestry have
bestowed upon me. It has been like trying to drive to capacity, and yet
in orderly fashion, a team of too many horses!"
Here is a rare glimpse of a woman who in the presence of genuine
greatness can acknowledge her own failure to achieve similar grace. "I
have taken a long time," she says, "to arrive at the self-knowledge
which [would] provide the necessary discipline" but she hopes that
now with his guidance, she will do better. "You have come at the right
time, so all is right . . . and I love you."
The following letter was written while Pearl and Danielewski were

coping with final arrangements for their trip to India to film *The Guide*.

Madison, Nov. 10, 1962

"My Pearl. Rainy, foggy, one feels like a chimney fire and a chat with my dearest. Been with her all the week via ESP.... I've been listening in on you and your friend dimly aware of your wrestling with a mountain of work (same as me only worser). Let me butt in, my love. . . . In a letter . . . I said that in a certain instant there was spun an immortal tie. As if the tie had no history! We know very well that there were years of history leading up to it. . . . But the remarkable thing is, that the new rapport was *indeed instantaneous!* Our earlier years of friendship were rich, and all within the proper distance of *politesse*—politesse being a perfect and silent limit . . . such that we might have gone on for all our further years, never taking the step into the immediate reality of our feeling, and we might never have known what we had lost. . . . Intolerable! My love. Your Ernest."

Perkasie, Nov. 17

"My Ernest: Your beautiful letter . . . I have read it again and again . . . what you say about our history is true. Else why should I remember so clearly through the years . . . the first moment I saw your face? I do not remember the surroundings although I know it was China, but I see your face with such clarity as it was at that instant. I had no premonitions then, no special feeling, even, except a sort of recognition which it did not occur to me to define, much less analyze. But wonderful and blessed that we have completed the recognition by fulfilling it. It is a wonder. I doubt it has happened before in human history!"

Sun-n-Sand Hotel

Bombay, India March 27, 1963

"My dearest, my Ernest: Your letters have such a miraculous way of arriving just when I seem to need them most. It is a strange and wonderful truth that nothing takes the place of knowing that one is centrally loved and loves the other the same way. . . . I love you, my darling, and please remember, day and night, that you are centrally loved. . . .

"I have my big Indian novel [*Mandala*] already in mind now and when I come home to you I shall want to work in your library for materials in history. . . . My love, only a few more months and I will be homeward bound. Wonderful staunch love you give me—life is filled with people and work, all interesting—but what you give me I have from no one else, and to you I give what I give to no other. I love you. Your Pearl."

Here are hints of the stressful relationship with Danielewski that runs hot and cold and lacks the peace that Hocking can give her and the respect she can give Hocking.

Perkasie, July 5, 1963
[She writes of plans to visit Hocking and study his books on India.] "I just want to be in your vicinity for a bit and I feel renewed at the very thought. I am surrounded by young people, all charming to me, but not enough in the way of mental and spiritual companionship—on a mutual basis, I mean."

Pearl has by now burned her letters to Danielewski, symbolically cutting him out of her life, and this letter is an attempt to convince herself that such "young people" lack the qualities that truly interest her.

Madison, April 29, 1964
"O my love, what a joy—just to get a word from you—and what a mystery; all the world changes—ceases to be routine, puzzlement, disorder, meaningless complexity, and becomes an inviting task—all the more interesting because it is formidable. That's the miracle wrought by a touch of love.

"Spring has now burst upon us; the ice 'went out' of the pond on Sunday the 26th, five days late. The roads are passable. Crocuses and daffodils sing their defiance to the vanishing snow piles. . . . And why does Germany choose this time to confer on me the Order of Merit? I dunno; but it's sort of nice. Oh my love, so much to say to you and such a yearning for a 'touch' instead of a 'say.' It will come. . . . I break off. I love you. Your Ernest."

The Order of Merit was bestowed upon Ernest Hocking for his book, *Experiment in Education: What We Can Learn from Educating Ger-*

many, in which he had set forth arguments to counteract the post-war hostility toward Germany.

Pearl told her sister Grace that Ernest Hocking had asked her to marry him. But, as one of her daughters suggested, considering his nineteen years' seniority, she did not want to repeat her experience with Walsh, nor did she want to hurt him by continual refusal. And with her burgeoning preoccupation it was easy for her to slip away.

> Daytona Plaza, Fla.
> Nov. 6, 1964

"My love. I am here in this delightful place by the sea, but only for two days before we move on to our next place. You will remember that I told you I was making a tour on behalf of the Asian-American children . . . traveling in my own car, Mr. Ottinger driving, so I am very comfortable. I am accompanied by two young men from the offices of the foundation in Philadelphia, so I am well looked after. . . . So darling, we are not out of touch and nothing changes between us.

"This morning I am quietly in my room. At one o'clock I begin television and radio interviews. At five a cocktail party, seven o'clock dinner, nine o'clock a ball. I like to dance. . . . My Ernest, I love you. Your Pearl."

> Dec. 4, 1964
> Snow snow snow poten-
> tial water. WELCOME

"O my love, how wonderful to hear your voice. . . . When I wrote you about 'my sun is sinking' I was talking literally—I grow aware of limits—but I think the demand to keep going helps the event, and so I say

> 'But sink in FIRE
> Song without end.'

Song to you, my beloved. And then one word I didn't write and don't intend to write just yet is the word Amen, which always properly follows the words 'without end.' I love you. Ernest."

He had become very ill. Pearl had decided not to visit him, wishing to keep her memory of him strong and vigorous in contrast with her last picture of Walsh.

Wed. Jan. 5, 1966

O my very Dear,
Here I am
motionless when I
want to fly, silent
when I want to speak,
but at least
moriturus saluto
and loving you,
as always.
I love you.

Ernest

His last letter to her was written on January 27, 1966.

"Beloved. How is it possible? 'She is thinking of me.' O my darling, can it be true? I must believe—'always with love.' In spite of all the turmoil in the world, 'love never faileth.' I must send her word at once. Beloved, nothing must prevent the world from reaching you. Your spark of life may be the only surviving message. I love you always.

"God keep you living and assured of life. Your Ernest."

His death occurred on June 12, 1966.

Pearl once talked about the men in her life with a friend: "While I keep talking about my living alone, and that I've done things by myself, which is true, on the other hand, I don't know what I would have done without the important men in my life. There have always been important men and there's always been one especially, and still is, for my real friendships are very lasting.

"Most men will say that there has always been a woman behind them. I can say there has always been a man behind me. So I would like to say here that I don't think I would have written the books I have, or have grown into the person that I think I am, or reached the success in my life that I have reached, or have the sense of vitality and potential growth that I still have, if it were not for the affection, love, or whatever one wants to call it, that has been given me from men. I am grateful, for I think these friendships bring something new into my life and have contributed a great deal to my growth. And I hope I have contributed something, too, to them."

18

Pearl Buck has often been compared to a factory in which one department can suffer a temporary breakdown while the other departments keep on humming along smoothly. Knowing something of Pearl's life, Dorothy Olding stated compassionately, "People like Pearl Buck in their sixties can be desperately in love, and the older you are the more vulnerable you are." But people like Pearl Buck can also bandage the wounded area and still function.

While the woman Pearl was undergoing the pain of heartache during the filming of *The Big Wave* in 1960, the humanist Pearl Buck, with brisk efficiency, traveled in Korea observing that country's wretched orphans of mixed blood, and the writer Pearl Buck gathered material for a Korean novel. And by the time she was home both a plan and a book had begun forming in her mind.

Years earlier she had admired the Korean refugees she saw in China, tall, handsome, fair-skinned, and fervently patriotic despite the onslaughts of their neighbors, Japan and Russia. Since Korea's history included the not too admirable part played by the United States, Pearl's nagging sense of responsibility rose to the surface, and back home she set Tsuta to assembling maps and books on folklore, social customs, history—everything necessary for a large-scale historical novel, which did ultimately emerge as the longest of her career.

The Living Reed is the multi-generational history of the wealthy Il-han clan who, cut down by constant invasions and defeats, nevertheless keeps springing up like living reeds. In its review *The Journal of*

278

Asian Studies wrote, "The remarkable novels of Pearl S. Buck have given the world an awakened understanding and appreciation of the Chinese people, and now she has wrought a like marvel for Korea. . . . The Korean people come hauntingly alive and the part that Americans have played is vividly disclosed. . . . Melancholy and fascinating, it is above all a drama of men and women whose hopes and dreams are caught up in the whirlwind of history. . . . A valuable book . . . about the popular struggle against corrupt and oppressive regimes."

The New York Times called it "absorbing and fast-moving. Not a great book certainly, but eminently readable, especially revealing of Korea and one of Mrs. Buck's best."

Pearl was working on *The Living Reed* in April 1962 when the White House gave a dinner for Nobel Prize winners and, the only woman laureate, she was seated at Mrs. Kennedy's table. In *The Kennedy Women* she described part of the evening. "After dinner we were all directed back to the East Room. . . . While we were waiting for the President and Mrs. Kennedy to rejoin us . . . a kindly elderly woman came to me and said, 'I enjoyed your book *So Big*.' Not wanting to embarrass her by telling her I had not written that book I merely smiled and thanked her. Fortunately the President had returned and it was he who interrupted with a sudden question.

"'What do you think we should do about Korea?' he asked. At that moment that troubled country was far from my thoughts. 'Why do you ask?' I countered.

"'Because we can't go on as we are,' he replied in his quick direct fashion. 'Japan must help us to rebuild.'

"'Mr. President,' I replied, 'I am writing an historical novel about Korea which explains the present situation in terms of the past. I'll send you the first copy.' Alas, when the first copy came off the press in 1963 and I sent it to him, he had gone to Texas. . . . My fondest memory of him and his attractive wife is that night when both were at the height of their youth and beauty."

In 1961 Welcome House, after years of peaceful growth, had acquired a new director and with her new impetus, so that eight or ten children a year were placed with parents, and an annual family Homecoming was held in the barn. The numbers grew yearly until a hundred or more mothers and children would spill out over the grounds.

"We would try to get a picture while all the kids were still clean," Mary Graves recalled. "I'd get them all set in place and then I'd bring

Mrs. Walsh over from the house. I remember once when we were walking across she stopped and said, 'Doesn't it seem to you, my dear, that the group is growing larger every year?'

"I could see in her face that it was a little frightening, when she'd see all the children and parents massed on the stage and know that she was responsible for the change in all those lives. The parents would tell her about this, they would speak to her in such gratitude, with a sort of adoration in their faces."

The fame of Welcome House had become widespread, and the governor of Pennsylvania made her chairman of his Committee for the Handicapped, which brought her further kudos. After the death of Eleanor Roosevelt in 1962, the public outpouring of love for that remarkable woman seemed to express the world's appreciation of her humanitarian contributions and Pearl Buck remarked that there must be thousands wishing for some tangible way to express it, some favorite cause to give to in her name.

By now the simple address, "Pearl Buck, New York," without even a telephone listing, was sufficient to bring mail from all over the world and the demands for her appearance in connection with public causes bespoke an international recognition. By now she was even courting such recognition. Not only did the doors of her limousine carry her monogram but so did her car's license plate. At special functions her Chinese robes caught every eye, as did her bizarre jewelry and the slightly theatrical make-up taught her by Danielewski. Thus, the plan she proposed to the Welcome House Board was not out of character.

After initiating the idea of an Eleanor Roosevelt Memorial Fund, she also suggested a Pearl S. Buck Memorial Fund for the support of homeless Korean-American children living in Korea. The board had already discussed possible ways of helping these orphans but the death of their powerful fund-raiser, Oscar Hammerstein, had dashed their hopes. A committee was formed to consult with lawyers about operating licenses and tax exempt status.

While the memorial fund discussions dragged on into the spring of 1963, Pearl set about pursuing a plan which she had considered earlier. Telephoning the Arthur Murray Dance Studio in Jenkintown, she told the director, "My daughters need to be taught the social dances. Please send a teacher."

And on July 5, Theodore Findley Harris drove up to Green Hills Farm. Red-headed, pale, with a dancer's walk and an actor's precise diction, he entered the house and looked around. In a flash he had taken in the grounds, the wealthy elderly woman with the foreign-looking daughters and no man in sight. With professional aplomb he combined the dance instruction with easy chatter, skillfully extracting the salient facts about his client.

In a week Harris had skimmed through her books and, while filing away her answers to his flattering questions, learned her history, her tastes and her philanthropies. The history of Welcome House impressed him, and her plans for a memorial fund inspired in him an instant desire to help. He professed to know all about fund-raising. He had raised thousands of dollars putting on charity balls at so much per couple including entertainment provided by professional dancers.

Pearl Buck was enchanted. Here was the kind of enthusiasm she loved, the instant verve to be found only in the young—and Harris was only thirty-two. A ball would be wonderful; it could be given right there in the barn.

Suddenly there was activity everywhere. The barn was swept and decorated and an orchestra engaged. Harris's friends from the Jenkintown Dance Studio were hired, Wendy Park and Frank Davis and Jimmie Pauls—though Jimmie Pauls, Harris's old friend, looked more like a bodyguard than a dancer.

The ball, held in October 1963, was a great success; seven hundred dollars were raised while Pearl Buck waltzed, astonishing her friends, and Harris and three colleagues performed a Shadow Dance to tremendous applause.

Stratton Productions' Anderson and Danielewski were both on hand to witness the emergence of a new Pearl Buck. Danielewski, searching out new film projects to promote and editing *The Guide*, was still part of the landscape, and he and she still met each other at the office. But the earlier intensity had shifted. Pearl's attention was now riveted on a second Welcome House ball because the first had been so successful. Pearl's horizons were widening in all directions.

An April ball of much greater dimensions was planned and many local people were becoming involved (a chance to meet Pearl S. Buck socially was a lure for both the rich and the curious). The Jenkintown Studio was abuzz, and all winter Harris was in and out of Green Hills Farm. For Pearl one of his charms was the fact that he seemed to think as she did. It was taken for granted that the ball would be planned on a lavish scale. No hotel ballroom would be big enough for it and only Philadelphia's Convention Hall would serve.

At this suggestion one Main Line matron shuddered. "But, my dear, you can't possibly hold a charity affair in Convention Hall. It has no prestige."

Pearl's smile was serene. "I take my prestige with me," she replied simply.

Throughout the winter Harris's audacity, his juggernaut quality exactly matching her own, delighted Pearl. "You can't" was an incitement to "I shall," and his dependable enthusiam for her every caprice, graced by little attentions and obvious devotion, restored her morale. After Danielewski, he was the perfect tonic.

As the hectic activity gathered speed, Harris's regular teaching duties suffered, and the Arthur Murray Studio began to complain. And the day he hung a banner over the door, "WELCOME HOUSE OF THE PEARL S. BUCK FOUNDATION," the manager exploded.

The board of directors of Welcome House went into a huddle. "There is *no* Pearl S. Buck Foundation as yet," they affirmed stonily. But in January they received a staggering surprise.

Among the awards pouring in on Pearl S. Buck these days was the Gimbel Award for Humanity. In January of 1964 she was honored for her work on behalf of retarded children and especially for Welcome House. The winner's identity was kept secret until the award luncheon, but Pearl had been tipped off and was present. Margaret Fischer, seated at a ringside table, saw a number of Welcome House board members and thought she knew the reason.

"I thought it was so nice that Pearl was being given a thousand dollars for all the years she had devoted to Welcome House, and of course I assumed she'd turn the money over to it. So when she stood up after the applause and announced that she was starting a new foundation to aid the Korean orphans and this money would be the first donation to it—well, I just sat there with my mouth open. And some of the committee who had voted for her were just as stunned."

Pearl's plans for the new foundation had crystallized two weeks before. For some time she had urged the Welcome House committee to get the memorial fund under way but the chairman had procrastinated. Furthermore, the Board had not been impressed with Theodore Harris, the young man Pearl had nominated for a place on the board. Her impatience mounting, on Christmas Eve during a foxtrot lesson she had answered Harris's chatty "Have you made any New Year's resolutions?" with a simple "Yes. Right after the first of the year I'm going to set up my foundation and I want you on it. I want you to be its head."

Pearl's first attempt to place Harris on the Welcome House Board had resulted in an investigation of him by one of the Board members, which described him as a "con man and a practicing homosexual." A furious Pearl Buck vigorously denied any suggestion of illicit relationships with young men. But, she added, who cared anyway? She could name a number of great men of whom the same thing had been said. She then proceeded with incorporating her own foundation.

On February 3, 1964, the Pearl S. Buck Foundation was set up as a Delaware Corporation with Pearl and Harris and a third party (who subsequently absented himself). The dance studio, with its firm rule against fraternization between teachers and clients, promptly fired Harris, and he moved into the Drake Hotel.

One of Harris's and Pearl's first acts was to decide on an attention-getting theme for their fund-raising appeals, and they chose a poem sent to Pearl by a reader in Korea.

Who killed Kim Christopher?
I remember the day he came,
Tied on a stranger's back,
Hamster cheeks,
Blue eyes huge with wonder,
Skin like brown cream.
A happy, silly smile,
On a trusting "love me" face.
Who killed Kim Christopher?
He had no name,
No birth date,
No record of existing.

His life story?
Birth,
Abandonment,
Pneumonia,
Death.
Time?
Six months.

Who killed Kim Christopher?
The father who gave him life in a moment of lust?
The mother whose race could not accept him?
The monsters who made a war?

Or the snug and safe who ignored him?
Who killed Kim Christopher?

Pearl drafted the first mailing piece. "After fifteen years in the field
of lost and needy children I am convinced that the most needy in the
world are the children born in Asia whose mothers are Asian but whose
fathers are American. In all family-oriented societies of Asia such
children have little chance of education or jobs. They are considered
foreigners and thus ostracized.

"We Americans are partly responsible for them. It is not good for
American prestige that our half-American children should grow up
illiterate, driven by destitution into criminality and prostitution. But
our troops are still there and so many more children continue to be
born, about a thousand a year. I plan to spend the rest of my life and
strength helping the Korean children right where they are. My foundation will place a permanent representative in Korea to find the half-
American ones and we will try to keep them with their mothers. And
we will try to help the mothers find work and make a good home.

"It is my hope that because each of the children is an American he
will be proud of our share in him and be an honor to our efforts on his
behalf."

With that mailing the Pearl S. Buck Foundation was launched. But
her thousand-dollar Gimbel Award was only seed money and just a
fraction of that needed. Shortly after the fund was incorporated, Pearl
and Harris accompanied by two strangers entered the John Day office.

Dick Walsh, Jr., and Tsuta were in London on company business
and editor Robert Hill was in charge. Tsuta described the events that
took place in a letter to her Austrian accompanist, Itkis.

"The Konigen [Empress] went to the J. D. office in N.Y. right after
we left with her lawyer and the head of a big private loan corporation
and her precious director and tried to get Bob to sign important
documents in our absence. He refused but she made him telephone.
She hounded us on the phone to authorize signing without our ever
seeing! Dick refused, so they read it word by word and fought on the
phone for *one and a half hours* across the Atlantic (hundreds and
hundreds of dollars). We were very shaken up by it, and then it
happened again one week later. It made life pretty tough."

Seeking funds for her Foundation Pearl had asked Hill to sign a
document which would assign her future royalties and earnings to a

corporation as security for a six-figure loan. Dick's refusal was based on experience, for after ten years of business dealings with his step-mother, he had learned that in money matters, Pearl must be carefully held on a very tight rein.

This refusal may have precipitated her next move. Since Walsh's death the chore of managing her money bored her. Her secretary Jackie Breen explained: "Money really wasn't a concern with Mrs. Walsh. She wasn't a good business woman; when she decided to trust someone she relied on them implicitly and wasn't interested in the details. So accountants were always after her about writing checks without re-cording them. And when the checks bounced, she didn't care; she knew royalties were always coming in so she'd get it somehow. She really didn't care about money, just wanted to spend it. And I don't believe she ever read the fine print in her contracts."

In particular Pearl Buck resented the Internal Revenue Service, which always seemed to be on her trail. Psychologically unable to accept the principle of the income tax, she failed to provide for it and would then have to borrow to meet payments. Of the men available for business advice, Dick always put the brake on spending, while Daniel-ewski, though willing to help her gamble, couldn't be relied upon to produce a winner.

But now, suddenly, here was a man with the initiative and brilliance she admired. Instead of collapsing before the John Day rebuff, Harris came up with a solution to end all her problems. He simply suggested she drop the tiresome accountants and longwinded lawyers who wasted her valuable time; he knew a lawyer who could handle every-thing for her. He would incorporate her into the Foundation, her copyrights would be transferred to it and her royalties deposited in its keeping. In turn she would become the Foundation's employee, re-lieved of all financial cares and drawing a salary in whatever amount she chose. It seemed simplicity itself to the beleaguered author, and it was no sooner suggested than accomplished.

On the pledge of her royalties, a loan was made with which to lease a mansion in the heart of an exclusive area of Philadelphia. Elegant furnishings were acquired plus an office staff of three; and for Theo-dore Harris, in appreciation for his help, there were gifts of a car, jewelry and several credit cards. By the end of 1964 nearly half a million dollars had been spent or pledged on Foundation properties and a "research and information program."

All of this had been quickly set in motion, even before the Convention Hall ball held in April, which yielded $13,000. Technically, the affair had been labeled a Welcome House benefit. Now, however, Harris announced that it was actually to be the forerunner of a new series of balls to be produced for the Foundation.

The Welcome House adoption policy had turned out to be a potent fund-raising tool and Pearl still hoped to combine the two agencies. One member felt strongly, however, that, "We have no question about the need for such a foundation, nor the validity of the purpose of the foundation. It's the *foundation* of the Foundation that we question." Thus the two forces remained unaligned.

To further allay fears or doubts about the Foundation, Pearl brought up her heavy guns. Aware of the comforting power of big names she used her own to entice a battery of others onto the Foundation letterhead: Steve Allen, Rear Admiral Philip Ashler, Art Buchwald, Joan Crawford, General Dwight D. Eisenhower, Arlene Francis, Huntington Hartford III, Robert F. Kennedy, Gypsy Rose Lee, Joseph Levine, Mrs. William Scranton, R. Sargent Shriver, Sophie Tucker, Fred Waring, General James Van Fleet, Her Highness Princess Grace of Monaco, Ambassador from Korea to the United States, Ambassador from the United States to Korea.

Backed by such towering luminaries, thousands of skillfully phrased appeals were mailed across the country, Pearl S. Buck stories and articles relating the tragic story of the little Kim Christophers of Asia. Inspired by Pearl's eloquent prose, money poured in. And an even more potent appeal was introduced—Pearl Buck in a series of personal appearances, telling in her melodious voice the moving story of the children, and Pearl in a beautiful evening gown dancing the opening waltz in ball after ball across the country.

By the fall of 1964 a cross-country tour had been arranged, twenty-one cities from coast to coast with newspapers and TV stations alerted and all local dignitaries on the reception committees. The drawing power of Pearl's name had never been more apparent.

Harrisburg was chosen for the initial personal appearance. First there was a meeting with reporters, followed by a cocktail party and dinner; then in the crowded ballroom at the appointed moment, with a fanfare Pearl was led onto the dance floor by Harris and swept into a majestic waltz.

They danced so late in Harrisburg there was barely time to be ready for the 7:30 A.M. plane south to New Orleans, their next stop. Though Pearl swore she had not slept, she was ready for the press and the TV tapings just as she was at the other nineteen cities. She returned home exhausted but gratified.

This royal treatment was proving to be a new high for Pearl after the shattering emotional blow she had experienced in June.

19

When John Anderson escorted Pearl Buck to Danielewski's wedding in 1964, he had been with Stratton Productions for three years. In his position there he had been one of the few close enough to witness the gradual disintegration of the Danielewski affair and the only employee to become Pearl's confidant. On many occasions he had seen the naked misery on her face and had tried, without embarrassing her, to let her know she had a friend.

His great value to Pearl was his youth. She had just been rejected by youth, and though she knew Hocking loved her, that was not enough. She needed youth itself, and the vibrant electricity it transmitted.

Her summers were spent in Vermont and her winters divided between Stratton Productions and John Day in New York, and Welcome House and now the Foundation in Philadelphia. In 1964, her relationship with Danielewski over and with Harris tied to the dance studio and, before his death, Hocking available only on an occasional weekend, she invited Anderson to Vermont.

While in Vermont they worked on the re-write of a screenplay of *Imperial Woman*, which Danielewski had written and tried unsuccessfully to sell to Sophia Loren.

By this time the Convention Hall Benefit Ball had taken place, but the twenty-one-city tour was still in the planning stage. Anderson was becoming aware, however, of Pearl's new fascination with ballroom dancing and her frequent references to "Mr. Harris." (He would be "Mr. Harris" until the end.) "Unfortunately," she told Anderson, "he's red-headed and I hate red hair." Anderson believed she was telling him he would not be supplanted, at least not by Mr. Harris.

At the same time, though, she seemed to be considering a new job for him. The Foundation, she informed him, did not want to offer Korea its services before learning what Korea really needed, and a vital young investigator was needed, someone with flair and sensitivity. Would John like to go to Korea?

Anderson, sensing the slow decline of Stratton Productions, was more than eager, so Pearl sent him off for a week-end of consultation with Harris. "By the way," she said off-handedly, as he left, "there's been a rumor Mr. Harris and Mr. Pauls are homosexuals. There's no truth in it. I just thought I'd set your mind at rest."

At Delancey Place in Philadelphia, life was lived luxuriously, with a full-time cook and a house-boy. Pearl's bedroom was on the third floor, Ted Harris's and Jimmie Pauls's above that, and though Anderson hadn't forgotten Pearl's farewell statement, he was not surprised at what he encountered. Over the weekend there was considerable drinking and with each additional glass, Harris's conversation became franker and more intimate. Though Anderson tried to stick to the subject of Korea, Harris kept returning to more personal subjects, probing for Anderson's reactions.

Suddenly he asked John if he knew just how rich this old woman really was? Not one million, my dear, he told Anderson, but many, *many* millions. Everything in the future looked extremely interesting, and he had it all sewed up, he continued. And later, after she was dead, he would be off to Europe. He would have to go, really, on account of her heirs. But, of course, he wouldn't go alone. Had Anderson ever been to Paris?

Anderson, appalled, kept up a noncommittal front and the weekend ended without further strain, but the job in Korea was not set either. Anderson suddenly saw Pearl Buck, "this old woman," as terribly vulnerable, even endangered and, as he had in India and after the Danielewski wedding, he silently offered a protective presence she was not aware she needed.

As Stratton Productions' business dwindled, there was less for Anderson to do. One day in 1964 he witnessed the beginning of the end. As Pearl left the office after a business conference, Danielewski, gallant as always, escorted her down to her car. In place of her usual Cadillac, a Chrysler limousine with a uniformed chauffeur stood waiting at the curb. She started toward it.

"Wait, Pearl," Danielewski called out, "that's not your car."

With a smile, she replied, "Yes, it is," and got in. As it drove off Danielewski saw the three silver initials monogrammed on the door—TFH.

"When Danielewski came back up to the office," Anderson recalled, "he was white. He looked like he'd just seen his house blown away. 'This is serious, John,' he said. 'What shall we do?'"

Finally when the last Stratton Productions' project failed to materialize, Danielewski called Anderson into his office. "John," he said, "you see how things are around here. We'll have to find you another job."

"Never mind," Anderson told him, "I've seen it coming. I'll find another job for myself." And he did—but not at once, for it seemed a résumé listing Stratton Productions was not an impressive recommendation.

And Pearl was no help, for by now her interest had moved off in a different direction.

Theodore Harris's influence was being felt in many places. One day Dick Walsh received an unusual call. Pearl had been looking through a pile of old manuscripts and came across some unpublished stories which had apparently never been submitted for publication. Wasn't this rather peculiar?

Dick reminded her that John Day had published a collection of odd pieces under the title *Fourteen Stories* some time ago. But if she liked, he would be glad to reread any others she recommended.

And, she told her stepson, she had discovered to her amazement that she had written a great many plays, *thirty* actually! And not a single one had been published. But here Dick dug in his heels. Publishers *did not* publish unproduced plays because no one ever *read* unproduced plays. Of course, if she insisted. . . . But she did not pursue the subject.

Contrary to the present custom this telephone call from her was not interrupted by Harris on an extension. It was becoming increasingly common for him to cut in with opinions and suggestions; he had also taken to escorting her to business meetings and her agent, Dorothy Olding, recalled one such occasion: "Some of Pearl's rejected manuscripts were being discussed because Harris was planning to dig up heaps of old stuff. Finally, I couldn't stand it, I said, 'Wait a minute— those books weren't good books in the first place. What are you trying to do? You're going to damage Miss Buck terribly if you bring out those books.' I was so mad at Harris. He told Pearl Buck every book was a masterpiece and she believed every word he said."

Ironically, it was among the "duds" that *The Time Is Noon* was discovered. Dick Walsh recognized at once the richness of some of the book and was happy to put it into production. But unfortunately the jarring memory of his father's suppression of the manuscript stirred up old resentments in Pearl, and she now saw him as holding back her good work merely on the pretext of relieving an overcrowded market. Old friends of the Walshes were amazed to hear her denigrate a marriage they had always thought a good one. William A. Smith, the artist who illustrated many of Pearl Buck's children's books, reported sadly, "I resented her disloyalty to Richard Walsh . . . saying she had always had to support both of her husbands and all that stuff. She didn't recognize Walsh's contribution to her career. That was Harris's charm, of course. Everything she wrote was perfection."

Inevitably the situation at John Day became the subject of gossip along Publisher's Row; their famous author was making noises of discontent. Since the ethics of publishing allowed an outside publisher to propose an idea to a contracted author who could legitimately accept it, a number of quickie books by Pearl Buck, under different publishers' imprints, began to appear. *Fairy Tales of the Orient* and *Children for Adoption* were published in 1965; *The People of Japan*, *Pearl Buck's Oriental Cookbook* and *The Little Fox in the Middle*, in 1966. Later publications were *Story Bible*, *A Book of Christmas*, and *America*.

For *The Kennedy Women*, she received an advance of $75,000. She wrote the book, she said, out of sympathy with the Kennedy family who were so conspicuously talented and successful that they unwittingly aroused the destructive element in people. She said she knew how they must feel.

These literary defections showed John Day how easily Pearl could be induced to jump over the fence, and a battery of high-priced lawyers was hired to negotiate an airtight contract in which everyone would get something. The John Day Company was given United States publication rights to her entire literary output with the exception of items previously committed elsewhere, plus a schedule of publication dates assuring a decent interval between books.

Pearl received a guarantee of a $75,000 advance for each novel with a straight fifteen percent royalty, but a somewhat lower rate on her children's books, non-fiction and collections.

At Harris's insistence a clause was included to provide that royalties from most of her previous books, and those now and in the future written as a Foundation employee, were to go directly to the Foundation.

All parties professed themselves pleased. But even after all the complicated contractual negotiations, if an outside publisher came up with a tempting offer, Pearl Buck was willing to listen.

In setting up the Foundation, Pearl and Harris, after acquiring their dazzling array of names for window-dressing, had gathered together a group of interested non-celebrities as a working board. The list, however, tended to change rather rapidly and one member explained why she attended only a single meeting. "At the board meeting I attended Mr. Harris, who as president was presiding, said, 'I'm going to leave the room now and ask Miss Buck to be temporary chairman.' After he left she said, 'Mr. Harris wants me to bring up the question of his salary. As you know he is now receiving only seventy-five hundred a year and very generously is giving half of that back. But now he would like to have a salary of forty-five thousand. And he would like it to be for life, so that whether he left the Foundation or whatever, he would always have it. I personally would like to see this resolution passed.'

"When the vote went round the table most people okayed it but when it got to me I said, 'I think this is unprecedented. No organization I ever heard of gave somebody a life-time salary whether he worked or not. I don't believe it is even legal. Why, he might decide just to go fishing or something all his life. What about that?'

"She said, 'I'd still like to have it passed,' so I abstained. At that point she sort of looked at me and then around the table and she said, 'Anything you do for or against Mr. Harris, you do for or against me.' I said, 'I still abstain,' but the others voted with her and it passed. A couple of weeks later I received a letter from Mr. Harris saying he was making room on the board for some new members and he was accepting my resignation—which of course I hadn't offered. So that was my involvement with the Foundation. Of course everyone else had thought that salary was all right so maybe I was wrong."

By 1966 the Foundation's expenditures had increased to the point that in order to raise money Harris had Pearl's Vermont property appraised. Over the years she had steadily bought parcels of land adjoining her home until finally she owned four houses and over four hundred acres. A mortgage for close to $500,000 was arranged on the property which put the Foundation in a comfortably solvent position.

On a trip to Korea with Harris and Frank Davis, another dance instructor, Pearl as usual visited Miki Sawada. In view of their mutual interest in the G.I. orphans Pearl announced to the Japanese press that the Pearl S. Buck Foundation was donating $50,000 to Mrs. Sawada's renowned home.

For Pearl dealing now in such large sums with a man of similar disposition who relieved her of all the tiresome details seemed to lift her spirits magically. "These young men," she told Dick Walsh, "are my kind, keeping me young." And life was exciting for her at this point. Three new college degrees, Doctor of Letters, Doctor of Humane Letters and Doctor of Law, were added to the ten she had already acquired. In 1966 the Gallup Poll listed her among the ten most admired American women. And *Good Housekeeping* magazine followed suit with its own Ten Most list, Pearl second only to Rose Kennedy.

John Mack Carter, the editor of *Good Housekeeping*, spoke almost reverently of the position Pearl Buck had held. "The response of the public, the millions and millions of readers, was as close to being absolutely guaranteed as any writer I've ever come across. And yet her literary quality was erratic and uneven. A story might happen to be very good or happen to be very bad, but there was something there that went beyond stringing words together and developing character.

"Running through Pearl Buck's work and the women readers' response to it, there was that thing every editor wants and good editors have—an unspoken, undefined rapport. It's almost an ethereal thing, a wave-length you're on with the reader and a sensitivity to it. Pearl Buck had that wave-length. It emanated from her. The readers knew it, they felt it."

Carter analyzed this special wave-length more fully. "I think what happened was that Pearl Buck had such a totally overwhelming *compassion for women* that no matter how it was cloaked with words or literary devices, that compassion came through. The reader felt it, whatever the story. She didn't even have to finish reading the story to feel it.

"That whole thing about Pearl and Harris is a mystery to me. When they were here together she absolutely *deferred* to him. He'd say something and she'd just sit back and look proud, like a mother seeing only the good in her child. There was a tremendous attachment there, not a man-woman thing; something deeper. He really dominated her. And she enjoyed it. She glowed . . . sort of glowed with pride. It was almost childlike and touching."

Harris's influence on Pearl Buck ran not only deep but wide, evidenced not only in her professional working world but in her expanding social life. The Welcome House Ball in the barn had introduced her to a new world of people and events, and soon Harris had her attending openings in a white mink coat with a full-length white fox snap-on extension. He had her frequenting cocktail parties (escorting her himself) and this social universe became an integral part of her life.

Meanwhile, other prestigious people were assembled for the Foundation, solid names who not only gave it prominence but who truly labored for the cause—Marvin Thorn, an officer of the Girard Trust Bank; Max Aronoff, Director of the New School of Music in Philadelphia; industrialist Norman Coates; Mrs. Donald Stabler of Pittsburgh and Mrs. Augustus Studer, Jr., of Montclair, New Jersey, the latter a member of the Vineland Training School Board and various other boards.

In December 1966, the scene of the Foundation activity widened. New York City was added to the list of benefit sites when the Korean Foundation and the Pearl S. Buck Foundation jointly undertook to put on a benefit dinner dance in cooperation with 20th Century Fox's premiere of their film *The Sand Pebbles*. Fox's public relations director, realizing she was dealing with amateurs, sent an SOS to an old pro at handling charity affairs.

Mrs. Donald Sills, wife of a prominent New York lawyer, was an ardent fan of Pearl S. Buck's and volunteered to lend her expertise to the affair. "The ball was the first time I ever met Miss Buck," Ruth Sills recalled. "Fox did the affair up with the usual glamour, Klieg lights and so on—the whole P. R. bit. There was a supper afterwards and I put Miss Buck with the Korean general and Mr. Harris at another table. He made a great scene and said, 'I'm always seated with Miss Buck' and so on, but somebody told him not to irritate me and so he calmed down and apologized."

A few weeks after the successful *Sand Pebbles* benefit, Pearl Buck invited Ruth Sills to Philadelphia for lunch and sent the Cadillac to pick her up. At lunch she asked Mrs. Sills to join the Board and help raise funds in New York where the real money lay. Ruth Sills was thrilled to be asked and the "Good Earth Ball" was planned for next winter.

Thus, with her name prominently displayed on the social pages, in the public opinion polls, on the best-seller lists and on her own organizations, Pearl S. Buck was sitting on top of the world. Furthermore, her image could hardly be damaged by the series of news items picturing her as a tremendous money-maker and an equally lustrous philanthropist. On February 15, 1967, *The New York Times* ran a short item, "Deal with Wolper Negotiated with Mrs Buck and Ted Harris for Over 200 Works." "Mrs. Buck is a salaried consultant to the Foundation. Wolper Productions, which plans to produce some of the works for TV and for movies, will act as the Foundation's agent in placing properties in the various media."

On the same day the *New York Post*'s columnist, Bob Williams, commented on the above item. "Ted Harris, Foundation President, estimated the benefits might range anywhere from six million to seventeen million. He said it was anticipated that ten or fifteen top TV shows might result from the arrangement."

On February 20 the *Chicago Daily News* interviewed Pearl Buck in the luxurious Lexington Avenue offices of Wolper Productions. The interviewer noted, "The alert dowager-writer wore a gray wool suit and a mink-trimmed Persian lamb jacket. Her silver hair was swept back beneath a Greta Garbo-style gray slouch hat and her perfectly applied subdued make-up gave her the appearance of a much younger woman than her seventy-four years. She announced the agreement with the movie documentary firm to develop an over-all program. Her share of the take will go to the Pearl S. Buck Foundation."

In May the Associated Press carried on its wires, nationwide, the story: "Novelist Pearl Buck has announced that she will give her one million dollar estate to the Pearl S. Buck Foundation devoted to furthering the welfare of half-American children living in Asian countries. The Nobel Prize-winning author, about to celebrate her seventy-fifth birthday, is preparing to make a trip to Korea."

And in July 1967 the *Doylestown Intelligencer* headlined, "Pearl S. Buck Foundation Donated Land by Founder. Pearl S. Buck, the first of the nationally and internationally famed literary celebrities to settle in the 'genius belt' in Bucks County has transferred some of her land holdings to the Pearl S. Buck Foundation. . . . The Green Hills Farm mansion and adjoining acreage were not part of the gift."

During these high-rolling years several cross-country tours were made in Pearl's enormous limousine. Thousands of miles were clocked on the speedometer while she and Harris sat taping lengthy conversations about themselves and the genesis of the Foundation which when collated would become the book *For Spacious Skies*. In Denver the limousine broke down and as Pearl later explained to a friend, "We were moving about the country so fast we had no time to wait for repairs, so there was nothing to do but buy another car."

Their fund-raising activities reached a climax in Tucson, Arizona. At one of the teas given by the wealthy of the community, Pearl described the tragic children of Korea so eloquently that Mrs. Richard Wilson pledged a $10,000 gift. The Wilson family was already familiar with Pearl Buck's work, having adopted through Welcome House an American-Indian and an Amerasian child to join their own four children. Within the year after his wife's contribution, Dr. Richard Wilson, who taught geology as an avocation at the University of Arizona, donated $525,000 and pledged $1 million to be spread over the next ten years. When he was asked to become a member of the Foundation board, he gladly accepted.

Not only was the Foundation reaching new financial heights but Pearl Buck's writing career, which seemed to have slowed down, took a sharp turn upward. In 1968 she published a novel, *The New Year*, which reflected the mood of the Foundation, the story of a mixed-blood love child. Then, having stayed close to China in whatever way she could, she wrote another Chinese novel, *The Three Daughters of Madame Liang*. *The Good Earth*'s Wang Lung had had three sons, each representing one of early China's three sociological classes. Now, Madame Liang, a modern Chinese woman, running a chic restaurant in Shanghai, has three daughters, who represent the three areas of modern Chinese women's lives. The Book of the Month Club selected the book, and that sum, when combined with money from the *Reader's Digest*, which condensed it, guaranteed the author $170,000. Things had never looked better.

But something unsuspected was brewing. An article in *Philadelphia*, a local monthly magazine, hit the stands the first week of July

1969, and immediately thereafter the local radio station, WIP, broadcast on three successive days some taped depositions of four Korean boys from the Foundation. Pearl Buck was suddenly faced with the most horrendous dilemma of her life.

Several years earlier Greg Walter, a reporter for *Philadelphia*, had asked Pearl for an interview. Critical of some of the magazine's content, she had refused, and Walter had pursued his story elsewhere, interviewing a vast number of people. The following is a digest of the resulting article.

Title: *The Dancing Master*. Subhead: *Famed novelist Pearl S. Buck has been waltzed into a heart-breaking story.*

Pearl Buck, known in Korea as Great Lady, has all Korean people puzzled; they hope she will come to her senses before it is too late.

Reason: friendship with Fred L. Hair, Jr., alias Theodore Findley Harris, thirty-two-year-old president of Pearl S. Buck Foundation who, leaving school in South Carolina after eighth grade, works thereafter as dance instructor, most recently with Arthur Murray Studio in Jenkintown, Pa. Having put on successful benefit ball for Pearl Buck's Welcome House he plans a cross-country dance tour for self and Pearl Buck, announcing it will be for benefit of Foundation under auspices of Arthur Murray studio. (Arthur Murray attorney immediately denies having made such commitment.)

Responding to Foundation's appeal for funds, Ross Forney, Dallas millionnaire, makes large donation and offers to underwrite a year's salary for Korean Pill Jay Cho as director of Foundation in Seoul.

Harvey Wright, ex-Marine, is engaged as Foundation's representative in Seoul. Given work but no plans and operating blind, Wright waits for specific orders and funds. After three months he quits, notifying Forney of his reasons. Puzzled, Forney writes Pearl Buck but receives letter from Harris canceling association.

Frank Davis and Alan Tate, dance instructors on Foundation staff, are sent to Seoul to investigate. They spend $4000 in one week while at same time ordering Pill Jay Cho to economize by working out of his home instead of a special office.

Second Foundation representative, ex-Marine William Scott, is engaged. Briefed at home office in Delancey Place he receives unfavorable impression of operations and personnel and writes Pearl Buck suggesting an investigation. Instead she orders him fired.

Harris announces change in operations. Besides housing orphans in Foundation buildings in Seoul they will support mothers and children in their own homes with sponsors' donations of $12 monthly.

Third Foundation representative, dance instructor Donald Anderson, engaged November 1965. He sells his house and goes to Korea. After four months he writes office asking reimbursement for funds he has laid out and is ordered fired by Pearl Buck.

Fourth representative, Gene Brooks, is engaged in Tucson after interviewing Pearl Buck for his paper. She and Harris are touring and take him along to San Francisco where Harris decides to open a western office. Brooks, installed in expensive office, secures many pledges of goods and properties for Korea and reports them to home office. Pledges are never followed up. He writes many letters, gets no replies. Finally writes full explanation to Pearl Buck and quits, leaving many unpaid bills.

During same tour Pearl Buck and Harris open Portland, Oregon, office with dance instructor Keith J. Berkley in charge. Local police recognize Berkley driving Lincoln Continental registered to Pearl S. Buck Foundation and expose him as ex-con James Jones Willis. Reporter for *Oregonian* writes investigatory article on Foundation and Harris citing questionable practices. (Article is seen only in Oregon community.)

Fifth representative, Richard McLaughlin, ex-Bell Telephone salesman met during installation of Delancey house phone system, goes to Seoul late 1966. Under instructions to decorate Seoul office using money donated for child support, he is reprimanded by Korea officials and is also attacked by Koreans when obeying Harris order to fire Pill Jay Cho. He leaves.

Early 1967, Pearl Buck and Harris, while vacationing at Bar Harbor, Maine, engage motel operator Warren Wakeman as representative number six. Under Harris's orders he fires Pill Jay Cho; again Koreans riot. He is sent to Okinawa as research expert.

Dallas minister Delbert Amos, spotted on local TV program by Harris, is sent to Seoul as representative seven, replacing Wakeman. He and wife go there and settle down.

June 1967, "Million Dollar Opportunity Center" in Sosa is opened to celebrate Pearl Buck's 75th birthday.

Spring 1968, disaster in Sosa; small child drowns in unguarded pool on Foundation premises.

In resulting confusion in Sosa social workers and counselors demand improvement in conditions, threatening to resign. Instead Harris fires them and puts in their place older adolescent boys to counsel mothers and children.

Board member Richard Wilson, disturbed by child's death, goes to Korea for personal investigation and on return institutes private audit of Foundation's books and prepares report of conditions for full Foundation's Board.

About this time a Korean newspaper publishes long, highly critical article on Foundation, its financial management, its director Delbert Amos, and its policy of sending boys to "counsel" in prostitutes' home.

Delbert Amos resigns, fall 1968.

Greg Walter's report on the Foundation's activities ends on this date. But during the course of his interviewing he also received a great deal of related information about the Foundation's finances and its personnel, including its founder, Pearl Buck. The article describes conditions as they prevailed at Delancey Place shortly before *Philadelphia* went to press.

As of late 1968 both Harris and his friend Frank Davis have lifetime contracts rising to $45,000 a year. Harris meanwhile gets a free home at Delancey Place, a limousine with handsome young chauffeur to whom he gives jewelry and money; he has use of American Express and travel cards, a $4000 yearly automobile allowance, and much expensive jewelry.

His manners in public are described by many observers who report shouting and tantrums, bullying co-workers, demanding excessive personal attentions, all of which Pearl Buck passes off with an indulgent smile, explaining that he is "very brilliant, very high-strung and artistic."

Besides the haphazard administration of the Foundation there are repercussions from unpaid bills and reports of employees having to pay office expenses out of their own pockets.

One very large obligation never honored is the $50,000 promised Miki Sawada and the monthly $12 support money for children and mothers. Mrs. Sawada, unwilling to let her friend be known in Japan as having defaulted on her promise, has herself been sending the checks out in her name.

Harris's private life has also become public. He has arranged, with Pearl Buck's assistance, to bring two adolescent Korean boys to the Foundation's Hilltop Home for Boys, promising to treat them like a father. They are astonished at American fathers' ways—undressing them, giving them liquor and pills, etc.

Harris, wishing to adopt one of them and knowing he cannot as a single man, begins courting his female secretary. Meanwhile a reporter on Philadelphia Station WIP-TV, having heard unsavory stories about Harris, has taped interviews with several of the boys.

Pearl Buck continues to support Harris's attempts at adoption, and Harris gets married on December 7, 1968.

At this point the magazine, to meet its deadline, was forced to leave the full story uncompleted. Summing up the events thus far it then returned to its opening theme, that Pearl S. Buck, a Nobel Prize recipient, had somehow, incredibly, let herself be conned into looking like a dupe and a simpleton.

Pearl Buck had a split-second decision to make—admit the facts or deny them. She could say, "My God, how deceived I have been! How horribly my confidence has been betrayed!" This tack would wash her clean and instantaneously reinstate her with the public and her friends. But it would also be tantamount to calling herself a senile fool taken in by a clever knave.

Other than that she could issue a blanket denial and threaten lawsuits. Even if she chose to temporize it would lend credence to the article and the broadcasts—and to the lethal document now in Dr. Wilson's hands, those three hundred pages of interviews with Foundation employees, reporters, school teachers, tutors, counselors, neighbors and a number of Korean and Japanese boys at Hilltop and the Opportunity Center.

With the boldness that had fueled her through forty years of public life she stared down the indisputable facts. "It's a lie," she declared. "Every word of it is a lie." A year before, it turned out, the four Korean boys had gone to Pearl Buck to report having been sexually solicited by Harris, and she had told them angrily, "There will be no talking about Mr. Harris or you will all go back where you came from." Distressed and frustrated, they had told their stories to two male employees of the Foundation and had in turn been taken by them to Paul Rust at Station WIP. Later, however, they had become fearful of what Harris might do, plus the fact that they were bringing shame upon the organization, and they asked Rust to withhold their taped conversations at least for the present.

Independently, Dr. Richard Wilson, now a member of the Foundation Board, had flown out to Seoul to inspect the local operation, and having become highly suspicious of the management, instituted a private investigation of Harris and the Foundation's books. In another separate area Mrs. Augustus Studer, experienced in the financial matters of other boards, began asking questions about the unusual number of staff personnel on this particular Board and its unusual expenditures—for instance, a private swimming pool for Harris and twelve cars in the garage, three for him.

Eventually, word of the boys' tapes and the Wilson investigation came to Harris's attention. By now he had presented one of the youths with a Thunderbird and allowed him special privileges while the other boys lived unsupervised in a sparsely furnished house where they ate TV dinners. Determined to obtain the boy's consent, Harris told him he had visited his mother in Korea and that she had "given him to Harris for adoption, no matter what he says."

The existence of the investigation appeared to give Harris further thoughts about his life style. He therefore bought, again with Pearl's assistance, a $32,000 summer home on the Maryland shore and a $6000 boat.

One thing he felt confident of was her unfailing support. When drunk, indeed even when sober, he never hesitated to boast that he had secured control of all her money and that whatever he did she would defend him. And nothing did seem to shake her support, even when she was told he spoke of her as a bitch and boasted of her unshakeable love.

Still driven by his desire for a complete hold on the Korean boy Hal (not his real name) and having learned that for a legal adoption he had to have a wife, he proposed to his secretary, Mrs. Clarissa Brown. When he informed Pearl of his intention to marry, though she "looked depressed," as one witness described it, she protested only feebly.

"A bachelor has no standing in society," he had explained to her, and so, as always, she did her best to help him, encouraging Mrs. Brown and making available to the couple a large barn on her property. To Mrs. Brown, Harris confided that Dr. Wilson's million-dollar pledge was "airtight and ironclad and could not be broken regardless of what happened to the Foundation." It was, he told her, "just what he needed to see that he was permanently taken care of for life." And as proof he showed her the plans for a $50,000 renovation of their future home. Their engagement was announced in *The New York Times* and Pearl Buck sent out engraved invitations to a wedding reception to be held on December 7, 1968.

That fall Mrs. Brown had spent her spare time teaching some of the Korean youths. Hal was one of her students, and when he learned that

Mrs. Brown planned to marry Harris, he warned her against such a step and told her why. Stunned, she broke the engagement and set about disclosing what she had learned.

Pearl Buck urged her to reconsider her broken engagement but she remained adamant. Harris then flew to California and on December 7, the day set for his wedding to Clarissa Brown, he took as his bride the fifty-one-year-old aunt of his friend, Jimmie Pauls. The new Mrs. Harris (nee Aurora Kekich) remained in California after the wedding (but with her new name Harris on the mailbox) and was only produced in person some time later.

During the first half of 1968 Dr. Wilson's investigation had quietly gathered testimony from many disparate sources. Finally in the late spring he introduced his report on Harris's administration of the Foundation at a Board meeting which included instances of his neglect of the boys' physical welfare and his sexual abuses. An audit of the Foundation's books was also produced indicating such chaos that no one could make out how much money had been taken in or how it had been spent.

An indignant Pearl summarily dismissed all the report's findings. Mrs. Donald Sills, fairly new to the board as a volunteer, at first could not believe what she heard, nor could Mrs. Donald Stabler of Pittsburgh. But Margot Studer, experienced in conducting her own investigations, was not surprised. Dr. Wilson, backed by an impeccable reputation and obvious goodwill toward the Foundation's overall commitment, made a formidable plaintiff, and those Board members who were, contrary to accepted practice, actually salaried staff personnel, must have felt the atmosphere growing increasingly heated. The non-salaried members demanded Harris's resignation; Pearl Buck and Harris refused to give it, and there the situation stood on the first day of July 1969. On the second, *Philadelphia* magazine appeared on the stands followed by Station WIP's broadcast of the boys' tapes.

On July 7 Theodore Harris resigned from the Foundation and disappeared while Pearl Buck, head held high and eyes blazing, promised lawsuits and wholesale vindication.

The Foundation Board, returning from the July Fourth holiday, faced a defiant Pearl. Margot Studer, who had known Pearl on the Training School Board and admired her, tried to reason with her. "She wouldn't listen," Mrs. Studer reported. "She said he'd done nothing wrong; that the Foundation was her personal project, that she personally had put him in charge and that she stood back of him completely. One day I tried to make her see that when you take public funds it's not your money, it's a very sacred trust, and that all those thousands of people who had sent their donations had thought they were adopting an Amerasian orphan. But she didn't like it at all. She actually demanded that the Board vote him $50,000 severance pay—'in gratitude,' she said, 'for all he had done'! (The Board refused, but later an examination of the books revealed a check for $3500 made out to Theodore F. Harris.)

The press scrambled daily for enlightenment and a few days after Harris's resignation a steely-eyed Pearl met a crowd of reporters from the Philadelphia and Bucks County area. The accusations against Harris, she declared, had been originated by a woman who had hoped to marry him. However, she said, he had discovered "certain facts" about the woman which made it unwise for him to marry her, so now that woman was bent on his destruction. Each of the witnesses against him, she stated, had in fact held some grudge against the Foundation. And, she added for emphasis, if anyone thought that this mess suggested that she, Pearl Buck, was a senile old woman, they should realize that anyone whose current book, *The Three Daughters of Madame Liang*, was a Book of the Month Club selection and a *Reader's Digest* condensation was hardly likely to be senile.

The following day Mrs. Brown made a statement of her own. Miss Buck, she stated, had urged her to marry Mr. Harris. And besides renovating a barn for the couple as a wedding present, she had planned to accompany them on a six-month world tour after the ceremony. As for her allegations regarding Mr. Harris and the young Korean boys, she stood firmly behind the facts.

Meanwhile the State of Pennsylvania authorities had not been idle. Seven months earlier the Commission on Charitable Organizations had referred the Foundation to the Attorney General when it failed to apply for a renewal of its license to solicit public funds. When it finally made application in May, six months late, its financial report was discovered to be unsatisfactory. Permission to operate in Pennsylvania was therefore denied and it was given two weeks in which to petition for a hearing.

The combustible situation was already smoldering when the magazine story broke and the newspapers printed their startling headlines. Pearl consistently protested Harris's innocence, and the board loyally elected her president in Harris's place, hoping at the same time to unravel the office's tangled affairs. Dr. Wilson, still dedicated to the Foundation's cause and desirous of continuing his support, joined with the non-paid members of the Board to find a reputable executive director and to adopt a series of reforms.

On October 9, however, after waiting nearly three months for some kind of constructive action, Dr. Wilson and his mother, both board members, sadly withdrew their support, followed by the new director and Mrs. Studer, Mrs. Sills and Mrs. Stabler, who also resigned. The commission chairman remarked wryly, "This leaves the Foundation in the hands of the same people who have been running it for years, the employees." Most employees hurriedly resigned and only a skeleton staff was left to keep operations moving on a reduced scale.

The commission chairman, leaning over backward in sympathy with what was up to now a worthy cause, gave them until the end of 1969 to produce certain required reforms. The deadline was not met. In January the chairman granted them an extension of another thirty days to supply satisfactory reports on their finances, current operations overseas, and the achievements of the previous year. By the end of February no new director had yet been found nor a full complement of legitimate Board members installed. However, the commissioner, in spite of all believing that honest efforts were being made, issued the necessary license and, though shaky, the Foundation was technically back in business.

During the months of waiting Pearl had kept a low profile. But now she called in reporters to announce the Foundation's revival and to ask them for their support. "All this smut publicity," she stated, "cost the Foundation three hundred and forty of its contributors and a reduction of $428,000 in income. I'm sorry I ever gave my name to the Foundation, it did it harm." And she disclosed that she was writing a book about the Kennedy family, a study on the disease in American democracy that likes to denigrate famous people and then read about them. "People like to read smut," she declared. Of the former Foundation president she said only, "We won't be so lucky as to find such a talented fund-raiser again."

Her brush with the press had been a traumatic experience. But actually, in light of the damage caused by some scandals, Pearl Buck fared pretty well. True, the Philadelphia and Bucks County papers hammered hard. And *Time Magazine* ran nearly a page-long story featuring a picture of Pearl and Harris dancing. But its focus was more on energetic *Philadelphia* magazine than on the person of Pearl Buck. And more importantly, the wire services ignored the story. The John Day Company, which had gone into shock at the initial blast of scandal, now breathed a bit more normally. And the scandal, potentially of major proportions, was soon dismissed and seemed to have no permanent effect on her reputation.

The Foundation recovered slowly. An experienced social worker was engaged to run it, but Pearl, with the glittering memory of Harris still in mind, could not tolerate the new manager, and he resigned. Finally, under Dr. Doris Howell, a pediatrician in Philadelphia, as chairman of the board, satisfactory personnel were hired. And at last the Pearl S. Buck Foundation became what Pearl Buck had always dreamed it, the savior of lost children, providing food, medicine and education to thousands in Korea, Okinawa, Thailand, Taiwan and the Philippines.

20

The Foundation did manage to survive but largely without Pearl Buck. Though she appeared at Board meetings that winter and there was no formal break, her heart was not in Philadelphia. Harris had been driven to Maryland (stories circulated that he hid on the floor of the car under a rug; others reported him in the trunk) to escape the charge of impairing the morals of a minor. Pearl joined him in Maryland to begin a brand new life.

Some years before she had said to Harris, eerily foretelling their future, "How fortunate we are, we who are born with certain talent. Wherever we go we are directed by that which is within us. . . . We recognize ourselves early and we pursue our own way. . . . When we face destruction we are resolute to save ourselves at all costs. I maintain that this is constructive, this courage to break away, to start again, to find life elsewhere when the environment imprisons. . . . Ruthless we can be when it is a matter of the spirit's survival. This is the liberating force of talent."

But one question had mystified all who knew Pearl Buck, one of America's most admired women, why a poorly educated social climber who lived by his wits and his feet? Why Harris? Her distressed friends had discussed this question by the hour. Many and varied were their theories, some sound and some fairly bizarre; "She was just plain lonely"; "It was his youth"; "It could be plain sex"; "She needed an escort and a sounding board for her ideas"; "It was a mother-and-son thing"; "I always think of Trilby and Svengali"; "When she danced with him she felt like she was flying through the air"; "He treated her like a princess, took her back to her Nobel days"; "He and his group kowtowed to her, made her feel important"; "She was the captive of those people"; "She was old and wanted to be taken care of"; "She could use him; if she couldn't use a person she wasn't interested in them"; "It could be blackmail; Pauls might have some damaging photos"; "She said he was the reincarnation of the Kennedy men"; "I think he had got her onto drugs and had a hold on her"; "She had lifted him up so high, taken him out of his safe little job and she felt a responsibility for him"; "To me she acted really as if she was under hypnosis"; "Some women want to give and he was her receptacle"; "She needed a dynamic man who would control her"; "She had always run everything; now she enjoyed being treated like a baby"; "It was loyalty, everyone else was against him"; "She was always seeking new experiences and new people to write about."

Many of the theories make sense, particularly those which center on his youth and her ego. "I like his kind of people, they keep me young," she had often admitted and there is no doubt that his flattery fed her vanity.

In view of her sex drive, ill-served early in life and then titillated and tantalized by Danielewski, her fascination with a practicing homosexual seems anomalous. But a conversation between Margot Studer, Ruth Sills and a friend provided some insight. Mrs. Sills had remarked, "Miss Buck told me she had thought once that she was going to marry Danielewski, you know, but he married someone else instead."

"Perhaps," the friend suggested, "she took Harris on the rebound."

"No. I believe she was entirely infatuated with him," Mrs. Studer said. "I really do."

"He catered to her," Mrs. Sills agreed. "He would come into the room suddenly and we would be sitting there and he would say, '*Oh*! I wish I had a portrait of you right now, the way you look!' And then he'd say to me, 'You know, the tragedy of my life is that I'm not thirty years older so we could be married. I adore this woman.' Then she'd make some light flirty remark. She was very flirtatious with him, very much the woman. And she was very jealous of him, always wanted to know where he was."

"She knew he was homosexual," Mrs. Studer recalled. "She actually preferred that, she spoke about how brilliant they all were."

"I suppose," Mrs. Sills contributed, "that active sex may have been something she wasn't interested in any more, that she was too old. But the courtship part, the adoration, the flattery, the kiss on the back of the neck without actually having to go through with it . . ."

"Yes, you may have hit on the truth," Mrs. Studer agreed. "But of course with him it was all for the money power."

The women expressed bewilderment that Harris had been so readily accepted by Pearl Buck's friends, but Mrs. Sills explained, "Well, you see, when you met Miss Buck you had this idealized concept of her from way back, and so it was like—say if Miss Buck had a wart on her face. It was Miss Buck's wart and so you didn't notice it. That's what he was, Miss Buck's wart, and you just accepted it."

But another important question remained. Where was Pearl Buck's searching, idealistic mind? If she felt a defense of Harris demanded that she lie, at least the mental processes are understandable. But she seems to have hypnotized herself, to have actually *believed* that the whole unfortunate affair was nothing more than a hate campaign against Harris and herself.

In article after article she inveighed against disloyal hero-worshippers. "We Destroy the Heroes We Create" ran a headline in the *Philadelphia Bulletin*, and in the *Richmond Times-Dispatch* she lashed out at America, "We Are No Better Than Other People." She disavowed her own early admiration for Americans. "My country is not a good country to live in for people of talent and the capacity to achieve. Such a person receives praise, awards, etc., but no genuine loyalty to greatness. Instead he arouses a jealousy and a desire, secret or overt, to do him damage, to bring him low or belittle his achievement." Obviously she aligned herself with Harris who, she once told Margaret Fischer, was more brilliant than either Hocking or Compton. "What one did to Mr. Harris one did to her" had always been the rule.

The depth of her wounds is reflected in a conversation she had with Janice and Janice's friend Joan one evening after a quiet dinner at their house. "We weren't talking about the *Philadelphia* story at all," Janice remembered. "She must have just thought about it out of the blue. She was sitting in this chair . . . and all of a sudden she just stood right up, walked into the middle of the room and started. It was like she was putting on a dramatic show. She shouted, 'I *am* a great woman. I am the greatest.' And she was pounding her chest with her fist. She had never done anything like that before and Joan and I just looked at each other. She went on and on about how people didn't appreciate her, they didn't understand her."

Joan explained, "She was replying to the editor of that magazine, of course, and trying to convince us the whole story was untrue. She should have known we knew it all, everything, even things that weren't in the magazine. We just sat there quietly listening but we never contradicted her."

Harris had remained invisible since his July 7 resignation, and except for confrontations with the press and certain authorities, so had Pearl Buck. Meanwhile, moving to their Maryland retreat and recklessly burning her bridges at the age of seventy-seven, she gave up home, family servants and friends and took up another life.

Witnesses to the new life are scarce and only a few facts surfaced about the period immediately following the move. The firm of Creativity, Inc., was founded almost at once, consisting of Theodore F. Harris, Pearl S. Buck and a lawyer. Its main function was to receive the royalties on all the future writings of Pearl S. Buck, and an employment contract to that effect was signed with the firm. The John Day Company in turn then contracted for the future Creativity books, their previous contract with the Foundation having expired.

On October 9 the *Rutland Herald* ran a story, with photos, about the sale of several buildings in Danby, Vermont, to Pearl S. Buck and her business manager, who planned to convert part of the village into a cultural center.

Other newspaper and magazine stories confirmed that Miss Buck, while driving with a friend, had seen the desolate condition of the small village of Danby, population 910—store windows broken, paint peeling and buildings abandoned. Lacking industry Danby was losing its young people and dying by inches. Her plan was to turn it into an antique center, which would bring work to painters and carpenters. Teenagers would also be hired to build a Youth Center.

Thus, three months after the debacle in Philadelphia, Pearl Buck fought back with another humanitarian idea. "She was," one Danbyite commented, "building her own posterity" . . . her own vision of greatness.

The past June, with his future looking uncertain, Harris had invested in a small store and gas station near Pearl's Vermont property, and after a brief stay in Maryland they moved to Mountain Haunt. Harris would open the antique business (Pearl could of course do her writing anywhere) off U.S. Route Seven in Danby, and with skillful exploitation of Pearl Buck's name it might become profitable. Harris sold his gas station at a profit and he and Pearl moved the Creativity group into the newly purchased Danby buildings.

Creativity, Inc., consisted of Jimmie Pauls, Wendy Park (the Arthur Murray dance instructor formerly married to Pauls), and Al Conklin, to whom Wendy Park was currently married. After the application of gallons of red and white paint, the Country Store was opened, followed by a sandwich shop called the Maple Skillet. Other buildings were restored for rental to antique dealers from outside Danby, and these shops comprised the new Vermont Village Square.

Pearl wrote colorful articles, gave interviews to reporters and touted the Village on radio and television. Commercials advertised the Antique Center and highway signs along Vermont's Route Seven pointed the way. Financing the venture was a problem, but Harris had his final $3500 check from the Foundation and possibly other monies. Pearl Buck owned hundreds of Vermont acres plus four houses, and had just finished *The Goddess Abides*, for which she received her usual handsome advance against royalties.

The main capital, however, was her name. The public's endless fascination for celebrities, particularly those close at hand, attracted the tourists. That brought dealers, one who prefers to be called Mrs. Lillian Gould, a professional antique dealer who alerted other professionals. "We had really very nice people there at one time," she recalled.

A portion of the General Store sold Pearl S. Buck books, and in back of the Square there was a flea market where a charming Pearl periodically wandered in and out chatting with the browsers. At other times she sat upstairs over the store and wrote, eating her lunch on the balcony where she would be seen.

For many months Pearl maintained Mountain Haunt, fifteen miles from Danby, as her residence and was driven back and forth to the village each day. The future of the project had looked promising in the beginning, but more cash was needed for expansion, so Pearl had offered her Vermont property for sale, including Mountain Haunt and the ski lodge Forest Haunt, deciding, however, to retain her right to life tenancy. Unfortunately, she failed to read the contract's fine print. After the papers were signed it was discovered that the life tenancy clause had been omitted. She was summarily evicted.

Only momentarily shaken, she soon got her nerve back. Partly to save face and to continue to maintain a solid front, she never publicly blamed anyone for the contractual oversight. The citizens of Danby simply assumed she had moved there from Mountain Haunt to eliminate the daily drive.

Harris did his best to compensate for her loss and found a square white house with a front door flush with the street, and decorated it to her taste. Sitting room, dining room and kitchen on the ground floor were all curtained against the shabby outside view. Up a little stair a suite was furnished luxuriously in pink with a handsome brass bed, delicate green chintz spread, white shag rug and chaise lounge beside a window overlooking magnificent Stratton Mountain. On the third floor were quarters for Harris and Pauls and, for a while, a young Korean upon whose arm Pearl Buck, like a queen, made her daily progress through the Danby crowd. At best Danby House was a far cry from Pearl's handsome residences with all their amenities. Furthermore, when they moved to Vermont, Harris had abruptly fired her long-time chauffeur and secretary, giving neither notice nor severance pay and leaving behind a bitter odor. So when a secretary was needed and Jackie Breen was not available, an ad was run in the local paper and Beverly Drake, the attractive, cultured wife of a teacher in a boy's school, was engaged on the spot.

Mrs. Drake became Pearl Buck's close friend, confidante and, later, practical nurse. One final addition to the group was Dolphus Crowe, a young ex-serviceman with a mild desire to write and a keen admiration for Pearl Buck, who attached himself as general factotum with a special talent for doing Pearl's hair.

More and more the entourage cushioned her. Lillian Gould remembered Pearl returning from a visit to Philadelphia with a sigh of contentment. "Those Foundation meetings are very stimulating," she told her, sinking into a deep chair, "but it's good to get back to this peace and quiet." Incoming telephone calls had always been monitored by a secretary, but eventually Harris and Mrs. Drake took charge so that even Grace had to identify herself. Many New York and Philadelphia friends interpreted her life in Danby as a subtle sort of captivity.

Mrs. Gould did not share that view. "She was too strong a person to let anybody do that to her," she commented. "She could always have escaped back to Philadelphia. No, I think she really enjoyed the slower pace here." Certainly there had to be some explanation for the new Pearl Buck whom Roger Baldwin, head of the American Civil Liberties Union, encountered. Over many years Baldwin had consulted with an earnest and serious Pearl Buck on civil liberties matters, and as vice chairman, she had been a sturdy right arm in defense of the underdog. After a long interval he sought her help once more and was given a phone number in Vermont. Following a lengthy interrogation, he was put through.

"But I thought I'd got the wrong number," he reported. "There was this voice, so gay and lighthearted she sounded as if she hadn't a care in the world. She laughed and joked, was almost sort of flirtatious. And the strangest thing, she even had a sense of humor. I don't recall what we talked about, certainly not what I'd called for. But it was nice in a way, to hear her sounding so gay . . . almost as if she didn't have any responsibilities any more and was enjoying herself."

Perhaps that was true. Certainly while Harris flattered, he also gave orders which she obeyed docilely. After holding the reins for fifty years, she was perhaps glad to relinquish them.

At all events, she didn't rebel. And her chintz-lined cage had its compensations. The Goulds, occasional dinner guests, reported that a typical dinner consisted of a lace tablecloth, fine silver and wine glasses, exquisite china and crystal finger bowls worth fifty-five dollars apiece ("I know because there were some at the shop," Mrs. Gould said). There were four courses, prepared either by the Korean or Pauls. "I do enjoy my meals," Pearl told her guests.

But despite the ease and cosseting, Pearl Buck was not idle. Rather like a champion racehorse groomed and kept in prime condition for the races ahead, her queenly strolls among the tourists paid off in her books being bought and autographed; her chats with children while parents beamed became anecdotes at home that spread the word. Pearl Buck was the star attraction and if she appeared in less than perfect condition, there were murmured complaints from the dealers. (Indeed, as her eyesight failed and bits of food spotted her clothing, Mrs. Drake attended to them on the sly.) Her make-up, once subtly and cleverly applied, had now become unsightly, finally drawing sharp criticism: "Isn't there *anything* we can do about those false eyelashes?"

She understood perfectly why she was there. Jim and Dorothy Farrell, who sold collectibles in the summer months, had become her friends and to them she occasionally opened up. One day, the only time on record, she confided: "I know perfectly well that Ted Harris made a fiasco in Philadelphia." And then she added: "But I want him to redeem himself and make a go of it here." And because of this she strolled through Danby, chatted with the tourists and scribbled "Pearl S. Buck" in her books. In the summer months there would be five or six thousand more tourists than normal passing through Danby, Vermont, "just to see Pearl Buck."

Even so the antiques business was still only a sideline. The main merchandise remained Pearl S. Buck's books. On May 8, 1970, Dick Walsh sent a MEMO TO ALL SALESMEN: "A recent statistic tells us Pearl S. Buck continues to be, as she has been for many years, the most widely translated contemporary author other than two unrivaled practitioners of the mystery story, Georges Simenon and Agatha Christie. Statistic appears in compendium issued by UNESCO entitled *Index Translatinuum*. Translations published during year 1968 in sixty-six countries—sixty-nine translated editions of PSB compared with sixty-four Hemingway, forty-eight Steinbeck. (Simenon had 134 and Christie 731.)"

Alongside her record for translations stood another for articles. *Modern Maturity*, the magazine of the American Association of Retired Persons, reported that her "Essay on Life" had drawn the greatest response in its history from its seven million readers. In it she summarized her conversations with Compton and Hocking and her own thoughts on immortality. And with her special gift for clarifying the abstruse she presented their conclusions in lay terms, easily understandable.

She wrote, "I have begun to live the eightieth year of my life. . . . I do not know what people mean when they speak of being old. I do not know because I do not know where life begins, if indeed there is a beginning, and I do not know when it ends, if indeed there is an end. I know that I am in a stage, a phase, a period of life. I entered this life at birth, I shall end this stage with death.

"For me, death is merely the entrance into further existence. I do not know what that existence will be, but then I did not know what existence in this stage would be when I was born into it. I did not ask to be, but I have been and I am. My reason tells me I shall continue to be. I am on my way somewhere, just as I was on the day of my birth. "Young" and "old" for me are meaningless words except as we use them to denote where we are in the process of this stage of being. . . .

"There will be those who question my certainty of a continuing existence. My belief is based on sound scientific reasons and long acquaintance with some of the greatest scientists and philosophers of our times. Religious faith and scientific hypothesis are much nearer to the same conclusions than is commonly realized. Serious studies in parapsychology are being conducted in various countries and the results are remarkable and will some day be made known. For the present, I content myself with two anecdotes which express in simple terms the silence between this life and the next.

"The first occurred in my own family soon after the death of my husband, who was much beloved by his grandchildren, Susan, then aged five, and Ricky, aged three. The occasion was a family picinic and I overheard the following conversation:

Ricky: Why doesn't grandfather come to the picnic?

Susan: He can't because he's up in heaven.

Ricky: Why doesn't he come down?

Susan: *He can't find the ladder.*

"It is truly spoken out of the mouth of a babe. He does not come down because 'he can't find the ladder.' The technique of communication is not yet complete.

"The second anecdote was given me through a letter by an unknown woman. In effect, it was as follows: 'When my small children could not understand the silence between their recently dead father and us, who loved him so dearly, I explained by describing the life cycle of the dragonfly. It begins as a grub in water. Then at the proper moment it surfaces, finds it has wings and flies away.

"'I suppose that the ones left in the water wonder where he went and why he doesn't come back. But he can't, because he has wings. Nor can they go to him, because they don't have their wings yet.'

"Something like that is true, I believe. We haven't our wings yet either. But some day . . . ?"

The gift of rendering the complicated simple and the cosmic personal helped make Pearl S. Buck universally accepted. These magazine pages were no doubt clipped and saved and re-read gratefully by many magazine readers who themselves contemplated such adventurous flights.

But magazine articles were not Pearl Buck's most important output during this period. *Mandala*, the novel researched during the torturous months spent in India, was to be her last "big" novel and, like the previous *Three Daughters of Madame Liang*, a book club selection. John Anderson, who traveled to India with Pearl, claimed it to be loosely based on the personal lives of Dev Anad, the star of the Indian film *The Guide*, and a member of a titled Indian family. Lush and romantic in an old-fashioned way, it reveals by its theme of reincarnation the trend of the author's own thoughts. *The New York Times'* reviewer faulted her for not having changed over the years, but admits that "for those of us who haven't changed, *Mandala* will prove an enjoyable and profitable experience."

For the thousands who found *Mandala* a splendid novel, however, her next, *The Goddess Abides*, must have been a sore disappointment. One of the few critics of a major paper who reviewed it stated: "Pearl Buck seems to be indulging in personal fantasy." About a beautiful middle-aged widow with two importunate suitors, one elderly but virile, and the other young, godlike and glowing with adoration, it was no doubt an embarrassment to those familiar with the facts of the author's own life.

Though *Mandala*, having been written under the old contract, contributed its royalties to the Foundation, this novel's royalties went straight to Creativity, Inc., and an eager Harris longed for other works. While going through Pearl's old manuscripts, he had come across an unfinished one and brought it to her to be completed. Originally, in *All Under Heaven*, the book's protagonist faced a situation with no solution; but now she quickly found one. While most of the characters are solemn and unreal, there are a few pleasant glimpses of humor in the depiction of a Russian girl suddenly faced with American kitchen gadgets. *Publisher's Weekly* referred to it as "a quiet and thoughtful novel."

There was another area in which Pearl's caretakers considered her capable of producing additional revenue. Some years earlier John Day had been incorporated into a larger company, Intext Press, whose publisher Theodore Dolmatch was happy to cooperate with Theodore Harris. Several of Pearl's early speeches on the technique of writing, "Advice to a Novelist About to Be Born," "On the Writing of Novels," "The Creative Mind at Work," and "The Novel in the Making," could be incorporated into the nucleus of *A Short Course for Writers*.

In 1972, the year of Pearl's eightieth birthday, plans were under way for a special public celebration. An eightieth birthday edition of her books bound in white leather was being readied, and a Pearl Buck Book Club about to be offered to potential subscribers.

When President Nixon suddenly announced his plans for a trip to

China, the repercussions in Pearl Buck's house in Danby were electric. With that great country being opened up anything could happen. Indeed, she was invited (for a $7500 fee and expenses) to appear as the guide and narrator on the National Broadcasting Company's documentary "China Lost and Found," thus reminding the world of her unique authority. In the resulting flurry offices in Hollywood, New York and Danby revved into high gear. "When I left China," Pearl had written years before, "my Chinese friends said, 'When you are old you will come back to us.'" And now two months after Richard Nixon's precedent-breaking visit, Pearl Buck's own trip was announced. "I had been invited to go with the President," she remarked calmly, "but I declined for political reasons." She preferred to go on her own. She answered the reporters' questions. "No, I never met Mao Tse-tung, but I knew Chou En-lai. A very brilliant man. I have written him recently and expect to visit him in May." She also wrote to Washington for clearance, then to Peking for a visa, and visited the Chinese Consulate in Canada. Finally, having laid the groundwork for her trip, she waited.

The various ideas of a dozen publishing, TV, magazine and advertising minds, paying court to a not-quite-eighty-year-old portly widow, were coordinated and the resulting program shown to her. Eyes shining like blue diamonds, Pearl Buck told them she could accomplish it all. The comprehensive plan went as follows:

Memo, May 10, 1972. Pearl Buck's China Trip. Projects:
1) Non Fiction: BOOK ON CHINA
   a) Reader's Digest—$40,000 advance. Manuscript to be available July 1972
   b) Book of the Month—$2500 option.
2) FICTION: NOVEL ON CHINA
   a) Book of the Month, $15,000 front money or more if it is a main choice.
   b) Reader's Digest—$5000 option.
3) READER'S DIGEST ARTICLES ON CHINA AND TRIP
   a) Articles developed from non-fiction book (above) $5,000.
   b) Article on Mrs. Gandhi and Golda Meir—$5000
4) TELEVISION
   A special documentary on trip, with camera crew.
     Total investment $350,000
5) NEWSPAPER SYNDICATION

Series of ten articles for NEA, $10,000
ADDITIONAL PROJECTS, SOME IN THE WORKS
1) *Once upon a Christmas.* Stories $5000 pd., $5000 due
2) Loretta Young type TV show. PSB hostess.
3) *All Under Heaven.* $15,000 pd., more due.
4) Antiques book, $5000 pd, $500 due.
5) *The America I Hate.* No description submitted.
6) Writers course—$2000 pd, $3000 due.
7) *Mrs. Starling.* Juvenile. $2000 pd.
8) China Juvenile. To be developed.
9) Vol. III of Harris bio. $5000 due on delivery.
10) Picture books plus prose on trip. *For Spacious Skies* type book, PSB in China, PSB in Jerusalem. To be negotiated.
11) Supplementary language arts material. PSB co-author. To be negotiated.
READER'S DIGEST ACCIDENT INSURANCE POLICY $100,000
Also Suggested for Negotiation: Projects:
a) Costume jewelry copied from PSB originals.
b) Christmas cards for Hallmark.
c) PSB commercials for Encyclopedia Britannica, Pan AM, etc.
d) PSB hostess for dramatic series of PSB works on TV.

Everyone dreamed happily, but on May 17, 1972, the dreams died. A letter arrived from the Embassy of the People's Republic of China in Canada.

"Dear Miss Pearl Buck: Your letters have been duly received.

"In view of the fact that for a long time you have in your works taken an attitude of distortion, smear and vilification towards the people of new China and its leaders, I am authorized to inform you that we cannot accept your request for a visit to China. Sincerely yours, H. L. Yuan, Second Secretary."

Hurt pride mixed with anger and keen disappointment as Pearl's exciting plans were scotched, not the least the old dream of a long talk with Chou En-lai and a possible warming up of their two countries' relations. Who better to speak for America than China's first friend in America?

The projected plans were filed away and the vision of immeasurable wealth forgotten. Ahead, however, loomed the memorable date for her eightieth birthday celebration.

The Pearl S. Buck Foundation, still attempting a comeback, grasped at every opportunity for respectable publicity, and Pearl, once again on *Good Housekeeping's* Most Admired Women's list (third after Rose Kennedy and Mamie Eisenhower), was a natural for attention. Though Danby was now her home, Green Hills Farm was kept staffed for an occasional visit and the morning before her birthday festivities Pearl, as in old times, sat at the little Pembroke table in the farm dining room chatting with Mrs. Florence Galla, who, with her gardener husband, was in charge of the estate.

Mrs. Galla congratulated her on her achieving her eightieth year in such good shape, and Pearl responded, "Oh, that's nothing. I'm going to live to a hundred." And in a sudden burst of confidence, she added, "You know, Mrs. Galla, I know that people are saying about me that there's no fool like an old fool. But I know exactly what I'm doing every minute. I always need to have new challenges, that's what it is."

That afternoon she announced to members of the press the Foundation's new division designed to facilitate international adoption of Amerasian children. The Foundation, she was happy to report, was operating successfully in six countries. Also prospering was her other project, Welcome House. "I'm always making future plans," she told the reporters. And as for the past, she had enjoyed it all immensely. "I wouldn't have missed a thing. Some was tough going, but everything seemed to have a meaning."

At a private gathering before the main formalities, Janice and Joan held a surprise party at their house which Janice described: "We had a picnic buffet supper. She had on a long maroon gown and she sat in a big red chair and her hair, very white, looked so pretty against the red. We have a picture—the best I ever had of her.

"Next day she was tired, really tired, more than just from the night before. But she was so happy that all the kids had gotten together. And away from the Foundation and her old house and all, it was just like old times. Just lovely."

Prior to the reception, with its slightly royal formality, the house resembled a beehive with workers buzzing about the queen—make-up, gown, position of her chair in relation to the refreshment table, all were carefully programmed. For hours the hundreds of guests passed her chair, and she gave them all the brilliant smile that made the old face young, then one brave but forced and finally one simply of pain.

At last it was over. She had done it, she had rounded out the eighty-year course and ended unbeaten. Now she could rest. So must her body have thought, for suddenly it said "Enough" and she collapsed.

21

That family gathering at Green Hills Farm was the last of its kind. Janice's "old times" were the days before children had turned into independent adults that no mother could control. One of these adults, asked to comment on Pearl as a parent, replied, "I think she *tried* to be a good mother, but that didn't come first. The writer came first and then the wife. The mother sort of tagged along at the end."

Actually she knew *how* to be a good mother, could write wisely and with compassion, so that mail poured in from a world of mothers. And daughters found in her books a certain understanding they missed at home. But to *live* the patience, the flexibility, was beyond her. She could love all humanity but single human beings got in her way, and opposition was something she had never learned to endure.

Green Hills Farm was nobody's home any more. She had adopted a new family in Vermont and there she demanded to be taken. In the Rutland Hospital, while tests were made, Harris and Mrs. Drake asked the reporters to make little of Pearl's hospitalization, and out of respect they did so. But somehow the news appeared on the radio in July suggesting she had had a heart attack. Grace and her husband had been out of town, but, hearing of it Grace called Harris. He said he had been trying to reach her but when she suggested coming to Vermont, he said her visit would only alarm Pearl. However, he would keep in touch.

Later she learned that Pearl had been put on a strict diet to lose twenty pounds. And when Grace did arrive in August, she found her very frail. Walking about her hospital suite in her Chinese robe. She showed Grace the beautiful mountain view, like her own at home, and asked about Grace's children. It was obvious she was making an effort to be cheerful about herself and all the work that lay ahead.

From time to time members of the younger generation came to visit for a day or so. One family brought their camper and camped out for two weeks in the woods.

There was one other visitor. After the intrusion of Harris into the John Day Company business the position of Dick Walsh and his wife, Tsuta, had become somewhat awkward. And when Theodore Dolmatch and Intext Press became the dominant publishers and Dolmatch worked closely with Harris, the Walshes' discomfort became acute. Dick confined his emotions to the business but Tsuta, utterly devoted to Pearl and anguished over Harris's influence on her, found herself in a volatile situation. Pearl's edict, "Whatever you do for or against Mr. Harris you do for or against me," was still in effect, and for a long time communication lines between Pearl and the Walshes were severed. At last Tsuta, putting love above pride, considered attending the birthday celebration but was dissuaded by her husband. What if she should be refused entrance at the door?

The situation was different now, however. Pearl was ill. On July 11 Tsuta caught the bus to Rutland, taking as a gift for her stepmother-in-law a negligee of unusual beauty.

Their reunion was apparently the warm reconciliation Tsuta had hoped for—except for the fact that Harris never left the room. One local resident commented wryly: "Afraid to let her be left alone." The following month Tsuta Walsh entered a hospital where she underwent a mastectomy operation. Eleven days later Pearl wrote her: "Dearest Tsuta: Today I called you to thank you for coming all the way to see me and bring me a lovely robe . . . and Dick told me what you have been doing while I have been resting and getting better each day. Now I must tell *you* to give yourself plenty of time to get back your strength. Of course I felt and feel terribly sad and upset over what you have been through, but luckily one *does* recover health and strength again and *you are brave.* That was all I could say to Dick, ['*She's so brave.*'] And so you are, my dear, and always have been. . . .

"My own regime is a stiff one, but I have excellent doctors and a most faithful and devoted staff—and family. . . .

"Now dear, I'll be thinking of you. I *wish* I could come to see *you*, but I only go downstairs once a day. The people here send their concern and good wishes—Mr. Harris especially. And I send my love, always. Mother."

By this time Pearl was back at home and working under great pressure. Under the Creativity, Inc., contract signed in October 1969 she was an employee of the Creativity firm and the income from her writings and lectures was deposited to the firm, i.e., Harris. In 1969 she had put up $50,000 to buy antiques and furnishings "in order [according to the *Rutland Daily Herald*] to make sure there was an ongoing organization Theodore Harris could run to keep himself self-supporting." Pearl Buck would receive a monthly wage for her labors.

This monthly stipend evidently had a short life for [again quoting the *Herald*] "on June 30, 1972 [exactly three days after her collapse] she had signed a release stating that Harris's firm did not have to pay her the back salaries due her, $101,000." This delinquency may help to explain Janice's remark that sometime when her mother dined with her in Bucks County "she didn't have a penny in her purse."

Far from recommending economy, Pearl Buck continued to spend extravagantly. Enchanted with Harris's antiques business she decided his establishment should be expanded into an elegant showroom for the display of quality merchandise. Plans were drawn up and work begun on the Annex, an extension of Danby House twenty-five feet in length and two stories high. It was to have marble floors and flagstone steps, a large fireplace and a huge window which overlooked a stream where a fountain played in the center court. A second floor balcony would contain an office and a writing room for Pearl.

Fascinated neighbors watched the building progress. Mrs. Raymond Stone declared, "It was going to be beautiful, huge windows that cost two or three hundred dollars apiece, shadowproof and everything. They were going to have an elevator up to her rooms, and I heard they'd ordered a grand piano."

For funding such expansions a bank loan seemed indicated. Pearl Buck had always indulged her financial extravagances on trust, relying on her royalties to bail her out. They usually did, although the Internal Revenue Service had once threatened to put a lien on her properties for a $70,000 tax bill. The $200,000 payment for a film (never made) of *Letter from Peking* had helped cover Danielewski's losses, and monies from *The Three Daughters of Madame Liang* covered Harris's $50,000 and the migration to Danby. Now, presumably backed by royalties both earned and guaranteed, Harris obtained a $110,000 loan from the First National Bank of Boston and Pearl Buck settled down to work it off.

The "Non-Fiction book on China" mentioned in the China trip prospectus and promised for July 1972 was probably her *China Past and Present*, an illustrated commentary which was published after the projected trip to China fell through. In it appeared the letter from the Chinese Consulate rejecting her proposed visit and her angry reaction.

The projected novel on China would likely be the long-planned sequel to *The Good Earth*, *The Red Earth*, as yet unwritten. Aside from these future books there was an unfinished novel, *The Schoolmaster*, and another uncompleted project, *The Rainbow*, which obviously harked back to the Danielewski era.

In order to undertake all this writing Pearl Buck had to be kept well and happy, with her every wish indulged. Mrs. Jim Farrell related how this was accomplished. "The Clan had a thirty-foot motor home for going to antique shows and Jimmie Pauls's occasional buying trips. They figured if they went on tour Miss Buck could work from the motor home, and on speaking engagements, if she wanted to lie down she'd be right there. Well, my husband Jim was just crazy about her, and he thought all this was awful. He said to her it wasn't right for a woman her age—and she was heavy, too, you know—to be climbing in and out of that motor home. He said she ought to have something more suitable. He said she was a grande dame and she ought to have a really fine car. So she listened to him . . . and the next thing you know, there, standing at their door, was this big black Rolls Royce. It had a beautiful suede leather upholstery and in the back an arm that let down and opened into a bar complete with sherry glasses and all.

"She really enjoyed that car. She took everybody for rides. She tried to take us but we were away on a trip and when we got back she was already back in the hospital."

The Danby townspeople speculated that the Rolls was only rented, and Harris wrote Dick Walsh that he didn't know why Pearl wanted a Rolls Royce at this stage of her life but that anything she wanted he was determined she should have.

Grace once expressed the opinion that during all of her sister's adult life her family had provided a sort of audience for her in front of which she always wore her cloak of superiority. And apparently she never removed it in their presence. On the other hand she could volunteer painful truths to casual strangers. To Dorothy Farrell she had admitted the fact, otherwise never acknowledged, about Ted Harris's fiasco in Philadelphia. To Paul Roebling she had volunteered her passion for a lost lover; and to a woman living in a Danby mobile home she laid bare the raw truth of her present situation.

A nun from the Philippines who had known Pearl Buck abroad and who was visiting Mrs. Sheila Sadowski in Danby, expressed a desire to see her again. After the usual news items were exchanged and they talked about the American spoils of war, Mrs. Sadowski asked the author some questions about her "philosophy." Evidently she had tapped an overflowing vein, for again Pearl Buck revealed inner thoughts rarely if ever heard by her intimates.

"She said to me," Mrs. Sadowski reported, "'You have no idea in your humble life what it means to once have been famous, to have been glamorous and sought after and to realize at this age that it was only money and fame that brought these people to you.' She said, 'I have very few friends. And I've reached the stage where I realize I have to pay for their friendship.'

"I asked her why she came to Danby and she never really gave me an answer. You know, I always thought this project here was not really *her* project, that she had people around her who used her for it. . . . I often think of her philosophy, that 'you can count your friends on one hand.' She held up her hand, fingers spread and palm out to show me. 'Just five,' she said, 'so choose them carefully. There's your mother and your father. Your husband will be your very best friend.' She said not to rely on your children, that they would probably not—she stopped there, she didn't finish that. Then she said 'you would probably have one good friend from your childhood and one from adult life. Five.' I remember her holding up her hand. 'And the rest of them,' she said, 'are just associates.'

"You know, after you read that magazine article and you saw her and then *him*, and you had a chance to talk to her, you saw that deep *deep* down, she knew. She had to. But I don't think she could afford to give up the one friend she could buy. Otherwise she was going to be alone."

However, Pearl remained a pragmatist, true to the words she had told friends long before: "You use me and I use you, that's what makes the world go round." And if you couldn't change something, you made it work for you. Her sister Grace had often wondered, "Was 'all this' really what she wanted? Or when she said it *was*, so vehemently, could she have just been trying to convince herself? You know, such vehemence makes you wonder. But at this point there was no other way left."

In honor of her eightieth birthday the state of Vermont, now that Pearl was officially a citizen, proclaimed September 17 to September 24 "Pearl S. Buck Week," and she made a public appearance at a program at the Fine Arts Center at Castleton State College in conjunction with the Crossroads Council of Arts. There was music and some of Pearl Buck's works were read followed by several laudatory speeches.

"Pearl looked beautiful," Lillian Gould remembered, "she had all the smiles and warmth and dignity and poise and happiness. She just blossomed." She wore a pink satin beaded gown, a fur cape and large pearls, and Dolphus Crowe had done her hair and carefully made her up. She had been away from audiences for a very long time and when she once again entered the spotlight on Harris's arm and heard the applause, she was a happy woman reveling in the moment. Seated near a side door she was given a hand microphone and after the speeches, almost intoxicated with pleasure, she told wry stories on her neighbors and, bright and witty, filled the hall with laughter.

A reception where she would shake her fellow Vermonters' hands had been planned but Harris, watching her intently, suddenly took her by the arm and, apologizing, led her away to the Rolls Royce.

It is good that she had this night. As on June 26, she seemed to have been saving up every shred of strength to blow on one last fling, for directly afterward she was taken to the Rutland Hospital and from there to the Burlington Medical Center.

At this point some observers prophesied that Harris would move out. Many people, like Lillian Wolfson of the original Foundation staff and Mrs. Dorothy Jones, a Danby acquaintance, remarked in wonderment at what actually did happen. Grace Yaukey summed up Harris's role at the end: "I know nothing about him personally or his integrity, but I know that nobody could have done as much for my sister in her dying months. He filled a very great need for her in terms of loneliness and of interest and of family. These were the things she got from him that were very important. And he didn't run out. He stayed.

"And," she added, "anything else aside, I do feel he was deeply and emotionally fond of my sister—loved her absolutely. I won't try to describe what kind of love, but in the last months I often saw him sit down and weep."

In the Burlington Hospital she underwent a gall bladder operation and seemed to be making a good recovery. Grace went up to see her. "And when I came in there she was, up and dressed and answering letters. Harris came in and Pearl said, 'I believe I can eat something today. What is there?' Harris said, 'There's chicken, of course.' She said, 'I think chicken is one of the most despicable of all foods,' and he said, 'What would you like?' She thought and said, 'Lychee fruit,' and he said, 'You shall have it.'"

Catering to her wishes posed a problem at the Burlington Medical Center. The Winnebago motor home was kept parked in the hospital's lot and the Rolls Royce commuted back and forth each day. Shortly the demands and expectations of their famous patient became a sore point with the staff. Richard Walsh's granddaughter, Jo Churchill, was a secretary at the Medical Center at the time and an embarrassed witness to the bustle and special orders, the spilling over of Danby personnel into the hospital corridors. Pearl explained to Grace, "I have all these letters coming in, publishers from all over the world and this enormous correspondence, it can't be managed in any ordinary way. It has to be done with a staff."

Jo Churchill, having watched Harris commandeer the Buck mail each day, passing along only what he chose, quietly initiated a private war to see who could catch the mail first, she delivering it intact to Pearl or he screening it beforehand. Jo conceded that he generally won.

It is possible Pearl was unconscious of the turmoil her presence caused the hospital, and indeed, her old sense of responsibility could still assert itself. When the principal of the local school's son landed in the intensive care unit with a broken back, ruptured spleen and collapsed lungs, Pearl offered Mr. Harris's or Mr. Pauls's help. Each day there was a phone inquiry, and from time to time large baskets of fruit and flowers and four of Pearl's books were sent down to the boy.

At long last sent home, Pearl enjoyed watching the Annex being built. And in the last months she had become fond of an elderly couple who lived across the street. Raymond Stone had brought her flowers and vegetables. "I think that she was happy here," Mrs. Stone recalled. "I think she liked having neighbors. She used to say she never had neighbors until she came here. She wouldn't come in the house though. She said, 'I don't want to come in your house because then everybody else will want me to come into theirs and that would be too much.'"

About this time everyone became aware that the gall bladder operation had not solved the famous author's medical problems. She was still working, writing a book about Vietnamese children, but not getting far. And she was still talking plans, Foundation meetings to attend in Philadelphia and deadlines to meet. Meantime, however, the antiques business was not doing well. Harris had said when the future of the business looked bleak that nothing was to interfere with her care, and a friend reported that "the business had done very well the first year . . . but when Miss Buck got ill . . . everyone just knocked themselves out, going back and forth, reading to her by the hour—she loved that—and fixing special foods and medicines. There weren't enough people to do everything."

In October she underwent another major operation. Even then she insisted on an office in the hospital and she continued work on the Vietnam book. But the news of her illness had seeped out, and flowers began to arrive from all over the world.

She wrote Tsuta in November. "I have been wanting to write you ever since I got your beautiful letter, but I am now dictating since it will be some time before I can write by hand. The operations, one after the other, have taxed my frame and now I am having a series of precautionary X-ray treatments. . . . The next step will be to get into shape to go back to Danby House, where all sorts of improvements are being made. . . . I am working some, daily if possible, and I am concerned now with the next book, *The Red Earth* . . . clarifying my characters and the action. We have also re-read *The Rainbow* and I have quite clearly in mind the amplifications which will make it into a full-length novel. . . . All this please communicate to Dick. Also I want to finish a novel, now about three-fourths done, called *The Schoolmaster*. I cannot work with all my powers yet but once these X-ray treatments are over I can really begin to build back. . . . I have good nurses, Mr. Harris, James Pauls, Mrs. Drake and our wonderful general factotum, Dolphus. The hospital let me have an office just across the hall from my room . . . and I am making an excellent recovery. I hope and know that you have too. We are both made of tough stuff and we are fighters. With love to you and to Dick, I am always, PSB." (The initials were written in a shaky scrawl.")

She was out of bed soon and taking walks through the corridors. Jo Churchill recalled a day when she was lunching in the cafeteria on Pearl's floor. "Suddenly somebody said, 'Isn't that your grandmother?' and sure enough, there she was between two nurses being led on her ambulations. My friend said, 'You know, I could tell, without remembering what she looked like, that it was she. She is so grand, even as ill as she is, being led by nurses. She just has such a *carriage* about her.'"

After nearly three months spent in and out of hospitals, she longed to go home, and they discharged her in time for Christmas. Some of her children had her suite decked out cheerily, and she was cared for twenty-four hours a day by loving friends. Says Mrs. Jones, "Wendy and Mrs. Drake nearly killed themselves nursing her, so she wouldn't have to have strangers in."

One day in February while lying thoughtfully in bed she suddenly said, "I want my Dickens books." She sat up while Mrs. Drake placed a frilly bedjacket about her shoulders and went for the old blue Chinkiang volumes. Ordering them spread out in a circle before her on the counterpane, she looked at them a long time in silence. Grace thought "she had probably been paying tribute to Dickens, thanking him for having stimulated her to write." And she may indeed have been reviewing all those years when she was trying to learn how to drive that "team of too many horses."

Sometime during February Harris told Lillian Gould that Pearl wished to see her. Mrs. Gould had been the backbone of the antiques operation while the others devoted most of their time to Pearl. Now Pearl greeted her from her chair and discussed the antique shop and the Annex being built. Their conversation was no different from previous ones. But when Mrs. Gould started to leave, Pearl rose and, going to her, took her in her arms. "I was stunned," Mrs. Gould admitted, "She hugged me. She didn't say anything special but she actually hugged me. She had never done anything like that before. It was the last time I saw her."

Shortly thereafter Harris called Grace long distance, his voice breaking into sobs. "She's sinking. She's going downhill fast." Grace hurried to Danby and found several of the children already gathered.

All of them had finally been notified of Pearl's condition. Like Tsuta some had indicated their distrust of Harris and like her they had been excommunicated. But, again like Tsuta, they had come hoping for a final reconciliation. The four who had traveled to Vermont, bringing flowers, sat downstairs in Danby House waiting for word. Harris was not around, having left Mrs. Drake in charge.

Grace had already visited her sister the day before. In the morning Pearl had seemed quite feeble but in the afternoon she had rallied a bit and asked to see her sister. Grace found her on her chaise lounge in a delicate lounging robe. "I was put to sit in a chair nearby and talk to her. But she was so tired that after a little conversation I saw it was just too much and I said, 'Pearl, I see you're tired. I'll say goodnight and go downstairs,' and I left.

"I was walking down the street when I heard Mrs. Drake running after me. She had a message to give me. Pearl had said, 'I want you to tell my sister that I think she is a wonderful person.' It nearly broke my heart. I felt she was saying goodbye and she wanted to be sure I knew she loved me. I never went back again. I felt she had been finishing things off the way she wanted it."

The next morning the children waited for Mrs. Drake. Finally she brought word that Pearl had decided to see them, after she was dressed. After another long wait Harris came down the stairs and hurried out to the antique shop. Returning with something small and gold in his hand, he went upstairs and, after more waiting, Mrs. Drake took the children up.

At the top of the stairs they found a nurse, formal in her crisp white uniform, and beyond her, Pearl Buck sitting erect in a large armchair. Wearing a long red and black Chinese robe with red earrings and necklace and the ruby bracelet Harris had just brought, she sat elegantly with her hair piled high and her face thin and ethereal, lovely in a way they had never seen her.

"There she was," Grace reported, "looking perfectly beautiful and totally in charge. They told me about it—she was sweet and chatted pleasantly, and she had her hands on the reins every second of the time." Harris had told the nurse to cut the visit short if Pearl sounded tired, because actually she was exhausted before they arrived, the dressing process had been torture for her. But as at other crucial times her will carried her through and the meeting went in perfect accord.

Janice, one of the four children present, went downstairs silent and shaken. Saying goodbye, each of them had bent to give Pearl a kiss and as Janice leant over, her mother looked up. Lifting her thin hand she gave her cheek a gentle pat. "That was the most demonstrative thing she ever did to me," Janice said.

Talking about it later Janice explained, "It was such a big thing because I felt that at that moment she had almost a whole lifetime of feeling she wanted to give me and that's all the time she had left."

She died early on the morning of March 6, 1973.

The news of Pearl Buck's death made the front pages and picture stories in *The New York Times* and most major newspapers, usually followed by an inside page on her life and achievements. President Nixon sent his condolences, calling her "a human bridge between the civilizations of East and West . . . a great artist and a sensitive and compassionate human being."

Following her instructions she was buried at Green Hills Farm under a large ash tree on the front lawn, and the small private service was held beside the library fireplace where she and Walsh used to sit surrounded by their children. The previous day the fourteen grand-children had been taken to see her lying peacefully in a beautiful white Chinese robe covered with a blue and white afghan crocheted by Mrs. Galla.

No friends were invited. "If you started, where would you stop?" Grace said. "She wanted only the families and people connected with the things she was working on." The adopted children had all come, and from Danby the Drakes and the Conklins attended. Harris and Jimmie Pauls, by prior arrangement, were not present.

At the graveside there were one or two farewell remarks and then a poem by Pearl was read. Written long before, it expressed her belief in a life having neither a beginning nor an end.

> I remember when I was born.
> I do remember!
> Through eternity I slept,
> By its quiet waters swept,
> In the silence safely kept.
> All unknowing, night or day,
> All unthinking, there I lay.
>
> Suddenly, by life compelled,
> I was free, no longer held,

Free to hear and feel and cry,
Free to live, or free to die;
Free to be that which am I.
I remember when I was born—
I do remember!

Epilogue

Many people wondered what Pearl Buck was really like. The dramatic final scene staged for the children, like a papal audience, had been directed by the public Pearl Buck determined to prove herself unconquered. But then at the last moment another woman had broken through for an instant of loving contact.

No one (except perhaps those young men who chose not to discuss her) knew her well. Actually, she was a paradox, pulled in two directions at once. She was fascinated by the pleasures of success and adulation and greedy for them at any cost. On the other hand, she had been vouchsafed, late in life, a glimpse of a peace and serenity more enriching than anything she had known before, and she had responded with humble gratitude. However, few beside the one who gave it saw that side of her.

During her last weeks she managed to maintain the public image of total command during the day. But alone at night with the nurse she seemed to be troubled and restless. "She'd be muttering, semi-conscious," said the nurse and it seemed as if she was arguing with herself, struggling with a sense of guilt . . . even scolding herself. She'd say, 'Look at me. Look at the way I'm living here. There are children hungry and crying in China, and I have all this here.' She'd say, 'This isn't what I want.' It upset me, I didn't know what it meant."

Here, it seems, is a glimpse of the woman, driven by a nagging sense of responsiblity, who, despite all her vanity and foolishness, managed to give so much to the world.

Palpably she was not one of the Immortals of history despite her yearnings for greatness. But one or two of her books may well outlast the present generation to keep Pearl Buck's name alive. And the solid fact of having pioneered China in America is a small but ineradicable monument.

There are other monuments, too, thousands of living monuments all over America—those mixed-blood children adopted into white homes as a result of her fight against 1949's restrictive adoption laws. In 1983 there were 3403 citizens who perhaps had never heard her name but who were provided with a family and a home through her efforts. And in turn the Welcome House adoptions helped to soften America's racial prejudices and open generous doors to thousands of Vietnam children following that war.

Overseas in Korea, the Philippines, Okinawa, Taiwan, Mainland China, Thailand and Vietnam there are thousands more who owe her thanks. The Pearl Buck Foundation, surviving its gruelling early trials, has since achieved its founder's original ideal of aid to the G.I.'s children *on their home soil*. Between 1964 and 1983 almost twenty thousand children have received aid and education, and four times that many family members have benefited indirectly.

These beneficiaries are, in whole or in part, Asian. In America her influence is just as pervasive though more subtle. There are probably very few blacks in the United States who realize that in 1932, when Pearl Buck first went to Harlem, any white celebrity who publicly fought discrimination, any white celebrity who spoke and wrote for Negroes, risked abuse and ridicule. By doing so steadily for forty years Pearl Buck helped alter the psychological climate, thus easing the way for those fighters who came after.

Most difficult for her personally, she gave the handicapped the gift of stature. As President Franklin Roosevelt took the stigma out of being crippled, so Pearl Buck, with her heart-breaking confessional *The Child Who Never Grew* lifted the shame from retardation. Bringing it out of the closet freed thousands of anguished parents so they could handle their problem in the open and thereby bring emotional and practical benefit to both parent and child.

Subtly her own sex too has felt her touch. Twenty-five years before Betty Friedan published *The Feminine Mystique* Pearl Buck was snarling at "lazy good-for-nothing middle-class women, over-privileged and under-motivated" who contributed nothing to their world but fashion news. Long before World War II made these women part of the work force, she had opened their eyes to the idea of work. Indeed, as John Hersey wrote in his "Commemorative Tribute," "she anticipated nearly every single one of the recent 'discoveries' of the Women's Liberation Movement."

After the grave was closed under the large ash tree at Green Hills Farm, a number of desperately anxious people remained to hear the reading of Pearl Buck's will.

Many years before she had promised her manuscripts to Randolph-Macon Women's College, at another time forgetfully promising them to the Pearl S. Buck Birthplace Foundation in Hillsboro, West Virginia. This active organization maintained the refurbished Stulting home, showing tourists through the house where she was born. The organization had been promised as well a selection of memorabilia including a special gown Pearl had worn at their convention.

The Pearl S. Buck Foundation had fervently hoped that, under a 1968 will made in their favor, it would inherit a sizable income in addition to the income from the books Pearl had written under their employment. They were probably aware that the foreign royalties had been assigned to Creativity, Inc., and would not be included in her estate, but they could not know the extent to which the U.S. royalties had been pledged to cover large loans to Creativity, of which Harris was sole owner. When the will was read, they learned that in addition to her royalties, Harris had inherited not only Pearl Buck's remaining personal and real property but her manuscripts and correspondence as well.

On publicatioin of the will Randolph-Macon bowed out gracefully. And the Birthplace Foundation, lacking the funds to contest the will, had to be content with a partial list of manuscripts. But her children were not so docile. They brought suit in court to break the will, charging Harris with exerting undue influence over their mother. Their suit was upheld.

However, this was not the end of the legal story. Other wills began to appear which pitted the Foundation's claim against the children and resulted in a giddy seven-year round of hearings and trials characterized by a Rutland judge as "the most complicated mess I ever had." The two sides finally reached an out-of-court settlement, the details of which are a zealously guarded secret.

The Pearl S. Buck Foundation, with no prospect of a continuing income, had to retrench. The Delancey Place establishment had already been sold, but Pearl Buck had some time earlier given Green Hills Farm to the Foundation to save paying taxes on it, so the Foundation moved there.

Creativity, Inc., was dissolved and its assets absorbed into the estate, the heirs being Carol, Janice, Richard, John, Edgar, Jean, Henriette and Chieko. The value of the estate, i.e., real estate, copyrights, jewelry, furs and cash, is not generally known.

After Pearl Buck's death Ted Harris, with Jimmie Pauls and the Conklins, traveled abroad for several months. After his return he spent a few weeks in a hospital in a state of severe depression. Thereafter he disappeared, his subsequent movements merely a matter of rumor. Various reports have surfaced of his selling antiques and offering Pearl Buck's jewelry as "Association Pieces" accompanied by a letter of authentication. Hillsboro, West Virginia, heard from him when he offered the Birthplace Foundation Pearl Buck's correspondence for a quarter of a million dollars. The foundation politely declined.

A few relics of Creativity, Inc., remain—the red and white trim on its former properties, and the white clapboard Danby house where Pearl Buck died.

The town of Danby, bereft of its bizarre centerpiece, returned to its former placidity with its older citizens breathing a tired sigh of relief.

Tad Danielewski, unemployed after the Stratton Productions demise, worked intermittently for NBC and various television producers. He and his wife finally moved to Provo, Utah, where he joined the drama department of the University of Utah.

Lossing Buck married Lomay Chang, a Chinese girl "of the twenty-fifth generation," and remained in China until he was forced to leave in 1944, returning later with the China-United States Agriculture Commission to oversee China's post-war restoration.

With his wife and two children he was posted to Rome as chief of the U.S. Food and Agriculture Organization. In 1954 he left FAO to set up the Council on Economic and Cultural Affairs established by John D. Rockefeller III with its focus on Asia and the Far East. In 1957 he and his family moved to Pleasant Valley and thence to Poughkeepsie, New York, where he died in 1972.

And Carol, the child who inhabits a sixty-three-year-old body, still passes her uneventful years playing with her companions. "At least," Pearl Buck used to say in comforting herself, "she doesn't know enough to be unhappy."

MISSIONARIES

Considering the period—the eighteen seventies—Absalom's choice of vocation was a natural one. The foreign mission field, opened in the early years of the century following the American expansion of trade and travel about the world, had been seizing hold of eager, thoughtful young men, breathing into them Christ's admonition to go forth and preach the gospel to every creature.

Travelers in the Near East, Far East and Africa returned home telling of the millions to whom Christianity was an unopened book. And after having had a personal experience of conversion themselves, these young of all denominations were inspired to share their vision with the unenlightened.

The places they went to were often completely strange to them. China, particularly, was a closed book. Calling itself The Middle Kingdom because it felt itself the center of the universe, it had a history of four thousand years of accomplishment in art and literature and science. Confucius and Lso-Tse had preceded Christ by five hundred years, and such inventions as gunpowder and printing were so old as to have been forgotten, only to be reinvented later. Curiously, however, half-way through the country's history its mind had frozen. Satisfied that it had reached perfection and thus could never be improved by change, it rejected the slightest adjustment to the sweep of time.

Except for a handful of explorers and priests, few white people had ever broken into this self-imposed isolation. But then in 1840 the British with warships broke in rudely, demanding an exchange of trade. After them came the missionaries. Many other countries had already been introduced to Christianity, and now it was China's turn.

To these missionaries their life purpose was a simple one and their theology earnest and uncomplicated. After death the soul of the individual had an afterlife that could be one either of bliss and peace or of a torment eternal and horrible beyond imagining. Therefore the most loving thing one could do would be to save the lost one from such a fate. This the missionary, in love for his fellow man, endeavored to do, sometimes at the cost of his own life.

In the many years since then the missionary idea has taken on many different functions. From its original thought of doing good by saving souls it branched out into the intermediary good of feeding and educating and healing bodies, to the point almost of dismissing the original intent. In China this had been especially noticeable, as Professor John K. Fairbank, the eminent authority on China, points out in his book, The Missionary Enterprise in China and America!

"The Chinese Communist revolution of recent decades has stressed the spread of literacy to ordinary people, the publication of journals and pamphlets in the vernacular, education and equality for women, the abolition of arranged child marriages, the supremacy of public duty over filial obedience and family obligations, increased agricultural productivity through the sinking of wells and improved tools, crops, and breeds, dike and road building for protection against flood and famine, public health clinics to treat common ailments and prevent disease, discussion groups to foster better conduct, student organizations to promote healthy recreation and moral guidance, and the acquisition and Sinification of Western knowledge for use in remaking Chinese life. Missionaries of the nineteenth century pioneered in all of these activities. Little wonder that the revolutionaries of China since 1949 have resented them in retrospect. The missionaries came as spiritual reformers, soon found that material improvements were equally necessary, and in the end helped to foment the great revolution. Yet as foreigners they could take no part in it, much less bring it to a finish, instead, it finished them. But in the Maoist message of today, 'serve the people,' one can hear an echo of the missionary's wish to serve his fellow man."

BIBLIOGRAPHY

Birch, Cyril, *Anthology of Chinese Literature*, Vol. 2 (New York: Grove Press, 1972).

Buck, John Lossing, *Land Utilization in China* (Nanking: University of Nanking, 1937).

Candlin, Enid Saunders, *The Breach in the Wall* (New York: Macmillan, 1973).

Chow, Tse-Tsung, *The May 4th Movement: The Intellectual Revolution in Modern China* (Cambridge; Harvard University Press, 1960).

Compton, Arthur H. *The Cosmos of Arthur Holly Compton* (New York: Knopf, 1976).

Cornelius, Roberta D. *The History of Randolph-Macon Woman's College* (Chapel Hill: University of North Carolina Press, 1951).

Craighill, Marian Gardner, *The Craighills of China* (Ambler, Pa: Trinity Press, 1972).

Daon-Cao-Ly, *The Image of the Chinese Family in Pearl Buck's Novels* (Saigon: Duc-Sinh, 1964).

Doyle, Paul A. *Pearl S. Buck* (New Haven: Twayne, 1965).

Fairbank, John K., Ed., *The Missionary Enterprise in China and America* (Cambridge: Harvard University Press, 1974).

Harris, Theodore F. *Pearl S. Buck, A Biography* (New York: John Day, 1969).

_____, *Pearl S. Buck, Vol. 2. Her Philosophy in Her Letters* (New York: John Day, 1971).

Hocking, William Ernest, *The Meaning of Immortality in Human Experience* (New York: Harper, 1957).

_____, *The Coming World Civilization* (New York: Harper, 1956).

_____, *Rethinking Missions*, (New York: Harper, 1932).

Kai-Yu Han, Ed., *Twentieth Century Chinese Poetry: An Anthology.* (New York: Doubleday, 1963).

Langner, Lawrence, *The Magic Curtain* (New York: Dutton, 1951).

Lash, Joseph P., *Eleanor and Franklin* (New York: Norton, 1971).

Lee, Leo Du-Fan, *The Romantic Generation of Modern Chinese Writers* (Cambridge, Harvard University Press, 1973).

Lin Yutang, *My Country and My People* (New York: John Day, 1935).

Nanking Theological Seminary, *Minutes of Annual Meeting* (Nanking: Board of Managers, 1932).

Nanking Station Report, *A Year of Tragedy and Triumph* (Nanking: Kiangan Mission, 1927).

Nanking Language School, Class of 1920, *The Linguist* (Shanghai: Commercial Press, 1921).

Nanking Woman's Club, *Sketches of Nanking* (Nanking: 1933).

de Riencourt, Amaury, *The Soul of China*, Rev. Ed. (New York: Harper Colophon Books, 1958).

Rouner, Leroy, *Within Human Experience* (Cambridge: Harvard University Press, 1969).

Snow, Edgar, *Red Star Over China*, Rev. Ed. (New York: Grove Press, 1968).

Sydenstricker, Edgar, *The Challenge of Facts* (New York: Prodist, 1974).

Time Magazine "Crumbling Foundation," (New York: July 25, 1969).

Walter, Greg, "The Dancing Master," (*Philadelphia* Magazine, July, 1969).

Williams, S. Wells, *The Middle Kingdom: The Chinese Empire and Its Inhabitants.* Rev. Ed. (New York: Paragon Book Reprint Corp., 1966).

Yaukey, Grace Sydenstricker (Cornelia Spencer) *Modern China* (New York: John Day, 1969).

_____, *The Exile's Daughter* (New York: Coward McCann, 1944).

INDEX

B
B9225s   Stirling, Nora B.,
    1900-

Pearl Buck, a woman
in conflict

B
B9225s   Stirling, Nora B.,   1
    1900-

Pearl Buck, a woman
in conflict

P18   MAY   1986

DATE	BORROWER'S NAME	

MAY   1986